Warren William

Warren William

Magnificent Scoundrel of
Pre-Code Hollywood

JOHN STANGELAND

McFarland & Company, Inc., Publishers
Jefferson, North Carolina, and London

LIBRARY OF CONGRESS CATALOGUING-IN-PUBLICATION DATA

Stangeland, John.
Warren William : magnificent scoundrel
of pre-code Hollywood / by John Stangeland.
p. cm.
Includes bibliographical references and index.

ISBN 978-0-7864-4878-4
softcover : 50# alkaline paper ∞

1. William, Warren, 1895–1948. 2. Actors—United States—Biography. I. Title.
PN2287.W4595S77 2011   791.430'28092—dc22 [B]   2010040274

British Library cataloguing data are available

Front cover: Warren William as he appeared in *Beauty and the Boss*,
his fifth picture with Warner Brothers, released in 1932

Manufactured in the United States of America

*McFarland & Company, Inc., Publishers
Box 611, Jefferson, North Carolina 28640
www.mcfarlandpub.com*

To my parents, Robert and Lorraine,
who encouraged my love of the arts,
and steadfastly supported my desire to avoid conformity.
They are the heroes of my life.

Also to my friends Chuck Furman and Rick Vitone,
not here to see this volume, but still alive in the inspiration
to observe, experience, and achieve.

Table of Contents

Acknowledgments

Sandra J. Lee and staff — University of Southern California, Warner Brothers Archives

Connie Pettersen — information, hospitality and research, Aitkin, Minnesota

Valerie Yaroz — Archivist, Screen Actors Guild

Sylvia Wang — Schubert Archives, New York

Barbara Hall — Interviews and Krech family photos

Patricia Lyon — Interviews and Krech family photos

Charles (Ted) Beisel — Interviews, Krech family photos and papers

Christine Arnold Schroeder — American Academy of Dramatic Arts, New York

Dorinda Hartmann — Assistant archivist, Wisconsin Center for Film and Theater Research

John McInnes — Des Plaines Public Library

Stacy Wittmann — Eisenhower Public Library

Staff — New York Public Library for the Performing Arts

Mary Jean Peterson — Aitkin, Minnesota, Historical Society

Mark Quigley — Manager, Research & Study Center, UCLA Film & Television Archive

K. Kevyne Baar — Tamiment Library / Robert F. Wagner Labor Archives, New York University

Rob Hudson — Associate archivist, Carnegie Hall, New York

Jenny Romero and staff — Special Collections, Margaret Herrick Library

Ana Martinez-Holler — Vice-President, Media Relations — Hollywood Walk of Fame

Steve Krech — Krech family history

Anthony Bozzi — Enthusiasm, support and lodging

Chris Caira — Legal documents

Carlos Alverio — Editing and advice

Don Anderson — Counselor

James P. Liversidge — Belknap Collection for the Performing Arts, Department of Special and Area Studies Collections, University of Florida, Gainesville

Academy of Motion Picture Arts and Sciences — for materials, photos and research access

Tom and Marsha Hasskamp — Interviews and Krech family photos

Staff—*Aitkin Independent Age*

John and Betty Fossen — Aitkin, Minnesota

Joe Lenius— Technical assistance

Kimberly Clement — Krech family, Aitkin, Minnesota

Randy Walls— Pictures and visual material, Aitkin, Minnesota

Magali Matarazzi — Special thanks for editing, encouragement and inspiration

Richard Vitone — Catalyst

Preface

The most famous resident ever produced by the tiny town of Aitkin, Minnesota, is virtually unknown there. Warren William, the dapper actor who spent ten years on the New York stage during the Golden Age of Broadway and starred in almost seventy Hollywood films — including three nominated for Best Picture Oscars — has been forgotten, even by those who would be expected to remember him best. A single visit by the young starlet Judy Garland has far surpassed his local heritage in city lore; Garland's appearance is mentioned regularly as Aitkin's brush with greatness. Almost always, the reason for her stop in Aitkin on the way to her hometown of Grand Rapids is conveniently forgotten: She wanted to visit the city that Warren William was from, and see where he worked as a boy. Grand Rapids has a Judy Garland museum. Aitkin has a collective blank stare.

This is not a peculiarity of Aitkinites, however. The line between remembrance and oblivion is mercurial, and people and events are constantly being evaluated by the collective psyche of a community for judgment. Some remain with generations of observers while others fade instantly, the moment we turn our attention from them. Warren William seems to have been consigned to our quickly decaying iconic memory — a momentary diversion in our cultural cache until something else came along to supplant it. He's lost in line behind innumerable more potent images, impressions and thoughts.

The tiny body of people who know Warren William today are mostly film buffs, specifically those interested in the rediscovery of pre–Code Hollywood — the years before new rules of film etiquette were imposed in July of 1934. For cinema, it was the epoch of indecency: standards were lax, censors were nonchalant and Depression era audiences were willing to forgive anything if they had the price of a ticket. At this time Warren William was at the height of his fame — on a par with Paul Muni or William Powell — and taking on roles unique and dangerous. During the early years of his career at Warner Brothers he was a singular presence on-screen, willing to be brazenly immoral and sometimes sexually predatory, but maintaining an uncanny ability to be sympathetic, even likable, in his wickedness. For four years he scammed, defrauded, boondoggled, deflowered and cheated his way across America's theater screens before Production Code czar Joseph Breen finally slammed the lid down on his peculiar brand of mayhem. It was bunco brought to the level of art.

Warren William is currently in the process of having his career interpreted, narrowed and defined largely by those four years. He is being boxed and packaged as the quintessential mountebank and cad. Although that is his indisputable metier, the reality is that he was a well-schooled, versatile performer who tackled almost any genre with charm and elan. During his twenty years in Hollywood he breezed through comedies, prowled detective stories and rode through westerns with equal conviction to his iconic shysters and businessmen swine. And, contrary to his modern image as the alpha male without a conscience, he just as often appeared as the second lead in productions built around strong women. Warner Brothers did

1

him no career favors with those assignments, and the actor did himself none in accepting them. But Warren was a professional and, more to the point, relatively free of ego as it relates to women; he was the beneficiary of much personal and professional help from women during his life and genuinely appreciated and respected the opposite sex. As a result he accepted roles subordinate to powerful actresses with humility and not a hint of male ego. Unfortunately this was not the path to an enduring screen legend when Hollywood was simultaneously grooming notoriously masculine icons like Clark Gable, James Cagney and Errol Flynn. Warren had the unfortunate quality of being a gentleman of the past when pictures were rushing headlong to modernity. His lack of ambition or star temperament conspired to divert quality projects to others with a deeper connection to the zeitgeist.

As a result, Warren William has no signature performance or showcase so powerful it can arc across the stylistic divide between generations. There is no *Casablanca*, *The Adventures of Robin Hood* or *Little Caesar* to be passed on to a new moviegoing audience. He headlined some outstanding films: *Lady for a Day*, *Imitation of Life* and *Gold Diggers of 1933*, to name a few of his best — but in spite of what the credits say, he is not the star of these productions, and not the driving force behind the stories. Consequently, his contribution to these minor classics is frequently —frankly, almost always— overlooked. The productions in which he was the uncontested focus of the proceedings are either "B" pictures, or those long suppressed gems of the pre–Code era — uniquely fun and stylish, but not always completely satisfying or relevant to a mainstream modern audience. Thus, he exists today only at the whim of fringe dwellers— still on the outskirts no matter how wide the fringe is getting.

It is only the curious interest of that fringe that now hosts the memory of his fame, and moment by moment, other events, people and things are crowding in, vying for space. Fortunately, the ongoing digital media revolution will likely ensure that Warren's films— along with other art great and obscure — will remain available to be viewed far into the future. But in that long-off era of cultural Alzheimer's— when not just a hundred years, but thousands of years of recorded media compete for our attention — who will know that they ever existed? For those that come after us then, it is our duty to remember those things we love — whatever they may be — and pass on the history, the art, and the joy of rediscovery.

Introduction

In late 1934 a young actor recently arrived from England was sitting on a set at the Warner Brothers studio in Burbank, California, waiting to make his American screen debut as a corpse in a film called *The Case of the Curious Bride*. The newcomer was then just a handsome, devil-may-care roustabout looking for fun in Hollywood, while Warren William, the popular star of *Curious Bride*, was at the height of his fame. Warren had made 25 films for Warner Brothers since arriving from Broadway in 1931, playing powerful businessmen, recalcitrant rogues and shyster lawyers, and was coming off three Oscar-nominated films over the previous eighteen months. In June, William had been announced for the lead in the studio's upcoming production of Rafael Sabatini's classic pirate adventure *Captain Blood*, and expected that the assignment would finally lift him to the top rank of cinema actors.

It was not to be. *Captain Blood* was indeed made the following summer, but it was not Warren William who shot to international acclaim as the pirate captain; instead it was Errol Flynn, the insignificant bit player from *The Case of the Curious Bride,* who snagged the role of Peter Blood. The film became a rare, once-in-a-lifetime confluence of style, personality, and moment. It launched the careers of Flynn and his co-star Olivia de Havilland, making them one of the great romantic pairings in the history of Hollywood. Director Michael Curtiz began his big-budget association with Flynn; they would share credits ten more times, including many of Warner Brothers' biggest successes. Erich Korngold, who was brought to the States to write the score for *A Midsummer Night's Dream*, stayed for *Captain Blood* and began a career that garnered two Academy Awards and a lasting reputation as one of the great film composers of all time. Even Basil Rathbone took great benefit from his participation, solidifying his reputation as one of the top film scoundrels of all time, and returning for an equally memorable part in Curtiz and Flynn's timeless *The Adventures of Robin Hood*. In short, *Captain Blood* was the exact type of film that carved a lasting memory in the public consciousness, and Warren William had nothing to do with it. He was instead making the eminently forgettable *Widow from Monte Carlo*.

Who knows what might have been if Warren William had swung across the screen as Peter Blood. Whether or not the studio genuinely intended for the film to be made with him is debatable. There are reasons to believe they did not, but in the end the circumstances behind the story are irrelevant: Warren clearly believed the publicity. The apparent loss of this superb opportunity ruptured the normal resolve of his quiet, reserved personality. That year the irate actor personally wrote to Roy Obringer, the general counsel of Warner Brothers, to demand release from his studio contract. "I consider that irreparable damage has been done to my standing in the motion picture industry ... by your reassigning other pictures that have heretofore been publicly announced as vehicles intended for me. I make particular reference to Rafael Sabatini's *Captain Blood*. As long as you so very apparently consider me unimportant in your forthcoming production schedules, I can most certainly see no reason why you should object to giving me my release."

Warner Brothers did not give Warren William his release. Instead, their response was to cast him adrift in a welter of cheap programmers, second leads and "B" mysteries. The studio's indifference to the career of their well-paid star was inexplicable and devastating. Their cavalier treatment may have been punishment for his attitude, or spite related to his difficult 1933 contract negotiations; or it may have been simple stubborn intransigence on studio boss Jack L. Warner's part. For Warren William it made no difference; after brushing past *Captain Blood* he never again had the good fortune to be near such far-reaching synergy. He had missed his greatest opportunity — however tenuous — to invade the permanent episodic memory of mainstream movie lovers.

Warren William's lost contribution to film history deserves reclamation. He counts among his many starring roles a genuine classic of the Hollywood musical; an important, archetypal tear-jerking soap opera; one of the all-time big-budget historical epics, and a seminal, perennially revived horror film. He was the first man to play a character that became one of the truly indelible icons of 20th century media, Perry Mason, and appeared as Sam Spade five years before Humphrey Bogart became a star in *The Maltese Falcon*. His early film persona as a ruthless and amoral bastard is a prototype for characters as diverse as Gordon Gekko in *Wall Street* and Daniel Plainview in *There Will Be Blood*. And no one, but no one, could be as bad and remain as likable as Warren William. He has been called "the best kept secret of the 1930s," and although that is indisputably true, I prefer to think of him as simply the most memorable forgotten man in the history of cinema.

1

The First Hundred Years

In central Minnesota, the Mississippi River proceeds in a southwesterly arc from the town of Grand Rapids to the Crow Wing County Seat of Brainerd. Two-thirds of the way there it passes through the tiny town of Aitkin, nestled among the vast array of forests and lakes that dot the Minnesota countryside. Only a hundred miles or so from the river's headwaters in Lake Itasca, Aitkin grew out of the fur and logging trade it serviced in the rugged days following the Louisiana Purchase.

Among the earliest commerce in the region was John Jacob Astor's American Fur Company, which supplanted the British Northwest Company's fur trading operations following the War of 1812. On Astor's payroll in the 1820s was a young man in charge of Minnesota's Fond du Lac territory, William Alexander Aitkin.[1] He arrived in Minnesota as a boy of fifteen and was raised among the Chippewa and Ojibwe Indians, giving him valuable experience that was put to use negotiating with the local tribes. He quickly became an important man in the fur trade, eventually gaining a stake in his employer's operations. Following Astor's divestiture of his holdings in American Fur in 1836, Aitkin ran afoul of the new controlling owner, Ramsey Crooks, and by 1838 was forced out of the company. But the wily businessman was nothing if not resourceful. Within two years he had rebuilt his business connections and returned to the area to take on his former company. For his new venture Aitkin chose a spot west of Fond du Lac, at the confluence of the Mississippi and Mud rivers, giving him a strategic advantage to and from the nearby Mille Lacs Lake.[2] With his operations as the base, the area that eventually became Aitkin took hold and flourished.

William Aitkin died in 1851. In 1857 Aitkin County was established and named for the local businessman who had spent his entire adult life in the area. It wasn't until 1870 that the town became firmly established when Nathanial Tibbetts, working for the Northern Pacific Railroad, surveyed the site and determined that it provided the first practical access to the Mississippi by rail from the city of Duluth. By this time the fur trade was in decline, and logging began to develop as the dominant industry in the region. River traffic was vital to the new lumber concerns, and the town quickly grew to support the needs of the men and businesses working the forests. In 1871, while the rail line was still being built, Tibbetts staked a claim and built the first house in Aitkin proper, the Ojibwe Hotel. He and his brothers Joshua and James nurtured the growth and became town elders, each fulfilling various jobs: county commissioner, postmaster, registrar, town chairman and sheriff.[3]

The threads of Warren William's lineage that eventually wound together in Aitkin began at Tennstedt, Saxony, in Germany, where his paternal grandfather Ernst Wilhelm Krech was born in 1819. The elder Krech was described as a non-conformist, and had many interests including astrology, music, philosophy and mathematics. Although deeply pious, he believed also in reincarnation and spirituality, including the ability to communicate with the dead. He hoped and expected to speak from beyond the grave when his time came.[4] During the German Revolution of 1848 Ernst worked with the popular front dedicated to the overthrow of the government.[5] In danger from a vengeful state following the failure of their cause, Ernst left Germany, first for France, where he became an ordained — then defrocked — Jesuit priest,[6] and then to the United States. He momentarily settled in New Orleans, then eventually made his way to the staunch German environs of Midwestern America where he returned to his chosen profession, teaching.[7] In Belleville, Illinois, he met and married another German émigré, the widow Mathilde Grow, who had come to the States with her foster parents at the age of seven after being orphaned in infancy. With Charles Grow she had produced two children, a son who died shortly after birth and a daughter whom Ernst adopted as his own. Mathilde was 21 at the time of their wedding in 1851 and the union would eventually yield six children, three of whom — two sons and a daughter — would also heartbreakingly die within their first months. The couple's first surviving child, Warren's father Freeman E. Krech, was born in Belleville in 1856.[8]

As a teacher, Ernst was constantly experimenting with new ideas about education. He taught and lectured on phonetics, music, language and religion, but his methods and his nonconformist nature often put him at odds with his employers. The family endured hard times as Ernst struggled to make ends meet, constantly moving — or being forced to move — to find better circumstances. After leaving Illinois, he took the family first to the German town of Hermann, Missouri (where Mathilde had lived when she arrived in the States), and then to St. Louis. Another move followed to Hannibal where a second son, Alvin William Krech — destined to be an important force in American business and finance — was born in 1858. Shortly after Alvin's parturition, Ernst again moved the family, first to Nauvoo, Illinois — once the home of the Mormon Church — and then to New Ulm, Minnesota. This final choice would prove nearly disastrous for the family, already quite familiar with privation and grief.

New Ulm was founded in 1855 by a group of German Americans, with the express purpose of providing — by dint of each man's labor — a home for every German who settled there. The spot they chose was situated on the Minnesota River in the south central part of a state teeming with American Indians who were enduring cavalier treatment by businessmen and gov-

Warren's grandfather Ernst Wilhelm Krech was a spiritualist, mathematician, teacher and defrocked Jesuit priest who believed that he would be able to communicate with the living after he died. When Warren's father died in 1931, he willed this portrait to his son. Courtesy Barbara Hall.

ernment alike. Ernst, Mathilde and their three children arrived by stagecoach in May 1861 and, in a house across the river from New Ulm, settled down to carve out a new life. That month Ernst answered a notice in the local newspaper for a German teacher and was appointed headmaster of the school, with almost fifty students under his tutelage, including his sons Freeman and Alvin. The two boys were served well by their father's teachings, including a strict intellectual discipline that undoubtedly contributed to their eventual success as businessmen and fathers. Ernst stressed learning and character above all else, and these lessons eventually filtered down to inform his grandson Warren's basic makeup of modesty, constancy and duty. It was also likely that Ernst's renowned inquisitiveness and curiosity became the model for Warren's own constantly searching mind.

In 1862, the smoldering resentment quietly building in the hearts of the Sioux tribes of lower Minnesota was fanning into a naked flame. After the *Treaty of Traverse des Sioux* was signed in 1851, the four Sioux tribes were relegated to a 150-mile reservation, bordered just outside of New Ulm. In the following years, the government and their business agents developed a financial system that kept the tribes in virtual servitude by offering yearlong credit to be repaid by their annual government stipends. Some saw potential for the fire to fan out across the region, but were given no heed. The local Christian missionary, Bishop Henry Whipple, wrote: "Our Indian system is an organized system of robbery.... It has fostered a system of trade which robbed the thrifty ... [and] left in the savage mind a deep sense of injustice."[9] The anger of the tribal youth finally overcame the caution and care of the elders on August 17, 1862. As the Civil War raged hundreds of miles away, five thousand Sioux Indians, driven to the brink of starvation by the government's refusal to pay their yearly stipends, resolved to take what was rightfully theirs. In the process, they also vowed, they would relieve their anger with blood.

Unlucky settlers near Redwood Ferry were the first to suffer the violence. The Indians cut a swath through the small farms and settlements there, and then destroyed a troop of Minnesota militiamen sent to quell the insurrection. Almost thirty soldiers were killed, with the Indians still on the rampage. The angry natives then turned to the town of New Ulm, where Ernst, Mathilde and their three children, aged fourteen, six and four, were situated just across the Minnesota River.[10] Before the Indians made it to New Ulm, frightened French trappers and other survivors from nearby skirmishes arrived in town with word of the rebellion that was taking place up and down the range. That evening, in the pitch-black Minnesota night, Ernst took the family across the river to the slightly safer environs of the town proper. The boys, Freeman and Alvin, were young enough, perhaps, to be straddled between fear and excitement, but the way their parents treated the event impressed upon them the seriousness of the situation.

In New Ulm, things were dire. If one were looking for the heroic image of the American frontiersman with a rifle over his shoulder and powder on his belt, you would expect that New Ulm would be a likely place for historians to begin. But the reality was something quite different: in a town of over 1500 residents, there were only twelve rifles among them, and no handguns. Almost forty miles from Fort Ridgely, the citizens knew they were on their own, and they set about dividing their meager resources for the defense of their homes and lives. The central four blocks were hastily cordoned off by makeshift fortifications (barrels, logs, wagons and lumber) and the weapons on hand — axes, scythes and pitchforks — were doled out to the able-bodied men. The only three brick buildings in New Ulm were designated as shelters for women and children. Mathilde took Freeman, Alvin and their half sister to the basement of the largest house, the Erd Building, to wait out — with hundreds of refugees from the surrounding area—the consequences of the fight.[11] On August 19 the Indians attacked in force, but were repelled by the townsmen, who knew that to lose would possibly mean a massacre of everyone inside those four blocks. The Native Americans then laid siege to New Ulm, making periodic forays into the town, hoping to break the will of the handful of remaining men who had not gone to participate in the Civil War. On August 22, the Sioux attacked Fort Ridgely itself, and inflicted more casualties. With trouble erupting all along the line of the Minnesota River and into Iowa, the U.S. Cavalry was engaged on many fronts, and New Ulm endured the siege for six days with no help in sight. In those six days the town was virtually burned to the ground, fourteen residents were killed and over 150 wounded. Krech family lore—heard again and again in years to come by the impressionable Warren—told of Mathilde's brave forays, sometimes under fire, to retrieve precious water for the huddled refugees from the town's only well in her battered coffeepot. Across the river, the Krech home was in ruins. Everything—including all family possessions—was lost.

The siege finally ended on August 25, when the Indians were driven off and the town was evacuated.[12] A caravan of over one hundred wagons made its way to Mankato where the citizens regrouped and tried to decide what to do next. The Dakota War of 1862 was hardly over, however. During the next few weeks, the Sioux and the U.S. Cavalry engaged in a bloody battle through three states, with as many as 800 dead before the army restored order. Many hundreds of Sioux prisoners were taken, with over 300 eventually convicted of war crimes. Following a commutation of most by President Lincoln—at the urging of Bishop Whipple—38 were hung on the day after Christmas, 1862. This act remains the largest group execution ever carried out by the U.S. government.

The uprising etched a deep and indelible mark on the people who survived it. As late as 1896—when Warren Krech was just over a year old—rumors flew around Aitkin that a new Indian uprising was in progress. Word spread that the nearby towns of McGregor and Kimberly had been wiped out, and that the murderous natives had commandeered the Northern Pacific train heading west to the next stop on the line, Aitkin. Freeman Krech couldn't help but think back to the fragmented images living in the part of his psyche that was still six years old. And when someone suggested that the men of Aitkin arm themselves, he picked up what he could find and went to the station with a throng of others who likewise remembered those horrifying weeks. The world was a different place by then, however. The train pulled in on schedule— an improvement over the Northern Pacific at least, if the natives were involved—and a grand total of two Indians stepped off.[13] Everyone went away relieved.

Although there is no record of whether it happened during the siege, 1862 is the year that Mathilde's only surviving daughter died at the age of fifteen. A mere youth of six, Freeman saw in his parents' grief emotions that would be mirrored in his own heart almost thirty years later.

Their home and all possessions destroyed, a daughter dead and the ugly memories of townspeople and friends killed—as well as the fear of possible new violence—was enough to send the family out on the road again. That year they made their way to St. Paul, where Ernst returned to teaching and tilting at windmills. The elder Krech was in many ways an intractable and rigid man, not easily suffering the actions of "knaves and fools" as he called them. His religious zealotry and unorthodox teaching methods caused regular troubles with the local school boards. During the 1860s he bounced from school to school in Minneapolis and St. Paul, taking the boys with him wherever they went, and in 1866 his final living son Paul was born. During these years Mathilde was contributing to the family income as a photographer, advertising quality glass slide portraits in the local newspapers.[14] Around 1870 Ernst took what he had saved since events in New Ulm and packed up the family for Kentucky. Freeman was now 14 years old and growing tired of the wandering existence he was obliged to live. Ernst's scheme for educating the illiterate miners of rural Kentucky was a disaster, and three years later he returned with the family to St. Paul broken financially and physically.[15] It was the end of his days as a vagabond and rabble-rouser. He continued to teach, with Mathilde always there in support, but by this time he was nearing sixty and his will for opposition was waning. In 1880 the family was still together in Minneapolis where regardless of Ernst's often dire circumstances they had a live-in servant.

As Ernst's life was settling down, his sons began to forge their own destinies. In spite of his intransigence, their father had set a powerful example through his dedication to study, hard work and ethics; one of his favorite sayings was "principle above expedient or compromise." The boys took these lessons to heart. Alvin began his working life in a flourmill at the age of thirteen, and later labored as a contractor and engineer for the gigantic railroad companies of the Midwest, by his account building more track than any other man in the history of American railroads. His rise to the highest levels of American business was astonishing, considering such modest beginnings. He was on the board of many powerful companies (railroads, financial institutions and insurance concerns), and eventually the chairman of the board of the monolithic Equitable Trust of New York.[16] Paul, the youngest, was the repository of his father's musical talent, taking it with him west to Spokane, Washington, and then to Chicago.

In 1881 Freeman, now 25 years old, struck out on his own. He was working as an accountant in a large dry goods store and was now ready to take stock of all that his father had taught and instilled in him. After a momentary diversion in New York, where he did some freelance writing and gained more experience as an accountant, the oldest son returned to Minnesota.[17] In the emerging town of Aitkin, less than 100 miles from Minneapolis, he found the place where he would raise his children and serve the community in business and civics for nearly forty years. The seeds of Warren William's destiny were sown deep in Minnesota mud.

The city that Freeman encountered in 1881 was still a raw frontier settlement, with taverns and brothels being the dominant form of business drawing in the spring and summer logging trade that traversed the Mississippi and Mud Rivers. The town's population swelled during those months, with rough-hewn men from local pinery camps looking for ways to gamble, drink, or party away their earnings. Watching the local sheriff regularly break up drunken brawls—as well as the not infrequent knifings and gunplay—could easily have dissuaded the new resident from putting down family roots in such a

Warren William's father Freeman E. Krech, circa 1880. Within a few years of sitting for this portrait he was one of the most important citizens of the small rural town of Aitkin, Minnesota. Courtesy Barbara Hall.

place. But Freeman, along with other locals, saw what Aitkin could become and set about turning the tide. The waning of the timber trade helped expedite matters; with fewer roughnecks in town the business trade began providing outfitting and services for the settlers who were taking over the newly cleared land to the north.[18] Within fifteen years Aitkin no longer evoked a Barbary Coast of the Midwest, but a steady, ambitious town with a telephone exchange, electric power, two newspapers, and prospects for a bright future.

Freeman Krech put his mind to becoming an integral part of the Aitkin business community. In his early years he was a cashier for the D.J. Knox lumber mill, sold insurance and operated other short-lived business concerns. But in 1885 Freeman saw an opportunity to make his mark on the community. E.F. Barrett, publisher of *The Aitkin Age*, the town's only newspaper — the paper that served all of Aitkin County, in fact — was interested in selling out his interests. Although the paper was only two years old and a marginal prospect at best, Freeman marshaled his business contacts, purchased the newspaper and set about using his writing and accounting skills to make it viable. Over the next decade, Freeman built it into a profitable entity, while selling and repurchasing the paper more than once. He also met Frances Potter, one of six daughters of Aitkin's most powerful merchant, Warren William Potter. A colonel with the Grand Army of the Potomac during the Civil War, Warren Potter was one of Aitkin's earliest businessmen, arriving in 1871. He had a hand in settling the nearby city of Grand Rapids, when he enterprisingly moved his general supply building closer to the local logging camps up river. When competition followed, the town grew from Potter's first modest structure.[19] The Potters were Aitkin royalty, owners of the Potter Hotel, among other enterprises, and Freeman was clearly a man on the rise. A union was almost inevitable, and the two were married on September 18, 1890.

In October, just about a month after Warren's parents married, Frances was pregnant. This was happy news for all involved, but Freeman had his worries knowing that three of his siblings and a half brother had all died in infancy. However things were quite different than they had been 35 years earlier; modern medicine was now reaching even the hinterlands of Minnesota, and Freeman calmed his own fears. The parents-to-be calculated that Frances would be likely to deliver in July, and dutifully prepared for the new baby throughout the late winter and spring, outfitting themselves with everything they needed. Frances delivered a baby boy on Monday, July 13, 1891. The son they wanted appeared healthy and happy, and the families were duly pleased. For two days the euphoria of a new addition to the family held sway. But on Thursday the boy, who superstitiously had still not been officially named, took ill. The next day, in spite of the best efforts of the family and doctors, he was dead.

The Age described it this way in the weekly edition of Saturday, July 18:

> Suddenly taken last night from the parents was the infant son of Mr. and Mrs. Freeman E. Krech. The baby first saw the light of day on Monday morning last — and until yesterday afternoon appeared to enjoy the best of health when he caught a bad cold, followed by sneezing and coughing spells, which resulted in his demise early this morning.

Ernst and Mathilde, still living in St. Paul, received word and commiserated with the couple. Of course they understood the loss of a child whom the parents never got to know. The following week, a ceremony was held, and the infant who would have been Warren William's big brother was laid to rest near the back of the local cemetery, in front of a large, rough-hewn stone with the inscription "Krech," adjacent to an area devoted to the Potter family. On the tiny tombstone was chiseled only "Baby" and the dates of birth and death, so heartbreakingly close together. Freeman and Frances mourned deeply, but were undaunted. Infant deaths were not at all uncommon, and parents knew that they might have to endure hard losses before their family was intact.

Meanwhile, things were slowly changing in Aitkin: more business was coming in, and the population was steadily increasing. In January of 1892 Frances was again — as Aitkinites might politely put it — in a family way. A fall delivery was expected, and the couple knew that it was now time for a new, permanent home of their own. Freeman began searching for a plat of land to develop, and quickly found it on what was then the far south side of town. Just beyond the crossing of the Mud River on Minnesota Avenue, the main north-south axis of Aitkin, were two large lots, nicely elevated to avoid the occasional floods from the river only an eighth of a mile away. The land had changed hands a few times over the years, most notably when Charles J. Birch had defaulted on his mortgage — possibly as the result of a clause in the contract explicitly forbidding "intoxicating liquors ... or immoral businesses or occupations thereon." But in 1892 the lots, along with a very modest home situated on the property, were owned by William Henguer, and Freeman negotiated the purchase for $200.[20] The deal closed on June 13, and the Krechs moved in just before the one-year anniversary of the death of their son. Once again, the pair set about to prepare the house for their new arrival. On October 26, Warren's older sister Pauline was born. Along with his mother and grandmother, she would become an important and reliable feminine influence in the actor's life.

With Pauline the picture of health, the fear of losing another

Warren's older brother survived only four days before he took ill and died. This marker and a small notice published in the Aitkin newspaper are the only existing records of his life and death.

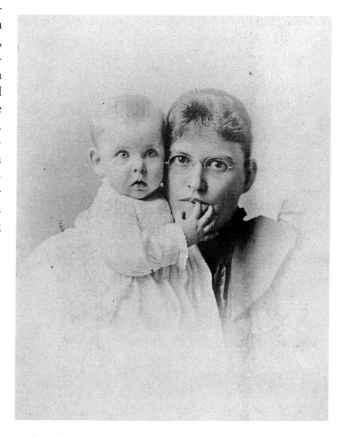

A playful portrait of Warren's mother Frances Krech with his older sister Pauline, made in 1892. These two women were the first of many important feminine role models for Warren William, who grew up with his grandmother, mother and two sisters. Courtesy Ted Beisel.

child wore off. Even so, she would wait over two years before having a baby brother in the house. In the meantime, Freeman continued to infiltrate Aitkin's social and civic society. He helped chair community organizations, dabbled in various local businesses, took membership in the Mendelssohn Society of Minnesota and continued on and off to be the publisher of Aitkin's lone newspaper. In 1894 the family was still living in the small house on Minnesota Avenue, and Freeman was selling fire insurance as an agent for large firms such as The Hartford. For entertainment, the couple might spend time around Aitkin taking in a road company performance of *Uncle Tom's Cabin*, or enjoying a few of the newest leisure activities. The phonograph was just then available to the public, and R.C. McMurdy purchased one and held parties exhibiting the new equipment. More entertaining still were the X-ray socials sponsored by the Methodist Church — X-ray pictures of your living heart, 10 cents— where you could also enjoy ice cream, cake and sodas.[21] There is no word available on the heightened incidence of cancer among those attending.

The Krechs eventually decided the time was right for another child and that spring Frances announced that she was again pregnant. This time the due date was in December. Aitkin was still having growing pains, and although it was more prosperous and less unruly than ever before, the town into which Warren Krech was about to be born was still essentially a small frontier outpost grasping its way into the modern world. Electric power was almost a year away. Public water and sewer facilities were only then in the planning stages, and for weeks at a time the only safe place to be was on the wooden sidewalks built high above the foot-deep mud of Aitkin's streets. Lumberjacks continued to flood the town around the spring breakup, when the Watson and Simpson Dams were opened to provide a head of water for logs to be floated to the Mississippi.[22] They raised hell, to be sure, but the general feeling among

The first appearance of Warren William Krech on film was in this picture with his sister Pauline, taken in 1895. The two remained close throughout their entire lives. It was Pauline who convinced her brother to pursue acting, and to change his name to Warren William. **Courtesy Barbara Hall.**

the polite element of the townsfolk was paraphrased by *The Age* in 1896: "Better let the boys have their own way for a brief session, and no one will be the worse off." There were still dens of ill fame, taverns, smokers and fights, but fewer blades and pistols to contend with.

It was into this changing world that a baby boy was born to the couple on December 2. Certainly Freeman must have been gratified to have a son. It was the time of deeply entrenched patriarchy, and fathers were expected to pass on what they had learned and acquired to their sons. Daughters might get a dowry, but not the family business. Warren William Krech was named—following a not unwarranted superstitious delay—after his grandfather Warren William Potter, the storied member of the great Army of the Potomac. Coincidentally, the future actor's given names mirrored those of the most famous actor of the era, the great Boston stage star William Warren.

Around this time, the Potter family, Frances' father and stepmother,[23]* purchased a lot directly across the street from the Krechs and built an impressive home on the site. Now in direct proximity, they could help with the rearing of the children and enjoy the advantages of grandparenting. Freeman himself began thinking about building a new home on his land and, while Warren was spending his days in a crib in the small home on Minnesota Avenue, he rolled the figures around in his head. While he calculated and saved, Freeman relished the opportunity to pass along family traditions to his children. His father came to America with a great affinity for Germanic and Norse legends, and had often recited those tall tales to his sons. The proud papa now repeated those nursery rhymes and stories for his children.[24] By the time Warren was toddling around the small house—inquisitive and curious, like most boys—he was completely fascinated with the stories, especially by the legend of Thor, the Thunder God of Norse myths.

The two-year-old Warren William Krech seems to be contemplating something bigger than himself in this portrait taken in 1896. Elsewhere in America, Henry Ford was starting his automobile company, the Dow Jones was first published and X-rays were discovered. Courtesy Ted Beisel.

According to Warren's Warner Brothers studio biography, one of his earliest memories involved acting, and put him off

*Frances' own mother Matilde had died in 1884, and Warren had remarried in 1891.

the very idea of it for many years. While still a young boy — likely under the age of five — the family hosted a gathering at their home. In the house was another young boy, perhaps a year older than Warren, who played a drum and "spoke a piece" for the assembled crowd. The boy made a tremendous impression on the future actor — Warren probably did not appreciate the attention the interloper received from his parents in his own home — and for years he harbored a great dislike of people who "spoke pieces." Although Warren claimed he didn't change his mind about actors until his first trip to New York in 1913, he almost certainly exaggerated; by then, acting was already becoming part of his life.

It wasn't until 1898 that Freeman was able to begin seriously thinking about building the house that he wanted for the family. His father Ernst had passed away on New Year's Day, 1897, following a long decline. Although Paul eventually claimed to have received a posthumous message, the old spiritualist's wish to communicate from the beyond was scuttled by the unfortunate finality of death. Freeman was now the *de facto* head of the family. He brought his widowed mother to Aitkin from Minneapolis where she would spend the rest of her days with the family,

telling tales of New Ulm, her travels in the Midwest, and the Fatherland, now so far in the past. It was clearly time for a new home that his family would grow up in. Around this time, Freeman had again released the newspaper and gone into partnership with another Aitkin businessman, W.B. Marr, under the name Marr and Krech. Marr had long owned Aitkin's only funeral parlor, and the two successfully operated various concerns including a hardware store, blacksmith shop and insurance agency, and had extensive real estate holdings in town. With business going well, plans were drawn up, and in the summer of 1899 ground was broken on the new house. It was to have all the modern conveniences then available: indoor plumbing with hot water, electric lights, telephone service and steam heat radiators.[25] All summer and into the fall, four-year-old Warren watched the massive house go up adjacent to their modest structure. He was absolutely entranced by the process, and a nascent curiosity and interest in how things work was surely spurred by the opportunity to watch it all close at hand.

Warren's piercing eyes are already evident in this photograph taken with Pauline when he was three. In Aitkin, the young boy grew up in what was still essentially a frontier town: dirt roads, no electrical power and no telephone system. Courtesy Barbara Hall.

Even more exciting to a young boy raised on tales of Norse mythology was the rumor that the burly man who used his hammer and other massive tools to fashion the boiler and plumbing system of the house was in fact the Thunder God himself, Thor. Aided by a summer notoriously active in thunder and lightning storms, the four-year-old took the story as deeply to heart as he would the idea of Santa Claus. In his young mind the man in the basement called down every rainstorm and gale. Every crack of thunder pealed from the sledgehammer he crashed against the pipes. The boy was in heaven, and the man he became never forgot the excitement of those months.

By the fall of 1899, the Krech house was finished. At a cost of $5000, it was—and remains—one of the great homes in the city of Aitkin. From its imposing and stalwart appearance, one would easily guess that it was the home of one of the important families of the area. It was built high on a bluff overlooking the street; a stairway and path winds up to the front door. The house itself is a magnificent, rambling assemblage of turn-of-the-century craftsmanship, interior design and engineering. Around every corner are the exact types of nooks and crannies that would fascinate a young boy like Warren: long, steep stairways, fireplaces, walk-in closets, enormous built-in sideboards, crawlspaces and a four-level dumbwaiter. The first floor entrance features a small vestibule that opens directly to a long hallway that divides the home neatly in two. On either side are the receiving parlor and dining room for entertaining guests, each with a fireplace, while the rest of the area is given over to servants' quarters, rooms for boarders (the Krechs usually had two) and a kitchen and bath. Stairways up to the second and third floor, and down to the basement — the lair of the Thunder God — are on the north side of the

This house, built by Freeman Krech during the summer that Warren was four years old, is still one of the magnificent homes in Aitkin, Minnesota. It was among the first houses in town to be constructed with hot water plumbing, electricity and telephone service.

divide. On the second floor are family spaces, with a sitting room and dining room for everyday use, a second kitchen directly above the first, as well as baths and sleeping quarters. The third floor then was the realm of the children, with three spacious bedrooms, a large storage room, a unique wrap-around closet underneath the eaves of the roof, and a large open area in the center where the stairs and dumbwaiter come up. This area, where Warren played and rambled during his formative years, also allowed him some of the first practical uses for his tinkering and invention. According to legend he fashioned a homemade rope ladder that allowed him to descend from one of the common area windows—some 35 feet from the ground—so that the teenage boy could visit his first romantic love, a local telephone operator. It's a pretty good story—but that one, and the other he later told about shinnying down a drainpipe for the same reason,[26] seem unlikely. Even a love-struck teenager would be daunted by those heights.

In 1901, about the time Warren was entering first grade, a man named B.L. Hollister came to Aitkin. He was an experienced newspaper publisher looking for an area in which to launch a new weekly tabloid. Word around town was that Freeman was the man to talk to, being successful—multiple times—with *The Age*. On an early autumn afternoon, Hollister paid a visit to Freeman in his office at one of the Marr and Krech buildings. The former publisher and editor was expecting the birth of his fourth child in November and not only had advice for the newcomer, but something even better: the hardware with which to begin. Freeman had kept, from his old days with *The Age*, a hand-operated, six-column "Pearl" jobber press, along with a few type cases and some news type. In short, everything Hollister would need to start a rival paper. Freeman was prevailed upon to sell the tools to the upstart and by November, *The Aitkin Independent* was born.[27] Amazingly, within a few months, another paper, *The Aitkin Republican*, began publication. Suddenly boasting three weekly papers, Aitkin must have felt giddy with big city aspirations.

In November, Aitkin also welcomed the newest member of the Krech family, Warren's younger sister Elizabeth. Warren was about to turn seven and he and his father were now outnumbered two to one—two sisters, mother and grandmother—in the new house on Minnesota Avenue. In the meantime, Hollister's new paper was performing well; during 1902 he also purchased *The Age* when the owners, Phremmer and Hoffstead, decided to sell out. Unable to work both papers, Hollister offered the editorship of the *Independent* to Freeman, while he would chair *The Age*. Freeman took the deal. Although he continued to keep his hands in many other endeavors—including acting as the vice-president of the 1st National Bank of Aitkin, and continuing in business with W.B. Marr—ink, as they say, was in his blood. From 1902, Freeman was the editor or publisher of one of Aitkin's papers continuously for the next twenty years.[28]

Warren Krech's formative years were a mélange of the proper and the playful. As the son of one of the city's wealthiest families he was sometimes pampered and cut off from the usual fun of the other kids in town. It didn't help that a young son of the Caseys, another prominent family who were half of the prosperous Potter / Casey company, had drowned while playing near the bank at the bend of the Mud River.[29] The death hit home for many families, and Warren, whose instincts were to run and play like every other boy—especially with the river only 40 yards from his house—was closely eyed by his father and mother. Warren usually shook off his watchmen, however, and in the spring and summer he sometimes blended into the crowd that followed the "River Rats"—lumbermen who herded log runs down river to the local sawmills. The Rats were fun to watch, leaping from log to log with the aid of their long pikes, but the real treat was what came behind them. The Wannigan, a large raft that held sleeping quarters and the cooks' kitchen that followed the run, providing food and lodging for the working men.

Warren and the children of Aitkin constantly hoped to convince the cook to allow them treats—usually fresh donuts—and often came away with their bellies stuffed.[30]

Warren's two lifelong passions were seeded and grown during these years. Tales of the seafaring Vikings and Norsemen that came down from his grandfather rattled around in his brain, and the rivers and lakes of upper Minnesota were like great oceans to the tiny boy. He became entranced by the romance of the sea. The Krechs had a cabin on Bay Lake where they often spent summers, and the aptly named Mille Lacs Lake—large enough to barely see across—was nearby. Warren began to fantasize about a life on the water, taking in exotic places and going wherever the wind took him. During the same time, his father noticed Warren's burgeoning interest in how things worked. His son was obsessed with understanding all things mechanical, and there was plenty of building and construction going on to satisfy his curiosity. In addition to the Krech home and his visits to the printing works at *The Age*, Warren's first ten years saw an incredible wealth of stimulus for his budding fascination with engineering. Around the growing Warren William, Aitkin installed its first public water and sewer system, watched a state-of-the-art sawmill go into service, constructed a modern high school building, finished their first electrical grid and erected an opera house. Although it is likely an apocryphal story, rumor has it that Warren's father was convinced of his son's aptitude for mechanics when the boy dismantled part of the family car, but hadn't yet the skill to put it back together. Whatever

Looking distinctly **unlike** the sheltered boy of wealthy parents, young Warren Krech (second from left) shows off his fishing skills, probably during a vacation at the family cabin on Bay Lake, Minnesota, circa 1907. Other men in unique headgear are unidentified. Courtesy Patricia Lyon.

the case, Freeman — a strict man, but a dutiful and caring one — didn't get mad, but rather encouraged the boy's aptitude by giving him a room in the old house for him to build a tinkering shop.[31] Many early pieces came out of the former Krech house over the years, including a table that Warren built for his mother when he was just nine. The boy's gift survived twenty years in Aitkin, then ten in New York before it eventually made its way to Hollywood with the grown-up builder.

As Warren developed into a lanky young boy — known around town as "Skinny" and "High Pockets" — he took more and more chances when he was able to steal away from his parents' watchful eyes. In spite of his image as a scion of a wealthy family, he made friends among the other children of Aitkin, and regularly snuck off to take a dip in the Keasley swimming hole, or in the Mississippi or Mud rivers. Ice-skating was also a common activity, as was sliding on what he and the boys called "rubber ice" in the late autumn and early spring. By far the most dangerous activity of Warren's youth — even if you're inclined to believe the rope ladder from the roof of his house — was when he and the boys imitated the log-hopping River Rats during the spring runs. "The River Rats had spiked shoes so they didn't slip," he remembered years later. "So I put long screws through the soles of a pair of shoes and went leaping along

On the far right, looking as if he's already practicing to take his first bow, is the young Warren William Krech. This picture was snapped with his Aitkin, Minnesota, grammar school class, circa 1906. Courtesy Randy Wall.

with them. They weren't as good as the spikes, but they must have worked. I'm still here." According to Warren, there were also some occasions when the screws didn't work so well. "If we fell in, we would build a fire and dry our clothes and go home as though nothing had happened," he said before his smile turned sour. "Then I'd get a whaling."[32] Corporal punishment, while not a regular occurrence, was definitely part of the Krech method.

Freeman was practically a town elder at this point, with fingers in everything from bank boards to a stint as the city auditor. He served on numerous committees, belonged to fraternal organizations and joined the Masons. Frances— now known as "Madame Krech" by most of the town — also became a member of the Masons, joining the women's arm, known as the Eastern Star. When Warren became old enough, he too became a member,[33] natural enough then for the social and financial opportunities it made available. It was a way of life learned during these years— Old World social intercourse — which Warren adopted when he made his way to New York and Hollywood. His desire for inclusion and the lessons his father showed toward charity and public service — as well as business contacts—filtered down into Warren's penchant for joining many clubs and organizations over the years. It eventually led to the star's participation in the formation of the Screen Actors Guild.

The young boy was now, however, just growing up and beginning to think about what he wanted to be. There has always been talk about Warren William's desire to become a newspaper reporter or editor, but it is entirely untrue that he either worked on his father's paper or held any desire to do so. In spite of Freeman's hope that his son would take an interest in the family business, Warren invariably developed "a headache" that kept him away whenever there was work to be done. His thoughts at this point were focused on the sea, perhaps visualizing himself as a ship's captain, or later—for a short time—a marine engineer. But it wouldn't be long before these serious diversions were put aside for something more frivolous and less taxing.

It seems odd to think that a small town in rural Minnesota would need an opera house, but that is exactly what Samuel Hodgeden calculated in 1903. The local entrepreneur decided that Aitkin was now prosperous and well populated enough to support the arts, and built a large building on north Minnesota Avenue. The first floor was devoted to retail space and the cellar to baser entertainments— illicit boxing and wrestling matches known as "smokers"— but upstairs was a large auditorium that Hodgeden called the Opera House. It became Aitkin's performance space for everything from music and movies to dances and travelling shows. And it was here that the fire of Warren's love of performance was ignited.

2

Stage Struck

When Warren William was still very young—probably not yet a teenager—a travelling show came through Aitkin. The troupe played the Opera House and performed a program called *The Flaming Arrow*. In attendance with his parents, the boy was astonished to see a genuine flaming arrow shot across the stage during the action of the play. It left an indelible memory, and was the spark of his interest in performing that grew hotter and brighter over the intervening years. At that moment, however, he was merely excited by the idea that he might like to do that kind of thing onstage himself someday.[1]

While Warren's elementary school years were uneventful, he had the occasional chance to perform in pageants to keep his interest in acting alive. "There was the episode of me doing a shadow pantomime of the great Paderewski playing the piano at some school function," he recalled at the age of 40.[2] During those years he was taking piano lessons (hence his ability to mime the great pianist) and enjoying typically boyish things, like studying the train that derailed in downtown Aitkin in 1908 (no loss of life to make his interest morbid).[3] But he had not forgotten that flaming arrow. It wasn't until the summer of 1911 that he entered high school—at the late age of 16—and began his stage career in earnest.

By 1911, movies were growing out of swaddling clothes and becoming the world's greatest mass entertainment. That year Aitkin followed the wave of enthusiasm and built their first theater, which they called The Moveum, configured for both film projection and live stage performances. In Warren's freshman year, Aitkin High began casting a new school play. Warren knew that he absolutely had to have something to do with it. He auditioned, and landed a part in the production that was performed at The Moveum; according to Warren, it was his first serious appearance on any stage. That flaming arrow was now lighting his path forward.

At this time, Warren was finding his way through the maze of adolescent connections, social and interpersonal, that everyone goes through during those years. He was sometimes socially reticent—not without confidence, but simply shy—and he found that it was easier to stand in front of people as someone else, rather than deal with the anxiety of talking to them directly. He also discovered that retreat into character released his inhibitions, making the opportunity to create and affect another personality highly desirable. It was the beginning of a trait that writers and friends observed again and again, and that drove his wife crazy during his Hollywood years: Warren hated the spotlight to shine directly on him, and often took pains to deliberately redirect it onto his work.

During his high school years "Skinny" Krech became absorbed in the art of the theater, from acting and staging, right down to painting scenery with his classmate Sarah Lowrey. Other stage appearances followed as Warren gained poise in front of audiences. When the class of 1912–1913 gave its senior performance of *The Kingdom of Heart's Content*, sophomore Warren was billed third as Sidney Hilton, "a student card sharp" in the production (featuring Sarah's older sister Annie) that played at the Opera House just 11 days after his 18th birthday.[4] (After

Downtown Aitkin, showing advertising for The Potter Company. Warren William Krech was the name-sake of his maternal grandfather Warren William Potter, the powerful Aitkin merchant who also had a hand in settling the city of Grand Rapids. Courtesy Patricia Lyon.

his migration to Hollywood, *The Age* recalled that Warren "enjoyed hamming it up to local audiences in every home theatre role he managed to get"; when she visited Hollywood in 1936, his teacher A.M. McMullin remembered that he took leads in all the school plays.) One time when he didn't manage to make it to the stage was when he had the lead in a production opposite his friend Elsie Spauldin; Warren took sick at the last minute and had to be replaced by the principal.

No one in the family knew it then, but shortly after Warren's performance with the senior class in December of 1912, his life was set on the final path to stardom. That winter, Freeman decided to take the family on a trip to New York City. He and Frances, along with the children, could visit his brother Alvin—now immensely successful with the Equitable Corporation—and take in the restaurants, cultural events and shows New York offered. Freeman had spent some time there before moving to Aitkin, but it was Warren's first chance to see the big city. The inveterate tinkerer and amateur inventor had never been anywhere farther than Duluth.

His trip to Gotham entranced him: soaring skyscrapers, elevated cars and subways, the Brooklyn Bridge, the Statue of Liberty and Times Square—everything was bigger, brighter and bolder. But the real thing Warren was dying to see was Broadway—then the unchallenged king of world entertainment. At the Globe Theatre, the family first took in a performance of *The Lady of the Slipper*, a massive musical fantasy with a cast of 85, including 65 chorus girls, and the vaudeville comedy team of Montgomery and Stone. Next they were in the audience of *Peg o' My Heart* starring Laurette Taylor at the Cort Theatre. The 19 year old was completely smitten with the leading lady, and utterly fractured by the comedy team. For him these stars

Standing at right with his hands on his lapels, the future Warren William strikes a pose as Sidney Hilton, a travelling card sharp, in the 1912 Aitkin High School production of *The Kingdom of Heart's Content*. Courtesy Randy Wall.

were, and always remained, the acme of the acting profession. "I doubted that I'd ever be as good as Laurette Taylor or Montgomery and Stone. But the glamour of the stage had caught me," he wrote in 1928.[5] These two experiences cemented his desire to become an actor. Although there were still hurdles, recriminations and detours, the young man who had bounded around the modest stages of Aitkin was eventually going to return to New York — to that very theater, in fact — to become a star.

Back in Aitkin, Warren continued his studies and his declamation, as well as his mechanical invention. During high school he built what he called "a motorboat operated by a bicycle," which he dubbed "The Pirate," and took it to the local swimming holes to run it. And although Ms. McMullin generously called him "a brilliant scholar,"[6] Warren was more of an average student. Good at English composition and poor at mathematics, he did not make it into the top 30 percent of his class and his grade average was below 80 percent. In those days his pockets were always stuffed with the very things young boys need for entertainment: knives, string, rubber bands, nails, bottle caps and so on.[7] He was on the Aitkin football team starting in 1913, and counted himself a good all-around physical specimen, continuing his athletic endeavors during his adult years as an excellent fencer, tennis player, golfer and yachtsman. By this time, Warren had shaken off his image as the sheltered son of wealth. When a call was put out for someone to take the class colors to the highest steeple available, Warren stepped forward and

By the winter of 1913, 19-year-old Warren William Krech was still a lanky high school student who excelled in athletics, mainly football and basketball. In the backfield, third from left (looking up) is the future Broadway and film star. Players and coaches are unidentified. Courtesy Patricia Lyon.

did the high climbing; perhaps he did make those sorties from the top of the Krech house after all.[8] Whatever the case, he became one of the boys—perhaps the genuine accomplishment of his youth, considering all that was stacked against him. This selfsame act of a wealthy boy working to fit in also infused him with a modest nature, never to be too ostentatious, call attention to himself or do anything that could be construed as arrogant or high-hat. The lesson he learned as a boy was: treat people on an even field, be decent and unaffected, and they will invariably appreciate it. His well-suppressed ego also eventually kept him from advocating too hard on his own behalf, limiting many career opportunities and driving his future wife to distraction.

Either following the school year of 1914 or after graduation in 1915, Warren somehow prevailed upon his parents to let him have a summer away from home. A group of his friends were going west to work in the Dakota wheat fields. Warren wanted to tag along but, considering his parents' long-standing reticence, he felt certain they would forbid it. As sometimes happened, they confounded him by agreeing to the trip. He was so surprised that in later life he confessed that he *still* didn't understand how his family allowed him that one absolutely free summer. According to Warren the work was mundane and not particularly difficult, but there were other hazards. His primary recollection of that summer was an accident he had while driving a hayrick back to the field from the separator. Deciding he was now an adult, he needed to partake in adult habits. To that end he took up the practice of chewing snuff while on the job. On this particular afternoon Warren put a large bit of snuff next to his gums just as he trundled the rig into the field. In short order the springless wagon hit a hole in the path, and Warren inadvertently swallowed his snuff whole. An hour later, someone realized he was missing and sent out a search party. They found him in terrible shape, but not much the worse for wear. Although unrecorded, it is assumed that he gave up chewing tobacco for good.

As Warren was nearing graduation, his anxiety over what he would do next was increasing. Although he loved acting, he once again expected that his parents would slough off the idea as a foolish whim and herd him into newspaper publishing. A compromise might have been his interest in marine engineering, which combined his two great passions—mechanics and the sea. But it was not to be. In an effort to mollify his parents, Warren took the entrance exam for the Military Academy at West Point. He looked back years later on the moment that might have changed the course of his life. "I just missed becoming a nautical engineer by flunking an exam in mathematics. I wasn't really as bad as the exam painted me—it was just that I was afraid of the quiz and everything I ever knew froze inside me when I came to it. If I hadn't been in mortal fear of examinations at that time, I wouldn't be an actor now."[9] During this period, father and son were quite close; residents observed that Warren took on the mannerisms and speech patterns of his father,[10] and the two participated in many civic activities together. In October of 1914 they were the only father and son in the newly formed 34-member choir of St. James Episcopal Church, which the Krechs regularly attended. Following graduation in 1915, Warren accompanied Freeman on a "sociability run"—an inaugural trip over Aitkin County's new highway which stretched from Duluth west to Brainerd. The men drove through Cloquet and other nearby towns—presumably with Freeman letting his son take the wheel occasionally—then had dinner in Cromwell with over 200 other automobile enthusiasts.[11] The mechanical-minded boy loved bonding with his father, and getting a look at all those flivvers parked near the restaurant in tiny little Cromwell. Getting Freeman to agree to let him take up acting was likely another matter.

Commencement was set for June 4, 1915. It is unclear why Warren started school so late, entering Aitkin High the summer he was 16 years old, but he was now 20, well above the average age of the other graduates, and ready to finish his education and start making his own way. In February, the Aitkin school board made an effort to address the new class divide growing in the town. For a number of years it was evident that the well-to-do families (of which Warren was one) were putting out an inordinate amount of money to outfit their sons and daughters with gowns, suits, flowers and gifts for commencement. The average family went to falling behind socially or making themselves bankrupt in keeping up. Across Minnesota, districts had placed monetary restrictions, or called for homemade clothes for all graduates. In 1915, Aitkin went a step further, limiting each graduate to a maximum of $2 for outfitting themselves, and limiting the senior banquet to one course. *The Age* was so disgusted by the penuriousness of the plan that they sarcastically lauded the board members, saying that the names of those "revered gentlemen" who endorsed the plan would go down in history. In 1915, however, Warren wore a $2 suit to graduation, where he danced with girls in $2 gowns.

The 1915 class of Aitkin High School numbered fifteen—nine girls and six boys—with Warren once again in the minority. Typically for small town America at this time, the festivities featured a strong dose of religion, beginning with a Sunday sermon and ending with the Friday evening commencement address from the Reverend W.E. Hammond. On Wednesday the class program in the school auditorium included speeches, music by the school orchestra, a performance of the Glee Club and the valedictory number "For Value Received We Promise to Pay." On Saturday, June 4, Warren picked up his diploma and was released into the world.[12]

Following graduation, Warren's future—at least where his parents were concerned—was not entirely decided. His father still had hopes that his son would go into journalism, but there was little chance of that. There was still the possibility of a career as an inventor, but Warren knew that it was an unlikely road to success. "I always loved tinkering around in a tool shop and I rather fancied myself as an amateur inventor, but I realized this would never turn into a particularly well paying profession," he remembered thinking.[13] Some months earlier, Warren had confided to his sister Pauline — and himself — that he had no desire for newspaper work, but he couldn't quite bring himself to disappoint the publisher-father he loved. "But because I was a reasonably dutiful son, I'd probably have done it," he later recalled, resignedly.[14] In their private conversations about the future, Pauline demonstrated a deep understanding of her brother's vaguely formed desire and began to encourage him to try his hand at acting as a profession. In an interview that appeared in *Movie Mirror* magazine in 1933, he stressed the considerable influence of his sister on his choice. "It was her prompting and support that finally induced me to say no to my dad's wishes. Acting was what I really wanted to do, but I don't think I'd ever had made the break if it wasn't for her."[15] The young man needn't have worried about his father's reaction: Freeman Krech was a surprisingly liberal man as it related to his children's futures. He admitted to his son that he himself had once fancied an opportunity to act — not a fantasy that many men would own up to in 1915, especially Midwesterners from small towns with respectable reputations.[16] When Warren's choice was finally out in the open, Freeman told the graduate that he was behind him and the family resolved to send him to the best acting school they could find. The praise that Pauline lavished on her brother was never forgotten; she was among the first of many positive feminine role models in the actor's life.

After a summer of research, including catalogues from various drama schools, they settled on the American Academy of Dramatic Arts in New York City. There were more than a few reasons to recommend going east. The Academy had been turning out talented and successful actors since its incorporation as the first professional acting school in the United States in 1894. It had a pedigree as the best institution in the east, and had lately graduated a group of actors who would determine the direction of the stage and screen craft for decades. Among the recent alumni were future Broadway and Hollywood stars William Powell, Edward G. Robinson, Spencer Tracy, Pat O'Brien and Joseph Schildkraut, as well as author Dale Carnegie, who used his Academy training to build an empire teaching public speaking.

In 1915, Manhattan was also the unquestioned mecca of entertainment in the United States. Broadway was at the luminous peak of its influence over American culture, and competition was sparse[17]; silent movies were only then entering the feature picture era (and they wouldn't talk for more than a decade). Practical broadcast radio was still four years away. The phonograph and the gramophone were barely moving past the parlor into living rooms, and television was just an embryonic idea in the minds of some foolish scientists. Across the country, road companies of the great Broadway successes toured towns grand and modest, bringing eastern entertainment to the majority that would never see the lights of Gotham. The Great White Way was omnipotent, unchallenged. If you were serious about acting, New York was the center of the universe.

Additionally, Warren's uncle Alvin Krech — Freeman's younger brother — was living in New York. He was a wildly successful and extremely busy man, now a top executive in the gigantic insurance concern the Equitable Corporation, but he could be counted on to look after Warren, and would be close by in case of emergency or trouble. So, in October, Warren boarded a train and headed east for his audition to enter the American Academy. Warren was typically self-effacing about the choice: "[My parents] were probably happy I was interested in anything. I wasn't a very hopeful boy."[18]

A few days later, Warren arrived at Grand Central Station and made his way northwest across Manhattan to a $10-a-week boarding house at 344 West 57th Street, between Eighth and Ninth Avenues.[19] The Academy — executive offices, students' rooms, classrooms, lecture halls, rehearsal space, and theater — was then headquartered in Carnegie Hall, the marvel of acoustic engineering built by Andrew Carnegie in 1891, located nearby at 57th and Seventh. On the cool autumn morning of October 26, Warren Krech walked east from his apartment to the 57th Street entrance of the auditorium and through the doors to the elevators. He made his way to the rehearsal room and sat nervously waiting to give his introductory audition. He was just five weeks from his twenty-first birthday, and beginning his life of performance.

3

Skyscraper Souls

The twenty-year-old who walked onto the stage in Carnegie Hall that afternoon was essentially illiterate in the ways of the theater. His modest training back home most certainly did not prepare him for the kind of intensive study that would be expected of him in New York. Like most young people who find their life's resonant path, however, the desire and dedication to succeed were tuned to a sympathetic vibration.

On that first day, Warren Kretch (as his name was misspelled on the audition form) was graded in 22 categories. Among the descriptions of his physical characteristics, he was listed as tall and heavy—odd, considering his lifelong ability to stay trim without dieting—with medium coloring and good proportions. The director noted his physical condition as "very good," and the general impression of his health and stature seemed positive. There is nothing in any of the other notations—all concerning his acting ability—to indicate that the school had a future star on their hands. His audition card was marked with the terse observations of a jaded tutor: Stage Presence: Good. Voice: Good. Pronunciation: Fair. Reading: Fair. Distinction: Good. Dramatic Instinct: Fairly Good. Imagination: Fairly Good. Pantomime: Probably Good.[1] In his final comment, the auditor gave the best recommendation possible for such a winning performance. "Acceptable" is all he wrote.

With something less than fanfare, Warren was now officially a student of the American Academy of Dramatic Arts. There was the matter of the tuition—$400 for the junior year—which his father paid and could hardly guess would be the best money he ever spent on any of his children.[2] The young man was on the path to following his heroes Montgomery and Stone and his idol Laurette Taylor, she who had so entranced him years earlier.

Just as it was at home, Warren entered the October semester at the AADA as a distinct minority. Eighteen of the twenty-five other students were women, and the shy boy from tiny Aitkin, Minnesota, must have had at least a little anxiety in the world's most exciting city among all those aspiring actresses. Again he was obliged to observe and interact with women — this time professionally — on an intimate basis. It continued to mold his attitude toward them, and give him respect for their work and dedication. There is no record of how he related to them on a romantic basis, although his courtly manners and good looks certainly would have caught more than a few eyes. It didn't hurt that he was also the spitting image of the clean-cut boy next door that was so popular on the silent screen in 1915. Bashful or not, the twenty-year-old only a few months past graduation was in precisely the right place to begin growing up quickly.

Monday through Friday for the next seven months, Warren would arrive promptly at the school at 9 A.M. for his four-hour morning class. After an hour for lunch, another four hours study between 2 and 6 P.M. rounded out his school day. Dispensing with the vague ideas Warren had learned about acting while in high school and replacing them with systematic, modern techniques was a time-consuming job. Each day was taken up with study in the various disciplines that were in vogue at the time. The curriculum was weighted heavily to the practical application of technique, and broken down nearly equally between acting, stagecraft, and physical presence. To prepare for professional assignments, Warren studied both makeup and costuming — indispensable tools for actors who would often be expected to prepare themselves for performances when travelling on the road in stock, or even sometimes in local companies before the days of union requirements. His training in costuming especially came in handy years later when he began providing his own wardrobe for nearly all of his Warner Brothers films. There was also study in stage mechanics and theater business to round out the professional side. The Academy even then believed strongly in training the body as well as the mind, and there were four classes tailored to honing the physical aspects of the art of acting. During the long New York winter of 1915–16, Warren studied health, action dancing, pantomime (crucial for aspiring film actors during the silent era) and fencing, which became a lifelong passion that he indulged often in Hollywood.

The Academy's acting classes were both intellectual and emotive. While technique was strongly accentuated in speech and diction (study of which turned Warren's voice into a magnificent asset), the faculty did not forget the art of observation or thought. Life study and interpretation were two of the most important classes in Warren's junior year, developing in him a passion for creating characterization. All of the disciplines came together in the reading rehearsals the school held regularly to hone the actors' instincts. The junior year at the AADA was a complete, all-in-one whirlwind of training in the art of theater.[3] Many students felt armed enough to venture out into professional assignments without navigating the senior program. However, when the semester ended on May 12, Warren had long since decided he was going to return. During his year in New York he and Pauline had engaged in "an orgy of sightseeing and playgoing,"[4] and the small-town boy was lucky enough to have the means and the opportunity to continue to enjoy the experiences and energy only New York could offer.

The senior year began on September 15, 1916. Although Broadway's dominance over entertainment in America was still at its apogee, the silent film was beginning to forge a mainstream image in the public mind. D.W. Griffith had scored one of the greatest hits in American media history with his unbelievable spectacle *The Birth of a Nation*. Charlie Chaplin had just moved from the Mutual Film company to Essanay, there to craft his finest short films, and become perhaps the most famous and well-paid man in the world. Theda Bara exploded into stardom as the original "vamp," and Pearl White — whom young Warren Krech was soon destined to star alongside — was fresh from coining an amazingly long-lasting addition to the American lexicon by surviving *The Perils of Pauline*. It wasn't perfectly apparent then, but the film had arrived as an art form in America, and the Great White Way had less than ten years before it was pushed aside by the new medium.

Year two at the Academy continued advanced study in the areas covered the previous year, building upon the lessons learned by Warren as a junior. The primary change for seniors was the organization of the class into the Academy Stock Company; a complete, working organization dedicated to gaining practical, onstage experience. Warren was drilled in the function of a working stock actor, taking roles large and small, learning them quickly and performing them in front of a live audience. The 1916 school catalogue described it this way: "Constant rehearsals under the varied and searching criticism of the ablest instructors and performances before audiences composed of people of culture, critics and managers, enable the student to learn easily in six months what it often takes six years and great discomfort to unravel and master in the profession itself." It was most certainly true: the Academy Stock Company mounted fifteen programs that season, the first coming only a month after class resumed in

September. Programs usually consisted of two and occasionally three productions; a full-length play was often paired with a one-act piece, or in some cases, excerpts from other plays. In all, the seniors offered thirty separate productions, from melodrama to farce and back again. It was then that Warren first encountered the constantly recurring bugaboo of his professional life: his inability to remember lines. The AADA taught him most everything a young actor could need, but they could not improve his memory. After school, his earliest assignment in a professional stock company was scuttled when he was let go for blowing cues, and his total lack of recall on film sets was legendary. Warner Brothers producer Hal B. Wallis was so disgusted with the time and money lost by Warren's retakes that he insisted that studio directors break up the actor's speeches into shorter, easier-to-remember pieces so there would be less film wasted.[5] Here, at the Academy, was the beginning of the forgetting. However, approximately every ten days from October 20 to January 12 — with a three-week break for a trip home at Christmas — Warren was obliged to read, rehearse and remember a new part in a new play, and sometimes — as in stock — two parts. It was hell for the beginner, but one can only imagine the difficulties he might have had onstage without the mental acuity gained over those grueling months.

In the basement of Carnegie Hall, adjacent to the building's gigantic boiler room, was the Carnegie Lyceum Theater. The first seven of the Academy's company productions were mounted there, as well as all the rehearsals for the senior class plays. In late November the company performed *The Land of Heart's Desire* by William Butler Yeats, and then began rehearsals for their next offering, Roi Cooper Megrue's *Under Cover*. The play had been a hit on Broadway in 1914–15, running 349 performances at the Cort Theatre. For nine days, Warren pored over the script and contemplated the characters. He took it home and studied it there, sometimes reading it while walking on the street between his boarding house and the school. Warren performed the role of Steve Denby on December 1 and quickly moved on — *The Far Away Princess* was following close behind. He had no idea of it then, but his knowledge of Megrue's almost forgotten little play would give him his first starring role and turn fate in his favor only a few years later.

In January 1917, the troupe moved their performances from the Carnegie Lyceum out into New York, and stepped up the frequency of their productions, now coming nearly every Friday. Warren and the other students got a serious taste of the life of working actors, putting on plays by Oscar Wilde, George Bernard Shaw and W.S. Gilbert at the venerable Broadway showplaces the Belasco, the George M. Cohan, and the Lyceum. Warren returned to the latter as a successful and well-regarded player with the musical comedy *Fanny* in 1926. His school memories may have been the only enjoyment he got out of it: the production was troubled, and even Fanny Brice's star power could only keep it open on Broadway for two months. The Lyceum, on the other hand, has gone on to become the longest continuously active space in New York City, hosting performances regularly since it was built in 1903.

The end to the grueling pace of senior class was in sight. Students were scheduled to graduate on Thursday, March 15, but performances continued on both the 16th and a farewell performance of *A Flower of Yeddo* on March 23, the final official day of school.[6] Simultaneously, however, events were taking place that would overshadow the commencement festivities, and dictate the near future for Warren Krech and millions of young American men.

During March, three American merchant ships were sunk in the Atlantic Ocean by German naval forces. President Woodrow Wilson had struggled mightily to keep the United States out of the Great War that had been raging in Europe for over two years, but these attacks severely loosened America's tightly held grip on neutrality. In the public dialogue it was no longer a question of *if* we would go to war, but *when*. Warren did not have the luxury of planning his immediate future beyond convocation. He had a very good idea where he was likely to be going.

The students in Warren's graduating class were a mixed bag: the serious, the dilettantes, the starry-eyed and those who simply had nothing better to do and the money to do it with. One, Margalo Gilmore, became a well-respected Broadway actress, working on and off from the mid–1920s through the early sixties, and appearing in original productions of the important plays *The Women* and *The Diary of Anne Frank.* Another, Jean Acker,[7] eventually married Rudolph Valentino and famously locked him out of the bridal suite on their honeymoon. Some returned to the towns and cities they'd come from, to act or teach in humbler settings. Most simply gave up on acting after a short and difficult period of struggle with hunger and ego. It was only the clear-eyed Warren Krech who vaulted out of his class to national stardom, taking a mere ten years to achieve it.

It is no exaggeration to say that the American Academy created Warren William. His continuing professional experiences molded and shaped him, but the actor was a product of the foundation he received in the school, and he never forgot it. In 1936, when Warren was asked about his approach to acting, he explained that it was important not to be mechanical in technique, but to genuinely try to win the respect, or admiration, or fear of other actors and characters. He gave the credit for this idea to the Academy: "At the school, we were taught that acting is far more than reading lines and going through

In this 1917 graduation portrait from the American Academy of Dramatic Arts, Warren is the spitting image of the clean-cut boy next door so popular in films at that time. Less than a month after it was taken, America entered the First World War and the young actor's professional career was derailed until the summer of 1919.

motions. It is something which depends on inspiration and closely follows the game of life."[8]

Today, Warren Krech's graduation photo hangs in the halls of the American Academy along with hundreds of other portraits of the celebrated and the obscure.[9] Almost no one who walks those corridors looking for famous faces stops and nods at his picture, and his name is conspicuously absent from the roster of other well-known alumni who entice aspiring stars from the catalogues and website. For the AADA, asking Warren William to speak across the years would be useless. It is quite naturally assumed that only the famous are heeded.

4

The Lone Wolf
Takes a Chance

In the spring of 1917 the United States was still struggling with isolationism, while Germany was fighting a war in Europe against American allies and American ideals. On April 1, just a week after Warren delivered his final performance with the AADA, newspapers across the country reported the discovery of a secret offer from Germany to the government of Mexico for a military alliance. Decoded by British cryptographers, the message, which came to be known as the Zimmerman Telegram, outlined a deal that engendered incendiary anger across the country:

> On the first of February, we intend to begin unrestricted submarine warfare. In spite of this, it is our intention to endeavor to keep the United States of America neutral. In the event of this not succeeding, we propose an alliance on the following basis with Mexico: That we shall make war together and make peace together. We shall give generous financial support, and an understanding on our part that Mexico is to reconquer the lost territory in New Mexico, Texas, and Arizona. The details of settlement are left to you.

In the face of such brazen provocation, America could no longer remain disengaged. The next day, Woodrow Wilson asked for a declaration of war against Germany. On April 6, 1917, Congress spoke and the United States finally entered the war that the president had campaigned so hard to avoid.

Like most other young men in the age before media recorded and disseminated graphic, bitter truths about war, the idea of duty and service seemed entirely obvious to Warren Krech. It was a logical extension to the ideals instilled by his father and grandfather. The self-righteous anger against Germany that swept the country pushed many young men to recruiting stations. Almost immediately, the 22-year-old actor resolved to join the exodus overseas to fight Germany. It was only two generations since his grandfather emigrated from Saxony, but already the family was fully integrated into the culture they had adopted. Although they were of German stock, there was no question where their loyalties lie. As the young enlistee would soon find out, however, the United States government was not so sanguine.

Only days after the declaration of war in April, and less than a month after his graduation from the AADA, Warren applied for a place in the Lafayette Air Squadron.[1] The romance of the skies and the opportunity to have an intimate relationship with state-of-the-art technology must have been an enormously exciting possibility for the amateur inventor. The Escadrille Americaine, as it was originally known, had been formed the previous spring as an ad hoc arm of the French military, made up of American-born flyers and adventurers unwilling to wait to join the fight against Germany. At the request of the German ambassador, the U.S. government had been persuaded to petition France to change the unit's name to something less provocative.

The French acceded and renamed the division the Lafayette Air Squadron, or the Squadron Escadrille. By the time war was declared, the American-bred unit had already seen extensive, but mostly insignificant action overseas. Stateside, however, they were lauded in the press as folk heroes, with some members of their ranks becoming national figures.

At almost the same time he resolved to become a flyer, Warren auditioned for and joined the Brooklyn Repertoire Company. While waiting for an answer on his status with the Lafayette Air Squadron, he played a variety of unrecorded roles in unrecorded plays, usually learned quickly and performed over a few nights. The company mounted two shows a week, paying the Minnesota boy five dollars per performance,[2] and giving him valuable experience that he would put to use when he returned from Europe.

Meanwhile, the Lafayette initially notified Warren that they had rejected his application for service, then once again made him eligible. Over the intervening weeks the Air Corps continued to give various stalling excuses to the young recruit until finally they set sail for France, leaving him without a unit in which to serve.[3] It wasn't long before Warren discovered the real reason he'd been denied an opportunity to serve with the Escadrille: his surname. France (as well as certain members of the U.S. military hierarchy) objected to the use of aviators of German descent. Krech, of course, was unmistakably German and, according to the powers that be, could not be trusted in the skies above Europe.

Once the aviation service was eliminated as an option, Warren visited the Brooklyn Naval Base to apply for a position in the submarine service — a perfect fit considering his love of technology and the sea. They rejected the skinny Minnesotan for being forty pounds under-weight.[4] It was a curious assertion, since although tall, he had a sturdy build to his frame; only two years earlier his audition record for the American Academy had listed his weight as "heavy." Whatever the case, he now had no other options to control his own destiny. So, in New York on May 28, Warren registered for the draft, listing Minnesota as his home state. His experience with the discrimination of the air corps had only nominally taught him a lesson — on his draft card, he first lists his race as "German," then crosses it off and instead offers "English." There in black and white, Warren had reiterated his reason for rejection by the Escadrille, but the U.S. Army, in this case, was not so particular; everybody was welcome for service. In the end, it didn't matter anyway — someone else filled in the real "race" information that they were looking for: "Caucasian." He also incorrectly listed his birth date as 1895.[5] This was the first of many confusing statements about his age, his birth date being variously ascribed to 1894, '95 and '96.

It was some time before the United States government collected the actor for service. During the spring and summer of 1917, Warren remained in New York. His tenure with Brooklyn Repertoire didn't last long, and by the end of May he was unemployed. After his failure to hook on as a pilot or a submariner, Warren worried where he would go upon induction. He was trying to avoid conscription into the infantry at all costs,[6] and hoped that his mechanical aptitude would qualify him for a ground position in the aviation service or duty with an artillery brigade.[7] In mid–August, however, the summons arrived ordering him to report to the local draft board in Aitkin where he would, in true bureaucratic fashion, be assigned to the infantry. A few days later, Warren boarded a westbound train and was on his way back to Minnesota.

The town was in full war mode when he stepped off at the train station. Earlier in August his parents held a reception at their home to raise money for the Red Cross, and the entire town was geared up. Warren and the boys who went with him would be the first group of Aitkin County's residents to enter the war.[8]

While the town elders dickered over festivities and circumstance, the mundane task of certifying hundreds of young men for service inched along with what might modestly be called regularity. The draftees congregated at the old sheriff's office to undergo their first test, the physical exam. Warren reported on August 22, and his body was deemed acceptable to Uncle Sam.[9] His name was passed up the line to the district draft board in Duluth, to wait the inevitable delay while they examined the applications. From there the paperwork went to the provost marshall in Washington, and so on. Nearly a full month of scrutiny and red tape passed before 47 "soldier boys," as they were known in the press, became the honored first contingent to represent Aitkin overseas.

Warren and the others were notified that when their mustering orders came in they would be heading first to Camp Dodge in Des Moines, Iowa, to become part of the 136th Infantry Division.[10] The 136th had a long and honorable tradition not lost on the young private. Originally known as the 2nd Minnesota Volunteers, the regiment was formed in June of 1861, only two months after the start of the Civil War. They participated in the battles of Mill Springs, Chickamauga and Missionary Ridge, as well as fighting under General William Tecumseh Sherman during his infamous March to the Sea, where they watched the burning of Atlanta. The youth of the mid-nineteenth century, just like the doughboys of modern industrial America, had joined what they thought would be a short-lived and exciting adventure. Instead what they experienced was hardship, privation, disease, mutilation and the never-to-be-duplicated vision of seeing men turned inside out. In 1917, the experience of the Civil War was still in the living memory of thousands of veterans who had endured the grinding wheel of a nation pulverizing their quite real horror into the grist of mythology. The millstones were again out in force, demonizing the enemy, celebrating the soldier, and doing their damnedest to convince the country it would all be over once we were "Over There."

To that end, the town was planning a send-off for the soldiers made up of equal parts county fair, ticker tape parade and Chautauqua tent revival. Minnesota governor Joseph Burnquist and former governor John Lind were invited to deliver an address, but both demurred because of other engagements. It eventually fell to Republican Senator George Sullivan, the zealous patriot from Stillwater, to prepare a speech on behalf of Aitkin residents. Also in the making was an enormous picnic and banquet for the boys, as well as the biggest parade in county history, to be followed by a massive rally at the train station.[11] This was heady stuff for small-town boys barely finished with high school, and even for the 22-year-old Manhattan resident Warren Krech. War was being waged everywhere.

An initial push was on for the soldiers to leave by September 5 but it was quickly put aside. Camp Dodge was not yet in condition to receive a large influx of men, and rail lines were choked with men and material criss-crossing the country. Additionally, the head of the local draft board, Aitkin County Sheriff I.E. Boekenoogen, was dubious of the provost marshall's ability to process the list of eligible candidates in sufficient time to notify and gather them in from around the county. A new itinerary was drawn up, but the sheriff supposed that the Aitkin contingent would be unlikely to leave even by the revised date, September 19. He was hardly a visionary in predicting delays because of red tape from the bureaucrats in Washington, but he did in fact guess the day of exodus almost exactly. The adjutant general sent notice for the final call of men on September 17, and the troop gathered in order to leave on the 21st.[12]

The day finally chosen by the city elders for the great celebration in honor of the soldiers was Tuesday, September 18. It began at noon with a banquet in the basement of the Methodist Episcopal Church. Along with 40 or 50 draftees (of 117 that had now been certified), families and friends listened to songs, speeches and toasts. Miss Helen Moork's rendition of *Keep the Home Fires Burning* was of particular note. At one thirty, "the most enthusiastic parade of Aitkin county citizens that has ever been seen on the streets of the town"—covering five blocks—started from the church. There was first a large marching band, followed by surviving Civil War soldiers of the Grand Army of the Republic. The drafted men came next, still in civilian clothes but beaming the proud smiles that soldiers muster only before war. Behind them was the Women's Relief Corps, the members of the Red Cross Society and the Spanish War Veterans. Then marched the Boy Scouts of America, and almost 500 students from Aitkin's public schools. In the rear came a contingent of town and county residents, including the entire staff of the Potter-Casey Company, and a fleet of cars in long procession. The caravan itself stretched almost as far as the five-block parade route, which ended at the local fairgrounds.[13] Warren stood in the midst of this unprecedented spectacle, perhaps thinking that it was all too much. He was, after all, only doing his patriotic duty—like every other good American.

At the parade ground Senator Sullivan bent the festivities to his political will. He took the opportunity to harangue union leaders like Robert LaFollette, and warn against the "Russianization" of America. He counseled for a vigilant eye against pawns of the Kaiser and homegrown seditionists. His lengthy remarks were well received, and were followed by a stirring rendition of "The Star-Spangled Banner" by the combined Aitkin-Ironton band. When the rally finally ended, many spectators remained with picnic lunches to take advantage of the blue skies and mild late-summer temperatures.[14] That evening, hundreds attended a free dance a few blocks away at the Opera House, above Hodgeden's store where Warren had his modest stage beginnings. In all, it was a highly memorable day in the life of Aitkin, Minnesota.

The draftees now had two days at liberty before they were to entrain on Friday the 21st. They were directed to report for final inspection at the headquarters of the draft board in the Aitkin County Courthouse no later than twelve hours before the train was to pull out, but no earlier than 24 hours ahead. As they arrived, they were assigned a place to eat and sleep, and given meal tickets and vouchers for transportation.[15] The draft board allowed locals who lived within one hour of the courthouse to stay at home until inspection. With the courthouse less than a half mile away from the Krech house, Warren ate home cooking and stayed in his familiar bed until he boarded the train and pulled out for Des Moines.

On the morning of the 21st, he reported to the courthouse with his bundle containing the essentials advised by the Army: soap, shaving kit, comb, brush, toothbrush and powder, towels, underclothing and socks. There would be no need for anything else, Uncle Sam providing all the rest. Even the clothes he traveled in would be shipped home. The company—now just forty members—gathered and, at 10 A.M., after a final roll call, stepped up behind the city band and marched a short hike to the train station. Once again Warren swept past crowds lining the streets wishing the young men *bon chance*. At the station, the platform was crowded with over 2,000 well wishers, who spilled out onto and along the tracks, making it very slow going for the incoming locomotive. There was considerable emotion in the crowd, and Warren said goodbye to his parents and sisters amid a din of whistles, bells, band music and singing. The boys all put on brave faces, giving spirited farewells, but even so, there were no cheers as the train moved away from the depot.[16] Deep down everyone knew some of them would not be back.

On the train the new recruits were feeling good. Locals had stashed four bushels of fruit, sandwiches and other food for the 200-mile trip, and the soldiers ate well.[17] Around 3 o'clock someone suggested that they might write a letter expressing their appreciation to the townsfolk. Each of the forty men signed it, Warren fifth on the list.

To Our Folks Back Home:

We, the undersigned, the boys from Aitkin's first contingent, wish to thank you for all you have done for us. We wish to express our deep appreciation for your many acts of thoughtfulness, kindness and loyalty, and wish to assure you that with backing like this from the folks back home, the boys will win you credit, honor and victory.[18]

There were no sleeping arrangements on the train and the men were obliged to catch winks in their chairs. Twenty-four hours later, the company was in Des Moines. In a letter to the *Aitkin Republican* (Freeman Krech's competition), private Ernest Buhler wrote: "We arrived here well and hearty ... on Saturday at 3 P.M. The boys are feeling well and favorably impressed with the prospects."[19] Camp Dodge was a massive facility, recently constructed with accommodations for as many as 50,000 men. The arrivals from Aitkin had a busy first day. Warren endured yet another physical exam, then took the oath to be sworn into the United States Army. He was now property of Uncle Sam, who pointed him to his billet in a two-story bunkhouse that held 160 other men. Inside were all the comforts of home, if you lived in a boardinghouse: community sleeping quarters, communal toilet, washrooms and shower bath. The camp also had a company store, YMCA buildings, a movie theater and a multi-denominational church. The Army wasted no time breaking in the recruits; the next morning they were obliged to fall out for calisthenics before breakfast — "just enough to learn how it was going to feel when we get down to business in earnest," Warren said. That day he wrote to his father at *The Age*: "We are treated well and are comfortable. The hard work will begin tomorrow." He was also convinced that the Aitkin contingent was well liked by the captain in charge. That same day, two pieces of news went around that would be enormously important to the young private. First was the company's probable reassignment for more training at Camp Cody in New Mexico, and second, the possibility of a raise in rank. "The captain told us in a body last night that some of us would be tried out in two or three days for the positions of non-commissioned officers, corporals and sergeants," he wrote, hopefully.[20] In a matter of days Warren was one of the men singled out to be groomed for a move to a higher pay grade and more responsibilities. The following weeks were hard work while Warren moved up the ladder, chasing a non-commissioned officer's rank.

It wasn't long before the Aitkin group began to break up. In early October, thirteen men with logging and sawmill experience — a common trade in Aitkin County — volunteered for the Forestry Service, a company that worked overseas cutting trees and building camps for armies in the field. They shipped out immediately and were in France within weeks. Four more were attached to units at Camp Dodge, with the remaining 23 set to move to Camp Cody in New Mexico, where they would be dispersed to various National Guard units that hadn't been recruited up to war strength.[21]

In late October, Warren and the remaining members of the 136th made their way by rail 500 miles to the town of Deming, in the far southwestern corner of New Mexico. In spite of the hot, dry climate, fields of cotton and chilies flourish in the valley that surrounded the town. The secret that sustains these beautiful plants, and the town itself, is the Mimbres River, which snakes underground just north of the city and nourishes the soil while continuing on its way into Mexico, where it reappears above ground in Chihuahua. The local landscape — where wind and water have carved massive monoliths of volcanic ash, and where unique southwestern desert plants flourish — couldn't have been more alien to the untraveled actor, used to the innumerable lakes and forests dotting the environs of Minnesota and the northeast. In later years, as a man of means, Warren returned again and again to vacation in Arizona and New Mexico, captivated by the contrasting topography he encountered as a young man.

In 1917, the town of Deming was a tiny enclave of about 2,500 inhabitants, dominated by a two thousand-acre training camp on its outskirts that the War Department had erected in December of 1916. Originally sanctioned as Camp Deming, during July the facility had been renamed Camp Cody, in honor of the recently deceased hero of the American West, Buffalo Bill Cody. At its peak, the camp was home to 36,000 soldiers, gathering National Guard units from Minnesota, Nebraska, Iowa, and the Dakotas.[22] These state units formed the basis of the 34th Infantry division of the United States Army, headquartered at Cody under the command of Brigadier General F.G. Mauldin. During September and early October the division was being assembled, and Warren arrived just three days before they began their systematic year-long training on October 29.[23] He was assigned to the 136th Headquarters Company,[24] with other of his fellow Minnesotans dispersed among six or seven separate units. The men of Aitkin professed to be delighted with the change, observing that the mornings and evenings were cool and the food excellent. Even the camp discipline, though strict, indicated to them that they were under seasoned officers who knew how to make good soldiers.[25]

Sandstorms whipped constantly across southern New Mexico that fall, bedeviling all training and infiltrating every tent, barracks and structure on the base. The storms were so common, in fact, that the regiment eventually adopted the *nom de guerre* "The Sandstorm Division." The year at Camp Cody was a long, arduous process of drilling, maintenance, monotony and drilling. Under these trying conditions, Private Warren Krech quickly became Sergeant Warren Krech, in charge of for the training and deportment of a platoon of men. Warren supervised recruits in the instruction of the Army's field manual: physical fitness, hand-to-hand combat, handling of casualties, rifle marksmanship and maintenance, use of grenades, deployment of balloons, basic first aid, hygiene, military rules—interminable but necessary drills to break down and rebuild each man who came through the gates. Before he left Camp Cody, Warren attained the rank of first sergeant, with responsibility for an entire company of men. It was proof that the boy who loafed through work at his father's print shop was no slacker, but rather someone who needed motivation and direction to perform at his best. The dedication required to make the grade of first sergeant was the same kind of hard work that made Warren into a successful actor when he returned from the war, and allowed him to excel in spite of his opposing desire for leisure and ease.

During the autumn and winter of 1917, morale waned, as the men objected to having to wait so long to enter the action they naively craved. In the spring they became downright angry when word came that the 34th division would not serve together, but rather be broken up and dispersed to other service units as replacements. Warren had already experienced the dissolution of the Aitkin contingent, and after building friendships, training and molding the men under his charge, being again separated was a grave disappointment.

In June of 1918, Warren dodged the first bullet of his war, when the 34th finally sent almost the entire division to France where they were splintered and doled out in the Allied Expeditionary Forces automatic replacement system. Only a skeleton staff of officers and NCOs was left behind at Camp Cody. Among those NCOs was Sergeant Krech, whose teaching and organizational skills kept him stateside to indoctrinate the new recruits coming in from Arizona, Colorado, New Mexico, Kansas, Oklahoma and Texas.[26]

On August 20, 1918, after almost a solid year in New Mexico, Warren and the newly reconstituted 34th Division, with the exception of the 59th Field Artillery, finally got their marching orders and embarked for Camp Dix, in Wrightstown, New Jersey.[27] It took seven days for the troop trains to reach the northeast, where the division established new headquarters on August 27, again under General Mauldin, who had returned in May after the unit had spent five months under interim Commander A.P. Blacksom. When they arrived, Warren may have wished he was back in the stifling southwestern desert. The area was in the midst of an unprecedented heat wave; earlier that month, drills had been cancelled at Camp Dix for two days when temperatures in New Jersey reached 124 degrees. The recently built facility housed 70,000 soldiers under Spartan conditions. Sixteen hundred barracks had been erected, each in ten hours, with a single potbellied stove for heat and a lone hanging light bulb. Fortunately, in New Jersey, less than sixty miles from Manhattan, Warren was once again close to his sister Pauline, now living in New York, and could entertain visits from her during the time before he shipped out. At Camp Dix, it was one of those visits that would introduce him to the woman with whom he would spend the rest of his life.

5

Madame X

During the time that Warren was training in New Mexico, Pauline was living in an apartment on Park Avenue in New York City. That year, a new boarder moved into her building. Helen Ferris was a petite, auburn-haired woman who had moved from Minnesota to pursue an acting career on Broadway. Although that career never materialized — she claimed in later years to have been too timid to go to auditions and quietly gave up her aspirations — she and Pauline Krech quickly became friends.[1] As single women in New York, the two bonded in the mutual challenges they faced in the city. America in 1918 was not yet prepared for the changes that would sweep across the nation following the war. Women still dressed very conservatively, with skirts rarely more than six inches off the ground and ankles daintily covered by spats or high laced walking boots. Makeup was only just beginning to gain acceptance, especially among the younger generation, and hairstyles were invariably long. Before the war changed America, short hair on a woman was a clear indication of feminine rebellion, naïve Bolshevism, or something else unspoken entirely. Although not short-haired, Pauline fell staunchly into the former category. Even in these early days she was already the firebrand of the family, loudly touting women's rights, refusing to observe the status quo and generally playing the nonconformist role. Both of Warren's sisters embodied strong personalities — Elizabeth was once famously escorted off a New York beach for refusing to wear the stockings that accompanied ladies swim wear during the teens.[2] Warren's respect and love for his sisters was deep, and Pauline's progressive ideas strongly informed his attitudes about women throughout his life.

Helen and Pauline quickly discovered that they had been reared practically next door to each other: Helen's family had moved to Brainerd, Minnesota, less than thirty miles from Aitkin, when she was just seven years old.[3] Naturally this engendered reminiscences about growing up in the great Midwest: places they had both visited, and the sights, sounds and smells of the rural countryside. The rest of Helen's story was very private. Even her closest friends and confidants never knew much of it over the next thirty years.

Helen Ferris was born Helen Barbara Nelson, about 30 miles from Chicago, in Michigan City, Indiana, on July 9, 1877.[4] It was an era of unprecedented immigration to the United States, and it showed in the Nelson family composition. Helen's father Louis was born in Indiana in 1852, of immigrant parents who had come to America in the 1840s. Her mother Rebecca had been born in Scotland and emigrated to the U.S. with her parents (mother Ellen, also a Scot, and father Thomas Stirrup, of England) in 1859, when she was just two years of age. Helen was the first born of the Nelson family, followed by two brothers, William, three years Helen's junior, and Frank, who was twelve years behind her.

Blessed with a remarkably youthful appearance, Helen was able to keep her true age a secret for the rest of her life. It is unclear when Warren William discovered the fact that his girlfriend, fiancée and wife was seventeen years older than he was. On their wedding certificate, Helen claimed to be 36 — a mere seven years his senior. On census rolls, passenger manifests and registration cards from 1885 to 1940, her age drifts from between two to seventeen years younger than what her birth certificate records. Whether it was vanity or fear that kept Helen moving the target, there is no question that she appeared far younger than she was. Photographs seem to capture a woman no more than a few years older than her doting husband — and in the mid–1930s, when the couple was in their Hollywood heyday and Helen was already over 55, she easily passed for a woman in her 40s.

Another secret that was shared only among family, and rarely with friends, was that of Helen's first husband. In January of 1902, just after Warren's seventh birthday, Helen Nelson was already in the process of becoming Mrs. Helen Ferris.[5] Very little is known about her first marriage, and it was a subject rarely talked about, and never mentioned in the press. Helen met Allen Ferris while living in Brainerd; when they were married she was already 25 years old. Allen eventually widowed Helen, although it is not clear how long they were married before he passed away. Whatever the case, Helen left Brainerd shortly after Allen's death, taking with her no more than some midwestern memories and a few Broadway dreams.

In 1918, Helen Ferris was living with her brother William in New York and failing to realize her dreams of becoming an actress. Both her parents and her husband were dead, and at 41 Helen had no profession and no job, relying on her brother's income as a brokerage clerk to sustain them. But she had a close friend in Pauline Krech, and spent many hours visiting with her. One afternoon in Pauline's apartment she noticed a new photograph adorning the dresser in the bedroom. In later years, she described what she called a "compelling magnetism" each time she saw the picture of the robust young man. Curious, but worried he might be her friend's new beau, Helen hesitated to ask about him. Eventually her preoccupation got the better of her, and she couldn't resist: "Pauline, who is that handsome fellow?"[6] Pauline explained that it was her brother, an actor who was in the service waiting to be shipped overseas.

Helen was determined to meet the subject of that photograph, and when she learned that he was now stationed only sixty miles away, the coy redhead resolved to tag along with Pauline when she next visited him. It took a few tries before the pair finally met — twice excursions had to be scuttled due to Helen's sudden illness — but finally in September, Pauline and Helen made the trek out to Camp Dix in New Jersey where Warren was on duty at officers' training camp. When they arrived, the soldier was unavailable and they were obliged to wait for him to finish his responsibilities for the afternoon. One hour turned into three and still no Sergeant Krech. When Warren finally did appear, he nonchalantly offered no explanation and no apology, which irritated his sister no end.[7] Helen, however, was thrilled. Her anticipation had turned to tingling excitement after all these weeks — and hours — of waiting. She'd had time to project all the qualities she imagined onto the personality of the man in the picture: dashing, eloquent, witty and charming. In short, her perfect man. The reality, however, was somewhat different.

Following Pauline's introductions, Warren sat down next to Helen and proceeded to say almost nothing for rest of the visit. The friends spoke. Helen spoke. But the man from Minnesota remained taciturn. His well-known reticence and shyness among strangers once again got the better of him. The Top Kick Sergeant who could mold young recruits into tough-as-leather war heroes, and the actor who could stand in front of an audience and declaim elaborate prose, was done in by the personal interaction which came so easily to others. Sitting next to his beautiful visitor was the best he could manage.

Eventually, the lopsided gathering had to break up if the women were to catch their train back to New York. At this moment Warren abruptly came alive and told them he'd drive them to the station. Then, after boarding the train and seeing the women to their seats, he suddenly and impulsively declared that he was also going to ride back to New York with them. Pauline was horrified as the engine jerked the cars into motion with Warren still aboard. He hadn't been given leave — and although a first sergeant may have somewhat more latitude in such matters than a buck private, U.S. Army Soldier #1426030 was now technically AWOL. It was a side of her proper and dutiful brother she'd rarely seen. Warren, however, was unconcerned. He casually sat next to Helen and enjoyed the ride.

Back in the city, the trio collected Pauline's beau and the foursome headed to a small Italian restaurant in Greenwich Village. In the course of the evening, Warren remained polite but reserved, offering little in the way of substance. Then, the man who so rarely showed any spontaneity unearthed his deeply buried sense of whimsy. At one moment during dinner Helen reached across the table, and without warning Warren impetuously leaned over and kissed the back of her neck.

Kismet.

Talking to Helen the following morning, an astonished Pauline told her: "Well, he isn't as slow and backward as I thought!"[8] Warren's sister probably still saw her brother as the small town boy she'd grown up with and looked after. The truth was that he was now a grown man of 24 who had spent two full years with eyes wide open in the modern metropolis of New York City, and had become a tough Top Kick Sergeant responsible for the lives of over 100 men in his company. He might still be proper and gentlemanly, but he was no longer the naïve boy she had to coddle.

The next day Helen received a special delivery letter from Camp Dix, dashed off as soon as Warren had made it back, saying that he'd visit her in the city again soon. It was the first of scores of letters Warren would craft for her over the next year, putting his thoughts and emotions into words too difficult to express in person.

At this moment, a massive and virulent influenza pandemic was running riot throughout the world. Soldiers packed close together on troop ships moving to and fro across the globe were getting sick in alarming numbers and spreading the disease wherever they went. Without modern medicines to check its progress, the lethal flu cut a swath through every continent, making it one of the deadliest events of the 20th century. By the time the epidemic had run its course almost a year later, a minimum of thirty million people were dead from its effects. After enduring an initial strike from the disease, a second wave of the flu made its way down the East Coast and hit Camp Dix on September 15, prompting an immediate quarantine of the facility. One in four soldiers in camps along the eastern seaboard were stricken with the disease, which affected young and old alike. Health officials knew that even one case allowed to travel outside the perimeter could prove disastrous. Warren was likely one of the fortunate group whose immune system kept him from contracting "The Grippe," but others in Camp Dix were not so lucky. The 2,000 beds in the camp hospital filled up quickly, with scores reporting daily. September 21 alone provided sobering statistics: That day, 179 new cases of flu were reported inside the camp, and 13 men and one nurse died in their sickbeds. Additionally, 15 soldiers developed pneumonia, a near death sentence, since no antibiotics were then available to stay the course of the disease. Men struck with pneumonia usually wasted away from the inside and succumbed in a few days. The crisis continued to expand exponentially, reaching its apogee on September 26, when 806 new patients were admitted to the infirmary. In total as many as 6,500 soldiers were infected — over 4,000 at the height of the epidemic — necessitating the annexation of empty barracks. The doctors at Camp Dix were stunned and overwhelmed by the crisis. A monograph published by the camp doctor revealed the severity of the situation: "The Disease was a veritable plague. The extraordinary toxicity ... and rapidity of development stamp this disease as a distinct clinical entity heretofore not fully described."[9] By the time Camp Dix was clear, 800 men and nurses were dead, and no one had set a foot outside New Jersey.

6

One Dangerous Night

Although the quarantine meant that Warren wasn't going to New York anytime soon, it was yet another stall that kept him safely away from the trenches of Europe. He satisfied himself by writing Helen on an almost daily basis, until finally the quarantine was lifted in early October. Excited to be at liberty again, Sergeant Krech sent a special delivery note to Helen saying that he'd commandeered a motorcycle, and would be in New York the following afternoon. Helen waited patiently for hours, but Warren never made it. The flu had reared its head and the camp was quarantined and shut up tight once again. Finally, on October 12, all restrictions were lifted — but it was now too late to matter to the couple. The very next morning, Warren stowed Helen's address in his haversack and boarded a troop transport with thousands of other doughboys setting off for France. The 34th Division sailed on October 13, in thirteen convoys, and took thirteen days to reach their first stop at Liverpool, England. After his safe return from the war, Warren claimed that thirteen thus became his lucky number.[1]

The flotilla arrived in dense fog and put in at Liverpool harbor. What remained of the 34th disembarked and made their way by rail to Salisbury Plain, where they encamped for a week. There, the division received the news that they were once again to be skeletonized, and not to see action as a reconstituted force. Little by little the various brigades were reduced or reassigned. Finally, Warren and the remnants of his unit, the 109th Engineers, were ordered to France. They made a dangerous crossing of the English Channel at night, in near total darkness. Luck was with them: Neither nature nor the Germans scuttled the ship, and they landed successfully at Le Havre in early November.[2] War was close now, and Warren was still of the mind that he hoped to find action at the front. No one knew that a deal was brewing to end the conflict before Sergeant Krech could see the sad sights ahead.

Quickly the men of Warren's company, men he had the ultimate responsibility for directing and looking after, were ordered on a southbound train to Bordeaux. They were now only miles away from the deadly action — marching distance — and could see and hear the effects of war first-hand. Warren must have had tense moments, when the direct field command of a company of men weighed on him, but there was scarcely time to think of it. Within a few days they were ordered to the front. They set out on foot and were waiting for new orders in the town of Castres when word rang out in the streets that the war was over. The armistice was signed on November 11. Warren William Krech had dodged the final bullet of his war. In a 1932 conversation with writer Gladys Hall, he claimed to have been disappointed at the turn of events, but the mature man who now had fame and love in his life naturally saw the foolishness of his youthful pique. "I'd beat it to the submerged continent of Atlantis before I'd take part in any war now," he unabashedly offered.[3]

Still overseas, but now safe and sound, Warren continued to compose heartfelt billets-doux to Helen, often accompanied by poetry. She found the sonnets terribly romantic, but Warren was mortified when his wife brought it up to a feature writer years after they'd made it to Hollywood. "Good Lord, don't ever admit that!" he howled.[4] The gallant in him couldn't resist pouring out his feelings in verse, but apparently his practical, proper side couldn't countenance the public knowing about it.

Following the armistice, Warren began to grow increasingly disenchanted with the excruciating boredom of Army life. The interminable preparation and maddening delays had sapped his interest, and he began thinking about how and when he could return to his interrupted career and new girl. One afternoon he stopped at a Y.M.C.A. to consider his options. There, he encountered a handbill announcing the formation of Corey's Singers, a chorus to be composed of enlisted men who would tour army camps and hospitals in the American area. There was more than just being relieved of pointless duties to consider, even if that were quite enough. Rumors were swirling around that his unit would soon be reassigned as a branch of the military police. Warren had already encountered the MPs a few times during his short tour; he disliked them and wanted nothing to do with any scheme the U.S. government had to make him part of the unit. So, he spoke to the secretary on hand, noted his qualifications and interests, and signed on.[5] "I didn't care what I did then," he later commented. "I just wanted to live a free life and keep on following every fool notion that came into my head."[6]

The man organizing the troupe was Madison Corey, a Broadway producer who'd had modest success with the shows *Justice* and *Erstwhile Susan* shortly before the war. Joining Corey's Singers, of course, meant that Warren would have to—well—sing. The actor could barely carry a tune, and during his interview he conveniently avoided, as much as possible, the subject of his voice. Once again, Warren's luck was front and center. The producer was also getting ready to mount a roving production of the Roi Cooper Megrue play *Under Cover*, which Warren had performed in during his senior year at the AADA. Corey asked him to audition for the play, to be performed by his "Over There Theater League." With his previous experience, Warren easily snatched the leading role of Steve Denby and applied for detached service from his unit. Once approved, Warren began touring the American zone with his first starring role being provided by the United States government. He later waxed nostalgic about that winter with writer J. Maurice Ruddy. "They detailed me to this Y unit. Grand!" he extolled. "A bed to sleep in, decent hours, recognition in a great work—ha, playing in airplane hangars, rickety old barns and quaint French municipal theaters with plenty of ventilation from shell holes. It was good fun and darn good training."[7] The men who knew Warren only as First Sergeant Krech were amazed at his histrionic talent. As usual, his personal reserve belied the greater depth and talent beneath.

For the next six months Warren tramped the villages of France, occasionally crossing paths with some of the 134 other companies of actors and vaudevillians entertaining the troops (including Buster Keaton, the not-quite-yet world-famous film star). It was a once-in-a-lifetime jackpot for the actor: a chance to get valuable experience in front of appreciative audiences and avoid the drudgery of daily military duty. He was also receiving an extra fifty francs a week in addition to his sergeant's pay, and with Uncle Sam footing travel and living expenses, it was highly profitable. Once the troupe had played almost everywhere else, the War Department finally allowed them to perform in the brilliant City of Lights, Paris. Warren drank in the electric energy of the French capital and, in a newspaper article, later called it his favorite city.[8] He enjoyed his relative freedom to the hilt: as a member of "Over There" he judged contests, auditioned actors and generally drank in the pleasures of an unattached American soldier in postwar France. There was just one problem: by this time Warren had well and truly fallen in love. He wanted to go home.

7

The Lone Wolf Keeps a Date

What was left of the 34th Infantry had been moving back to the States during early 1919; only the 109th Supply Train and Warren's unit, the 109th Engineers, remained to be shipped out. In early June the actor said goodbye to his fellow troupers and rejoined his company. Over three million men had already made their way home and the 109th was among the final few hundred thousand left behind. They made their way to the point of embarkation at the port of St. Nazaire on the Bay of Biscay, where Warren picked up his billet ticket, grabbed a bunk in the heated barracks and awaited the orders to return stateside.

One could easily look back on Warren Krech's service record and feel that time after time, the young man had fate weight the dice in his favor. Both the Escadrille and the submarine service had rejected him for no good reason, stalling him in New York for precious months. Once home, the provost marshall's red tape kept him from shipping out far longer than expected. In Iowa, his opportunity to make sergeant meant that he remained behind in New Mexico with a mere handful of enlisted men and officers in June when thousands of his fellow soldiers headed to the front. His request for assignment to a field artillery unit was likewise scuttled, keeping him in New Jersey when the artillery units shipped out to France in September of 1918. And the deadly influenza epidemic that hit Camp Dix — but not Warren — twice delayed the timetable for his unit to travel overseas, allowing him to miss action by mere days. As a complete force — those not broken off and assigned to other units — the 34th Infantry had the second shortest service record in France, arriving the second latest and leaving the third earliest.[1] If one were summing up Warren's service record in the World War in a word, that word would certainly be "fortuitous." Even his introduction to Corey's Singers and the Zen-like coincidence of his experience with *Under Cover* seem unreal when added to everything else. Years later, the actor professed that the war hadn't disillusioned him or made him bitter, like so many others who returned. It didn't hurt that he hadn't seen direct action, but the casualties and carnage he undoubtedly encountered while touring — or even the 800 men who died around him in Camp Dix — apparently did not make an indelible impression on his psyche. He claimed simply that he never bothered to analyze it.[2] Warren William Krech may be one of the few enlisted men who came away from the war better off than when he went in.

The ship carrying Warren back to the United States left St. Nazaire on June 17. During the two-week voyage, the actor had plenty of time to consider what he wanted to do next. As much as he had enjoyed touring the villages and arrondissements of France, he was anxious to return to the two things he had grown to love most during his sojourn overseas: acting, and his beautiful correspondent Helen Ferris. The returning troops steamed slowly towards the East Coast, bound for Newport News, Virginia. Although he recalled for his 1932 studio bio that the ship landed on July 4, it appears more likely that it docked on June 29, carrying the 109th Engineers and various stragglers from other units.[3]

The Victorian, pre-war America that the 25-year-old soldier had left was already being compromised, confronted carelessly by modernity. The Jazz Age, which had its early beginnings in 1911 with Irving Berlin's "Alexander's Ragtime Band," was passing into popular consciousness through Jelly Roll Morton, King Oliver and George White's *Scandals*. The Golden Age of Sports' first superstar was born only five days after the actor's return, when Jack Dempsey bounced Jess Willard around a prize ring in Toledo, Ohio, annexing the World Heavyweight Championship in the process. And the men returning from Europe saw the world in a new and startling way that would quickly infiltrate literature, film and the stage. Warren himself seemed largely to belong to the earlier age. His midwestern upbringing, with parents and grandparents who had instilled in him a great respect for tradition, humility and modesty, continued to inform his character in spite of the tidal wave of change sweeping across the cities of America, especially New York.

When Warren's ship docked in Virginia, he was surprised by a most unusual proposal. According to a newspaper article of 1933, the young soldier was met at the pier by his Uncle Alvin, then the president of the Equitable Corporation. Alvin had an offer — almost an ultimatum, if one is to believe the newspaper account: If Warren would consent to remain unmarried, Alvin would see to it that his nephew would inherit the lion's share of his estate — potentially over a million dollars— when he died.[4] As absurd as this arrangement seems in retrospect — like the machinations of a capricious silent movie patriarch — this was still the era of old money. Alvin may have merely wanted to motivate someone in the family to follow him into the business, and felt that only a "free" man could devote the time and energy necessary to protect his hard-won advantages. His own son Shepard had married in 1916, possibly putting him out of the businessman's will and leaving Warren as the only male heir unattached. If the story is true — and forgetting that Alvin himself was then married to his second wife — the arcane deal did not interest Warren. He was thinking about another thing entirely. When Alvin died suddenly nine years later, of a massive heart attack sitting at his desk in the Equitable building, the bulk of his estate went to his wife Angeline and a portion also to Pauline and Elizabeth, but none to their uncooperative — and happily married — brother.

In Newport News, Sergeant Krech went about the business of reverting to the civilian Warren Krech. Before leaving France he had written to Helen, letting her know that he would be spending a month visiting his family in Minnesota following his release. First he had to wait to be mustered out, along with the thousands upon thousands of other doughboys who had disembarked to Virginia's Camp Lee with him. It was an excruciating two weeks before the sergeant became the civilian, finally signing separation papers on July 12, 1919 — just two months shy of his second anniversary in uniform. In his pockets were the two things the army left him with: one was a $60 bonus from the United States government. The other was a small wad of folded paper he kept with him for the rest of his life: the typewritten "sides" he used to memorize his part as Steve Denby in *Under Cover*.[5] The young man from Minnesota was also sent off with a World War I Victory Medal and a Bronze Victory Button, both given to every soldier as an emblem of participation in the Great War.

Returned to the ranks of the civilian world, Warren boarded a westbound train to Minnesota. On July 17 he arrived after a long trip through Chicago (there likely visiting his other uncle, Paul) to the tiny town he'd grown up in and hadn't seen but a handful of days since he moved to New York four years earlier. The *Duluth News Tribune* ran a photo of the sergeant in uniform, emblazoned with the caption "Was Entertainer" touting his service following the armistice. Although anxious to see his parents, Warren wanted to see Helen worse still. It was

This is the scene Warren encountered at the Aitkin Depot when he returned home from Europe following his service in The Great War: a brass band and the thanks of a throng of grateful citizens. Courtesy Randy Wall.

a wonderful homecoming, but after only a few days he couldn't wait any longer. After just 33 hours in Aitkin he cut his trip short and trooped back to New York,[6] hoping that the girl and the career were both waiting.

When Warren arrived in New York, Helen was indeed waiting with open arms, and for good reason. At 42 and widowed, she was not the most marketable single woman in New York. The interest of a young, handsome actor from a well-to-do family must have felt like having a winning sweepstakes ticket in the lining of her purse. Notwithstanding that she had likewise fallen in love with the doughboy through his letters and correspondences, he was an island in the storm.

To the general public the returning soldiers represented a great unknown. The wartime economy had developed its own rhythm and rules, and those who were gainfully employed wondered what the influx of ready labor might do to their jobs. As millions of men returned to civilian life, rampant inflation took over in many areas: prices for food, housing and services endured increases of as much as 40 to 90 percent. Warren struggled to find an apartment in this saturated market, likely staying with his sister for a short time. Meanwhile, liquor prohibition, which was designed as a wartime measure and was belatedly imposed on July 1—long after the war was over—also shot the price of alcohol sky high.

As the two reignited their courtship, Warren began to construct the framework of his interrupted career. His first official act as an aspiring Broadway star was to join the theatrical union Actors' Equity. Only days later, the organization went on strike, leaving Warren with nothing to live on but his bonus money and the savings he had accumulated while in France. Serendipitously, Warren's parents and his sister Elizabeth arrived in New York for a visit at almost that exact moment.[7] With nothing to do but walk a picket line and wait for the end of the dispute, Warren was able to visit with his father and introduce Helen to the rest of the family. It was not an auspicious beginning, with Freeman and Frances immediately dubious of their son's choice. The difference in age between the couple remained a troubling problem for Warren's parents from then on. The Equity strike raged from August 7, when players walked out on a dozen shows in New York, and spread through Chicago and other cities before it was settled three weeks later, with the actors' union winning only a partial victory. Once the dust cleared and the family was packed off to Aitkin, it was finally time for Warren Krech to begin his professional career.

In April of 1919, a little play fetchingly called *I Love You* was bringing in reasonable business first at the Booth Theatre and then at the 48th Street. It was a pleasant comedy about a Harvard-educated man who has fallen on hard times and is reduced to being a butler for a wealthy family. In due course he falls in love with the daughter of the house — winning a wager about the power of love in the process. The play had a remarkable jigsaw of Hollywood connections. It was produced by the recently retired G.M. "Broncho Billy" Anderson, the star of countless enormously successful two-reel westerns during the early days of American cinema. Anderson had left the film industry and was now concentrating on legitimate theater, with varying degrees of success. The writer was William Le Baron, a former editor of *Collier's* magazine and future head of production at Paramount and independent producer at 20th Century-Fox. The lead was Richard Dix, also recently returned from the war and soon to be an important star in silent films. The New York run of *I Love You* ended in July and, following the strike, Anderson mounted a travelling production to send out on the road. Here again Warren's curious luck was working for him. The manager of the company had seen him in *Under Cover* while both were in France and he remembered the actor's performance as Steve Denby very well. He hired the ex-soldier on the spot and the tour began in September of 1919. Although it was reported in many places that Warren took over the role vacated by Richard Dix, there is no verifiable record of his performance in the lead. Indeed, there is no mention of Warren Krech in the surviving reviews of the period, indicating that he likely had a small part in the company, possibly taking over the lead later in the run, or on a one-time basis. Whatever the case, Warren was now on the road, at last making a living in his chosen profession.

Once again Warren was obliged to be apart from Helen. The two stayed in touch through the mail and the occasional phone call while Warren drank in the experiences of road life. The company trudged into Pennsylvania and the near west where they played through the month of September. In October they swung to the south and made their way through small towns in Georgia. Reviews in each town were kind, but seem to indicate that Anderson's press agents were probably spreading around a little payola here and there for the copywriters. The *Columbus Enquirer* noted, "It can be truly said that it contains not a single objectionable line or incident,"[8] while another Columbus rag noted, "Let it be said that none of the laughs were accompanied or followed by a blush."[9] In Pennsylvania they claimed the show was "not blemished with a single blush," and even the advertising touted it as "sweet and wholesome."[10] Even in 1919, the idea that small-town America was paranoiacally wary of the propriety of anything coming out of the cesspool of the east, New York City, was not likely to be this uniform. After twelve weeks on the road, this bland, unoffensive milquetoast of a play limped into Flint, Michigan, and promptly closed, leaving the company flat. It was Warren's first experience being left high and dry in the sticks, and it taught the young actor an important lesson: be prepared; you never know what is just around the corner.

After making his way back to New York, Warren received word from Aitkin that his father was ill. Freeman was now 63 years old — not exactly considered spry in 1919 — and in late November he suffered a serious stroke that paralyzed the right side of his body.[11] With Elizabeth away attending

St. Mary's Academy at Faribault, in central Minnesota, Frances was left with servants to tend to his needs. Both thought that his days of activity were over, and felt that they couldn't continue to live in the big house. Almost immediately Freeman made plans to move east and be near his brother and children. It was time for the threads of the Krech family to unwind from Aitkin.

In the meantime, Warren had hooked up with a stock company based in Erie, Pennsylvania. Among their repertoire was the well-worn stage standard *A Stitch in Time*, the story of a scrub woman who falls in love with the man she works for and helps shape his success from her humble position. Frighteningly for the notoriously forgetful actor, he would be expected to learn and memorize this role and a variety of others quickly, just as he had in the senior year at the AADA. In France he had played Steve Denby in *Under Cover* for six months, and whatever modest facility for memory he had gained during his schooling seemed gone once again. For over two months in Erie he worked and studied every night. He developed a technique of always watching himself in a mirror while studying in order to simultaneously perfect his actions. "Gradually I found myself mumbling my lines and peering over my shoulder into the broad windows of the brownstone houses and shops I passed [while walking to the theater]," he reminisced. "I've never been able to break myself of the habit."[12] The technique was only partially successful — he still often blew his lines during the first few performances of each production. He eventually adopted a trademark delivery to compensate, one that you can hear throughout his film career: he takes short pauses during lines in order to momentarily find his bearings.

Warren described that season in Erie as "a long, hard winter,"[13] and he was under constant harassment and ribbing from the company — including Florence Eldridge, the future Mrs. Fredric March — about his faulty memory. At Christmas they gave him a model airplane with the suggestion that he "try going up in it instead of in his lines." And when the company reorganized in February, the forgetful actor's option was not renewed. The young man was more relieved than disappointed — he wanted to truck back to New York and look for a part he could learn once and — so to speak — forget about. However, just as he was preparing to head to the train station, a member of the troupe intercepted him and said the company now wanted him back. Warren looked evenly at him, thought about that long, hard winter and refused. He was heading home — it really was home now — and to Helen.

Back in Aitkin, Freeman was disposing of his local interests and preparing to leave his home of almost forty years. On January 1, the *Aitkin Independent Age* slipped out of Freeman's hands for the final time. When he made the deal public, the long-time publisher was quoted as saying, "It wrenches the soul to make the announcement,"[14] and many residents of Aitkin felt similar pangs. No less than his direct competition, *The Aitkin Republican*, wrote a glowing retirement article in their January 1 edition, in which they lauded the businessman and civic champion: "It will be some comfort to him to feel that his service to the public has not been unappreciated by the citizens of the town. *The Republican* esteems Mr. Krech very highly. Always he has been an honorable competitor, and we trust ... that he may be spared many years of usefulness." Over the next few months he recuperated and received the good wishes and plaudits of various clubs and organizations that honored him with going-away parties and galas. Fifty-five members of the Commercial Club gathered for a testimonial where Freeman was given a handsome cane and treated to "eloquent addresses ... attesting to the high worth and character of the guest." In response, he emotionally offered that he hoped the cane would "now and then guide his footsteps back to the best town and the best people in the world."[15] That spring the superb house he built in 1899 was sold to a family with which it still resides, and in May he and Frances — and the Krech name — finally made their way out of Aitkin, Minnesota.

8

Times Square Playboy

When Warren returned from Erie in February of 1920, he began auditioning for something more stable and closer to home. He secured a part in Joseph Klaw's production of *Mrs. Jimmie Thompson*, a new comedy set to open on Broadway at the Princess Theatre in March. It was here — in his Broadway debut — that Warren embarked on what could literally and figuratively be called his "women's work." *Mrs. Jimmie Thompson* was the model for many Warren William productions to come: written by a woman (Edith Ellis, with Norman Rose), centered on a woman and women's issues (in this case the reluctance of men to commit), starring a woman (Gladys Hurlbut), and even bearing a distaff title. The influence of women in the actor's life was woven into him through his mother and grandmother, his sisters — especially the artistic and progressive Pauline, who helped him decide to pursue a career in acting — and the women he worked with while in school. Now, professionally, he would continue to be influenced by working with female writers, directors and actors over the course of his stage and film career. By the time he reached Hollywood, his attitudes about women were already amazingly generous and even-handed for the time. He subscribed to the idea that women were usually behind great men, and duly credited those who made his career successful. He also believed that women should be afforded the same opportunities as men. "If a woman wants to be economically independent," he reasoned, "more power to her — she has as much right as any male, right? Women have greater mental agility, keener wit and as sound judgment as most men."[1] Eleanor Warren, the clever girl who "married" the non-existent Jimmie Thompson in order to make herself more desirable to men, was among those who had proved it to him.

The new production rehearsed through February, and began road try-outs on March 8 at the Cort Theatre in Springfield, New York. Warren breathed a sigh of relief, now able to concentrate on one set of dialogues and forget about everything else. The play toured through other towns in New York, New Jersey and Pennsylvania while tinkering with the timing and pace of the staging proceeded. The out-of-town notices were solid, with Warren singled out by the reviewer of the Wilkes-Barre preview of March 24 — the first mention of his name in print as a professional actor anywhere. After a dozen or so out-of-town appearances, the show, sharpened over the weeks of try-outs, docked in New York City for Warren's Broadway debut on March 29. His parents were still wrapping up business in Aitkin, and likely did not make their son's maiden performance. They and the rest of Aitkin read about it in the paper on April 3. "Warren Krech, an Aitkin product ... is making a notable success in the East. His greatest success has just come, when [*Mrs. Jimmie Thompson*] opened at the Princess Theatre, New York. Many Aitkin friends will extend congratulations to 'Bill' and his parents...."[2] Attendance in person was left for Helen and Pauline, perhaps with his Uncle Alvin in the audience as well. Now 23 years old, Warren must have felt he had finally arrived; a part in a Broadway show produced by half of the legendary Klaw and Erlanger team was heady stuff. During April and May the show played to solid houses, eventually closing after a modestly successful 64 performances. Like many shows in this period, the road called and Joseph Klaw responded. Once again, Warren packed up his valise, stashed away his script, said goodbye to Helen and headed to points west. Performing in *Mrs. Jimmie Thompson* offered an excellent income for most of the spring and summer, giving Warren the opportunity to bank some savings for the inevitable lean times ahead, such was his careful and steady nature. The production finally petered out — probably in September — and the Broadway actor headed home with a solid success under his belt.

Returning from the road to New York again — the cycle of his working life throughout the 1920s — Warren and all of America were shocked by the events that took place in New York City on September 16, 1920. Just before noon that day, a man drove a horse and wagon through the intersection of Broad and Wall streets and left it in front of the United States Assay Office, across the street from the J.P. Morgan offices and near the New York Stock Exchange. Moments later the cart exploded in an enormous ball of flame, killing thirty people and spewing an estimated two thousand pounds of shrapnel across the heart of America's financial community.[3]

In his office a few doors away at the Equitable Corporation, Warren's Uncle Alvin was hit by flying glass when his office windows were shattered by the force of the blast.[4] Even in the days before radio and television, word spread quickly through the city, and the family worried about Alvin's status until they were able to talk to him by phone. He soon moved his office upstairs to the 30th floor of the Equitable Building. The next day on Wall Street, the opening bell rang and trading went on as if nothing had happened. Money has no memory.

Intermission: The Firefly

The Wall Street bombing was not an isolated incident, but rather the tangible release of the immense pressure and frustration that had been building between labor and business for many years. When Actors' Equity went on strike in 1919 — just after Warren became a member — they joined almost a million other Americans on strike that summer and fall. Coal workers, carpenters, telephone operators, longshoremen — a veritable tidal wave of discontent and anger gripped the working men of the nation. Fear-mongering against anarchists, immigrants and communists — those that the powers-that-be blamed for the divisions being sown — grew to proportions that dwarfed McCarthyism or the terrorist hysteria of the Bush era.

Fear was easy to engender that year. In April, a quick-thinking postal employee had averted a series of 36 mail bombings after the first of the packages was delivered and mutilated a woman in Seattle. In Washington, DC, the home of the attorney general was bombed, killing a man who happened to be standing outside the front door. There were riots with Socialist groups in Cleveland and New York, and a police strike in Boston caused near-anarchy throughout the city. Coordinated government operations, known as the Palmer Raids — where 6,000 citizens were summarily arrested and jailed without charge on the mere suspicion of being communists — were justified by manufactured evidence of a non-existent Red conspiracy. As in the aftermath of September 11, America began to believe things were headed towards an inevitable cataclysm, and forgave the government many transgressions.

It all boiled over on September 16, 1920, with the explosion in front of the Federal Assay Office in New York City. The powerful blast was the deadliest terrorist attack on U.S. soil until the Oklahoma City bombing in 1995.

The public devoured what little evidence the papers offered. Police recovered the fragmented remains of the horse and cart, including two hooves that were traced to a blacksmith shop in New York. People imagined anarchists and mad bombers behind every door and window. Local and federal authorities were very thorough, but the trail eventually went cold, and New Yorkers began to forget about the story. Wall Street for their part swept it all under the rug—no memorials, no plaques and seemingly no memory of the day. The Communist hysteria was already dying down and the country was beginning to resume a sense of decency and proportion. No one was ever named or charged in the murder of over thirty people that September afternoon, and America today has no collective recognition of the incident, not even a dimly understood slogan like "Remember the *Maine*" to repeat. But in the façade of the J.P. Morgan building on Wall Street the evidence is still there, etched deep into granite, where thousands pass daily with no hint of the meaning behind it.

In October, fresh from the road, Warren auditioned for a part as The Director in Sven Lange's production of the play *Samson and Delilah*. The role was not to be his, instead going to a fast-rising star of the New York stage and future Warner Brothers stablemate, Edward G. Robinson.[5]

Warren's next professional outing lasted a mere five performances, but it was an important and heartening experience nonetheless. The play *John Hawthorne* was produced by perhaps the single most influential group of the Golden Age of Broadway, the Theatre Guild. The Guild was an outgrowth of the Washington Square Players, who had been mounting meaningful plays in New York until the Great War sent them in different directions. The Guild's mantra was "The play's the thing," and though undercapitalized, they insisted on producing only plays of superior quality with superior talent. There were no egos allowed in the Guild—no names above the title, no exorbitant salaries and no pandering to the commercial audience. Although the group was only just starting, they'd had a series of solid successes with plays by foreign authors, and now were obliged to capitulate to the pressure that they put on a work of American origin. Warren auditioned in December in front of the Guild's unique board of directors: six principals who approved every play as well as the casting of those plays. Even at this early time in their history, a play by the Theatre Guild was recognized as an important production for an actor. Warren was thrilled to be cast as John Hawthorne, the eponymous character who murders his lover's husband and buries him in a coal bin. Unfortunately, the play too should have been interred there. Opening and closing during the last week of January, it was the Guild's first major failure, prompting the great critic Heywood Broun to remark: "The Guild must permit itself some form of dissipation. *John Hawthorne* is enough for the year."[6] In the final scene of the play, Warren's cornered murderer jumps off a cliff to his death, and the actor may have felt that it was not an entirely distasteful fate. When the *New York Times* reviewed the show, they called it "uncommonly lugubrious" and pointed to at least two instances of inappropriate laughter from the audience, both elicited from lines—although not a fault of his acting— delivered by Warren. Alexander Woollcott was kind enough to observe that this response was merely "the unconquerable rebellion of common sense against hifalutin' nonsense,"[7] but it was still painful. The play closed after a series of carefully planned matinees and, but for the smug satisfaction of jealous Guild-haters, was quietly swept under the rug. Oh, and neither Warren Krech nor Warren William ever worked for the Theatre Guild again.

That spring, director Harry Millarde was preparing a feature film for the William Fox company, *The Town That Forgot God*. It was to be shot in New York, and would use many Fox regulars in the cast. Millarde had seen Warren around New York, and was interested in making a test of the actor for the part of a simple but wise carpenter who befriends the main character.

The film debut of young Warren Krech came in the 1922 William Fox production *The Town That Forgot God.* Warren played a simple man who wept at the sad plight of humankind. Director Harry Millarde practically had to use onions to get the inexperienced actor to cry on cue. Warren William is upper left, clockwise with Bunny Grauer, Jane Thomas, Harry Benham and Edward Denison.

Although some stars of the legitimate stage still often scoffed at movies, Warren simply wanted to work and, after "resting" for a couple months, finances were dwindling. When he went to the Fox studio to make the test, the director told him a little about his character. He was a dimwitted, pious carpenter, the only decent person in a town of sin. He lamented the state of mankind, and cried often at the sadness he perceived around him. Of course Millarde needed an actor who could essentially cry on cue and, fortuitously, under the intense brightness of the kleig lights at the studio, Warren's eyes watered. It was exactly what Millarde wanted, and he signed Warren to perform the second lead in the picture, the young man's first film role. But when it came time to shoot, no matter how hard Warren tried, he couldn't tear up. The effect of the lights had worn off. "They practically had to use onions to get me to cry,"[8] Warren later chuckled at the experience. There was more laughter regarding the beard that he was obliged to raise for the part. The director insisted that it remain scraggly and unkempt, and to that end the budding film star trimmed it daily with a nail clipper. He — and Helen — endured the endless snickers and staring of pitiless New Yorkers, Warren remembered with conspicuous amusement. Bothered or not, immediately after the shoot he shaved and no beard adorned his face ever again.

The film itself is a third-rate Cecil B. DeMille knock-off, the centerpiece being a lightning storm and flood that wipes out faithless citizens of "the town that forgot God"—except for the humble carpenter and his equally pious friend. The message was hard to miss, and the Hollywood hypocrisy front and center. The *Boston Globe* observed that the floods "had been put in the film purely for spectacular purposes," and the *New York Times* sniffed: "[The storm] is supposed to have been sent by God to a town that has forgotten Him — and thus revealed again the sermonizing propensity of the movies. They can't even have a storm without giving it a moral purpose."[9]

On the strength of his performance, Fox offered Warren a contract. He considered it for a little while and with the foolish confidence of youth turned it down. He admitted to assuming that if they offered him a contract, that he'd "always be able to get one."[10] It was a grave miscalculation. Warren spent the next ten years trying to break into films, doing test after test, with no contract offer forthcoming. For now, he decided to return to the stage, figuring blithely that the silver screen would wait patiently until he was ready.

In early September of 1921 Warren auditioned for a role in Marc Klaw's production *We Girls*. It was another play flavored, if not dominated, by women. It was co-written by Fanny Hatton (with her husband Frederic) and again featured women at the center of the action. The "Girls" of the title are the widowed Mrs. Carter Durand and her daughter Harriet, recently returned from many years abroad. While Harriet was away, Mrs. Durand has reached the Neolithic age of (gasp) 46. So desperate is she to act young that she embarrasses her daughter, and is embarrassed herself when her twin brother — looking like he was disinterred from an Egyptian tomb — arrives unexpectedly. His wizened appearance convinces her to accept that her youth is fading and take a new husband who is the impossibly frail age of fifty. Warren played Tom Brown, a timid young M.D. who lands Harriet at the end of the play after being handcuffed to her by a Cupid-loving cop.

We Girls began rehearsals on September 18, and opened in Bridgeport, Connecticut, on October 21 before heading to New York on November 9 for its engagement at the 48th Street Theatre, there competing with George Arliss at the Booth and Al Jolson appearing in *Bombo*, at — where else — Jolson's. In the advertising for the New York run, the producers ran a pull quote from the *New York Sun*: "Lots of ginger, and it has speed enough to carry it along for months." Most of New York disagreed. George Jean Nathan, the mordant drama critic of the *New York Times*, was more reserved in his estimation: "The play descends to the outworn tricks of the music show and the two a day stage until nothing is left of the initial idea save a thin spiral of smoke." Warren, along with others in the cast, were described as "distinctly mediocre."[11] The show didn't make liars of the *Sun*, though: It limped into the first week of the following month before closing after thirty-odd performances.

It was six months before Warren resurfaced again. He had banked some solid dollars from his time on the road and his salary on *The Town That Forgot God*, and may have decided to take a few months off. He was usually careful with money — he eventually purchased an annuity with film earnings to be certain he'd have a lifelong income — but also would sometimes go on alternating thrifty and extravagant binges, most often spending money for custom-tailored clothing, which was now becoming a vital interest. In July he attended the wedding of his sister Elizabeth, all of 21 years old, at the Little Church Around the Corner in Manhattan. Her husband Charles Lyon had been a pilot during the war and was also an avid sailor, giving Warren someone to kibitz with on his visits to the couple's new home on Long Island.

On September 3, 1922, George B. Seitz announced Warren Krech as the leading man for the new serial *Plunder*. The star of *Plunder* was the important and immensely popular Pearl

White, who became a major star in the teens portraying strong-willed, athletic women who, rather than relying on men, got themselves out of danger. Following the success of her starring role in *The Perils of Pauline* (1914), White was an international sensation, but was now returning to her serial roots after several less than successful years making features. The fifteen-part film had been shooting on location in New York as early as the beginning of August — meaning that Seitz's PR department was moving somewhat slowly. But his publicity machine now got into the swing of things, touting their new star's supposed resemblance to a well-known and popular French boxer of the day, Georges Carpentier.

> The leading man ... is Warren Krech, "easy to look at" on the screen because of his handsome face and clean cut athletic figure. Miss White says that on first meeting Krech at the Seitz studio on her return from Paris his resemblance to Georges Carpentier was so striking that her first thought was that the celebrated French prize fighter had chartered an aeroplane and "beaten her" to America.[12]

Warren was well flattered. Carpentier, known as "The Orchid Man," was nearly the height of masculine beauty in 1922. The artist Neysa McMein believed that Carpentier was such a perfect specimen that Michelangelo himself would have fainted at the sight of his body. Less than a year earlier, he had challenged Jack Dempsey for the heavyweight crown and was world-famous for having staggered the Manassa Mauler with a right hand in the second round. Rather than faint, Dempsey got angry and quickly ground the upstart Frenchman into the canvas. Such was the price of fame for the Orchid Man. Warren had a considerably easier road to his celebrity, but not as much of it.

The circumstances behind Warren's involvement with *Plunder* are dimly lit. The actor claimed that he "selected" the job from among numerous offers to make a film,[13] but this was just youthful ego; no other offers were on the horizon, no matter how high up he was while looking. The picture did afford him another chance to make hay while things were good: Seitz was paying him $150 a week, a princely sum at a time when the average working man's salary was about $25 a week. Warren played an enigmatic stranger who helped Pearl in her efforts to uncover a fortune in pirate gold buried under a New York skyscraper. For a good portion of the summer — including location work in Nova Scotia and Washington, DC — he helped the heroine get into and out of hair-raising, cliff-hanging, nail-biting adventures.

Plunder opens with a superb automobile chase shot on location in the streets of downtown New York City. Pearl speeds her car through an unexpected thunderstorm (location shooting can be entirely unpredictable), before crashing it through an office building where she traps the thief she spied grabbing a man's bag. A flashback reveals that the man's bag contains diamonds discovered under the foundation of a Manhattan skyscraper, and — surprise — Pearl owns shares in said skyscraper. The fifteen chapters are a mad dash by competing factions to obtain unfettered title to the building, putting Pearl and the 29-year-old Warren in various perilous situations around the world. There is an electric chair in New York, deadly black mists in the jungles of South America, an enormous man-eating octopus beneath a cutthroat smuggler's lair, a mad scientist with a Frankenstein monster, fire, floods, fistfights and, in the end, romance.

As Warren's first major acting job on film (*The Town That Forgot God* was a featured part), he comes off very well as the type of young go-getter prevalent in silent cinema at the time. He first dramatically appears from behind a curtain to warn Pearl not to sell her stock to the villainous Jude Deering, then drifts in and out of early chapters as a mysterious figure known as "Mr. Jones," who may or may not be working with her enemies. When Pearl at last finds that he is her benefactor — sent by his father, who has also invested in the building — Warren's profile increases, occasionally carrying entire chapters almost by himself. His acting is typical of the time, occasionally overwrought, but using the basic tools of pantomime that then dominated the art of silent film acting. He is still learning the craft, looking excellent but visually declaiming in a way that would not cause audiences to forget about great stars of the era like Henry B. Walthall or Richard Barthelmess. When Warren encounters the narcotic fumes of "The Pit of the Black Ash" in episode thirteen, his histrionics are — well — excessive. Physically he is displayed to good effect, doing some outstanding work on horseback, and displaying many of the Warren William mannerisms and body language of later years.

The producers knew they had an athletic man on their hands, and Warren was game enough to engage in rough, sturdy fights and some difficult stunts without a double. In a sequence where Pearl is trapped on the second floor of a countryside hideout, the confident climber from Minnesota scaled the façade and mounted the roof with the sure hand he had learned in his youth. But, back on August 10, the real price of the risks of those stunts was fatally driven home. That afternoon, John Stevenson was doubling Pearl for a scene being shot in New York at 72nd and Columbus. Dressed as the adventuring actress, he was to leap from the top of a double-decker bus onto the overhead girder of an elevated track. A large crowd, including the cast and crew, had gathered, many thinking Pearl herself would perform the stunt, as publicity had always insisted she did. Unfortunately, as Stevenson made his leap, his hands slipped on the dust and grime covering the girder. He fell 25 feet and cracked his head on the pavement as cameras continued cranking and bystanders worried that Pearl White had taken the fall. Stevenson was moved to a nearby drug store, then taken by taxi to Roosevelt Hospital. After an operation to relieve pressure to the brain, he died without regaining consciousness. The physically fit and semi-fearless Warren — he who had climbed high to hoist the school colors in Aitkin and supposedly descended from the third floor of his house via a homemade rope ladder — learned a valuable lesson. He would perform many vigorous athletic scenes himself, but any thoughts of serious stunting were left to the professionals. Stevenson's leap, but not the fall, remained in the film.

Plunder is somewhat old-fashioned for 1923, with the production following Pearl White's longstanding serial formula, thus lagging a few years behind the stylistic leading edge of Hollywood filmmaking as exemplified by D.W. Griffith, Henry King and Erich von Stroheim. Audiences did not flock to see her as they had in the past. She was already a relic of another time. The present and future were looking towards an even more modern construction of American women: more urban, and not just physically, but also emotionally daring. Colleen Moore, Joan Crawford and Clara Bow would take deeper personal risks than Pearl White ever dreamed of. It wasn't until Sigourney Weaver and Angelina Jolie hardened women into tough-as-nails adventurers that some semblance of Pearl's persona jumped over the decades and returned to cinema.

With Warren's naked submission to a dominant female figure — Pearl was then still an icon of feminine empowerment — *Plunder* is the ultimate template for the actor's career relationship with women. Mr. Jones is depicted as Pearl's helper, not truly her equal. And while he is competent and brave, she saves his life on multiple occasions, occupying the typical masculine figure in the narrative. Even in the end, when they've bested the crooks and secured the treasure, the impression is that Pearl chooses the romantic union between them, not the other way around. It is an insidious pattern that will occur again and again in the future.

After *Plunder* wrapped in October, Warren supposedly turned down some tentative offers to go to Hollywood. The likelihood that these offers were somewhat dubious is pointed up by the fact that the actor eschewed them in order to take a very small part in the road company of Henry Bataille's *La Tendresse*. The play, about an actress who has an affair with a young film star, had been a tremendous success for Henry Miller and Ruth Chatterton, who played it in cities from San Francisco to New York during the summer of 1922. Reaching Broadway in September, the stars settled in for a three-month run, then retooled with some new faces—Warren among them — and hit the road again. When the company opened at the Broad Street Theatre in Philadelphia on November 20, Warren's part was so small that his name is not even on the cast list. In Washington, DC, his name is likewise absent. Once again, however, his luck was lurking in the wings. Tom Nesbitt, who was playing the role of Alan Sergyll — essayed by Ronald Colman in the original production — decided to leave the company following the Washington run. Warren was offered his part for the rest of the tour. On to Chicago they went, with Warren and company hitting the Windy City on December 11 for a month-long stay at the Blackstone Theatre. It was Warren's first real chance to see and experience Chicago, with its magnificent architecture, and the beautiful lakefront walking distance from the theater.

The Chicago engagement continued through the holidays, and Warren was more aware than ever about how his absence from Helen affected him. During the run of this play about love and infidelity, he made a decision: when he returned to New York, he would tell her his feelings in person — and ask her to marry him. On January 8, *La Tendresse* played its last performance in Chicago, and shortly after, Warren boarded a train from Union Station headed toward matrimony.

9

The Secret Bride

Although Warren had often revealed his feelings to Helen through poetry and prose, his personal manner of courtship was still somewhat shy and reserved. There is every reason to believe the couple had a complete, intimate relationship since his return from the war, but he was a self-contained, taciturn man — never one to exhibit euphoric highs or be mired in emotional lows. Helen knew that she was respected, even loved, but Warren's feelings were not often expressed directly, either in words or in deeds that she might recognize as important to her. Of course she sought the advice of her best friend, Warren's sister Pauline, about her prospects. Pauline loved her brother, but did not shy away from telling Helen what she thought: "He'd make a terrible husband," Pauline warned. She also noted that Warren's personality was sometimes maddening: "so complex, inclined to be stubborn and indifferent to many ordinary inclinations."[1] Like others who hear news other than what they hope for, Helen pretended it didn't matter. It was academic, she told Pauline; she hadn't the faintest intention of marrying Warren Krech.

Having returned to New York, Warren prepared his surprise. The two were still living separately at the time, and the night he returned they were together at Helen's apartment. During dinner, he interrupted the meal and in his stolid, straightforward way he proposed. The woman who hadn't the "faintest intention" of matrimony said yes immediately. Helen recalled later that she felt not just love, but a compelling urge that seemed to draw her — a feeling that he was headed for important things, and that she would find her happiness helping him to do it.[2] Both were thrilled, but the engagement was to be kept quiet. Warren's involvement with Helen continued to be a sore point between father and son. Freeman and Frances still believed that the gap in age between the two was inappropriate and told their son in no uncertain terms that they did not approve of the idea of marriage.[3] Pauline was already 31 and had no inclination towards providing grandchildren, and if Warren married Helen, who was already 46, Freeman knew it would be extremely unlikely that his family name would be passed on. They also did not like the fact that Warren was still a struggling actor at the mercy of the whims of fate that haunt the theater. But Warren's sense of self-determination was highly developed, as it was handed down through the personal examples of his grandfather and older sister. He would do as he pleased, not as it pleased others. So, in order to avoid drama and misgivings, Helen and Warren resolved to elope.

Quickly and quietly, things were put in order. Warren wanted to be married where Elizabeth and Charles wed, at New York's Little Church Around the Corner, a beautiful neo–Gothic chapel with a tiny English garden on the grounds, built in 1849 at 1 East 29th Street. The church had long been associated with the theatrical profession, hosting weddings for many famous actors and stage professionals. Warren's Episcopalian roots and the recommendations of professional friends had brought him to the Little Church many times, and later that year he would join the newly formed Episcopal Actors' Guild which held its first meetings there. The next day, January 10, Warren and Helen made their way to the chapel. It was the perfect setting for their nuptials, situated in the heart of New York, in a liberal Episcopal church that loved actors and the stage. When it came time to fill out the proper paperwork, 29-year-old Warren Krech and the self-declared 36-year-old Helen (who was actually 46 — 17 years older than the groom) were asked about their parents' consent. Thinking nothing of it, Warren said his parents were unaware of the impending union. Even in 1923 it seems incomprehensible, but the rector then declared that there would be no marriage — even of consenting adults— without the formal consent of the surviving parents.[4] Warren and Helen were stunned. They would have to go elsewhere.

The very next day Warren and Helen presented themselves at the Church of the Incarnation, situated at 35th and Madison Avenue. Navigating similar questions with carefully vague answers, the couple were given a license and married in front of two requisite witnesses by the Reverend Charles Belden on January 11, 1923.[5] In spite of the trouble, the simplicity of the ceremony must have pleased Warren, who hated to be on display except when acting in character. Standing in front of a massive assembly of guests at his own wedding would have been sheer horror for the retiring actor.

The newlyweds immediately made their way to Atlantic City for an impromptu honeymoon, with friends and family still unaware of the union. When they returned to New York, Warren gave his parents the news. He hoped that they would realize that his feelings were genuine and accept Helen as their daughter-in-law despite the difference in their ages. However, unlike the other times that the couple had surprised him with their understanding and help, no such sympathy was forthcoming. Freeman was adamant, and the marriage created a rift between father and son that lasted most of the rest of their lives.[6] The situation made things difficult for Elizabeth, who adored her brother but wound up seeing far less of him than she wanted to during the next few years because of the trouble between father and son. It may have been the origin of the inhospitable relationship that Elizabeth and Helen maintained even after Freeman passed away.

Now Warren's rare bad luck conspired to further make his parents' case. One of the primary things his family worried about — the mercurial and fickle nature of the acting profession — reared its head. As a successful film star, Warren later postulated that most young couples who marry on a wave of prosperity eventually endure adversity. Here, immediately, was his and Helen's: beginning in January of 1923, almost to the day he was married, Warren did not work as an actor for one full year. There was a minor financial panic that year and Broadway was enduring difficult times. Warren went on the standard auditions and casting calls during the spring, but none were successful. Helen later remembered those struggles: "We had fun in those early days when Warren was invading Broadway. We learned to make the best of simple things, to give and to take. Perhaps sometimes we were happier than now, with the responsibilities that money brings."[7] Between the couple's savings, Helen's salary and some support from the family — as well as some possible help from the Episcopal Actor's Guild Fund set up for just such emergencies— the newlyweds were never "in want," but as the months dragged on, Warren had to consider what was next. He eventually decided to once again try to break into the movie business. By now, however, movies were almost exclusively a West Coast prospect, with Los Angeles being the mecca of production. That summer, Warren decided to once again pack up and leave Helen in New York, this time to fish for offers in Hollywood.

Meanwhile, both *The Town That Forgot God* and *Plunder* were appearing across the country, and each eventually made its way to rural Minnesota. "Warren Krech Gets Rousing Welcome" was the headline of the *Aitkin Independent Age* in March. "Home boy as screen star to be seen in weekly serial." *The Age* reported that "the first appearance of Warren William Krech in his hometown theater drew a large and appreciative audience Wednesday night and again Thursday. The minute he was on screen enthusiastic applause greeted him, and the kids, many of whom had never seen him, joined in the din with home loyalty. Aitkin people will turn out in throngs to welcome the homecoming of the old town boy...."[8]

For three months Warren made the rounds in California, testing, schmoozing and cajoling, but without success. The foolish optimism that led him to reject offers from Fox and others now proved among his last indulgences of ego. His cavalier choice had taught him a lesson: never allow your head to get too big.

While Warren was on the West Coast that summer, the New York stage was gradually gathering the actors and personalities who would soon migrate west to become the next generation of film stars. Edward G. Robinson was already on his way to full-fledged stardom. Producers were just beginning to take notice of a youthful Humphrey Bogart. Ruby Keeler, then all of fifteen years old, was already "dancing her heart out," and Aline MacMahon — so wonderful later as Warren's co-star in *The Mouthpiece* and *Gold Diggers of 1933* — was performing in *This Fine Pretty World*. Among Warren's other future co-workers on New York stages in 1923 were Edward Arnold, Ned Sparks, Mae West, Mary Boland and Fannie Brice.

With no interest from the Hollywood production machine, Warren packed his wardrobe and boarded the eastbound train back to New York.

Warren and Helen rang in 1924 hoping for a change in their fortunes. Their first anniversary was rapidly approaching, and both of them knew it couldn't continue this way much longer. Warren's only work since their wedding had been a momentary stint with a small theater company where he wore a stuffed shirt and played a Member of Parliament. He'd received some good notices, but almost no money. Finally, in January, Warren auditioned for the new production of a group known as the Players Company, Inc. A confluence of events conspired to make his casting in *The Wonderful Visit* an important event in his career.

Returning empty-handed from Hollywood in the summer was a blow to the actor. Now almost thirty and with a new wife to support, he began thinking about his prospects, and wondering why success had recently eluded him. He also began contemplating steps that he could take to help change his circumstances. According to Warren's 1932 studio bio, a discussion with friends conversant with "the occult, numerology and similar pseudo-sciences" led to the suggestion he might consider changing his name. These "friends" probably included Pauline, who inherited a lifelong interest in such disciplines from her grandfather Ernst.[9] The practical Minnesota man resisted the idea, as he often did when someone told him that he ought to do something; it had been part of his nature since he rebelled against his father's desire for him to take over the newspaper in Aitkin. "I got in the habit of rebelling against anything preconceived, cut and dried, foreordained,"[10] he said, examining his own intractable nature. Warren was doubly dubious in this case, since he considered the various supernatural disciplines to be so much bunk. There were, however, other reasons in favor of a name change beyond the esoteric. In addition to the undercurrent of anti–German sentiment still lingering beneath the surface of American life, the simple fact was that Warren's name was constantly mispronounced (it rhymes with "wreck"), and occasionally misspelled. But Warren was very fond of the family name, and had misgivings about leaving it behind. Conflicted, the actor again sought the counsel of his older sister. He knew that she could always be counted on for clear-headed, logical advice. She was the reason he was acting at all, he felt, and he trusted her expressly. Pauline endorsed the change, convincing her younger brother to put aside his misgivings and take a chance. And, once Warren had resolved to begin the New Year with a new name, it was Pauline who suggested he simply drop his surname and use the sobriquet Warren William. Professionally he acceded to the change, but personally his identity was still with family and heritage forged in Minnesota. Everywhere but on stage and screen, from friendships to legal contracts, he remained Warren Krech for the rest of his life.

There was another change in the New Year of 1924. Warren Krech certainly wasn't aware of it then, but he needed one more thing to officially launch his new persona as "Warren William." In 1933 he gave the background behind the origin of his most famous personal characteristic: his moustache. According to him, it was a woman who convinced him to grow it. "She told me, in that complimentary way women have of getting men to do things, that although I really was very handsome, I'd be handsomer still with a moustache. I fell for her wiles and grew a moustache, and believe it or not, it was the moustache that won me the part in my next play."[11] Warren doesn't reveal the identity of the sly female who charmed him, but the facial hair — a neat, razor-thin chevron without which Warren was rarely seen over the next 25 years — became an unmistakable trademark. Feature writers could hardly resist the opportunity to comment on his most obvious physical feature; the Canadian film director Guy Madden deftly likened the appendage to a sharpened Gillette Saber. Another Hollywood wag noted, with a disconcerting degree of seriousness, that the actor "flicks one drop of hair tonic onto his moustache every morning before work." It aided, for good or ill, his eventual comparisons to John Barrymore, and inspired Jack Warner to later declare in an interoffice memo: "We want William to definitely keep the moustache on for the rest of his natural life, so he won't look undressed."[12] The studio head more or less got his wish; Warren gave only two film performances without his hirsute trademark. Appearing in Cecil B. DeMille's *Cleopatra* sans moustache was both appropriate and forgivable, even though the director (in spite of his protestations to the contrary) rarely encountered an anachronism he didn't film. However, seeing a hairless Warren William in the late Warner era offering *Dr. Monica* is indeed, as Jack Warner described, like watching him perform nude: uncalled for, inappropriate and downright weird.

The final important element in Warren's signing to *The Wonderful Visit* was the beginning of his lifelong friendship with its director, Eugene Lockhart. Lockhart, later known to movie audiences from superb character performances in classic Hollywood films such as *His Girl Friday, Algiers* and *The Sea Wolf*, had been on Broadway since 1917. He had recently come out of the Players Company's enormously successful production of *Sun Up*, and late in 1923 he received his first directing job when he was chosen by the Players to helm their adaptation of *The Wonderful Visit*. In January, Lockhart and the producers called for auditions. Just before his first wedding anniversary, the newly christened Warren William was still desperate for work and earnestly appeared for an audition. The drought was broken. He sauntered out with a modest role as Sir John Gotch, Knight of the British Empire, and the beginnings of a relationship that would end with Gene Lockhart acting as a pallbearer at his funeral.

The first production to feature Warren William began life as a short story penned in 1895 by master fantasy writer H.G. Wells, concerning the appearance of an angel on earth. In 1921 Wells enlisted the aid of Saint John Ervine, the English dramatist, to turn the satiric story into a stage production. In their adaptation, an angel appears in the garden of the Reverend Richard Mendham; the ensuing social intercourse with various members of the little town of Siddermarton confounds and vexes the angel. Class distinction, sin, violence, greed, and human arrogance are only a few of the things that the angel is obliged to understand in the short time he mingles with Man. Ultimately, the angel is asked to leave Siddermarton, when his embarrassing and "inconvenient" questions become too painful for the locals. Although there was some momentary confusion about the provenance of the stage play — many reviewers attributed the adaptation solely to Ervine — he immediately set the record straight in a letter to the *New York Times*, printed March 16, 1924, during the middle of the play's run. "I am anxious you should not misapprehend the facts about authorship of *The Wonderful Visit*. The play was written by H.G. Wells and me in collaboration and not by me alone. Wells did most of the work."[13]

The production received mostly positive reviews upon opening on February 12, although its engagement at the Lenox Hill Theater likely limited its exposure to the greater New York public. The Lenox, a small space on East 78th Street, was well off the beaten path for most Broadway theatergoers, used to the best productions taking place below 53rd Street. But word of mouth kept *The Wonderful Visit* open for a respectable 56 performances despite the hike it required of its patrons. Some fans of the play were devoted enough to write to the newspapers with praise, encouraging adventurous New York theatergoers to trek north. "It would be a pity if lovers of the best in the drama should miss this truly artistic performance just because it is a few blocks removed from Times Square," one wrote.[14] "It is well worth the trip to the Upper East Side." Another reader expressed similar feelings: "It is a relief beyond expectation to see, in a tiny, out of the way playhouse a production so smooth, vividly cast and altogether professional."[15] Warren himself was singled out for neither praise nor scorn; the play belonged to Margaret Mower as the angel. She basked in the glow of many fine words about her difficult role as the supernaturally charming and ignorant visitor. For two months the production siphoned enough business from the downtown shows to stay alive. It was an uphill battle, however: the tiny Lenox production was competing with legendary Broadway figures. The First Lady of American Theater, Lillian Gish, was performing at the Lyric. Eddie Cantor rolled and fluttered his eyes every night in Flo Ziegfeld's enormously popular *Kid Boots*, while pianist Sergei Rachmaninoff was performing in Warren's old stomping grounds, Carnegie Hall. The King of Broadway, George M. Cohan, was still packing them in after 30 years in show business, and the luminous Jeanne Eagels basked in the glow of her long-running hit *Rain*. At the end of April, finally, word of mouth had played out and nothing was left to do but close the show and hope to have the chance to mount it again in a higher profile house.

The Warren William experiment was deemed a success, although the new name was not without its own problems. The inevitable consequence of the last name "William" is that everyone unconsciously adds an "s" to it. That included the *Aitkin Independent Age*, who re-christened their erstwhile resident in the March 29 edition. "Warren William is Warren Krech," announced the headline. "If any Aitkinite should chance to see Warren Williams among the names of actors on a theater program, they will know that it is Warren Krech, formerly of Aitkin." The mistake was so prevalent during his career that it would be no exaggeration to say that roughly 25 percent of the time his name was used — in advertising, programs, press releases, reviews, even in studio memos— it was misspelled. It was so common an error, in fact, that Warner Brothers literally begged Warren to allow them to change his surname to "Williams." By that time he was quite attached to the moniker, and stubbornly refused.

At around this time, one of the great scandals of post-war America was just beginning to unfold in front of the American public. Almost immediately following President Warren Harding's death, information began to leak out about a group of sweetheart oil deals that his administration had arranged. Quickly, the background behind what became known as the "Teapot Dome" affair took the front pages of American newspapers. The eponymous "fall guy" of the case was Secretary of the Interior Albert B. Fall, who had received hundreds of thousands of dollars from well-connected oilmen for engineering no-bid contracts from the Interior Department. Eventually Will Hays, the future czar of motion picture censorship, and the Equitable

Trust, where Warren's uncle was chairman of the board, were nominally involved in the proceedings. Through 1924, Senate hearings, Congressional testimony, editorials, articles and rumors dominated the public discourse. It would take years for the full facts to be revealed, and punishment—then, as today—was modest. Meanwhile, just as *The Wonderful Visit* was closing, a production was taking shape that proved another important step in Warren William's career, and again magnified the positive influence that women had in his success.

In 1924 Rachel Crothers was one of the few genuinely successful women on Broadway who was not an actress. She had written a remarkable series of plays over the previous 18 years—complex and challenging stories of modern women, sexism, divorce and double standards in a time when these issues were rarely raised on stage. Although often frankly feminist (but not without sometimes questioning the tenets of feminism), Crothers most often used humor and wit to make her point, allowing her audiences an evening's entertainment with her message. She had also been occasionally afforded the opportunity to stage her productions, and hoped for the same level of control on her new offering, *Expressing Willie.* The author beat the pavement of the big Broadway producing concerns, looking for an angel who would not only put up the money, but also allow her to direct. In spite of her pedigree, there were no takers. It was not just that they didn't want a woman directing, but many were dubious of the play itself. It was written off by most as hackneyed, trite, or hopelessly old-fashioned. After reading the manuscript, one producer told her that it was barely "an eighth of a play,"[16] and a reviewer later observed that the plot "was stale even before *The Saturday Evening Post* or the movies."[17]

Even so, the veteran Broadway insider felt confident in her work; if *Willie* was short on novelty, it was long on Crothers' brand of incisive, crowd-pleasing wit. Eventually she consummated a co-producing arrangement with the Equity Players, a small group devoted to mounting plays that were "too distinguished in merit" to appeal to commercial producers. The contract for *Expressing Willie* was designed on a revenue-sharing arrangement, with the author receiving one-third of the weekly profits while Equity took the rest. Meanwhile, stung by the rejection from the mainline producers, Crothers proceeded to spread the rumor that she had deliberately bypassed the commercial arena, taking her new offering directly to Equity because she would be afforded an opportunity to direct. It was not remotely true, and the *New York Times* critic John Corbin, an admirer of the play, used his column to explode her manufactured myth shortly after *Willie* opened. It was irrelevant. However she managed it, Crothers was now in complete control of her career. She was the producer, writer, director and casting agent—an unprecedented nexus of power for a woman at the time.

In late March, *Willie* was navigating casting and rehearsals for its April opening at the 48th Street Theater. Uptown, as *The Wonderful Visit* was winding down, Warren began looking for a new situation. He heard about the upcoming production on the main stem and auditioned almost immediately after the Lenox show closed. His reading for the part of George Cadwalader went well, and he was told by the producer that he might have the part. Then quickly he was told that he might not have it. "It went on that way for days. I was actually in and out of that role almost a dozen times," Warren later remembered wryly.[18] He eventually wound up with the part and the beginning of a profitable professional relationship with the author that he never forgot. He and Crothers worked together again two more times, including one of Warren's greatest stage successes.

Rehearsals continued on through late March and early April, and many were still as dubious of the sturdiness of the narrative as those reticent producers were. One of her own cast members, Louise Hale—not without enormous cheek, it might be added—took the author-director aside and told her that she had best prepare herself for disaster; that the production wasn't "a ghost of a show."[19] But the naysayers were over-thinking it; the public was happy with a good time and some rich laughter, which the production delivered to a sparkling champagne fizz. *Expressing Willie* opened to enthusiastic audiences and good box office on April 16. Reviewers called it "stale," and proceeded to complain that it had all been done before — but once they got that out of their systems, they praised *Willie* as a crowd-pleasing, feel-good comedy with a touch of weight to the ostensibly airy proceedings. A letter in the *New York Times* capsulized the critical response perfectly: "There is not much depth to *Expressing Willie*. Neither is there much novelty. But there is a Crotherian sense of humor which casts a magic spell over otherwise unenchanted situations and makes it one of the cleverest comedies that Broadway has seen for several seasons."[20]

The story concerns a small-town woman named Minnie who is unexpectedly invited to the weekend party of a Long Island millionaire (the eponymous Willie) who she grew up with and has always loved. It's Willie's mother who has engineered the reunion to scuttle her son's impending engagement to a snobbish gold digger who is after the family's newfound millions. During the course of the evening, Minnie's folksy charm and unconscious decency humble the host and his guests, so used to the petty certitudes of their insular world. Of course by the finish Willie and his old sweetheart are in love all over again. The script gently derides Long Island mores, with Warren playing a modest role as one of the party guests, the inept George Cadwalader. It would be interesting to know how Warren felt about the playful chiding, since his sister Liz and his mother and father were all Long Island residents precisely at this time. Chances are he saw the transplanted Aitkinites, who had recently moved together to Port Washington from Brooklyn, as far more like small-town Minnie than social-climbing Willie.

Expressing Willie offered another, entirely different thing to the rising actor: a chance for the man with no voice to sing in front of notoriously tough New York audiences. The piece was "Express Yourself," and Warren had to rely on the — ahem —"training" he had received during his oh-so-short tenure with Madison Corey's Singers overseas. Although one finds no review of his vocal interpretation, the song was an important element to the theme of the story: "Standing out distinctly is the song 'Express Yourself.' It is calculated to excite the emotion which would be aroused in any human being where fear played a part."[21] The song stayed in the show and Warren was good enough to keep it as his own throughout the run.

During the spring of his first big Broadway success, Warren impressed the management and crew as a professional and inventive trouper. With his dressing room on the third floor of the 48th Street Theatre — proximity to the stage being in direct proportion to one's importance to the production — the stage manager, Mrs. Lawson, was obliged to tramp upstairs during each act to give Warren his cues. Immediately the resourceful technocrat devised a solution to ease the lady's pounding heart. While in France he had purchased a wristwatch that could also be set as an alarm. During each act, Warren would set the alarm and take care of the business of preparation in his aerie on the third floor. When the watch sounded, he scampered down to the wings and awaited his entrance, to the stage manager's delight. The technique proved so successful that Mrs. Lawson resolved to purchase a consignment of the watches and rest her tired heart from then on.[22]

Expressing Willie lasted in New York for more than seven months alongside a Broadway lineup featuring Howard Carter (the discoverer of King Tut's tomb), Anna Pavlova, the legendary star of the *Ballet Russe,* and the notorious "Girl in the Red Velvet Swing," Evelyn Nesbit. It was the beginning of a very profitable end to the drought that bedeviled Warren in 1923. He would now work almost continuously on stage for the next eight years. The Equity Players

In 1924 Warren Krech appeared in the second stage production under his new professional name, Warren William. The play was Rachel Crothers' *Expressing Willie*, the story of a wealthy toothpaste magnate who falls for an old flame. From left to right: Louise Hale, Alan Brooks, Crystal Herne, Richard Sterling, Warren William and Molly McIntyre.

resolved to make *Expressing Willie* a summer run, and in July the show celebrated its 125th performance with a party and a special performance with souvenir fans given away to keep patrons cool. It stayed at the 48th Street Theatre until new productions appeared in the fall season.[23] When the show finally closed in Manhattan, it went on an extensive subway tour of the New York area for the final months of 1924. It opened to excellent reviews in Boston just after New Year's Day of 1925 and the *Daily Globe* noted, "Mr. Williams [sic] as the blundering Cadwalader and Miss McIntyre ... were each excellent impersonations."[24] The Boston run closed in time for Warren to return home to celebrate his second wedding anniversary with Helen. Three days later the actor picked up where he left off when *Willie* returned to Manhattan at the Shubert-Riviera Theater on 97th Street. The play nobody wanted trudged to its last stop in Brooklyn almost ten months after opening. Rachel Crothers' creation was so successful it even spawned a second company that toured the Midwest — to far less success than the New York company, it might be added — during 1924. When the New York cast disbanded early in February, the Krechs had a tidy nest egg, Warren William had two solid productions on his résumé, and his confidence was sky high.

The success of *Willie* gave Warren more opportunities with casting directors, and he found new work immediately in Henry Stillman's newly formed Art Theatre production of Frank

Swinnerton's *Nocturne*. The presentation was troubled from the start, with the original opening of February 9 postponed for a week. When it opened at the Punch and Judy Theater on the 16th it played only matinee shows while *The Small Timers* held evening performances. Stark Young in the *New York Times* lauded the adaptation but condemned the cast as being out of their depth. It would be bad enough to be singled out for scorn in the lead, but after deriding Sydney Thompson and Mortimer White, Young tersely proceeded to dump Warren in a mass grave: "The three other principals are faced with tasks nearly always beyond them."[25] The entire experience seemed like an exercise in humility. *Nocturne* closed after only three performances. The promised matinee performances for March never happened. Nobody complained.

At this moment, a man named Edward Goodman was forming a new company called the Stagers, which would soon provide Warren with some of the most complex and interesting roles of his career. Goodman had been a successful writer, director, critic, and the founder of the Washington Square Players, the forerunner of the Theatre Guild and an important Broadway company before the war. He was also widely known as a shrewd judge of young talent, having given many actors their first jobs, including the great Katherine Cornell, then at the height of her popularity and critical acclaim. Since 1919 he had been teaching and directing the senior class performances at Warren's alma mater, the American Academy of Dramatic Arts. In the Stagers, Goodman wanted to build a resident company that could tackle quality projects, not unlike the Washington Square Players or the Theatre Guild.[26] It would be a good group with which to be associated, promising steady work and meaty roles if they were successful.

Goodman's first Stagers production was *The Blue Peter*, the story of a former adventurer in colonial Africa who finds himself restless and dissatisfied with his quiet domestic life back in England. Warren auditioned and won the part of David Hunter, the nominal hero of the play, trying to decide between proper obligations to his family and the responsibility to take care of himself. The actor's name was now important enough to be included in the print advertising, but again it followed three women: Mary Kennedy, Marjorie Vonnegut and Margaret Wycherly. The production opened on March 24 at the Stagers' home base, the 52nd Street Theatre, and received middling reviews from the New York media. United Press was lukewarm, noting, "The hero is played by Warren William, who does an excellent job of acting, handicapped as he is with such an avalanche of conversation."[27] Stark Young delivered this ambiguous appraisal of the male lead: "The part of the restless hunter was played with a fair amount of convincingness at times by Warren William, in spite of many stiff inflections, physical and emotional."[28] One critic who was not so reserved in his praise was Alexander Woollcott, the fine theater critic of the *New York Times*. After seeing Warren in *The Blue Peter*, he penned a notice that simultaneously energized Warren's career and created a lifelong source of intense frustration.

The influential writer, having seen Warren begin to blossom as an actor and personality, made an observation: that here in New York there was an actor who was the spitting image of a young John Barrymore, "but without the Barrymore mannerisms." It was most certainly meant to be a compliment — at that moment there was no bigger sex symbol on the metropolitan stage, or any actor more lauded than "The Great Profile." "He has a Barrymore accent in his voice and a Barrymore tone to his voice and looks the very image of the young John Drew who played Petruchio," Woollcott wrote, quickly putting the name of Warren William on the lips of the Broadway cognoscenti. In Port Washington, Freeman Krech saw Woollcott's comments in the newspaper and was so impressed that he momentarily put aside his pique and wired a telegram to Warren in New York. In it, he jokingly advised his son to "lose all thoughts of engineering and stay in the theatre with the Drews and the Barrymores."[29] Helen, who was continually vexed by her husband's pathological lack of interest in courting publicity, was walking on air.

It was all exhilarating and fun, of course, but within a few months the whole thing was on its way to becoming an inescapable fetter around Warren's neck — an unintended, but irksome challenge to his highly developed sense of individuality. For the next 25 years, the comparison was never off the lips of the public or the media. It became one of the only things that could always be counted on to get a rise out of the actor, normally so sedate and self-possessed. When interviewers mentioned it — as they invariably did — he always became a bit grim. In a 1931 interview with Otheman Stevens he made his feelings as clear as possible: "It always makes me feel self-conscious when I am compared with anyone other than myself, no matter how complimentary. From what people I meet say, I must look like twenty-odd different actors."[30] Later, he expanded on the idea: "They began saying I looked like a lot of other actors. It was rather disturbing. If I looked not only like Barrymore, but like so-and-so and so-and-so, I began to doubt whether I could possibly have any personality of my own."[31] He grew so tired of the analogy that he even tried to steer feature writers and publicists away from the angle. When Gladys Hall was preparing an article about him for *Modern Screen* magazine, she sent a copy of her manuscript to Warren for proofreading. He returned it with a petulant note written in the margin where she had mentioned the long-standing comparison: "Must we have this Barrymore business?"[32] He did have a sense of humor about it at times, however. After he and Barrymore later became friends, the *new* Great Profile quipped: "I wish they would stop comparing me to Barrymore — and so does he!"[33] Although he loathed the situation, Warren couldn't avoid putting his own share of fuel on the fire: He eventually wound up starring on stage and screen with two of John Barrymore's wives, and one of his brother Lionel's for good measure.

The Blue Peter (so named for the tavern where much of the action takes place) continued into late April — not entirely successful, but neither a complete bomb. Goodman liked Warren's performance — not to mention the publicity he was bringing to the group — and smartly gave him the lead in the Stagers' next production, Henrik Ibsen's *Rosmersholm*. Warren was thrilled, as this was the kind of work he had been longing to do since he arrived on stage; intelligent, challenging characters that would stretch his ability. The company began preparing for the new offering while *The Blue Peter* was still running. Exhausted from the regular evening performances of *Peter,* daytime rehearsals and readings of *Rosmersholm*, and his own devotion to learning, memorizing and performing two complex roles, Warren took to sleeping at the 52nd Street Theatre during the weeks leading up to *Rosmersholm's* premiere.[34] It was the most intense period of his professional life until he submitted himself to the Warner Brothers sweatshop in 1931.

As the *Rosmersholm* cast and crew geared up to take over the 52nd Street Theatre, *The Blue Peter* was rumored to be moving to another space on Broadway. The swap never happened, and *Peter* simply evaporated at or around the time *Rosmersholm* opened on May 5. The cast of the new show again included Margaret Wycherly (widely remembered as Cody Jarret's mother in director Raoul Walsh's intense crime drama *White Heat*) and Arthur Hughes from the Stagers, and J.M. Kerrigan, the fine character actor who later worked with Warren in *The Wolf Man* at Universal. *Rosmersholm* received plaudits as a welcome diversion from the populist fare dominating the main stem. John Daly wrote in the *Washington Post*, "It is safe to say that lovers of drama ... will find more food for thought in this study of the individual soul than in most of the drama foisted and fashioned during the current season."[35] The champion — and bane — of Warren's career, Alexander Woollcott said the production was "one of the essential experiences of the persistent playgoer who ought not let slip this chance to see a rare and memorable play." Others were less enthusiastic. More than one reviewer called it dull, and the political message that Ibsen wove into it must have seemed heavy and ponderous to audiences of the kinetic Jazz Age of 1925. It didn't help that the plot saw Johannes Rosmer, his wife, and his mistress commit suicide; even the modern bohemians couldn't get behind it very strongly. *Time* magazine summed it up with deadpan simplicity: "The general public will probably regard it as an unnecessary bore ... Warren William, a discovery of [the Stagers], looks like John Barrymore, and brought to the central part a personality that whispers of a sound future."[36]

Now becoming successful and famous, the young man from Aitkin must have marveled at the contrast from the era of mud streets and gaslight he was born into. It was an amazing time in the American theatre. Just two blocks away, the grand old vaudevillians Weber and Fields — later to co-star with Warren in *Lillian Russell* — were at the Colony. Within walking distance he could take in Fred and Adele Astaire at the Liberty, while W.C. Fields and Will Rogers were nearby headlining the *Ziegfeld Follies*. George Arliss, Jeanne Eagels, Joseph Schildkraut, Alfred Lunt and Lynn Fontanne all had popular offerings, and Paul Whiteman could be seen at the Hippodrome. And Warren was part of it — living the dreams of his youth in the greatest city in the world, amongst talent never to be duplicated.

Rosmersholm held its own though May. Then, starting on June 1, New York experienced a week of scorching temperatures unprecedented in contemporaneous memory. Shows across the city reported a drop in receipts of 50 to 90 percent, some taking in less than a thousand dollars for the seven days. Doing a show in that heat and under the powerful stage lights was a brutal experience. The cast of *Rosmersholm* got through it, but the show never recovered. It limped on until June 13 and closed with the knowledge that they had attempted something good.

From here, Warren moved on to another enormous stepping stone in his career. That summer, William Anthony McGuire, a comedy writer who had prepared the book for two *Ziegfeld Follies* productions, was working on producing his first drama. The show was then called *The Hi-Jacker*, a story of two men — one a rum-runner and the other a modern-day pirate — who argue, with prerequisite violence, over a married woman's affections. In August, following a two-month vacation, Warren signed on as the rum-runner Gerald Fay, opposite Frank Shannon as his archenemy. The play, also known before it opened on Broadway as *Somewhere East of Gotham,* spent almost three months rehearsing and playing try-outs across the Northeast, buffing the action to a high mirror shine. Some elements were simple tricks of stagecraft born out of necessity. For weeks War-

This portrait was taken at De Barron studios during the autumn of 1926, when Warren was starring in the popular drama *Twelve Miles Out* on Broadway. Courtesy Barbara Hall.

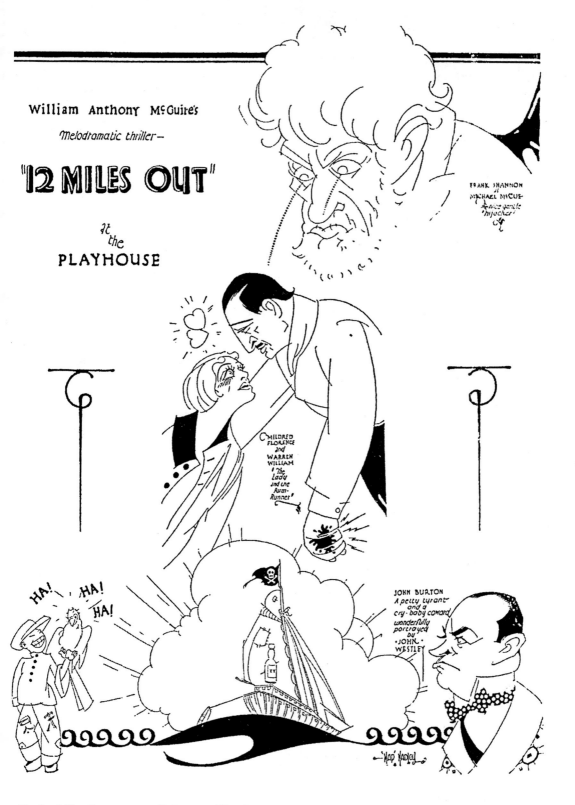

Twelve Miles Out was one of Warren William's greatest successes on Broadway. He played a tough-as-nails rumrunner who kills the villain and wins the girl. This outstanding caricature appeared in the *New York Journal* in 1926.

ren and Shannon worked on choreographing the final scene, a brutal fight to the death between the two. No matter what they tried, they couldn't find a way to make it look realistic — except in those times when they accidentally did hit each other, which would do no one any good. In frustration, McGuire, who was also directing, tried the oldest trick in the book: "Just turn out the lights, slap your hands and grunt," he told the pair. The climactic fight in darkness stayed in the play through the entire run. When it at last made its way to Baltimore on October 26 — now known as *Twelve Miles Out*— for a final engagement before opening in New York, the play had taken on many of the comedic elements that writer McGuire was known for in his *Follies* days. At the Broadway opening on November 16 it was an immediate smash. "At the close of the second act ... there was as prolonged and enthusiastic a demonstration as has been heard in local theatres for many months," the *Times* wrote. "It was honest and deserved." The play became one of the biggest hits of the winter season, running almost 200 performances through April of 1926. With Warren's salary on the production at almost $400 a week, the engagement was a massive success, netting almost $10,000 for the Krechs' bank account.

In late February, the Stagers called on Warren once again. They were preparing a dual bill of August Strindberg's *Easter* and Joseph Conrad's one-act play *One Day More,* and wanted him for parts in both. Warren knew that *Twelve Miles Out* was nearing the end of its Broadway run, and that McGuire was planning to take it on the road after it closed in New York. He had a choice: stay with the show and make some easy money, but leave Helen again for months, or remain in the city and try to parlay his recent successes into something more. Additionally, in order to make the opening of *Easter* on March 15, Warren would have to begin learning and rehearsing the double bill while starring in *Twelve Miles Out.* The chance to play Strindberg was too alluring — Warren decided to return to the Stagers and began the grueling process of working on three roles simultaneously. He was reunited with his friend Arthur Hughes who had appeared with him in both *The Blue Peter* and *Rosmersholm,* and a new recruit to the Stagers, actress Michael Strange, who just so happened to be Mrs. John Barrymore. There must have been a lot of good-natured ribbing about Warren's Barrymore connection, none of which could have pleased him. It certainly wouldn't have helped alleviate the stress of the task he had set himself to. He quickly realized that he could not do justice to the Stagers' program divided between the two shows, so on March 6, Warren gave his final performance in *Twelve Miles Out* just a month before it closed on April 10.

Strindberg and Conrad arrived in New York City a tad late, pushed back from the 15th to Thursday, March 18. Again the Stagers garnered a mixed reception, with critics giving plaudits for attempting serious drama, but the public not warming up to the ponderous mood. A letter in the *Times* said both plays were "perfectly cast and directed with rare sensitiveness and sympathy." Brooks Atkinson was more measured in his estimation, thinking *One Day More* a weak effort from the author that had been helped immensely by the cast. Of Warren he said, "As the misanthropic son, Mr. William conveyed force verging at times on truculence." *Easter* was judged by Atkinson to be among other things: gloomy, ghastly, melancholy, heavy, hypochondriacal, dismal and desolate. Yes, a fun night out at the theater. It's no wonder the bill folded after only 28 performances.

As *Easter* ground to a halt, Warren watched his sure thing — *Twelve Miles Out* — close and head out on the road without him. He was out of a job. There was little reason to worry, however. If not a bona fide star, he was now riding a wave of popularity from the success *of Twelve Miles Out,* his work with the Stagers and the publicity surrounding Woollcott's Barrymore comparison. Casting directors now knew his name and experience, giving him a decided advantage that he didn't have before.

Just as *Easter* was ending, David Belasco, then the most successful producer on Broadway, was mounting a new production starring the toast of the Ziegfeld Follies, comedienne Fanny Brice. It seemed like an unbeatable combination, and Warren snagged the male lead in the show, as — of all things — a Jewish cowboy. Once again he was playing support to a strong female lead, in a show named for the star: *Fanny*. Rehearsals began on May 4 (pushed back from April 20), the cast then spending four weeks of Belasco's money getting ready for out-of-town rehearsals. The production was troubled from the very beginning. As a vaudeville star who told jokes and sang bawdy songs, Brice was a sensation. However, as the star of a musical comedy — one that required the creation and control of a genuine character — she was lost. She could not act. Things were so bad in rehearsals that the second lead John Cromwell was forced to take on the unenviable task of coaching the star in her own show.[37] Meanwhile, Belasco himself rode Brice, mercilessly drilling her and Warren in an endless repetition of the second act curtain. It had become so burdensome that when the second act ended "successfully" on opening night, Brice broke character and kissed Belasco in front of the entire house.[38] Late in the month, Fanny's husband, the noted swindler Nicky Arnstein — who'd previously spent time in federal prison for bond theft — was again arrested and put in New York's notorious jail "The Tombs." Breaking rehearsal, Fanny visited her husband and bailed him out. Drama was *de rigueur* in the company of *Fanny*.

Try-outs began on May 31 in Atlantic City. It was disastrous. The production was panned, with Belasco and Willard Mack receiving the brunt of the flak for the execrable script they had penned. Brice got off no better. If the immensely powerful Belasco were not involved the entire show would likely have been scuttled. As it was, the producer closed the show and, refusing to give up, withdrew to retool. Brice went off to the West Coast on a short vaudeville tour while Belasco and Mack rewrote the scenario. Warren had most of the summer off until

The inexplicable casting of Warren William as a Jewish cowboy was just one of the reasons that *Fanny* was a dreadful failure for producer David Belasco and its star Fanny Brice in 1926. The actor lined his pockets while the producer kept the play running in a futile attempt to convince New York theatergoers that *Fanny* was not "rubbish."

rehearsals on the revamped show started on August 10. More try-outs followed in Washington, DC, and Baltimore but nothing was going to save this abomination, the worst reviewed play of Warren's career. Of the Broadway opening on September 21, the *New York Sun* had these words: "A stagnant, highly stupid, sometimes malodorous piece of play making." Alexander Woollcott was similarly impressed: "A rubbishy play, which, upon inspection, turned out to be just a rather inferior musical comedy libretto, written by Willard Mack and Mr. Belasco and they both ought to be ashamed of themselves and each other." "Warren William has a dull time," the *New York Post* declared, "being no more than a target for the beanbags of Miss Brice's mockery."[39]

On Tuesday, September 28, just a week after opening and being grilled by the critics, Warren received news that put the reviews of *Fanny* in clearer perspective. Early that morning he was woken by a call from his father — an unusual occurrence that instantly made him nervous. Freeman gave him the bad news: Warren's mother — his wife of 36 years — had died suddenly during the night. She was just sixty. Warren was in shock. Although she had been ill on and off for some time, there was nothing that would have indicated the possibility of a quick death. The wedge that Warren's marriage to Helen put between mother and son had never quite been removed, and it must have been frustrating for him to have her disappear from his life without a resolution to the conflict. With his father also having health problems, it was left mainly to Warren and his sisters to make the funeral and burial arrangements. With their help — and some flexibility from the *Fanny* company — everything was taken care of. At his daughter Elizabeth's home where he lived, Freeman Krech now felt as alone as he ever had in his life.

Meanwhile, in the face of the thrashing that the New York press gave *Fanny*, David Belasco still refused to give in. He had the most popular comedienne in America and the power and money to force her on the public. In October the producer "anonymously" told the *New York Times*, "Regardless of what business *Fanny* does at the Lyceum, it will continue there until March."[40] When it was forced to close in November after only 63 performances he didn't blink, but rather took it on a subway tour through Upper Manhattan, the Bronx and Brooklyn. That was okay with Warren; he didn't have to like the show or the producer to take the considerable money Belasco was wasting on the project. Having finally alienated everyone in New York, *Fanny* moved to Newark and then to Philadelphia, where it closed — at long last — on January 8. It is likely — but unconfirmed — that Warren never made it to Philadelphia, having been removed from the production in an effort to shore up a revamped comedy sequence in the third act.

Now at liberty after eight months wrestling with *Fanny*, Warren learned in early January that William McGuire was getting ready to send out another road company of *Twelve Miles Out*, this time to Chicago and the Midwest. Warren was now available, and McGuire quickly signed him for the tour. Most of the original cast was intact, including Frank Shannon and Mary Carroll, making it easy for Warren to slip back into the part with the timing and rhythm they'd developed the previous year. By January 16 they were in Chicago at the Cort Theatre. The play was received well, but Chicago in January was not quite the same city it was during the summer Warren appeared there in *La Tendresse*. It was cold and about to get colder.

Chicago audiences liked the play, but did not embrace it the way New Yorkers had. After six solid weeks at the box office, things began to slow down. Road manager Lee Morrison soon informed the cast that there was not enough revenue to pay the actors, and offered to issue IOUs against future receipts to keep the show running. After a discussion, Warren and the other players decided to continue, hoping for better attendance when the weather warmed.

For two more weeks the cast labored, usually being paid out of the previous week's receipts, then finally accepting reduced salaries. After another month, on April 16, the show closed with no money in its coffers and a cast of thirteen sitting in Chicago's Hotel Ambassador trying to figure out how to get home. Things were bad. The McGuire / Baer Corporation — legal producers of the show — had not procured the customary bond insuring themselves against just such a problem. Many in the company, including Warren, were flat broke or refused to spend their own money to return east. Actor's Equity eventually fronted almost a thousand dollars to bring the actors and crew home (a first class ticket from Chicago to New York was $30.70). But getting back pay — of which Warren was owed $504, an amount equal to one week's salary and some change — would be considerably more difficult.[41]

Even with the loss of his final week's pay from the Chicago run — which he likely never received — Warren was doing very well. His salary had risen to over $400 a week during *Twelve Miles Out*, at a time when the average American was making about $1,400 per year. Now that he was working regularly (since breaking his post-marriage drought with *The Wonderful Visit* he had worked 32 out of 37 months), he and Helen were in excellent financial condition. He took the opportunity to return to Hollywood, hoping to parlay his recent successes into a movie contract. He visited MGM just as they were preparing a big-budget film version of *Twelve Miles Out* with John Gilbert in Warren's old part. The originator of the role on Broadway wound up with a bit part in the film just for fun, but no contract. He headed home empty-handed again, but this time with a real career to fall back on.

Warren dumped his things at the apartment he and Helen now occupied at 1730 Broadway. It was time to go back to work again. In June he auditioned for a new play produced by Sam H. Harris, the former partner of the prolific King of Broadway, George M. Cohan. *The Conflict* told the story of two married couples who share a passion for golf. When the club pro falls in love with one of the wives, she rebuffs him, until she discovers that her seemingly faithful husband is playing in the rough with another woman. Louis Calhern (Ambassador Trentino of *Duck Soup* fame) played the feckless husband and Warren was the slick golf pro who came between him and his wife. Rehearsals began on June 19 pointing to an October debut in New York. Although it limped through summer try-outs in Atlantic City, Long Branch and Asbury Park — now known as *Among the Married*— it never quite pulled together as a cohesive story. Harris worried about the weak third act and the author Vincent Lawrence tinkered and tampered, but could never quite get it straight. The surviving reviews seem to bear out Harris' misgivings, noticing that the play fell apart on the back nine. The company soldiered on into the early autumn, announced to begin in New York on November 1. Instead they continued out of town in Baltimore and then Washington, DC, starting on Halloween day. It was then rumored to open on November 7 at the Theatre Masque. But Harris had seen enough. With Lawrence unable to solve the third act puzzle, he closed the show after only a few days. In an effort to sway Harris, the author delivered yet another rewrite and the producer said if he liked it, they'd revive the show. There was no revival.

Warren's next three productions combined lasted a total of eighteen performances on the Great White Way, the most dismal record of consecutive flops on his résumé. Oddly, this personal nadir came just as Broadway reached the muscle-flexing peak of its Golden Age. Legend (and reality) points to the plateau of Broadway hegemony being Christmas week of 1927, when eighteen shows opened within six days. Eleven of those, including Warren's new play *Paradise*— opened on the single day that is widely thought of as the pinnacle of the apogee, as it were: December 26. Warren spent his holidays that season in rehearsals, including a Christmas Day preview of *Paradise*, the sad tale of an Ohio girl who goes to New York to find a husband

and winds up faking one instead. The play, along with thirteen more of the Christmas week debuts, was a flop. It lasted almost as long in dress rehearsals—six performances—as the eight it mounted with the public attending. It was no surprise. *Paradise* was not terribly interesting. But compared to what was going on at the Warner Brothers Theatre on Broadway and 52nd Street, it was downright old fashioned.

The Jazz Singer had arrived.

History has compressed, formed and wrapped the story of *The Jazz Singer* as the first "talking picture," but even as shorthand history, it is taking grave liberties with reality. Talking pictures had been contemplated and tried almost from the birth of cinema. Warner Brothers themselves had been making commercially released short films under the Vitaphone banner for a number of years. If inventor Thomas Edison hadn't been so uncharacteristically myopic about the marriage of sound and film (he didn't see the value of combining the two ideas of the phonograph and the motion picture), there might never have been a silent cinema at all. But in 1927 the power of Broadway, in the form of Al Jolson, provided the spark that ignited the public's interest the way all other experiments had failed.

It is immensely odd symmetry that at the exact moment Broadway reached its fullest expression of power, the talking picture was sitting just down the street wooing their audience away. For the public, talkies were a no-brainer. In Manhattan the price of a ticket to see *The Jazz Singer* was 65 cents, while admission for a theater production averaged around $3.50, with some as high as $6 on weekends. Why pay six bucks for Jolson when you could watch and hear him for 65 cents? It wasn't quite apparent yet, but Warner Brothers was delivering hard blows to the body of the legitimate theater—punches that would be felt as the rounds wore on and its strength ebbed. Within a year, New York's theater industry would have the dubious moniker "The Fabulous Invalid."

The first consequence of *The Jazz Singer*'s influence was the studio talent scouts looking—or rather, listening—for new blood. During the Christmas holidays of 1927 they were like sharks swimming around a sinking ship that had used raw meat for ballast. Everybody was being tested for voice on film. One of Warren's co-stars in *Paradise,* the lovely Helen Flint, was called in before the studio cameras. That day she invited her friend Warren to come and help her read lines, each hoping that he might get some exposure as well. The ruse worked perfectly, with both actors receiving tests at the sound stage in New York. The indifference of the agents was overwhelming. The two returned to the stage, and then to the rolls of the unemployed: by early January, *Paradise* was closed.

After a few weeks off to celebrate his fifth wedding anniversary—and it is interesting to note that Warren often seemed to be *just* out of work when that date rolled around—the actor landed a job in one of the most unusual shows of his career. The play was *Veils,* a musical in twelve episodes about twin sisters, one a nun and one a criminal, who change places during the course of the narrative. There were no fewer than 35 parts—amounting to cast salaries of almost $4,000 a week—making the production an unwieldy, sprawling, and expensive mess. Warren dove into rehearsals in mid–February and to no one's surprise, the show almost immediately ran into financial trouble. A new producer, A.A. Snyder, infused some needed capital, and the play opened for previews in Worcester, New York, on March 5. After some vague and contradictory reports as to where it would land, it finally opened in New York City at the Forrest on March 13.

It is entirely unknown—or perhaps deliberately unreported—if Warren had a singing part in this production. Assuming that he was not being overly modest when he claimed to have "athlete's voice" during his stint in Corey's Singers, it would be unlikely. His only other musical performance was when he sang the song "Express Yourself, My Boy" in *Expressing Willie* early in his career. Here however, with 34 other performers, they could likely afford to keep William's mouth shut.

Here again Warren was playing support to a story of feminine themes, with Elsa Shelly headlining in a dual role as the twin sisters. Shelly had little experience, being cast chiefly for her position as the wife of the writer, Irving Kaye Davis. The critics called it "sprawling," "loose-jointed" and "a bit preposterous," and the *New York Times* said that opening night seemed like a "tank town [production of] *Miracle*." Meanwhile, kinder hands mentioned: "Warren William and Arthur R. Vinton ... chiefly aid in bringing the play and its projection closer together." After six dismal performances, money and energy were exhausted. On the afternoon of March 20, the producers announced that there would be no performance that night, blaming it on the sudden illness of fourth lead Hilda Spong. Warren knew the handwriting was on the wall. There was talk of moving on to another theater, but it was all face-saving for the papers: when the management won't even let the understudy go on for a Hilda Spong, you know things are dire. *Veils* was never seen again.

It was around this time that Warren developed his interest in marine prints—art of ships and sailing vessels that he collected and showed off throughout the rest of his life. His love for the sea had not abated as he matured and he had lately been thinking of investing in a boat to sail in Atlantic waters. Working regularly and now established as a leading man with a salary to match (he again made $400 a week on *Veils*), he could afford extravagances beyond his burgeoning wardrobe. He started looking for a ketch in earnest.

Within a few weeks Warren was again engaged, this time by John Tuerk for his production of *The Golden Age*, a story of Indians and whites living together peacefully in the wilds of Utah. Their blissful remove from civilization is interrupted when Warren arrives in the guise of a bearded stranger who turns out to be an escaped convict who had killed an officer during the war. It opened on April 24, and Brooks Atkinson's review helped the play make it all the way to six performances: "It is, by turns, naïve, painful and speciously introspective. In the long run it is perhaps mostly painful ... Warren William sees his embarrassing part grimly through," he wrote. The shameful aspect of Warren's character, at least according to Atkinson, was the fact that he had been castrated during the World War. It was not entirely standard material on stage in 1928, to be sure, and the revelation was a particularly tense moment, waiting to discover if audiences were sympathetic or merely put off. "The painful admission," Percy Hammond wrote, "was a feat of acting as uttered by Warren William in a difficult role."[42] By the end of the month the play was withdrawn and Warren's embarrassment was over.

The following Thursday, as Warren was taking a break and deciding what to do next, news came that startled the Krech family and the New York financial world. That morning, Warren's Uncle Alvin arrived at his office in the Equitable Building where he had been the chairman of the board for five years. At 11 o'clock, in a meeting with the president and vice-president of the company, he was seized by a tremendous heart attack and died instantly. By the afternoon Freeman called Warren to give him the awful news. Although not typically demonstrative, the actor must have been gravely disappointed; after his father, Alvin was the next most important male figure in his life. The wealthy businessman's dignity and self-possession were clearly models for Warren's own personal manner. And Alvin's unstinting support of the arts—he was a director of the Metropolitan Opera and the New York Symphony—informed Warren's choices as a patron of "good" music throughout his life. At least part of his performance as the rich banking brother in *Gold Diggers of 1933* may have been based at his uncle's controlled, sober personality.

Alvin Krech was a major force in American finance and plaudits rained in from across the world. One of his daughters had married a nephew of President Teddy Roosevelt, and at the funeral Warren saw captains of finance, government officials, ambassadors and businessmen all pay tribute to his uncle. There was tremendous sadness, but tremendous pride among the family. Freeman's youngest brother Paul had died in Chicago a year earlier, making him the last of Ernst and Mathilde's eight children. Warren knew his father was getting no younger, and although some of the cracks in their relationship were healing, they were still far from the team they had been through the war.

After taking most of May off with family duties, Warren achieved a career milestone when he signed a long-term contract with the Shubert Organization. As his *de facto* management, they would provide the actor with carefully chosen roles, massaging and shaping his image. Their first assignment was not much of a change from what Warren had been doing on his own: He was cast in chief support of Irene Fenwick, also known as Mrs. Lionel Barrymore, in a play called *The Domino Parlor*. The production was set in one of the many gaming houses that substituted for the then-banned billiard halls and bowling alleys of rural Oklahoma. Warren played Jude Summer, the owner of the establishment, a man hiding from his murderous and cavalier past. When his old flame conveniently arrives in the guise of Ms. Fenwick, all hell breaks loose. Rehearsals were underway by the first week in June, and troubles quickly arose between the writer Lynn Riggs, the director, and the Shuberts as to the tenor of the work. In New Jersey, the Newark police nearly shut down previews at the Broad Street Theatre when the language proved too much for the sensitive ears of the locals. The Shuberts had no intention of antagonizing their audiences or the constabulary and insisted on changing lines against Riggs' will. They also changed cast members, rewrote the final act and played poor Ms. Fenwick so clearly against type that every reviewer complained. While the disputes simmered, the production bounced through Connecticut and New York during June. It was clear that the play needed work desperately, but the Shuberts were losing the will to salvage it. The unkindest cut of all was left for Warren himself, expressed in a review following the Newark engagement on June 24. "Nor did Warren William unduly impress as Jude. A synthesis of the Barrymores, but lacking in the peculiar distinction attaching to that family even at their worst, he gave a performance remote from ideal."[43] Given all the tension, legal troubles, arguments and strife, no one was surprised or disappointed when *The Domino Parlor* suddenly disappeared. By July 8 the *New York Times* reported that the play was "cold," and would not be offered in New York or anywhere else. The last word may as well have come from the finale of the play, where, after Ms. Fenwick has murdered the villain of the piece and then committed suicide, a bumpkin reporter unknowingly asks Jude if anything interesting ever happens in the place. "No," he says gloomily; "you'd better move on to a live town."

"DOMINO PARLOR" CAST IS NAMED

Supporting Irene Fenwick in "The Domino Parlor," a play by Lynn Riggs, Oglahoma pet, which Lee Shubert will soon produce, will be Edward Massey, Warren William, John Brawn, Edith Arnold, Zelma Tiden.

Warren William

The Domino Parlor never made it to Broadway, but Lynn Riggs' tale of murder and revenge gave Warren William a few months of work while he was under contract to the Shubert Company during the summer of 1928.

Shortly after *The Domino Parlor* died, Warren was given liberty by the Shubert Company to take the lead in a stage version of Joseph Hergesheimer's novel *Tampico*. Govett Bradier is the head of an oil company working south of the border, where he is simultaneously fending off Mexican bandits and business rivals, as well as trying to seduce the wife of an employee. (The hard-driving, merciless Bradier was a prototype for Warren's later characters in *Skyscraper Souls* and *Employees' Entrance*.) The play was doomed to failure. It had been on the schedule of producers A.L. Jones and Morris Green for over a year and was only now getting started in earnest. With Warren in an actual starring role for once, the production limped through Newark and the Bronx, then lost traction and closed late in August. Meanwhile, the Shuberts were looking for something new for their sophomore contract player.

While Warren waited for a script to read, he continued looking for a boat to buy, but nothing was yet to his liking. It wasn't until early November that the Shuberts presented him with a part in the first American production by Edgar Wallace, the prolific English writer of novels, plays and criticism. By all accounts *Sign of the Leopard* was a standard crime whodunnit with little to recommend it, but the Shuberts were convinced that any man who could sell five million books in the British Isles (as Wallace did in 1927 alone) must have something they could peddle to New Yorkers. As usual the production opened out of town, this time in Brooklyn on November 19. It followed the standard circuit, including Philadelphia, and the *New York Times* reported the city's flattering response: "They say it's good." On Broadway *Leopard* prowled the National Theatre for 34 performances, but Wallace failed to impress American audiences with his wit or originality. This production was solely notable for two of the 35 members of its immense cast: Thurston Hall, the fine character actor with whom Warren would later memorably banter during his appearances in Columbia's *Lone Wolf* series, and Nina Gore, mother of the great American author Gore Vidal.

Just as *Sign of the Leopard* was closing in early January (once again, just as Warren and Helen's wedding anniversary was about to arrive), casting was about to begin on Rachel Crothers' new comedy, *Let Us Be Gay*. The author had an arrangement with the Shubert organization that allowed them the first look at all her manuscripts, and the company readers thought highly of her latest offering, about a divorced couple who inadvertently find themselves reunited at a society party. During January, Warren's name came up in production meetings—Crothers remembered well his contribution to *Expressing Willie* five years earlier, and *Let Us Be Gay* seemed like a perfect vehicle for his underrated light comedy instincts.[44] With him under contract to the company and just then at liberty, he was an obvious choice. But just as casting was about to get underway in earnest, the Shubert organization thought better of their decision to back the play. The season just ended had been a dismal one, and some voices on their own staff had termed *Let Us Be Gay* "hazardous," reasoning that a so-called "smart" comedy was almost impossible to judge in manuscript form. They demurred.

Crothers was disappointed; she felt in her bones that this play could be one of her biggest successes. She had two principals she felt quite confident in: Warren William and Broadway stalwart Francine Larrimore. Some producers thought the actress unsuited to the role as the flighty, shameless Kitty Brown, but Crothers knew she could rise to the occasion. And Larrimore had other talents that made her a valuable choice to the author.

In January of 1929, impresario John Golden, like everyone else on Broadway, was coming off a lackluster season. He was focused in on escaping the long New York winter for a two-month hiatus in Palm Beach. Two days before he left, Larrimore braved the cold Manhattan winds, trudged up to Golden's offices, shook the snow off her shoulders and accosted the producer. At that moment nothing could have been further from Golden's mind than getting

Sign of the Leopard was an extremely modest success on Broadway during the 1928–1929 season. Warren's co-stars were Flora Sheffield and Campbell Gullan.

involved in another production; he was only interested in sun, swimming and golf. But Larrimore had a way with producers and convinced him to accept a copy of the script to look at. Golden passed the script to one of his trusted readers, and the following morning he received a review that was so effusive he resolved to back the play. The decision didn't stop his vacation, however. He directed his general manager, R.E.H. French, to make arrangements to mount the show, with Crothers to have carte blanche over all decisions, and to bother him with nothing for the next two months. The following morning the producer left for the Sunshine State. Golden's vacation was restful and happy. While he was away the play became an enormous hit, eventually running for ten months and 353 performances at the Little Theatre. His only connection to *Let Us Be Gay* that winter was to read regular telegrams informing him of the play's gratifyingly large overnight grosses.

Let Us Be Gay opened on February 19 after a preview in Washington, DC. The action opens at a society party on a country estate, where Kitty Brown has been surreptitiously invited in order to vamp the footless suitor of the matriarch's granddaughter. What she doesn't know is that said suitor — played by Warren — is Bob Brown, Kitty's own ex-husband. In lesser hands this scenario could emerge helplessly old-fashioned or hackneyed, but in Crothers' script humor and irony hold sway, upper-class mores are playfully chided, marriage and divorce receive humorous if not deadly observation, and everyone goes home satisfied by the end of the night. Although Warren was the male lead, he once again he played second fiddle to the distaff star of the production. Even with his well-developed comic timing and flair for light comedy, the focus was unquestionably Francine Larrimore. Critics adored her and ignored Warren. It continued the standard dynamic of a great many of the actor's career productions.

Meantime, there was trouble brewing. The Shuberts still held Warren's contract and, although they had tacitly allowed it, were furious about him appearing as the lead in a smash hit that they had passed on producing. Talks started between Golden and the Shuberts to allow Warren to stay with the production. The negotiations dragged on through the early run of the play, but by the middle of summer the contesting parties reached an impasse. Shortly after, the Shuberts demanded he leave the show. Warren's very own management had forced him out of the biggest hit of his career. The actor was understandably disgusted — and although he understood the positions of both parties, he was still out a hefty salary of almost $600 a week on a hit production where there seemed more than enough money to go around. As always with Warren, though, he decided to make the best of it, finding a way to spend his time that was far more important than the triviality of acting.

During the spring and early summer Warren was still looking for a boat. It would be his first real boat — not a makeshift contraption like *The Pirate* which he had built and launched back in Aitkin. With a friend and fellow investor, Warren scoured the classifieds, perused sales catalogues and haunted boat yards until they found a vessel that both liked and could afford. The ship they eventually settled on was a blue-nosed Nova Scotia schooner that the partners named *Cutlass*, and moored in a slip at the New York Yacht Club. Warren and Helen spent most of the time left idle by the Shuberts' pique on the boat that summer, sailing away their cares on the hefty savings that they had amassed during Warren's recently steady and lucrative years. It deepened and infused his love of the sea more than ever, with he and Helen often spending days on the water. During those months Warren also found, in his "mean ability to scramble an egg" for breakfast, another personal enjoyment that would last for most of his life: cooking.

In the fall, Warren was finally released from his obligation to the Shuberts. It had resulted in more trouble than it was worth. Although it was reported that Warren rejoined the cast of

Let Us Be Gay, it seems unlikely that this was the case; by September he was in rehearsals for *Week-End,* yet another parlor room comedy-drama of conflicting personalities at the French estate of a wealthy couple. It opened on October 22 to modest reviews. Brooks Atkinson summed it up with admirable brevity: "There is blackmail. There is scuffling. There are frantic plans to set bad matters right. The host and hostess agree to separate, and the most amiable soak in the company shoots himself. [But] it never comes into clear focus [and] you are constantly expecting more than you get." Warren played a short story writer who becomes the armchair psychologist for the assembled gathering. He worked again with Margaret Mower, the friendly angel from *Wonderful Visit* five years earlier, and personally received positive reviews. The show closed after just eleven performances, almost all of them mounted for charity benefits, the Boy's Clubs, the New York Society for the Prevention of Cruelty to Children, the Institute for Crippled Children and the Community Council of New York among others. The children of New York most certainly made more money out of the engagement than did first-time producer Bela Blau. Hereafter Mr. Blau confined charitable efforts to the back end of his productions.

At almost the exact moment that *Week-End* crashed, Wall Street did the same thing. On October 29, 1929, known as Black Tuesday, stocks dove on the exchange, causing a worldwide panic. Within days it was apparent that this was not to be a short-lived correction to the market. Stock prices continued to plunge and investors— many thousands of small, first-time speculators who staked life savings on the Bull Market — lost everything. The Krechs may have had investments based on the advice of the family's own financial genius, Alvin. But Warren maintained a reasonably conservative attitude towards money over the years, and likely kept his funds relatively fluid. Pauline and Elizabeth were both in stable situations, but it was impossible to predict how badly the economic downturn would affect Broadway. People immediately began holding onto their money more cautiously, meaning fewer regular theatergoers, less capital available for new shows and greater competition among actors for the remaining jobs. Producers began lowering ticket prices to recapture audiences, which resulted in reduced salaries for the actors and technicians lucky enough to have work at all. During November the Krechs dealt with the crisis the way most of the country did: watching, waiting and hoping. President Hoover's response — eerily familiar to observers of the modern counterpart — was to insist that conditions were "fundamentally sound," and that "American business is steadily coming back to a normal level of prosperity." The secretary of commerce went a step further away from reality, saying, "There is nothing in the situation to be disturbed about." America had almost ten more years of disturbance to endure.

In early December, Warren was gratified to be reunited with producer John Golden and his personal good luck charm, Rachel Crothers. The play was *Anchors Aweigh,* formerly known as *Let Us Be Good,* the title likely changed for being cynically close to her other hit of 1929. Unfortunately, this time Ms. Crothers was no charm. The play began rehearsals on December 2, opened in Brooklyn on December 23, then moved to Newark for a week. It was expected in New York on January 6, but simply evaporated into thin air when it left New Jersey. Its failure was at least partially a casualty of the cancerous economy. Warren took only a few days off and immediately auditioned for a very promising production to be directed by the great British actor Leslie Howard.

The story of how *Out of a Blue Sky* came to be produced is a fascinating example of the iron being struck while it is hot. On Christmas Day, while Warren was working in *Anchor's Aweigh* at Werba's Jamaica Theatre, actor Gregory Ratoff barged in on the morning slumber of former press agent Tom Van Dycke. Van Dycke had recently left the staff of Gilbert Miller's production company to strike out on his own. Ratoff, an ambitious young man who later became a film director of some note — including Fox's execrable 1937 offering *Day-time Wife*, featuring Warren William — had the rights to a German play he wanted Van Dycke to consider for his first production. Perhaps feeling a sense of urgency after having chosen the very onset of the Great Depression to mount his first production, or being merely drunk with good cheer, Van Dycke promised to read the script instead of indulging in Christmas festivities. Later that day, the fledgling producer sent for Ratoff and gave him as fine a holiday gift as the actor could want: He waxed enthusiastic about the script and resolved on the spot to produce it with an excellent part for Ratoff to boot. When they discussed who might direct the germinating project, Ratoff brought up the name of Leslie Howard, one of the hottest stars then on Broadway. The next day the two men boldly sought out Howard during his regular performance of *Berkeley Square* and convinced him to read the script. On Friday, December 27, Howard, unabashedly enthusiastic, agreed to direct, and to adapt the German script for American audiences. By Monday the Booth Theatre was engaged and casting began — all before Howard had even begun his translation.

Having just finished *Anchor's Aweigh* at the end of December, Warren might normally have taken January off to celebrate his anniversary. Instead, the sense of fiscal urgency sweeping the country led him to head out on a new audition, and only days into 1930 he corralled a part in *Out of a Blue Sky*. The conceit of the script was that the company that was to present *Camille* failed to show up and the director of the show "randomly" recruited new players out of the audience. Quite naturally, he happens to choose a husband and wife, and — what a coincidence — the wife's lover to play those very roles in the impromptu scene taking place on stage. Warren played Paul Rana, the lover in "reality" and on the stage. Unfortunately neither Howard, nor the wonderful Reginald Owen — who received the only kind notices from the New York press — could save the day. Warren's performance was singled out for devastating, if amusing derision: "Warren William as the lover merely declaims. His resonant importunities have all the ardor of a drawing room loudspeaker." *Out of a Blue Sky* lasted all of 17 performances, closing on February 22. Warren next saw Ratoff three years later in Hollywood, when both appeared in *Skyscraper Souls* for MGM. Howard became one of his greatest friends, sometimes accompanying Warren on visits to the Krech family home on Long Island.[45]

Following *Blue Sky*, Warren's luck — and talent — were once again in play, as he walked practically from one show into another. Just as the Howard production was ending, *Those We Love* was opening at the John Golden Theatre. The director and author, George Abbott, was temporarily playing the lead following the loss of the original headliner — Warren's future Warner Brothers contract mate George Brent — only a week before the February 19 opening. Both he and producer Phil Dunning were looking for someone to step into Abbott's role quickly. When Warren became available, he was asked to read for the part, and Abbott knew he had his man. The director immediately put him in a series of intensive rehearsals, and Warren took over the part of Frederick Williston, author and — possibly — philanderer. It must have been the kind of scenario the forgetful actor had nightmares about: learning a new play and being expected to perform it in front of a New York audience with only ten days reading and rehearsal. He was helped by a familiar face among his co-stars, Helen Flint, who had taken him on his first sound screen test just two years earlier, while they were working in *Paradise*. With her help, his American Academy training, and all those years in stock, Warren walked out onto the stage at the John Golden on March 1 and made the role his.

The production ran a respectable 77 performances through March and early April. During the run there was another chance for Warren to take a screen test, this time for Paramount.

Scouts were still trying to discover new blood for talking pictures, and Warren, with his forceful, trained voice, seemed like a natural. He continued to lament the fact that he had passed on his other opportunities years before, and still wanted to break into film — if for no other reason that to relieve the pressure of having to memorize every line of dialogue and be letter perfect every time, every day. At the Paramount studio space in New York, Warren ran through the audition, hoping to make an impression. Instead the impression was made on him. His test was so bad that the local talent scout actually brought the would-be matinee idol into a screening room and showed it to him. Warren later said he "almost broke down and cried" when he saw it. He knew immediately that he was not going to Hollywood — at least not with Paramount. He still had a lot to learn about the craft of screen acting.

In spite of the beleaguered economy, it wasn't all work for the Krechs. In addition to sailing when his schedule permitted, Warren was continuing his father's example for social intercourse. He was a member of the Masquers Club, the long-standing organization for New York actors, begun by Edwin Booth — yes, the brother of Abraham Lincoln assassin John Wilkes Booth — in the 1880s. He was also involved in numerous charity activities, including the opening volley of his lifelong passion for animal rights. The Episcopal Actors' Guild counted him as a fellow, as did the Veterans of Foreign Wars and the Theatre Club, which made him the guest of honor at their spring luncheon that March. He was also interacting and engaging with an amazing array of people, including friends of his eclectic sister Pauline: gadabouts, raconteurs, writers, artists, bohemians, and occasionally those with alternate lifestyles.[46] From all appearances, Warren's years in New York instilled a surprisingly liberal social attitude in the outwardly reserved actor. While Freeman Krech was quietly whiling away his days in Manhasset, his chip off the old block was duplicating and updating his example in New York City.

When *Those We Love* closed early in April, Warren once again wasted no time "resting." He quickly hooked up with the Philadelphia Theatrical Corporation for their production of *Lysistrata*, the classical play by Aristophanes about women who try to stop a war by withholding sex from their soldier husbands. Again Warren was a tool to feminine themes, with the power of women's will over their men being examined. Appearing in *Lysistrata* meant spending over a month in Philadelphia, but with the economy continuing to sag and the added inducement of a juicy role in a Greek classic, Warren packed his bags, said goodbye to Helen and headed south. The play opened on April 21 at the Walnut Street Theatre for a limited three-week engagement. The star was veteran trouper Blanche Yurka. On Broadway from 1910, Yurka had been a successful opera singer before switching to drama, and was a character fixture in New York for over fifty years. After coming to the United States as a young girl, she grew up in St. Paul, Minnesota, where Warren had spent many seasons visiting his grandparents. The two enjoyed the opportunity to reminisce about young days in the Midwest and maintained a friendship for many years thereafter. Following a critically and financially successful engagement in Philadelphia, Yurka invited her new friend Warren to play Sigurd to her Hjordis in a production of Henrik Ibsen's *The Warriors of Helgeland*, which she would direct on Broadway.

The Vikings — as it became known on Broadway — was one of Ibsen's early offerings, written in 1858. It concerns the tragedy of circumstances when Sigurd conspires to create a false image of his friend Gunnar, so that he might win the heart of Hjordis, whom Sigurd also loves. The production (known affectionately by the cast as "The Veekings") was, like *Lysistrata*, conceived as a limited run, expecting that mainstream New York audiences would not support it in the long term. Again, the female lead is the focus of the proceedings, with Miss Yurka directing and having her name plastered above the title in print and on the marquee. Even Ibsen's theme, explicated by Gordon King in the *New York Times*, places Sigurd in the secondary position: "In this play there is expressed the view that men have no right to deceive women. Women have a right to love men honestly, and men have no right to deny."

Along with once again working with his friend Margaret Mower, Warren had the added diversion of a fascinating mechanical device that was essential to the stagecraft of *The Vikings*. Thomas Wilfred, the avant-garde inventor of a machine called the Clavilux—a keyboard instrument that produced light rather than sound—co-directed *The Vikings,* and performed on a nightly basis with the play. His instrument, through the use of light, provided a visual counterpoint as the emotions of the characters were played out on stage. *The Christian Science Monitor* described the effect: "Under Mr. Wilfred's Clavilux accompaniment, the invisible flames flared up in echo of [Hjordis'] great emotions. The same mechanism provided a changing vista of sea for the first and last acts, with the sky and waters providing a visual frame around the spoken word." Wilfred also experimented for the first time with projected scenery during this production, being one of the early pioneers of the technique. All of this was of interest to Warren, still captivated by engineering and invention. The chance to admire and perhaps even

In *Stepdaughters of War,* Warren William played a soldier literally and figuratively emasculated by his experiences in the War. Katherine Alexander (left) was an equally damaged Red Cross volunteer.

tinker with this unique contraption — as well as compare notes with the man who built it — was tremendous fun for the little boy who took his father's car apart back in Aitkin.

The Vikings received wonderful reviews and surprisingly robust support from New York audiences during its weeklong engagement starting May 12. As usual for Warren, his female lead was the center of attention, with Yurka's portrayal of Hjordis called "a performance heroic in scale and always forceful." And although Warren's work was lauded as well, it was largely judged in diminutive relation to the star: "Warren William's Sigurd [was] heroic enough in mold to be worthy of Miss Yurka's characterization." After eight shows, Wilfred packed up his equipment and returned to giving colorful but silent recitals with the Clavilux. Some of his original machines still exist and occasionally tour museums and theaters throughout the world.

Before May was out, Warren appeared in the cast of Geoffrey Kerr's *Ring Three Times*— the title being an allusion to the signal for discrete speakeasy patrons who want illegal hooch. It opened in Atlantic City on June 16; the *Atlantic City Daily* liked it well enough, but audiences weren't so sanguine. It contributed a few weeks salary to the Krechs' coffers, then disappeared entirely.

Warren next found work at the Millbrook Theatre in Millbrook, New York. The facility was in its first season devoted to restaging recently closed Broadway hits, often with members of the original casts. They mounted two productions that summer; Rachel Crothers' *Let Us Be Gay* and another outstanding success from the previous Broadway season, *Holiday.* Under other circumstances Warren might have remained at liberty looking for a new Broadway production, but after a modest recovery in the stock market during the first quarter of 1930, April saw deep losses start once again. Since October three million men had been thrown out of work with no unemployment insurance to back them up, and American industry was slowing to a crawl. So, when *Ring Three Times* closed, Warren quickly shifted over to his familiar role as Bob Brown, needing only modest rehearsal to refresh his memory and hammer out timing with the new cast headed by Katherine Warren. It opened at Millbrook on Independence Day, then spent time in Cape Cod and at the Newport Cascina in Rhode Island.

By the end of July the *Let Us Be Gay* engagement was over and jobs were scarce. Those who did have work found their salaries dropping as well. From late 1929 through 1930, average income in the United States went down almost 40 percent. In August, after a series of unsuccessful auditions, Warren finally joined the cast of an "underworld comedy"[47] called *The Up and Up*, written by Eva Kay Flint and Martha Madison. In the early stages of rehearsals, *The Up and Up* looked like it would collapse upon itself. Cast members were announced and removed. First the show was going directly to Broadway and then the producers opted for out-of-town try-outs. The leading lady took ill and had to be replaced. When the troubles mounted and a postponement of the New York opening threatened to sink the play, Warren jumped ship. He was offered a part in *Stepdaughters of War,* a new play based on the novel by Helen Zenna Smith being directed by 26-year-old Broadway wunderkind Chester Erskine, a youthful Orson Welles of his day. With Warren being the male lead among a cast of sixteen women, it was undoubtedly the vertex of his professional submission to feminine themes and ideas.

The action of *Stepdaughters of War* concerns a subject that Warren knew quite well. It follows a company of Red Cross ambulance drivers in France, women who volunteered to go overseas and drive to and from the front with the human remains— physical and spiritual — of the World War. The women bond in their disillusion and bitterness, becoming callous and hard, removed even from their families, who they now view as hopelessly naïve and sheltered. In a moment of emotional need, Kit Evans turns to Geoffrey Hilder (Warren) and the two fall in love, wrecking her politely arranged engagement back home. By the fourth act the war has literally and figuratively emasculated Geoffrey, psychologically destroyed Kit and thrown the couple into a future of barren, loveless marriage.

Although Warren hadn't seen any direct action in France, he spent many months in and around the hospitals and clinics of the American zone, watching the toll that the war took on the men and women he encountered. He understood quite well the price paid by those who weren't as lucky as he had been. It made his portrayal of Geoffrey Hilder a resonant, deeply felt characterization. Moreover, Warren's willingness to play a man castrated by war and accepted by his lover only because the war has likewise made her spiritually sterile was a bold choice. It is difficult to imagine many other high-profile actors willing to compromise their image in such a nakedly subordinate role.

Stepdaughters of War endured difficult pre-production, including the staging of an air raid that the characters endure on the second floor of their living quarters. Erskine's clever direction and innovative stagecraft created a wonderfully tense scene that every reviewer hailed, but the show also needed a lot of tinkering with the large cast. To that end, Erskine often lounged backstage with the actors after rehearsals, talking about the characters and soliciting ideas for changes in staging or blocking. He was well liked by the cast members, who were very grateful for his thoughtful and open nature.

The Broadway opening was twice postponed while Warren and sixteen ladies tramped through Hartford, Baltimore and upstate New York. On September 17, producer Charles Frohman placed ads in the *New York Times*, announcing the opening on September 23, but Erskine told the press that *Stepdaughters* "was not quite in shape" and it was again postponed, staying in Baltimore for more work. Finally, Warren and company returned to Manhattan for an opening at the Empire Theatre on October 6.

The successful Broadway star proudly looks over his new Cord L-29 Sedan, parked near his Central Park West apartment, circa 1930. This model was the first front-wheel drive American production automobile, and cost $3,095 when offered in August of 1929.

Stepdaughters of War was only a modest success. Broadway audiences were already looking for a pleasant diversion from the daily news of economic collapse and business failures, not the grim dirge of hopelessness Erskine was mounting each night, regardless of its high level of craft. In spite of the lukewarm response from audiences, Warren's work did not go unnoticed. Burns Mantle observed that with Warren playing Geoffrey Hilder, the character was "guaranteed a certain upstanding manliness."[48] That manliness was entirely necessary to make the deformed character sympathetic under difficult circumstances. Meanwhile, Brooks Atkinson saw something of Warren's own personal qualities infused into Geoffrey when he remarked: "Warren William acts [his part] with modesty, directness and reticence."[49] He might just as well have been describing the actor as he was describing Geoffrey Hilder.

The production was just a diversion, however. Within a few weeks Warren would be in one of the great successes of his career, while enormous, jarring changes both personal and professional were lurking in the wings.

10

Go West, Young Man

Before *Stepdaughters of War* opened early in October, Dwight Deere Wiman, the erstwhile producing partner of William A. Brady Jr., was making a deal to acquire the rights to Paul Osborn's unproduced play *The Vinegar Tree*. Theater impresario Billy Rose — the current "Mr. Fanny Brice" — had earlier purchased an option on the property, but was now having second thoughts about mounting the play when Wiman stepped in and offered to buy him out. With Rose now out of the picture, Wiman moved to create a Broadway smash.

Wiman had his leading lady chosen even before he closed the deal with Rose. Mary Boland, a fixture on Broadway for 20 years and later an attraction in the early days of sound film, was made-to-order for the flighty, scatterbrained Laura Merrick, namesake of the Staghorn Sumac, or Vinegar Tree, the scourge of all surrounding vegetation. The play follows the metronomic cues of a great many others that Warren starred in during his Broadway years: old money; a getaway at a country estate; family intercourse upset by outside forces; infidelity, affairs and the comedy of manners. Rehearsals began on October 5 — the day before the curtain went up on *Stepdaughters of War* — and continued through October, shooting for a road premiere on November 3. However, casting did not quite gel, and the previews were pushed back by a week. The *New York Times* of October 19 announced — even though he was still employed by Charles Frohman in *Stepdaughters of War* — that Warren would join the cast of *Vinegar* before it opened in try-outs. Then, on October 25, *Stepdaughters* closed, and Warren's management closed the deal for the actor to move to the Wiman production as Max Lawrence, the eccentric, if slightly aristocratic outsider whose presence throws six lives into disarray. Even the *New York Times* noted the urgency with which Warren "hurried" from *Stepdaughters* to *The Vinegar Tree*.[1]

Just two weeks after Warren left *Stepdaughters of War*, *The Vinegar Tree* opened in Hartford, Connecticut. Delays had already scuttled performances in Jackson Heights, New York, and the proposed Broadway debut on November 10, possibly because the newly engaged "Max Lawrence" needed more time to get ready. The Hartford audiences were large and enthusiastic. In spite of limited time for preparation, director Winchell Smith had drilled the cast perfectly and left no loose timing or inarticulate staging. Although there would be some trimming of scenes and tinkering with cues, the play was already nearly polished enough for Broadway.

As Max Lawrence, Warren accompanies his married companion Winifred Merrick to the house of her older sister Laura (Boland). Somewhat scatterbrained and flighty, Laura comically mistakes Max for a long-lost lover that she had before her marriage, and vows to leave her husband of 20 years to reunite with him. Not only is Max confused by her attentions — to Warren's incomparably acted bemusement — but he has simultaneously fallen for Laura's daughter (and his mistress' niece), Leone. So, the younger sister Winifred tries to hold on to Max while simultaneously making a play for Leone's young blade; Max wants to dump Winifred in favor of Leone while the boyfriend makes effort to block Max at every turn; Laura wants to leave her husband Augustus (an idea that Max strongly discourages), and the bemused husband sits by absorbing it all.

With razor-sharp direction by Smith, the situations crackled with comedic energy. Boland and Warren positively shined in scenes where Laura confronts an utterly baffled Max concerning their supposed long-ago tryst. As he did when properly directed, Warren played Max with understated aplomb, finding humor in the spaces between proper manners and social anxiety. It was left to Boland to provide volume for the comedy, barging through every scene like an arctic icebreaker. By the time *The Vinegar Tree* opened on Broadway at the newly refurbished Playhouse Theatre on November 19, it was highly anticipated. Boland was receiving plaudits for her trip wire timing and outrageous characterization, while Warren, as usual, soaked up the scraps. "Warren William plays with admirable tact and deference," observed Brooks Atkinson, indicating the bland reserve the Minnesota actor was bound to conjure when placed adjacent to the star's sparkling commotion.

The Vinegar Tree made an immediate impression on the box office. It was observed that the opening night audience "laughed until it burst its stays," and that the play itself was "confusion worse confounded and discharged from the stage like a barrage of laughter." *Time* magazine called it "sustaining, sophisticated, recommendable." It lasted seven months and 229 performances; however, Warren would not be there to see all of them.

Although he also played bootleggers, hunters, oil barons, soldiers and cowboys, the dominant image of Warren William during his Broadway years was that of a sophisticated and refined gentleman.

As the play gathered steam from rock solid reviews and superb word of mouth, it buzzed through the holidays with a New Year's Eve top of $5.50, holding its weight against Paul Muni in *This One Man* and Edward G. Robinson in *Mr. Samuel*. Along the main stem Warren's future co-stars Ginger Rogers and Glenda Farrell sat poised to jump to Hollywood. Al Jolson, Ed Wynn, Clifton Webb, George Jessel and young Anna Mae Wong — a close friend of Warren and Helen when they made it to Hollywood — all gathered after shows and toasted the great good fortune of beating the Depression with their success.

During the run of *The Vinegar Tree*, Warren was enjoying life in his idiosyncratic way. He was still an engineer and inventor at heart, but within his New York apartment there was very little opportunity to

The Vinegar Tree was a major hit in the fall of 1930. The following spring he was signed by Warner Brothers and never returned to Broadway. In Warren's theatrical embrace is Helen Brooks.

fire up the lathe, power saw or arc welder. In the summer of 1930 he made an arrangement to work as the official assistant to a man named Maurice Holland, who was the director of the Engineering Division of the National Research Council with offices in Manhattan's Engineer's building.[2] Warren kept semi-regular hours at his office (Holland knew better than to expect him there all the time) learning the art of engineering during the day and entertaining theater audiences at night. On the weekends he regularly sailed *The Cutlass* down the Hudson and out into the blue Atlantic, usually with Helen, Pauline and their friends. Warren's ship was lost

Although undated, this photo was likely taken about 1930: Warren and Helen standing alongside the actor's New York–based Nova Scotia schooner, *Cutlass*. Close inspection reveals a rare candid portrait of Warren William without his trademark moustache. Courtesy Patricia Lyon.

the following spring when it ran aground on a sandbar; Warren had to be rescued by the Coast Guard.[3] It was not the disaster it might have been if the Krechs were not soon to leave New York.

At a salary of $650 a week, Warren was pulling in an amount equivalent to the yearly income of the average American every fortnight. Although he had not achieved true headlining stardom in the theater—never once did he have an uncontested lead, or see his name above the title—he was well-known and respected. After all his success, however, he still craved the opportunity to take his craft to a wider audience in motion pictures. The popularity of *The Vinegar Tree* led casting agents and scouts to reconsider him for film tests. In the three years since *The Jazz Singer* shook up the power structure in Hollywood, Warren had tested twice for studio contracts, but with no takers. In February, they came calling again, this time from Warner Brothers. The studio casting director Rufus Lemaire was looking for a leading man to star alongside Dolores Costello in her new film *The Passionate Sonata*,[4] and a New York scout decided Warren might be that man.[5]

At exactly this time, Warren's father was lying ill at Elizabeth's home in Port Washington, New York. On February 28, the 74-year-old patriarch gathered neighbors to witness the signing of his will. The family knew it couldn't be long before he was gone. In spite of their cool relationship since his marriage, Warren made sure to find time between performances to visit his dying father. With two such reserved and taciturn men, discussion of their love and care for each other could not have been easy. But it is likely that they both also understood innately how the other felt. If words were unspoken, a lifetime of experiences— mostly positive — were deeply held.

Only days after Freeman signed his will, Warren trekked to the Warner Brothers sound stage in New York. After the several opportunities that had dissolved into nothing over the previous ten years, Warren was not sanguine about his chances. While Warren was sitting in the makeup room waiting to be tested, the local Warner executive asked him if he would mind helping make a test with actress Violet Heming, who was starring in *Ladies All* just three blocks from where Warren held court in *The Vinegar Tree*. The ever-polite actor naturally agreed, and there was manifest yet another example of the William luck. His own test reel from that afternoon made no impression, but the film he shot with Heming secured him an offer from the studio. On March 6, Warners tendered a contract. It was worth $750 a week for a period of six months, with options built in for four more years; if the actor stuck with the studio, his salary would top out at $2,000 a week by 1935. With such numbers to calculate and consider, Warren thought well of having an agent to manage the details of the contract, and Warner Brothers gave him time to consider the offer. The aspiring film actor was not going to let this one slip through his fingers. After some discussion among friends and business associates, he engaged theatrical agent Ben Boyar, who also worked as aide-de-camp to Broadway producer and impresario Max Gordon. Boyar spent the week negotiating with Warner executives, and they quickly reached an agreement. But Warren still couldn't leave the cast of *The Vinegar Tree* until a replacement was found for him. Producer Dwight Deere Wiman and director Winchell Smith held auditions during the week and finally signed Kenneth Hunter to take over for the freshly minted motion picture star. With that, Warren signed his new contract — backdated to March 6 — on March 12.

In spite of their disagreements about his marriage to Helen, Freeman Krech couldn't have been more proud of his son. Warren had achieved his childhood dreams beyond anything that either of them could have expected back in the mud streets of rustic Minnesota. New York had been good to both of them, but still Freeman's mind reverted back occasionally to the boy who survived the New Ulm Indian uprising and the young man who sold insurance and published a small town's only source of news. Just a few years earlier he revealed his not-so-deeply hidden sentiments in a letter to an old friend back in Minnesota, E.C. Knieff, whom he had not seen in ten years:

> I have been wanting to write to you for some time, but you know how it is, I put it off until I can make excuses to myself no longer. The present impulse is due to the fact that I have in my possession a water color picture of Lake Minnetonka, Crystal Bay, painted in 1878 by your father, and it occurred to me that you would prize it dearly for its associations as well as its artistic merits. If you care to have it I would be only too glad to forward it to you with my compliments, as a cherished momento of our youth.

The day Warren signed his contract with Warner Brothers pictures— Thursday, March 12, 1931— Freeman Krech died of a heart attack while asleep at his daughter's home in New York.[6] The next day Warren's understudy went on at the Playhouse. In front of 1 West 67th Street, the swanky address on Central Park where Warren, Helen and Pauline lived, the family piled into a car and took the long drive out to Port Washington. There, the girls and the sole remaining Krech man — there would never be another from this part of the family — made the final arrangements for their father. As executor of Freeman's estate, Warren took care of most of the details surrounding his will and all legal questions. On Sunday the 15th, Warren, Helen, Elizabeth and her husband Charles gathered at the Nassau County Surrogate's office for the registration and formal reading of the will. Freeman's bequests were simple, leaving everything to his children, including forgiving a $10,000 loan given to Elizabeth and Charles for the purchase of their home. To Warren he left his "old-fashioned" gold watch, and a grand oil painting of his father Ernst that remains with family to this day.[7] The only truly personal bequest of Freeman's will was typically Old World in its sentiment: Freeman made fit to pass on "the set of collar buttons which I have worn almost continuously for fifty-one years to my son; I would like him to wear them with such knowledge and see if he can equal my record." Warren took the request to heart and wore the collar buttons — but he didn't come close to equaling the record.

That same afternoon the family returned to Elizabeth and Charles' home for the funeral. Friends and family gathered to grieve and remember the decent man whose charity work and public service gave them all reflected pride. His death was reported in the Aitkin newspapers, and many there wished they could have been in attendance to send off their old friend in style. There were few movers left from the early days of the city, and each one who passed took those remaining further from the cherished memories of quaint, sleepy Aitkin.

Under normal circumstances, the newly signed contract player would have hopped on a cross-country train to Hollywood to begin work the following Monday. But with legal and funeral arrangements to be taken care of, Warren could not leave just yet. Warner Brothers understood the situation and re-jiggered the shooting schedule of Warren's first film (eventually released under the title *Expensive Women*), so that their new player's first scenes were put off a week. Meanwhile, Warren returned to *The Vinegar Tree* while he was taking care of last-minute details. That week was a mad spree of family arrangements, nightly performances, contract details, preparations for the trip to Hollywood, and study for his maiden Hollywood production. The details were likely helpful for the 37-year-old actor to keep his mind off his loss. The questions about what would happen in Los Angeles kept his practical side busy with "what if." At the moment, all Warren could be certain of was twenty weeks of work and six weeks of vacation on the West Coast; if he would stay, return east, succeed or fail, was unknown. He was so busy that he barely had time to consider the certain and irritating repercussions which would inevitably come from the fact that he was starring in his first picture with Dolores Costello, the new wife of his bothersome doppelganger, John Barrymore.

On March 19, just one week after his father passed, and only days after his funeral, Warren gave his last performance in the New York production of *The Vinegar Tree*. His first scenes at Warner Brothers were set to begin on Monday, March 23, far too soon now to make by cross-country train. The studio called on Wednesday the 18th and asked if he could be ready to leave for California on Friday. Warren told them he was "perfectly sure" he couldn't, but he found that Hollywood rarely takes "no" for an answer. Warner execs decided to charter a passenger plane to fly him from coast to coast — a costly three-day journey, but an expense they recouped many times over in the publicity it brought their latest find. On Thursday night there was a going away party, and on Friday morning Warren climbed aboard the aircraft — presumably excited by the finely tuned example of engineering and industrial design — and took off slowly toward stardom.[8]

Back in Minnesota, the *Aitkin Age* took note of the new success of their native son. Yet even the locals who would be expected to get it right couldn't help adding that nettlesome consonant:

Warren Williams [*sic*] has been signed by Warner Brothers as a leading man for Dolores Costello Barrymore in *The Passionate Sonata* [subsequently renamed *Expensive Women*]. He quit the east last night and left by plane for Hollywood. It is understood that Williams [*sic*] was selected by Mrs. Barrymore's husband Mr. Barrymore.

It is *exceedingly* unlikely that John Barrymore had anything to do with Warren's assignment to his wife's latest film, much less his signing to a motion picture contract. But the publicity wags were already at work and Warren would learn to tolerate it, although not always with good grace.

On Monday, Warren's plane landed at the airport near Hollywood and a Warner Brothers representative picked him up for his first visit to the studio. He was scheduled for shooting that afternoon and had digested the script during the flight, an effective way to take his mind off his troubles and the anxiety of starting a new project. Only an hour after touching down in California he was sitting at a makeup table on the Warner Brothers lot, getting ready to go on the set for his first scenes in Hollywood. Before he even set foot on the stage, columnist Hubbard Keavy started the torrent of reductive comparisons that dogged Warren for most of his Hollywood career. "You certainly do look like Barrymore," Keavy blurted out.[9] Warren sighed, saying wearily but diplomatically that he had heard it all before. Trying once again to head off the nonsense he had endured in New York, the new contract player told Keavy that he would rather stand on his own two feet as an actor than on his resemblance to the Barrymore profile, "excellent though it is," Warren politely added. Moments later he was on the sound stage, making love to John Barrymore's wife, while on an adjacent stage Barrymore himself was shooting *The Mad Genius* with Marian Marsh, herself a near dead ringer for Miss Costello. More than a few people noted the irony.

The very next day Warren learned the wicked power of the Hollywood publicity machine. The *Los Angeles Times* ran an article about Warren's first day at Warner Brothers titled "Can You Pick the Barrymores?" It featured side-by-side pictures of the two "Great Profiles" and the two leading ladies, with a detailed description of the startling resemblance that the newcomer from the east bore to the legendary star. Warren had been in California precisely 24 hours and already his image had been reduced to that of a second-rate Barrymore. The individualist who hated anything to be presented to him as "cut and dried or preordained" was only just beginning to see the geometric expansion of scrutiny that Hollywood represented above Broadway. He was none too happy about it, but even he couldn't deny the resemblance. When he saw the rushes of his first scenes at Warner Brothers, he groaned loudly in the screening room and exclaimed: "Gosh! I really *do* look like John Barrymore!"[10]

For a short time after he finished *Expensive Women*, Warren had liberty between pictures. He and Helen began making plans to relocate to the coast, at least temporarily. Warren found he loved California, with yearlong sailing weather, plenty of sunshine and fresh air that one did not encounter in New York during the 1930s. He also helped out at the small training school that Warner Brothers was offering (in conjunction with their recently acquired subsidiary, First National Pictures) to new film actors. His Academy training and long stage experience as well as the tools gained as a sergeant in the war made him a natural teacher. After a minor diversion to shoot an episode of the Bobby Jones short subject *How I Play Golf*[11] (wherein a hilariously exasperated Warren breaks his one-iron over his knee, then seeks Jones' help with his fairway woods), Warners assigned him to *Honor of the Family*, known in script stage as *Honor of This House.* The film was ostensibly based on a story by Honoré de Balzac, but bore a far closer resemblance to hoary Hollywood melodrama than to any French literature. Warren played Captain Boris, the swaggering Legionnaire of an old Austrian clan. The aristocratic and blustering Boris arrives just in the nick of cinema time to settle the family's honor in a duel with Alan Mowbray. Eventually Warren developed into one of Hollywood's best sword handlers, but here Mowbray took some mean hits from Warren's errant blade.[12] It was not altogether unexpected that the studio would experiment with their new star in cultured roles. His aris-

H.F. 209

Honor of the Family (1931) was Warren's second film in Hollywood. His cultured look and trained voice initially led Warner Brothers to consider him for aristocratic roles, but it wasn't long before they reconfigured his image as an amoral businessman, shyster attorney or cagey detective. He is seen here embracing Bebe Daniels.

tocratic features and perfect diction continued to convince his employers of the possibility that they might have — surprise — a second Barrymore on their hands. Clearly, at this moment the Warner Brothers machine has no indelible picture of what to do with him. That month he was mooted for a part in *Larceny Lane*, a proposed sequel to *The Public Enemy*, with James Cagney and Marian Marsh.[13] And as early as May 21, the studio already announced that they were preparing his first starring vehicle as lawyer Jimmy Fallon in *The Mouthpiece*.[14] Later that year they would find a winning formula, selling him as the amoral businessman or callous rake that modern audiences have come to know, but for now it was a matter of testing the waters and seeing what developed.

While *Honor of the Family* was shooting late in May, the theater producers Belasco and Curran announced a Los Angeles production of *The Vinegar Tree* to feature the great stage and screen actress Billie Burke. With Warren's Hollywood stardom still just an indistinct blur on the horizon, he decided to exercise a clause in his original contract allowing him to take time off for legitimate stage productions and join the show. Although Burke was clearly the star, having an original Broadway cast member was a coup for the West Coast production, which had spent three months in casting. Warner Brothers drew up a contract on May 28, and when Warren finished shooting *Honor* on June 10 he took a week off, then trooped over to the Belasco Theatre to begin rehearsals for what would be his final stage appearances until 1943.

The Vinegar Tree opened at the Belasco Theatre on June 29 following two sold-out previews at Santa Barbara's Lobero Theatre. The show received glowing reviews, although the pattern of unbalanced accolades that Warren endured was still clearly in force: "Billie Burke, elfin spirit of gayety ... shone as the most deft queen of laughter who has appeared on stage this season." Then followed the filtered dregs: "Warren William, somewhat of a Barrymore type ... is a reserved and efficient actor."[15] As his first appearance in front of a West Coast audience, the response was tepid at best — and maddeningly similar to what he experienced in New York. While Warner Brothers was doing yeoman's work in touting the new player, he still couldn't break through the stranglehold that strong women had on the public's attention when placed next to him. Regardless, he maintained his humble outlook irrespective of any efforts to trip him up. When Otheman Stevens interviewed him in June of 1931, he asked the star: "What makes you so notable in *The Vinegar Tree*, Mr. William?" Warren shot back, unblinking; "Why, Miss Burke and the play, of course."[16] *The Vinegar Tree* continued through July in Los Angeles, then moved to San Francisco on August 6. When the production went out on the road later that month, Warren returned to Warners' Burbank studio and bid farewell to the stage that had been so good to him. He believed that his ultimate future might still be in the theater, but it would not be long before his film success took him far from that idea.

For a few glorious years following the advent of sound, Hollywood had the opportunity to reflect at least some of the inner life of American society. Almost from the beginning of the motion picture, censors and pressure groups had dictated the content and tone of most films. When producers or writers troubled anyone with a bad word or salacious scene — or a series of orgies, in Cecil B. DeMille's case — the public raised political capital and spent it on crushing the impulse towards change. Each time that the creative bar was raised higher — or lower, depending on your perspective — new rules were put in place to return the bar to status quo. Each time, of course, the genie was out of the bottle and the new line was never quite capable of being level with the old one. In the early sound era, Hollywood found itself still under the restrictions of the latest production code, a relic from the last explosion of outrage over film manners in 1930. However, more and more producers, writers and directors were then exploring what it meant to live in a world that had endured a World War and the social calamity of the

Great Depression. Unlike previous movements towards modernity in film, this era engendered less resistance from the public and only nominal interference from censorship czar Will Hays' office but for adhering to general ideas of good taste and decorum. If adult subjects were treated implicitly — hinted at, misdirected, couched in metaphor or insinuated — fair game was wide-ranging and in open season. With this tacit understanding, many writers took the opportunity to test the limits of where they might roam, and when no game warden appeared to check their license, they kept right on going. In 1931 and for the next four years Hollywood pushed the line further than they would at any time over the following fifteen. It was the era of relative permissiveness known imperfectly as the pre–Code, and Warren William was about to be unknowingly deposited in its lusty, violent, earthy center.

When he returned to work in August, Warners executives were just starting to tease together the successful screen persona of Warren William. Their first choice was to feature him in a small but pivotal role in *Under Eighteen*, starring Marian Marsh, fresh from her success in *Svengali*. Warren's performance is the seminal role in what became his dominant pre–Code persona — the wanton, amoral man without a conscience. And although not yet fully unregenerate, not yet entirely unprincipled, Raymond Harding is nonetheless the prototype of the shady and libidinous characters for which Warren William has become widely known.

Like many other Warner pre–Code pictures, *Under Eighteen* burrows deep into the seamy lives of poverty-stricken urbanites, reflecting the blue-collar audience the studio regularly courted. Sisters Sophie (Anita Page) and Marge (Marsh) struggle against the dehumanizing effects of Depression life, facing jealousy, abuse, privation, seduction and the law, all uncompromisingly lensed by director Archie Mayo's camera.

An early portrait taken shortly after the actor arrived in Hollywood. The inscription says: "To Margaret Kingsley with all good wishes from Warren William." Courtesy Barbara Hall.

From her place as a seamstress in the wings of the moneyed world of high fashion, Marge sees the models on staff enjoying the high life — food, money and excitement — on the arms of rich and powerful men. Marge clearly knows the carnal price for such favors, but still covets the lifestyle it could lead to. As decent as her fiancé Jimmie might be, the Depression ensures that he'll never be able to give her the comforts and experiences she craves. Stirring this little soup of discontent is Marge's sister Sophie, married with child to Alf, a ne'er-do-well whose gambling has resulted in the loss of their business and livelihood. When the bickering couple comes to live with her, Marge's sad image of marriage as a trap of poverty and misery is reinforced. And when Alf becomes physically abusive to Sophie, Marge feels she's made an awful mistake in accepting Jimmie's proposal. In order to save her sister's health, honor and sanity, the girls must raise money for divorce proceedings. Marge resolves to get the funds even at the expense of her own virtue.

Enter Warren William.

As the wealthy rake Raymond Harding, Warren positively oozes charm: his manner with women calls to mind an insect being caught by slow-moving amber. When Harding first encounters Marge she is momentarily pressed into service to model a coat with nothing underneath but a delicate silk slip. After the tycoon inadvertently gets an eyeful, he sits back, drinks it in and luxuriously strokes his moustache. While Harding is still contemplating his private view of paradise, the camera moves into a close-up on Marge. When it pulls out, he is standing so close to her that he can hear the rustle of her scanty lingerie. The prey is now in the path of the inexorable flow of his lust. No one — including poor Marian Marsh —can miss what he's looking for.

Knowing his interest, Marge resolves to go to Harding's penthouse apartment to trade herself for a loan that will relieve her sister of an abusive marriage. She finds him hosting a wild, orgiastic party. When Harding's butler inquires if he should admit her, the wealthy cad eyes her from across the terrace and says, salivating: "Serve it here." Marge is then ushered into the tangled crowd where she encounters the businessman in his swimming pool, bouncing a drunken woman on an inflatable toy that resembles nothing so much as a massive phallus— just to make sure we all understand what is about to happen. And it is then that Warren William delivers one of those deathless lines of the pre–Code that still has the power to startle: "Ah, Miss Evans, what a pleasant surprise. Why not take off your clothes and stay awhile?"

Almost in that moment, Warren William became unique among film actors: simultaneously capable of uncommon sleaziness and inescapable magnetism. Although we are deeply sympathetic to Marge's plight, we can't help but admire the predatory instinct of this urban hunter.

In *Under Eighteen*, however, Harding's pedigree as a cad is in question; he is incapable of closing the deal. Once he has Marge in his boudoir and she has made the decision to betray herself for the $200 that will help her sister, Harding has an attack of conscience. For him it's easy to barter sex for money when both sides understand the exchange rate; the experienced girls know the price and are perfectly willing to swap what they have for what they want. But Marge has a quality that even he values above money and toys— decency — and he knows it isn't right to take it so cheaply. He demurs and tells her she can have the money with no strings attached. Warren plays the scene wonderfully, going from willful profligate to principled gentleman with little more than a shift of body language and the lowering of an eyebrow. Unfortunately, a sharply observed and fairly intelligent picture quickly veers off course at this point. Jimmie winds up wanted for murder after breaking into the scene and impulsively taking a swing at Harding. Following some cheap melodrama, a silent-era denouement finds Harding alive and well after all, Alf and Sophie reconciled and with $1,500 to regain their business, and Marge with a wad of cash, a new job and a forgiving fiancé. Reviewing for the *Washington Post*, Nelson Bell saw the precise problem with the picture. "The principal objection to [*Under Eighteen*] is that almost invariably when it seems to be getting somewhere in a worthy dramatic way it goes either maudlin or farcical and has to begin all over again to reconstruct its plausibility and salvage its claim to realism."[17] The *New York Times* was not as thoughtful, but no less accurate: "When the honest grocery clerk bursts into the room and fells his man with a half hearted punch, the climax falters badly."

Under Eighteen embodies more than a few of the starker elements of the pre–Code, but the finale has the appearance of the censor's hand. After sixty minutes of misfortune and grief, marriage, fidelity and chastity are arbitrarily rewarded and the scales are balanced. There is no question the Hays office was more active at this point than modern film scholarship suggests, and writers Kenyon and Fulton would have known better than to degrade lovely Marian Marsh and expect to get away with it. But we do have the start of a singular male construction of pre–Code Hollywood, one that did not go unnoticed in the press. "Warren William is especially deft in his performance of an inferentially dangerous character who is moved by the events here depicted to disclose his nature's better side."[18] Once Warners' writers and directors saw this picture, they quickly refined the idea, eventually creating a unique and challenging portrait from this first blurry image.

Next Warren starred as a stalwart but cheating naval officer in *The Woman from Monte Carlo*, also known as *The Captain's Wife*. Lil Dagover was the wife and Walter Huston the captain. Warren is the second in command on Huston's ship, as well as second in command in his bedroom. Dagover was clearly being modeled as the newest version of Greta Garbo, and she books more time on screen with Warren than with Huston. The story involves secret naval maneuvers, a clandestine rendezvous between the captain's wife and his second in command, and a military trial where only an admission of infidelity can save her husband's career. It is all somewhat quaint, even for 1932, but the picture does feature a very exciting and well-staged sea battle between World War I dreadnoughts, and a spectacular moment when a wounded and delirious Warren shoots sleazy John Wray dead in the middle of a packed courtroom. It was solid entertainment designed to sell Dagover, but did little to hone the image of the new Hollywood star.

Warner Brothers quickly re-teamed Warren with Marian Marsh in *Beauty and the Boss*, a version of Ladislas Fodor's play *A Church Mouse*, about a down-on-her-luck waif who makes good as a stenographer for a high-powered businessman. It expanded upon the businessman-rake of *Under Eighteen* and pulled focus closer still to his primary pre–Code image: magnificent bastard.

Baron Von Ulrich is a high-flying Continental financier, introduced by director Roy Del Ruth returning from business in the States via his private plane. The baron has devised a novel system to allow himself to be single-minded, but about two things. During the day, he thinks only about money, during the evening about sex. When his daytime secretary Olive shamefully upends the divide by being entirely too attractive, he fires her from his office and neatly ensconces her in his evening boudoir to restore order.

The avalanche of innuendo, insinuation and implication that occurs in just the first ten minutes of *Beauty and the Boss* is worth the price of admission: the baron notices Olive's skirt hiked up above her knee as she takes dictation. "Yes, I see it," he says, exasperated. "But I've seen better." Olive lowers her eyes. "But I didn't think you could see my, umm...." "No, of course not," the baron reassures. He reaches out and pulls the skirt down. When she moves suggestively on the divan, he grumbles, "Don't squirm! I know you have hips!" Olive explains that she does it when the baron dictates too fast. "I do everything rapidly," he barks, and she playfully raises her voice an octave: "Oh, baron!" Later, she deliberately bends over to show him her cleavage, and after an interruption to admonish her, he's lost his place in the letter. "Where was I...?" he wonders, then once again eyes her bust. "Oh yes, I saw [*long pause*] the directors yesterday...." After he's fired Olive and proffered six months salary to set her up in an apartment, he instructs: "Give your phone number to Ludwig. I'll call you when I'm in a proper — or rather an *im*proper mood."

If the mind of the picture was modern, the body of the story was old-fashioned even in 1932. When Marsh arrives, looking like a disheveled Eliza Doolittle, we are indeed treated to a second-rate *Pygmalion*, wherein the ugly duckling becomes a swan, reforms the wayward baron and is likewise fired so that she can stop being a distraction and become the baroness. It is only Del Ruth's quick direction, the sturdy work of the cast and the censor's laxity that make *Beauty and the Boss* memorable today. It was however a juicy part for Warren, and in spite of being billed third after the ossified David Manners he is clearly the lead. The feminine focus, this time Marian Marsh, is once again the star of the proceedings.

Things were moving quickly for Warner Brothers' new leading man. His first few months in Hollywood were a whirlwind of sound stages, studio interviews, photo sessions, publicity appearances, personal plans, business arrangements and microscopic scrutiny. For a modest, unassuming professional like Warren, getting used to the attention and demands on his time was a chore. He was fortunate to have come to Hollywood as a mature, fully formed man. At the age of 36, he'd had his share of fame and celebrity in New York, and as a result he was better able to handle the pressures and temptations that went along with becoming a newly minted film star when Hollywood was the unquestioned king of world excess. The lore of Warren William, in the press and among his family, is that of a faithful, decent man who never strayed from the path of fidelity. By all accounts—well, almost all—the lore appears to be largely true. From the day he arrived, it appears Warren insulated himself from the temptations and siren calls of the film capital, or at least managed them very well indeed. He was helped by a schedule that left little time for anything but work. From March until the end of December he shot five feature films, one short subject, taught in the Warner Brothers–First National drama school, spent ten weeks on Los Angeles and San Francisco stages and navigated a full-scale move from New York to Hollywood. In between he somehow managed seven weeks off, probably dedicated largely to locating and outfitting a new apartment that he and Helen took at the Chateau Elysee in Los Angeles. "At least I can't work in more than one picture at a time," he sighed.[19] The pace would not stop for the next five years.

In early September, the first hiccup of his relationship with Warner Brothers manifested itself. Irritated by the chronic misspelling of his new star's name, Warner Brothers head of production Darryl Zanuck called a meeting. He had tried to get the troops at Warners' New York advertising agency in line, admonishing them to stop unconsciously making Mr. William into Mr. "Williams." When they argued that they could not control the "natural inclination" of regional printers and copywriters to add the excess consonant, Zanuck asked Warners' legal council Roy Obringer to instead convince Warren William to change his professional name to Warren Williams. On September 9, just days before his contract was up for renewal, Warren met with Obringer, who made the full court press for the change. The Minnesota boy who never liked to argue was having none of it. He steadfastly refused, saying that the name was a distinction in itself, and that he was already well established in the theatrical world as Warren William. Ever polite, he allowed that he wanted to help the studio in any way possible, but he would not go along in this instance. Obringer knew they were stumped; their contract gave them no legal grounds to impose the change without Warren's permission.[20] The matter was permanently settled, but New York was right: For the next seventeen years that appendix "s" continued to turn up at the end of Warren's name with maddening regularity, including studio correspondences, advertising, publicity materials, newspaper articles, fan magazines and even the Warner Brothers payroll log.

Another problem that September was the issue of the six-month option on Warren's contract. The original document called for a raise in salary to $1,000 a week, but Warner Brothers balked at committing to such a fee when their new contract player had not even been seen on theater screens yet. The Hollywood office of the William Morris Agency was then representing Warren on behalf of his New York–based agent, Ben Boyar. The parties agreed on a compromise and Warren's renewal was adjusted to $850 a week, with options to continue up at a slower rate than originally planned. He wasn't happy about it, but there was no leverage with which to bargain.

It wasn't until October that the national public got their first look at Warren William. The opening of *Honor of the Family* and then *Expensive Women* provided the new contractee a mixed introduction to film audiences. His reputation as a debonair clotheshorse was immediately cemented. Since his success on Broadway, one of his few sincere indulgences was clothing, and he was blessed with impeccable taste. He became an almost instant fixture on Hollywood's ten best-dressed lists, along with William Powell and Adolphe Menjou, and eventually owned over 100 suits, 30 overcoats and 50 pairs of shoes. In 1933 the tailors of London, New York and Hollywood voted him a runner-up as one of the ten best-dressed men in *the world*.[21] In spite of already being 36, the Warren William of 1931 looks youthful and fresh. Unfortunately in *Expensive Women* was created the prototype for his auxiliary career persona: the passive and ineffectual good guy. In this guise Warren is typically a neglected husband or the third wheel in a love triangle — the man who quietly waits for the leading lady to realize that it is *he* whom she has wanted all along. It is a thankless role repeated again and again during William's career — see *Smarty, Living on Velvet, Three on a Match, Madame X* and many others — to his everlasting detriment. In the case of *Expensive Women*, Dolores Costello spends the entire movie ignoring William as Neil Hartley in favor of Hartley's friend Arthur Raymond. After Costello is acquitted of murder charges in Raymond's death (while her lies conceal the unpunished murderer — this is pre–Code, after all), Hartley nobly and inexplicably takes her back. The continuing power of women over Warren William — whatever we might see in his future — is undiminished.

Expensive Women was a restart of Dolores Costello's career after two years away from the screen. It endured drastic cuts from the censors because of its sexual content and did not find favor with audiences or critics.[22] The dialogue and scenario were correctly derided, but the press did take favorable notice (sometimes at the point of a billfold, to be sure) of Warner Brothers' new player. In reviews of each of his early films in fact, Warren is singled out as a fresh face on the cinema landscape. Not fresh enough, however, to avoid being compared to Barrymore with metronomic regularity. While Warren piled up plaudits in these embryonic appearances, the Depression was tearing the world economy apart. In September alone, 305 American banks went bankrupt and closed. In October, 522 more followed. More than ever, Warren and Helen prayed for his success in the film industry. Everyone in the country was afraid of what would come next. They couldn't know it then, but at that very moment Warner Brothers was preparing the film that would make him a full-fledged star.

11

Living on Velvet

The Mouthpiece was loosely based on the life of criminal lawyer William Fallon. Notorious in New York as a libertine, gambler and drinker, the flamboyant Fallon defended many underworld characters including the racketeer Arnold Rothstein. Although the role had been mooted for Warren as early as May 21,[1] memos from November show that Warner Brothers still considered it a possible project for Edward G. Robinson. Robinson reportedly turned it down with much to chose from following his massive success in *Little Caesar*. It was then supposedly offered to all the other Warner–First National actors before Warner Brothers fell back on it as a star vehicle for Warren. The fictional Fallon combined character elements that had been so successful for him thus far: the powerful, amoral businessman; a bankrupt conscience; predatory sexuality and a deeply buried kernel of decency. *The Mouthpiece* was everything an actor could want — except all the other actors at Warner Brothers. "I just play the roles that everyone else won't play," Warren said later, smiling.[2]

Shooting began on January 18, 1932, just a week after Warren and Helen's ninth wedding anniversary, and continued for five weeks. It is doubtful that anyone thought of *The Mouthpiece* as anything more than the latest in the line of Warner programmers, but with the snappy direction of James Flood and Elliott Nugent, a script full of sulfuric dialogue, and the full expression of Warren William's range and character, it became a major hit for the studio.

The Mouthpiece opens in a courtroom where assistant District Attorney Vincent Day is delivering a summation to the jury. Warren is at a theatrical fever pitch as he struts the floor, rolls his consonants and bellows accusations at a frightened teen on trial for murder. The poor criminal justice system is clearly no match for this cyclone of jurisprudence, and the boy is sentenced to death while Day basks in the soothing warmth of another capital conviction. In short order, however, the boy is discovered to be innocent, and the DA's office is too late to stop the execution. Lights dim, and justice — deaf, dumb *and* blind, in this case — takes its course. Day is beside himself with guilt and shame; he quits his job in disgust and within minutes of the opening frames has drunkenly resigned himself to the sleazy fringes of New York's saloon culture. In the very next scene (after a few words of encouragement from his bartender), he's cynically reinvented himself as the champion defender of reprobates, criminals, predators and other human filth of New York. From there things *really* get going.

Vincent Day is the first genuinely profane rogue in Warren's oeuvre. In *Under Eighteen* he was secretly a decent person. In *Beauty and the Boss,* he was an honest businessman who simply had a penchant for beautiful women. Here, however, is a man of deformed principles; a man who knows the right thing and chooses to do the wrong thing, in a sense punishing himself for the mistake of caring. If he doesn't care anymore, Day rationalizes, he can't be hurt again. In an orgy of perverting justice, he wins freedom for swindlers, pimps and murderers. He revels in his power, chiseling the strong and weak alike. When he saves a timid bank clerk from prison after he embezzles ninety thousand dollars, the clerk asks what he'll do now that

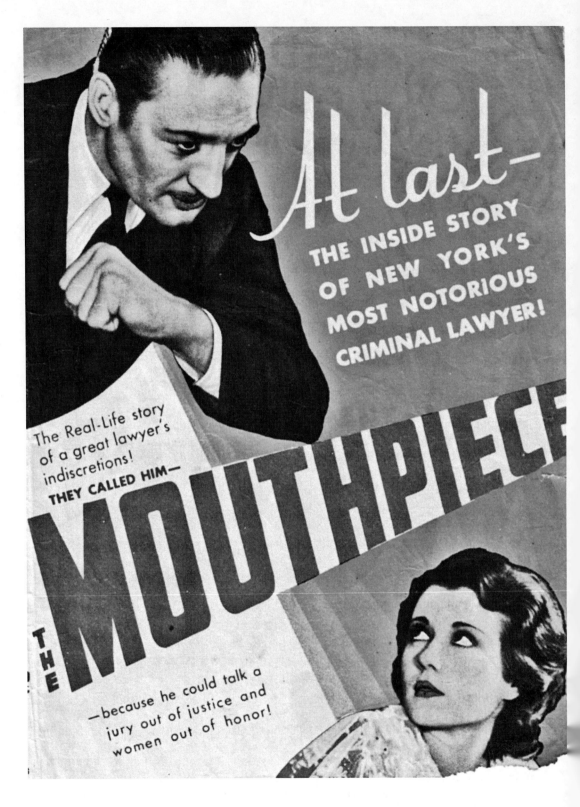

The Mouthpiece is the film that made Warren William a star. Based on the life of New York lawyer William Fallon, the story was salacious enough to encourage Fallon's daughter to sue Warner Brothers, unsuccessfully. Cowering below is Sidney Fox.

his boss knows what's happened. "Go out and jump in the river, you cheap tinhorn crook," the lawyer growls. Day's lack of scruples does not stop in the courtroom. His crusade to demean himself takes the quickest route to the bottom when he brazenly resolves to seduce his underage stenographer. Day's loyal secretary Hickey (played by the magnificent Aline MacMahon) has seen this all before and instantly warns him off his salacious course. "There's two reasons to keep her away from you," she drawls from under sleepy eyes. "She's jail bait, and she's dumb." Unfortunately Day is so obsessed with self-punishment that he refuses to listen. And when circumstances later demand that he begin to care again, it is inevitable that he must get hurt.

In spite of its pre–Code pedigree, the cynicism of *The Mouthpiece* is upended in the final reel. Day redeems himself through a noble sacrifice, something that few others in Warren's rogues' gallery deemed necessary. Most often they simply flaunt their errant ways, while the Hand of Justice occasionally offers a stern rebuke. But Vincent Day's reclamation made for good drama and *The Mouthpiece* found a tremendous audience among Depression era moviegoers. It momentarily swept Warren near the top rank of leading men, just underneath names like Clark Gable, William Powell and James Cagney. "In this picture Warren William proves himself to be one of the most talented actors of the screen,"[3] proclaimed *The Washington Post*, kicking off the unanimous acclaim accorded his performance. Mordaunt Hall praised Warren's turn as the criminal attorney as "one of the outstanding interpretations that has been contributed to the screen,"[4] and later led an essay in the *New York Times* with the observation "Few screen performances have equaled Warren William's superb characterization in *The Mouthpiece*."[5] The *Westfield Leader* said Warren had a role that "fits him like the proverbial glove, and gives him a chance to demonstrate the great dramatic talent which made him a legend on Broadway."[6] Another columnist offered: "Warren William plays the role for all it's worth. It establishes him as one of the genuinely important newcomers, a skilled actor and a stellar personality."[7] He was simultaneously called "wonderfully engaging," "magnificent," "electric," "forceful" and "extraordinarily entertaining." For once Warren even came out ahead of John Barrymore. When the Great Profile's *State's Attorney* was released the week after *The Mouthpiece*, critics inevitably compared the pictures and found Warren and his vehicle more to their liking. "*State's Attorney* is much on the order of *The Mouthpiece*, in which Warren William so recently distinguished himself," wrote the *Chicago Tribune*. "*The Mouthpiece* was the better picture because characters were more forcefully drawn [and] Warren William was a far more convincing lawyer than Barrymore."[8] That spring a new star was born at Warners, hot on the heels of the recent rise of James Cagney and Edward G. Robinson, and Warren William was suddenly a household name.

Even before it premiered in April, Warner Brothers production chief Darryl Zanuck knew that he had something with *The Mouthpiece*, and wasted no time in maneuvering Warren into another starring role. The studio was now convinced that they had a working model for their new contract player. Memos crossed the lot concerning the next option on Warren's contract, due in April. Producer William Koenig was eager to re-sign him, but made sure that everyone knew to play it close to the vest. "I do not want to give him the impression I'm in a hurry," was his directive.[9] After Warren and Helen had a two-week vacation in late February and early March, the studio immediately began production of the actor's second headlining role.

The property was *The Dark Horse*, a political comedy that would play to the budding image of Warren as a con artist and promoter. The script began life in January of 1932 as a sequel to the recently finished (and not then released) William Powell vehicle *High Pressure*. The original picture followed Powell's manic con man Gar Evans as he devised a scheme to manufacture and sell a dubious concoction of artificial rubber. *High Pressure* moved a mile a minute and had a breezy, likable rogue as the main character — someone the writer in Zanuck knew was a natural for a sequel. Confident of the film's success, Zanuck commissioned a story from Sidney Morrison then sat himself down at the typewriter and banged out the screenplay. By January 7 he had a script in hand (written under the pseudonym Mark Canfield) titled *The Further Adventures of Gar Evans.* Quickly, however, things were derailed. The writer of *High Pressure* had a contract that lacked a clause for sequels. With this leverage he was determined to hold the studio's proverbial feet to the fire in negotiations. Warner Brothers eventually offered to buy out the name Gar Evans for $2,000, but were refused.[10] The writer and his agent clearly wanted more money than Warners felt the property was worth, so the studio propagated their own confidence game. The script went through a series of rewrites and was eventually extruded from the Warner assembly line as *The Dark Horse,* featuring Hal Blake, the nominal stand-in for Gar Evans. Although the focus of the new script shifted from promotion to politics, the legal department decided that Powell's appearance in the film might convince the writer and his agent that "Hal Blake" was a mere smokescreen (he was) and that a lawsuit was in order. So, discretion being the better part of valor, Warners reassigned the actor and began looking for someone else to take over. Zanuck immediately thought of Warren to fill the role vacated by Powell. Zanuck and the rest of the Warners machine were already positioning him as an analogue Powell: someone who could play those smart, snappy, confident roles Powell excelled at and look good doing it, but for less money. A significant part of the Minnesota actor's early film identity is in fact predicated on his similarity to the star of *The Thin Man,* far more so than those often-repeated comparisons to John Barrymore. So, Warren stepped for the first time into William Powell's shoes (something he would do again when he took over the role of Philo Vance after Powell left Warner Brothers), and on March 14 they started shooting.

To direct, Warners assigned Alfred E. Green, a sturdy, solid craftsman who was in films as early as 1912. Although nearly forgotten today, Green is responsible for a handful of genuine pre–Code classics, including the notorious Barbara Stanwyck vehicle *Baby Face,* and the immensely underrated *Union Depot.* His direction is efficient, if somewhat tonally inconsistent. The real problem is the script, as a wonderfully cynical, trenchant and amusing comedy degenerates into an unruly domestic farce in the third act.

The Dark Horse was among the first Hollywood pictures to deal directly with politics in a comprehensive way. In early 1932 the Depression was worse than in 1931 and America was entirely disgusted with the sad fact that their leaders seemed unwilling or incapable of doing anything about it. It was an election year and scorn and derision were the order of the day. A book of glib and ultimately idiotic prophecies about the Depression called *Oh, Yeah* was selling well on the basis of making the average reader feel smarter than the cognoscenti, while the magazine *Ballyhoo* basked in circulation over a million copies by ridiculing politics and big business.[11] *The Dark Horse* tapped into this undercurrent of discontent, mercilessly lampooning elected officials as brainless dunderheads, and offering their behind the scenes puppet masters as chiselers and thieves. The fun in pre–Code Hollywood wasn't always just about sex and violence, after all.

If there is a film that proves the adage "Everything old is new again," *The Dark Horse* is it. Anyone who believes that politics have changed in the last eighty years will find the scenario as timely as ever. The story concerns Zachary Hicks (Guy Kibbee), a hayseed representative to the local party convention who is nominated for governor following a deadlock in the floor vote. The insider hacks reckon if they can get him elected, they will be the power behind the power and Hicks will be none the wiser. After some prompting from a party staffer (Bette

Davis), they resolve to hire the best political strategist in America, Hal S. Blake. There's only one hitch: Blake is serving a term in state prison. This is where we encounter Warren William; in full siren cry, behind bars, exhorting his fellow inmates (already) to "Vote for Hicks!" Never mind that the convicts have no rights to cast ballots in the election. For Blake, it's an audition. He's all about the ballyhoo.

At Hicks' headquarters the newly released campaign manager meets his candidate for the first time. Hicks is a perverse, cherubic man-child, someone you would report to the police if you saw him hanging around a schoolyard too long. Blake privately chokes out his opinion to the party bosses. "He's the dumbest human being I ever saw," the huckster offers, as if he's inhaled some obscene efflux. "Every time he opens his mouth, he subtracts from the sum total of human knowledge." Blake is undeterred, however. Hicks' slack-jawed, vacant stupidity has given him the key to victory: "Sure he's dumb. But he's *honest*. That's how we'll sell him." The cynicism in *The Dark Horse* is as dry as kindling in the desert, and no one is safe from spontaneous combustion; politicians, advisors, party bosses, reporters and civil servants are torched with equal glee. Even the voting public—who you would expect to be exempt, since they have paid for the seats—are obliquely derided. They elect Hicks governor.

The Dark Horse was Warren's first chance to headline a full-fledged comedy (*Beauty and the Boss* being part comedy, part romantic fantasy) and he made the most of his opportunity. He is snappy, funny, wry and energetic, and he cements his uncanny ability to make even the basest liar and cheat likable. Green understood that Warren worked best at a fast pace, and he makes sure that Hal Blake steams through the scenario like a Coast Guard cutter in choppy waters. Most of the difficulty in tone is the fault of the script, which flags badly in the last reel when situations turn from political to domestic. *The Dark Horse* is only two-thirds of a memorable picture.

Production lasted just under a month, wrapping in the early morning hours of April 14. Warners went all-out for the premiere, with a gala debut featuring the entire cast at the Warner Brothers Hollywood Theatre. By early July *The Dark Horse* was in theaters nationwide, less than a month after the debut of *The Mouthpiece*. With the fall election nearing and audiences still buzzing about the new star, the film did excellent box office and Warren continued to ring up accolades. "Warren William swaggers through his promoter's role with an insincerity that is overwhelming," was the position of the *LA Times*.[12] The *Chicago Tribune* said that he was "one of the best bets the screen has on tap," and everpresent Warren William fan Mordaunt Hall claimed he was "as much the master of his role as he was in *The Mouthpiece*." Quoted in the *New York Times*, a London critic was even kinder. "Warren William is, without doubt, one of the most promising young stars in America. He has an intellectual quality which prevents him ever becoming dull, however obvious the material he has to handle may be."[13] It is a comment that recurs again and again with critics throughout Warren's career—that of consistently performing above the material he is given.

One person who was not so high on Warren was his *Dark Horse* co-star Bette Davis. According to her—and only her, as far as anyone can tell—the predatory nature of Warren's screen characters was evident in the man himself. Davis claimed that Warren mercilessly attempted to seduce her during the course of filming,[14] and while they were on a personal appearance tour promoting the film that spring. The story has been repeated in many Davis biographies, often without attribution, and is a troubling anomaly that is not supported by any other indication of misbehavior. He and Davis worked together three more times: that summer in *Three on a Match,* in 1936's *Satan Met a Lady* and attendant publicity tour, and on a 1942 radio appearance on *Gulf's Screen Guild Theatre*. It seems incomprehensible that the outspoken actress would consent to resubmit herself to such unwanted attentions, much less go on the road with someone she describes in such unflattering terms, but this is exactly what Davis did. In Lawrence J. Quirk's 1990 biography, the author states that the actress even believed that Darryl Zanuck cooked up the *Dark Horse* publicity tour as a favor for the allegedly amorous actor.[15] Davis did not evidence any particular enmity in 1940, when Warren was invited to, and attended, a dinner in her honor at the Trocadero nightclub. It would have been eminently understandable for the notoriously vindictive actress to keep him off the guest list for such transgressions, but this she did not do. Warren also became a member of the Tailwagger's Club, a charitable organization for animal rights, working with president Bette Davis on various occasions, to the friction of none. Davis often seemed to find enemies and rivals in places where they did not exist, making adversaries of many co-workers for no other reason than her massive ego. Perhaps her notoriously harsh temper festered over the years and she manufactured a more salacious story than actually occurred. Possible but less likely is that Warren was momentarily distracted in those early days with a particularly beautiful woman in his path. If it was true, it was not normal behavior, and certainly was not likely to be repeated.

During the first quarter of 1932, after a minor upswing in the economic outlook, Wall Street took another steep dive toward anarchy. Although Warren had occasionally thought of returning to the stage, the enormous success of *The Mouthpiece* made it clear that he would not be venturing back to Broadway anytime soon. For all his professed love of the stage, it could not compete with the riches or the lifestyle offered by Hollywood. In April, Warner Brothers rewarded him for his breakout role by picking up his option and raising his salary to $1,100 a week, far more than he had ever made during his greatest New York successes. Even so, Warren was still unhappy about his salary having been reduced from his original contract. Irritated, he contacted his representative from the William Morris agency and they discussed the possibility of trying to renegotiate, but Mr. Feil of their office felt that the economic condition was not conducive to forcing Warner Brothers' hand at that time.[16] It would have to be left for another moment. Regardless of his compensation, Warren was now a film star, and that meant that he and Helen were also now permanent residents of Hollywood. Roots were inevitable.

The only real home Warren had ever known was the one his father had built in Aitkin during the summer when he (Warren) was four years old. Since then he had led the fractured life of a soldier and vagabond actor; moving from army bases to overseas camps, then touring the States for months at a time and returning to New York to start again in a new apartment in a new neighborhood. Now, for the first time, he and Helen had the luxury of deciding where and how they wanted to live. Late in 1931 the Krechs had taken possession of a feisty wire-haired terrier named Jill. The dog became a surrogate child to the couple, and after a playmate terrier named Jack arrived on the premises, they found their rented apartment was entirely too small. After just a year in California, and in spite of the continuing erosion of the Depression economy that spring, the Krechs began looking for a home to buy.

Almost immediately they became intrigued by a new subdivision of Newport Beach being developed by the well-known Southern California architect, Franz Herding. The Swiss-born designer responsible for the Los Angeles neighborhoods of Hollywood Knolls and Leimert Park was now in the midst of his latest project, a beachfront community about 60 miles from Hollywood, known as Lido Isle. Herding's designs were based on the quaint resort village of Lido, situated on a tiny eleven-mile-long sandbar on the Adriatic Coast of Venice, Italy. Naturally, Warren could hardly resist the opportunity to live directly on the ocean, with a view of the Pacific and a private pier for the new boat that would replace *The Cutlass*, which had been run aground and smashed in New York. So, by June, the Krechs had purchased an oceanfront lot in the subdivision for about $1,500, with Herding engaged to design and build a modest beach house on a budget of about $5,000.

That summer while Warren was working long hours shooting *Three on a Match* and *The Match King,* plans for the house were expanding, along with costs. Herding had suggested a more ambitious design for a bigger house that required another lot adjoining to the first. Warren purchased the second lot, and looked with great interest at the blueprints the architect showed him. They included a flagstone loggia resting on the main floor of the house, spilling out onto a white sand beach that led directly to the ocean. On the flagstone you would find dressing rooms for houseguests and a massive fireplace adjacent to the kitchen for convenient outdoor entertaining. The house loomed two more stories, with four bedrooms, large bay windows, wide decks looking out onto the ocean, and spiral stairways leading down to the beach. A five-car garage, with car ports for another five vehicles, sat behind the house. As impressive as the plans were, Warren and Helen began to have second thoughts when the budget quickly ballooned to an estimated $10,000. Warren's new prosperity hadn't clouded his logic; he knew that this was only the beginning. "It's a swell plan," the *Hartford Courant* quoted him as joking at the time, "and it could probably be built for $20,000."[17] During July, Herding used the star's name to stoke publicity, and stories began to appear in Los Angeles newspapers about the Williams' new home in Lido Isle. Just then, Warren's cold feet were turning icy. In an article in the *Los Angeles Times,* Herding indicated that he expected the cost of the house to be approximately $25,000, but — likely in an effort to mollify his client — added that it could be "executed less luxuriously ... for about $15,000."[18]

At this point, Warren began hauling anchor. Special tax assessments on his vacant Southern California lots were costing him an amount of money he wouldn't have countenanced only a year before. Furthermore, he worried that the cost of his home would mean scaling back or postponing something far more important: the question of when and how he would get his new boat. Now that he realized that he was a permanent resident on the West Coast, he could think of little else.

He and Helen decided to scrap the expanded plan proposed by Herding and return to something more modest, in keeping with their character as a couple. "I find," William told a reporter, "that I could buy a very respectable boat for $3,000. Now a good boat for $3,000 sounds better than a house for $20,000 to me. I could, you know, anchor my $3,000 boat right in front of my $5,000 cottage on the one lot."[19] They put the second lot back on the market in August, and plans for the house limped along into the fall. Eventually, Warren got his boat, but not the house. Lido Isle would have to do without the publicity and charm of the Krechs being in residence. In short order they instead decide to rent a house in Los Feliz, where they would stay for two years. In the meantime, Warren would be able to get his boat, and before long he and Helen would have a permanent home they could call their own.

Shortly after Warren finished *The Dark Horse,* he and Helen took off on a well-deserved three-week vacation. In the interim, Warner Brothers made an arrangement to loan him out to Hollywood's premier motion picture studio, Metro-Goldwyn-Mayer. The Lion had seen Warren's recent work and wanted him for the part of the heartless financier David Dwight in *Skyscraper Souls,* based on the 1931 novel by Faith Baldwin. The contract called for four weeks work at his new rate of $1,100 a week, plus three weeks salary that Warners described as a "carrying charge." The film was designed to capitalize on the enormous success of *Grand Hotel,* released earlier in the year, by ingeniously substituting the intertwined lives of the denizens of a massive New York City hotel with the intertwined lives of the denizens of a massive New York City office building. Although *Skyscraper Souls* is not in the class of *Grand Hotel,* it is a highly entertaining picture, and in it Warren William gives one of the essential performances of the pre–Code era.

Skyscraper Souls begins with an establishing shot of the massive Dwight Tower looming high over the puny Empire State Building on New York's skyline. It is a painfully obvious metaphor, but one that more than applies to the owner of the structure, David Dwight. His ego, his manhood, his very essence is intertwined with the possession and control of his building and the people around him. Even his personal appearance — upright, rigid, perfectly erect and straight — reinforces the connection between the man and his masculine *raison d'être*. He will do anything to keep his status, consolidate his position and strengthen his grip on power. It is social Darwinism taken to the nth degree.

Like many pre–Code films, *Skyscraper Souls* luxuriates in a lubricious olla podrida of sex, scandal, suicide, adultery and murder. Dwight is happily keeping company with his long-time secretary Sarah Dennis (Verree Teasdale), while his wife maintains a lucrative pipeline to his bank accounts so that she can carry on her own liaisons. Miss Dennis is convinced — foolishly, blindly and dangerously — that her lover will eventually divorce the wife and become hers full-time. In spite of their years of working and loving together, Dwight has no intention of marrying Sarah. He lies to her about asking his wife for a divorce, and we can't help but wonder why someone so intelligent would fail to see that Dwight is only interested in one woman, his building. When a fresh-faced new stenographer named Lynn (Maureen O'Sullivan) comes to his office, it takes Dwight all of thirty seconds to resolve that after all their years together, Sarah must go. He has set his sights on something new and he must have it. There's nothing personal; the same rules apply to business.

With his building in danger of being foreclosed, Dwight conceals the financial problems and cons an old friend named Norton into merging his bank with Dwight's own highly lever-aged interests. He and another business associate then conspire to kite the subsequent stock offering and sell short, bankrupting Norton and his board of directors (each of whom is involved in insider trading). The complete and utter ruin of his friend is an incidental detail: once he has control of the bank, he'll be able to save his building, and that is all that matters. The moment that Dwight resolves to crash the stock, we see only the merest hint of contrition, just a slight furrow of his brow the instant before his predatory instinct takes over. In the end there is no contest. It is the simple choice of nature: kill or be killed.

For Dwight, the moral is in the intent. After he's destroyed his friend and regained control of the building in the illicit stock deal, he delivers a wild, messianic speech about the value of creation over mere capitalism. He justifies his actions because he's leaving something concrete and valuable behind. "That's the difference between a man who makes money for the sake of having money ... and a man like me," he spits at the financier who helped him cheat his partners. Then he scowls and pointedly adds: "You crook." In that moment the audience discovers that Dwight is a man with principles, even if they are twisted and tangled. In his mind, creation justifies the casualties. He rationalizes his actions because he believes that man has a duty to advance, not just survive. The money men, on the other hand, reach into our pockets where we find nothing left behind, and we hate them for it. Depression audiences could understand a man who tried to build, but not the kind of men — swindlers like Charles Ponzi or Ivar Kreuger — who took money from others with nothing compensatory in return. The moral hier-archy is clear: a bastard who cheats for mere greed is an infinitely greater bastard than one who cheats for a practical purpose. Dwight's final act in the drama is to brazenly reveal the identity of his silent partner to Norton and his board of directors, thus moving himself further along a radius away from the center of avarice.

The finale of *Skyscraper Souls*—which I will not describe here—still has the power to shock modern audiences. It is so deliciously cynical that even the acrid taste of an arbitrary and pyretic happy ending is scarcely enough to erase invigorating enjoyment of the sinfully rich meal just consumed. The buffet of vice offered up in *Skyscraper Souls* may not be nutritious, but it certainly is filling.

With the release of his third star vehicle, reviewers and audiences were now beginning to observe Warren as a unique character on the screen, noting that his performances were skewing regularly toward the dark side of the moral scale. He was labeled "Hollywood's Most Dangerous Man" by *Movie Mirror* magazine, and was asked what he thought of the idea. "Oh, I hear occasional rumblings in that region," Warren conceded in his typically humble way, "but don't they call everyone that?"[20] Some were curious as to how and why pictures of this type could be so tawdry and so compelling at the same time. "It is a pity that Warren William was not cast in a role on the other side of the fence," Mordaunt Hall wrote of *The Mouthpiece*. "For many persons will agree with one man who, after seeing this shadow story, said that he regretted to say that he liked it."[21] Phil Scheuer of the *Los Angeles Times* felt *Skyscraper Souls* "guilty of much that is tasteless and ill advised. [There is] an intangible coarseness ... that permeates the entire *mise en scene*, communicating itself to the characters and losing for them the spectator's sympathy." And yet in his next breath he offers: "Mr. William continues to be, for me, an acting phenomenon. I admire his sense of theatre immensely—he is charged with it to a dynamic, almost alarming degree."[22] In the *Washington Post*, Nelson Bill called *Skyscraper Souls* "thoroughly tawdry," and then offered this mouthful: "Warren William has another role no less expository of the suave perfection of his polished histrionics than the character of Vincent Day in *The Mouthpiece*." The influential columnist Louella Parsons called Warren "one of our better villains because you always like him no matter how wicked his role,"[23] and another noted, "Warren William continues to be liked in spite of his depredations on screen."[24] These captious, hard-nosed writers are under the same spell as audiences: the uncanny ability of Warren William to be likable no matter what he did on the screen. If the great silent-era villain Erich von Stroheim was "the man you love to hate," Warren was becoming "the man you hate to love."

For their part, Warner Brothers had the publicity machine running at full speed for their new star. In spite of his general reticence to participate in personal ballyhoo, Warren did believe that he had a responsibility to help the studio whenever possible. Just after *Honor of the Family* opened, he emceed the premiere of *Five Star Final*, introducing the cast (and himself) to the audience at Warner's Western Theatre. His occasional attendance at stage openings, movie premieres and social events was enough to elicit a mention from the local wags, happy as they were to take the low-hanging Warner payola for their trouble. New York was treated to his appearance at the premiere of *Skyscraper Souls* and later that year he and actress Bebe Daniels lit the Christmas tree in the lobby of the Hollywood Theatre. Gradwell Sears, a low-level Warner Brothers executive, proudly proclaimed: "We have never had a player who stepped to the front so rapidly as has Warren William. William's first year has been an exhibition of a player catching the public's fancy."[25] One overeager young publicity hound even planted a story insisting that Warren was becoming a rival for the King of Hollywood, Clark Gable. Gable seemed unconcerned and the rhetoric was ever so slightly dialed down.

Just before *Skyscraper Souls* wrapped, Warner Brothers agreed to loan William to Paramount for Rouben Mamoulian's *The Song of Songs*, starring Marlene Dietrich. He likely would have played the second lead eventually taken by Lionel Atwill, as the wealthy reprobate who marries Dietrich even though she is in love with Brian Aherne. The loan-out was never consummated. One can only wonder what Warren would have done under the meticulous direction of Mamoulian, far away from the headlong rush of the Warner machine.

Warner Brothers sent Warren and Bette Davis out on a five-city tour to promote the July 2 release of *The Dark Horse*. During late July he and his reluctant companion trouped through cities in the east, including Warren's first trip back to New York since he left the cast of *The Vinegar Tree* early in 1931. Stories in many Davis biographies indicate there was more friction between them on the junket, but none offer attribution or context. They performed a specially written short stage drama, made easier for the fact that both had a theatrical background. In Washington, DC, they performed at Warner Brothers' Earle Theatre and Warren had the chance to see thousands of his fellow veterans of the World War as they gathered near the capitol to petition the government for early payment of the deferred War Bonuses that Congress had authorized in 1925. Warren, a proud veteran of the AEF, sympathized with his fellow soldiers who were enduring unprecedented hard times. That week Congress denied the Bonus Army their funds and Herbert Hoover ordered the U.S. Army to forcibly remove the remaining protestors who were living in makeshift camps near the Capitol. On July 28 the troops moved in, firing tear gas and driving American men, women and children off Pennsylvania Avenue with horses and truncheons. That night Warren could look out from his hotel and see the Washington sky glowing with fire from the burning of the Hoovervilles and shanty-towns. The tour moved on, but the sergeant from Minnesota's proud 34th Infantry could hardly avoid being disillusioned by his government's uncaring response to the plight of his fellow vets.

When Davis and William returned from the *Dark Horse* tour, Warner Brothers again teamed the pair when they assigned Warren to a meaningless role in *Three on a Match*, a project designed to feature a trio of the studio's up-and-coming actresses, Ann Dvorak, Joan Blondell and Davis. Here again the actor fulfills his secondary screen construct as the ineffectual husband who is thrown over when his wife descends into drugs and illicit sex. According to his professional nature, Warren accepted this insignificant part, one which almost certainly undermined his burgeoning star image, without complaint. Although he would have been better off to advocate for roles befitting his talent and status, he maintained his passionate lack of interest in self-promotion. His overriding personal modesty was a defining characteristic that he could never overcome. Helen, on the other hand, was immediately dismayed that her husband was being reduced to a mere studio prop. A *Washington Post* critic might as well have written what Helen was feeling for her husband on the film's release: "Warren William ... finds himself called upon to confront what amounts to an empty zero in opportunity."[26] Try as she might over the years, Helen could never convince him to fight for his own career. Even when Warren knew that a role was not to his benefit, he preferred harmony to strife and this intransigence eventually contributed to the public's indifference to him as a star. But those days were well out on the horizon and for now he continued to ride high as one of the top-ranking stars in filmdom.

Although maligned at the time as "tedious and distasteful," *Three on a Match* stands as one of the starkest of pre–Code pictures, and boasts a genuinely menacing Humphrey Bogart in his first role as a gangster on film. Director Mervyn LeRoy is really the hero of the production, however, pulling no punches as he delves into a squalid little world of narcotics and sex. His quiet observation of the disintegration of a marriage is a wonder of economy, in marvelous contrast to the unblinking camera eye that follows Ann Dvorak's suicidal ten-story plunge from a hotel window. He even found time for humor in his character shorthand, introducing gambling boss Edward Arnold through a close-up (shot in a magnifying mirror) as he plucks his nose hairs. Critics of 1932 may have been put off by it all, but LeRoy's uncompromising realism has allowed the picture to stand the test of time.

The title *Three on a Match* hailed from a common superstition at the time, that it was bad luck to light three cigarettes on the same match. Coincidentally, the man who supposedly coined the phrase became the subject of Warren's next assignment. Ivar Kreuger, known as "The Match King," was the next quacksalver to ooze from the actor's cast of characters.

Intermission: The Match King

If there were any mortal man who embodied the vulgar excesses of Warren William's pre–Code persona, it was the Swedish industrialist Ivar Kreuger. "The Match King," as he came to be known, was no ordinary businessman; during his heyday, he controlled an empire valued today at 100 billion dollars, and during the depths of the Depression he loaned the governments of Europe millions to save economies which were then in shambles. Unfortunately, for the people who placed their hope and faith in this titan of finance, it was all a sham; smoke and mirrors. The Great Depression knew no boundaries, brooked no excuses and had no pity; thousands were stripped of their life savings, honor and reputation through his machinations. But unlike a Hollywood movie there was no last-reel salvation or even honest repentance on Kreuger's part, just a self-inflicted 9mm hole through his heart and a tangle of stock swindles, ruined lives and worldwide incredulity.

Kreuger's life had been incendiary and short-lived, much like the matches he used to control an empire that had stretched across Europe and America. Before the stock market crash of 1929, he had cornered the global market in matches. One ingenious scheme to boost the sales of his product involved the worldwide dissemination of a simple superstition: that lighting three cigarettes on one match was bad luck for the final smoker. Kreuger calculated that the phrase "three on a match" translated into millions for his empire. But his larceny far exceeded mere ballyhoo. In 1932, Kreuger's apparent ownership of the Swedish telecom giant Ericsson was thrown into question through circumstances that necessitated he repay an eleven million dollar loan. The man who supposedly controlled Ericsson and 200 other companies with hundreds of millions of dollars in assets could not raise the modest sum: his empire was an empty shell of pyramid schemes, worthless investments and phantom accounts. On March 12, just ten days after his fifty-second birthday, Kreuger retreated to his Paris apartment and contemplated the situation. It was inevitable now that the world would discover his Machiavellian swindles. The man who had been deified throughout the continent as a savior of the world economy fingered his 9mm Browning pistol, then shot himself through the heart, leaving the world to absorb the financial fallout and pass legislation that would supposedly stop it from ever happening again.

It was a fortuitous happenstance that the unrepentant, conniving Warren William had been created just in time to play *locum tenens* for Kreuger. Following an investigation into the circumstances behind his death in 1932, no less a source than *The Economist* dubbed him "The World's Greatest Swindler." For the actor who had already conned, defrauded and scammed his way through a series of pictures, nothing could have been more appropriate. By the end of 1932, Warner Brothers had *The Match King* in its theaters, and William added another unregenerate mountebank to his *oeuvre.*

By the time World War II obliterated standard lines of trade, finance and business, Kreuger was already forgotten. There were far bigger problems, personalities and horrors to contemplate. In the new decade of the 1940s, the American character was looking forward, not back. Although criminals and hustlers are still occasionally embraced as folk heroes, they have most often been mythologized as iconic individualists, or as eccentric visionaries. John Dillinger and P.T. Barnum spring to mind. Kreuger was rightly seen as the driver of an economic machine designed to prey on the average man, and as a result engendered no grudging respect or curiosity, merely contempt.

It is extremely unfortunate that Ivar Kreuger's crimes were ground down to mere anecdote over time. Those who do not remember history, the saying goes, are condemned to repeat it — as the names Jeff Skilling, Ken Lay and Bernie Madoff, soon to be forgotten themselves, no doubt — so abundantly prove.

Following Kreuger's death, everyone in Hollywood wanted the story behind the century's greatest swindler. Greta Garbo, one of Kreuger's Swedish compatriots and a short-lived companion, temporarily toyed with the idea of purchasing rights to his life story and producing the film with MGM. While Garbo was visiting Sweden that summer, Warner Brothers secured the rights to Einar Thorvaldson's novel *The Match King* and moved quickly to develop a screenplay. On August 8 they had a first draft, and that week Jack Warner corresponded with Garbo via cablegram about her possible participation in the film they were preparing.[27] The studio also floated the rumor that if Garbo were to accept the part, Warren would travel to Sweden to shoot his scenes with her. But there was very little chance of that. Garbo had recently signed a lucrative contract with MGM for $250,000 per picture,[28] a figure that was almost double the entire production budget of *The Match King*.[29] The notoriously penurious studio head had no intention of paying that kind of salary for an actor, but happily scammed some free publicity for the project, and Warner Brothers quietly began looking for an appropriately continental replacement for the great Swedish star.

The Match King began shooting on August 22, 1932, with French-born actress Lili Damita — the future former Mrs. Errol Flynn — essentially playing Greta Garbo to Warren's entirely undisguised stand-in for Kreuger, Paul Kroll. Shooting took 33 days and the finished product made it to theaters before the end of the year, premiering in early December.

The Match King starts with an unusual pre-credits montage sequence detailing the importance of the humble matchstick. From an opium den in China to a condemned man's final cigarette on Death Row, matches are seen to light, warm, nourish and protect the world. In Chicago we meet a man who understands the unparalleled value of this inexpensive commodity. Paul Kroll is a simple custodian at baseball's Wrigley Field, but he is also ambitious, conniving and sly. On the job he hatches a scheme to get each of the members of his five-man maintenance crew an unauthorized day off by everyone agreeing to pick up the slack for the periodic missing man. He confidently tells his skittish co-workers: "Don't worry about anything until it happens — and I'll take care of it then." Of course he doesn't wait for something to happen, but rather blows the whistle on the first man who takes advantage of the scam. After his boss fires the shirker, Kroll convinces him to keep the man on the books so that *they* can split the extra salary. In short order they have four ghost payrollers and Kroll is also payrolling the boss' wife on the side. When a cable arrives from distant relatives in Sweden looking for help from their "highly successful" nephew, he steals the fake payroll account, uses, then throws away the wife and heads for Sweden.

Overseas, where Kroll bluffs his way into taking over the family match manufacturing business, he has plenty of opportunity to fulfill the promise of his personal motto: "Don't worry about anything until it happens — and I'll take care of it then." His pitiless rise to power is the greatest sustained carnival of larceny in any pre–Code picture, starring Warren William or not. He cleverly amasses bank loans worth hundreds of millions of dollars, leveraging them

The Match King was based on the career of Ivar Kreuger, one of the greatest swindlers of the early 20th century. Having already scammed his way through *The Mouthpiece, The Dark Horse* and *Skyscraper Souls,* Warren William was a natural for the role of Paul Kroll, the ultimate con man.

against company stocks that are nearly worthless. He uses his loyal and caring lovers as carnal spies, manipulating them into sordid trysts with competitors, degrading them until they are used up and tossed away. When he is told of an elderly inventor who has created an eternal match — one which can be lit thousands of times without fail — the look on his face calls to mind a vegetarian visiting an abattoir. He takes an evening to consider an appropriate course of action, then has the old man declared insane, cast into an asylum and placed in solitary confinement as in *The Man in the Iron Mask.* Even murder is not a bridge too far: after he buys fifty million dollars in phony government bonds to barter himself out of ruin, he disposes of the forger by drowning him in a lake. Kroll is the world's greatest sociopath, interested in no one but himself; even his affair with Marta Molnar (Damita) is predicated on his single-minded obsession that he must have her, rather than any real feelings for her as a person. As in *The Mouthpiece* and *Skyscraper Souls,* however, Kroll pays for his transgressions. His poetic demise, lying flecked with matches after falling from his balcony with a bullet through his heart, is a moral balancing of the scales but not an admission of guilt. Before his suicide, Kroll reviews the ugly events of his life but he does not repent, and he does nothing to save his loyal and innocent friend Erik, caught up in the machinations of his evil empire. Death is simply the easiest way to avoid the degrading hell of prison. In this sense the script follows Ivar

Kreuger's last days—self-pity, humiliation and anger, but no remorse. Those things are for lesser men, not for those who are above the law.

The Match King offers Warren one of his great roles, and allows him a characterization that few actors could safely tackle. He begins as a seedy, insignificant little man, not much more than a cheap hustler, and plays it with a subtle body language that testifies to the tawdriness of his character. By the time he's become "The Match King," all vestiges of the petty, parochial crook are gone, replaced by a self-assured, Continental businessman. His grandiloquent pronouncements roll from Warren's lips with absurd confidence: "I'm going to sell matches to *the world*. And with them, I'm going to *buy* the world." With the exception of— forgive me—John Barrymore, no other actor of the era could pull off such operatic theatricality.[30]

Critics were divided about the film, complaining of a disjointed, episodic quality, and of too much emphasis on the business aspects of the story. But again Warren was lauded for performing beyond the limitations of the script. "Warren William is the perfect article as Paul Kroll. He makes *The Match King* an entirely credible and a completely, repellently fascinating person," was the opinion of the *Chicago Tribune*. "He's expressive from his head to his toes."[31] Norbert Lusk found the film entirely unconvincing, but noted: "Warren William plays with his accustomed smoothness. The failure of the picture cannot be attributed to him."[32] The public didn't seem to agree that the picture was a failure. *The Match King* performed well, receiving an honorable mention in a list of the top box office performers for 1933.

At the time of shooting *The Match King*, Hollywood was continuing to grapple with the enervating effects of the Depression. Studios were looking for cost-cutting measures, and Warners decided that the stars should take some of the burden. In August, United Press revealed the salaries and reductions that the Warner Brothers stable were expected to take. According to the article, William Powell was at the top of the salary list at $6,000 a week, expected to be reduced to $4,000, while Warren was listed at $1,250 weekly, to be chopped to $1,000.[33] UPI was not entirely reliable in their sources. On August 6, Warren was still making $1,100 a week as per the second renewal of his contractual option, and whether as a result of his refusal or the threat of a massive walkout of contract players, there was no reduction.[34] The next move on the studio's part to tighten their belts came early in 1933 and inadvertently resulted in a very lucrative change in Warren's contract.

Following *The Match King*, Warren was again obliged to work with Bette Davis when they appeared together in a short promotional film for General Electric. *Just Around the Corner* was nonsense about a newlywed couple inviting their boss (Warren) home, and impressing him with their modern appliances. None of the Warner stars enlisted to this deal were happy, least of all Davis, the prissy, easily offended hothouse flower, but things were relatively quiet and the pair soldiered through. After shooting was finished, Warren was so disgusted about the assignment that he sent a letter to Warner Brothers demanding that the film "never be shown to a paying audience." Although the studio refused, Warren needn't have worried. Nobody would pay to see such cheap ballyhoo.

It was now October and Warren had been working almost continuously since late May. The studio kept him going at an exhausting pace, building his audience profile and continuing to turn out product for the studio machine. The Warner Brothers lot during the early 1930s was essentially an assembly line sweatshop for movies, with highly paid indentured servants working at the whim of the corporation. The studio left no idle time for their stars during the forty weeks a year they were on salary. Warren's original contract with the studio specifically called for a minimum of "six films per year as a featured player, or five as star," and they regularly exceeded that minimum. In 1932 Warren completed seven movies, one short subject and was sent on a two-week promotional tour. He was busier than his contemporaries James Cagney and Edward G. Robinson, who had already begun to raise a ruckus over long hours and stockyard conditions. Among the few who were busier was Joan Blondell, the supremely perky girl next door who teamed with Warren three times during their tenure on the Burbank lot. "We helped each other at Warners," she said. "We were always on time and there were no star complexes or temperament. We seldom said hello or goodbye — it was just a continuation. We were a very close group."[35] Straight from finishing *The Match King* on September 25, Warren went to his sixth production of the year, the pre–Code classic *Employees' Entrance.*

Although 1933 and 1934 might have been more financially and artistically successful for Warren, 1932 is the year that modern audiences—those who are aware of his career—love him for. Beginning on January 18 with the first shots of *The Mouthpiece* and continuing through the year-end schedule of *The Mind Reader,* he made seven incredible pre–Code gems: wry, caustic, bawdy, risqué films that still have the sting to excite audiences 75 years later. It was like a deliciously sleazy version of Albert Einstein's three great theories of 1905 or the Babe Ruth homerun hitting machine of 1927 — a moment when everything aligned in perfect, sordid order. The next year would begin a softening of his image, but for now he was Hollywood's unquestioned king of vile thought, ignoble action and supercilious attitude. "Do you think they'll ever permit Warren William to be a good boy again?" asked Mae Tinee on the opening of *Employees' Entrance.* "I doubt it!"

The story of *Employees' Entrance* is simple: Kurt Anderson (Warren) is the obsessive, tyrannical, and uncompromising director of the gigantic Franklin Monroe department store. He hates inefficiency. If his workers can't keep up, they're ceremoniously terminated with a wave of his hand and a bellow: "*Get out!*" When a vendor is a day late on his contract, Anderson ruins him by canceling the contract and suing him. The only thing the autocratic executive hates more than inefficiency is women, who he believes are a fatal diversion to a man's work ethic. He isn't above using women as sexual toys, however; he makes a conquest of a down-and-out girl named Madeline (Loretta Young) with the bait of a job, which he then dangles over her head to keep her "available." After a short time she winds up secretly married to Anderson's right hand man Martin West (Wallace Ford). West is a go-getter who wants to make good and Anderson needs a protégé he can mold in his image. The two men bond in their desire for success, with Anderson unaware that West is already compromised by marriage. Since this is a Warner Brothers picture, it all will most certainly unravel just in time for the final reel.

Kurt Anderson is a direct descendant of David Dwight of *Skyscraper Souls.* On the surface Dwight and Anderson are each consummate bastards. However, this surface merely serves to conceal the *true* men hidden beneath: base, arrogant, remorseless, consummate bastards. Like David Dwight, Anderson is also a doer — a man who believes in hard work and dedication to the job. In his world there is no other way to succeed, with the Depression turning people's pockets inside out and thousands of his employees fighting for their lives. The pair are social Darwinists through and through; they believe that to slow down is to die, and their creed, in Anderson's words, is "smash, or be smashed." And yet, in spite of their high positions, haughty attitude and cavalier treatment of their employees, audiences identify with them because they are ultimately champions of the working man.

It was never more apparent than during the Great Depression that the vast majority of Americans saw that society was divided into two classes: those who have money, and those who work. Although powerless to do anything about it (except organize unions, which they

Behind the scenes on the set of *Employees' Entrance*, Warren goes over Robert Presnell's script with Alice White. Behind them is the model of the building that houses the massive Franklin Monroe department store, where the action of the film takes place.

did in increasing numbers), workers saw themselves as the tools of money: the bankers, investors and tycoons who benefited from their labor and were responsible for the collapse of the system the two sides had built together. Anderson and Dwight have audience sympathy because they identify themselves as workers—men who came from nothing to carve out a position in the towers of business by dint of honest labor and who take pride in it. Their work defines them. When the board of directors insists that Kurt Anderson purge hundreds of workers from the department store payroll so they can keep profits up, he speaks the truth as millions of Americans saw it. "You bankers make me sick! You don't know how to run your own business and you want to tell everyone else how to run theirs. You're a banker, not a producer. You haven't done a thing to deserve one penny of profits this business has put into your pockets. You couldn't go out and earn a nickel." It is also no random chance that the men who are portrayed as the villains of *Employees' Entrance* are senior citizens—bastions of old money. The clear message is that old money is dead money; it stays within the gravity of those inert bodies and does not circulate outside their system, where so many could use it. Anderson and Dwight want to use that money for something other than just to make more of it. They are trying to hold together some semblance of stability in a rapidly decaying society. Anderson sees himself as the last defense against anarchy, and he treats every decision that affects his store and employees with a martial attitude, something Warren William understood from his war years as a tough, uncompromising top sergeant. "Every experience in life helps an actor in the portrayal of the characters he represents," he observed when the film was finished. "And nothing could have fitted me for this part as well as Army life. No one has to be meaner, or tougher, to accomplish things than a top sergeant, unless, perhaps, it's a mule skinner. I felt right at home in the picture."[36] That heartless sergeant whose ultimate job is to insure the survival of his soldiers is seen again and again in *Employees' Entrance*. When an old man commits suicide after he's been fired, Anderson deadpans: "When a man outlives his usefulness, he *should* jump out a window. This is war, you understand? *War!* He's just one of the casualties." The men and women of the Depression knew that it was exactly that — survival of the fittest — because they lived it every day.

Employees' Entrance is not all downbeat, dour and depressing. Like most of Warren's other pre–Code vehicles, it brims with invention and humor. The juxtaposition of Anderson's intense seriousness against absurd situations made for some excellent business, as when he tests out a children's frog jumping toy, or regards Alice White's tiny Pekingese before depositing it in a waste basket. And it contains more than a few priceless *bons mots*, including Warren's confused response when his former *fille du jour*, Polly (White), arrives at the office: "Oh, it's you. I didn't know you with all your clothes on."

But the humor was not what critics were looking at when it was released in January of 1933. They saw again the tough, uncompromising cad that Warren was becoming widely known for. "Warren William is at some risk of being typed, becoming noted for his characterizations of the ruthless businessman."[37] "Admire the man, you will not," the *LA Times* insisted. "Admire the characterization, which deviates not one whit from the outline set forth at the opening of the picture, you must. It is a fine example of forceful, expressive acting. It is a consistent, carefully etched portrait of an interesting if unbelievable man."[38] The *Hartford Courant* compared Warren to James Cagney, lauding the duo as "two of the most forceful personalities in pictures today," while simultaneously observing something else entirely fascinating. Although we tend to think of the pre–Code era as a land rush of unpunished larceny, the truth is that a personal moral code — as well as a published, semi-binding one — was in play in Hollywood. Whether by design or by edict, most of Warren's famous rogues have a moral comeuppance: by the conclusion of

Skyscraper Souls, The Mouthpiece, The Match King and the soon to be released *The Mind Reader*, each is either dead or in prison. But not Kurt Anderson. "In the ordinary film, Mr. William would sooner or later be overtaken by the same kind of unhappy fate that he has dealt out so mercilessly to those in his power," the *Courant* noted. "But *Employees' Entrance* is not that kind of picture. It sticks closer to the facts of life as it is, and the conclusion of the picture finds Mr. William carrying on just as belligerently as ever."[39] Indeed, Kurt Anderson survives even after he has driven one man to suicide and willfully molested an inebriated Loretta Young (who likewise attempts suicide). It makes the film the *ne plus ultra* of the Warren William pre–Codes—uncompromising and undiluted.

It would be remiss to discuss *Employees' Entrance* without noting the brazen streak of misogyny that permeates the script by Robert Presnell. There is a minor intimation of homosexual bonding between Anderson and his assistant ("Don't you ... *like* women?" West timidly asks). But there is nothing so arcane in his design; Anderson simply hates the female gender and what they do to men. His attitude is like a much-jilted suitor who works out his sexual frustration through cheap liaisons and outbursts of corrosive anger. "Love? It's all a lotta hooey!" he tells Martin in an effort to dissuade him from the diluting effects of marriage. "A wife makes a slave of you!"

In Anderson's world, women are merely tools. Without a hint of conscience he whores out his old flame Polly to spy on a store executive, and when she starts blackmailing him, said executive comes to Anderson, pleading for advice. "Why don't you kill her?" he suggests, only half-joking. After Madeline puts off Anderson's advances, he bellows: "What do you want me to do, marry you? Bunk! When you dames get your claws in a man, you don't let go until you've dragged him to some altar and ruined his life!" And when he finds Madeline alone at a company party, he takes advantage of her drunken state to get her into bed once more. He's delighted when it nearly breaks up her marriage to Martin, furious as he is that his assistant is being "ruined" by her. Later, after he's exposed her to Martin as a cheater, he venomously lashes out at her: "That's what you call love. You women make me sick!" Unlike Warren's other cads, this man doesn't seduce women because he desires them; he does it because he hates them. In another life, Kurt Anderson could have been Ted Bundy. After all his years on stage supporting strong women, *Employees' Entrance* is undoubtedly the professional nadir of Warren's relationship with them. The only place to go from here is up.

When *Employees' Entrance* wrapped in late October, the Krechs took a jaunt on the S.S. *Santa Teresa*, down the coast of Baja California to Mazatlan on the Pacific Coast of Mexico. A few days of sun and relaxation were in order. The North Pacific and points south were an adventure land to the young Warren Krech, still residing within the nationally famous film star. From his earliest days reading literature of the sea, he was intrigued by the idea of roaming those great expanses, seeing the exotic locales and meeting the peoples of those far-off places. It was just at this time that Warren was contemplating a trip much further south, to Tahiti—smack dab in the middle of the South Pacific, 3,000 miles from both the United States and Australia. "I have a friend who has been trying to persuade me for months to go with him to Papeete and the South Sea Islands," Warren giddily revealed. "He's a friend of Victor Berge [author of the novel *The Pearl Diver*], who knows the South Seas as probably no other white man today knows them. My friend wants me to go down there and spend some weeks with Berge. He promises plenty of excitement." It is presumed that the trip—proposed by a man who once captured both a shark and an octopus, then released them into a fresh water lagoon to watch them fight to the death—would not include Mrs. Krech. Warren's boss Jack Warner would have been apoplectic at the idea of his star sailing off to a speck of land in the middle of the vast South Pacific, and Helen was positively *not* going to put up with it. In this situation she was the octopus and Warren, the shark. The octopus prevailed and the shark never made it out of that lagoon alive.

In November, the New Deal President Franklin Roosevelt was elected in a landslide over the incumbent Herbert Hoover. As a longstanding Republican (although the voter registration roll of 1932 indicates that he "declined to state" his affiliation), Warren did not support Roosevelt. In future elections, Warren invariably backed the Republican cause, including loyal support of Al Smith, whom he claimed to "greatly admire." But Roosevelt would soon bring a new charisma and confidence to the office, something America desperately needed as the economy continued to sag going into the New Year.

Warren's career year of 1932 ended with his final truly outstanding pre–Code gem, *The Mind Reader*. The film concerns the occult con artistry of Chandra the Great (Warren). No ambiguity here, folks—just plain, old-fashioned fleece-the-hayseed bunco. The film was co-written by a former associate of Harry Houdini, Wilson Mizner, who helped the great escape artist to debunk fraudulent psychics (are there any other kind?) during the 1910s and '20s.[40] Mizner's interest in fraud extended beyond merely the esoteric. In New York he promoted fixed boxing matches, and was a friend of the great middleweight champion Stanley Ketchel, later murdered over breakfast by the irate husband of his morning companion. At age 29 Mizner famously married an heiress who was 51 years his senior. Most notably, he had a hand in engineering the artificial Great Florida Land Boom (and subsequent genuine Great Florida Land Bust) of the 1920s; the dangerous legal fallout sent him from Florida to Hollywood.[41]

As a look into the world of parlor spiritualists *The Mind Reader* is a tepid exposé, concerned more with the lies and deception between Chandra and his assistant (and later wife) Sylvia. The film is primarily noteworthy for the abject cheapness of its leading character. Chandra is a petty, common huckster, unworthy of the grandiloquent, preening charlatans who came before him. But this very quality—coarseness—is somehow a compelling character trait in the hands of Warren and Roy Del Ruth. When Chandra momentarily retires to the stultifying life of a Fuller Brush salesman, we feel genuine sympathy for him. Not just because Chandra has been consigned to a profession that anyone would abandon in favor of bunco, but because a man of his inspirational baseness is being wasted on the straight and narrow. Warren is at his best crooked— and, to paraphrase the great boxing trainer Cus D'Amato—"a guy born crooked don't die straight." Sitting on the sidelines while there are yokels yet to be clipped is just unacceptable.

Like most other of Warren's pre–Code characters, Chandra is not primarily interested in wealth or what it can bring. He does not cheat to amass a fortune, but rather to survive. He and his assistant Frank (Allen Jenkins) attempt various tried-and-true methods to grift enough cash to make a living: painless dentistry, hair tonic for Southern blacks, and a stint trying to interest an audience in watching Jenkins set a world's record for flagpole sitting. (When it fails, Warren moans: "We're a bust. If the whole population was lyin' on its back, it wouldn't look up at you.") It isn't until they see a traveling mystic raking in the dough that "Chandra" is born. And once they're successful, their circumstances don't change significantly, except that they now have money to drink, play dice and periodically bet on horses. The boys do not wave it in anyone's face. They simply don't have to *worry* about money, something that would have thrilled most Depression era families.

Critics were lukewarm about *The Mind Reader*. Some complained of a danger of typecasting in William's performances, but most agreed that he was still the best thing about the picture. "*The Mind Reader* hands [Warren William] an opportunity to prove versatile, and he fulfills all the great expectations of his rooters," enthused the *Chicago Tribune*.[42]

By the time *The Mind Reader* wrapped shooting, 1933 had begun. Once again Warren was at liberty to celebrate his wedding anniversary, now marking ten years of May-December happiness with Helen. As spectacular as the previous year had been, 1933 would be better still. During the next twelve months Warren would appear in two of his greatest successes and bask in the reflected glow of headlining an Oscar-nominated film. But first, the moribund American economy would deliver Warren a new manager, a more lucrative studio contract, and a legal battle that lasted four long years.

Just a week after his anniversary, Warren was the best man at the wedding of his close friend Alan Dinehart. The two came up together in New York and made their way to Hollywood within six months of each other. The friends were similar in many ways. The modest groom hosted the wedding in his Los Angeles home, and when it came time for the ceremony, Dinehart and his bride quietly retired to another room, followed by the best man, maid of honor, and the groom's mother. Before anyone else in the house knew it, the deed was done and the couple re-emerged as man and wife.

In February, Warren and a superb cast of Warner Brothers regulars began shooting the classic musical *Gold Diggers of 1933*. That season was a tumultuous time for America. The national economy was still in shambles and getting worse all the time. The governors of Michigan and Maryland declared statewide bank holidays, and more were expected to follow suit. World markets for loans, business capital and stocks were frozen and panic had set in among small investors and depositors. So much money was being withdrawn from American banks that armored cars were in constant motion, bringing cash to institutions whose resources were dwindling.[43] On February 15, Franklin Roosevelt was nearly assassinated in Florida; the mayor of Chicago, Anton Cermak, sitting in the car beside him, died from gunshots meant for the president elect. The next day, the Senate voted to repeal Prohibition. In Germany, the Reichstag burned and Adolf Hitler took supreme power over his government. Amidst all this, Roosevelt was getting ready to take office on Inauguration Day, March 4. One can only imagine the carnivorous coverage the events would have spawned in the era of instant communication and the 24-hour news cycle.

At the beginning of March, Warner Brothers chartered a train that they called the "*42nd Street Special*" and stocked it with stars who would cross the country to attend the inauguration. Oh, and while they were at it, they would also promote the release of Warners' new film *42nd Street*. On March 5, the day after the new president took office, he issued a proclamation for a national bank holiday. Across the country banks would close for one week, giving officials time to institute new regulations and quell the panic that was building in the public. This maneuver by Franklin Roosevelt unwittingly gave Warren the leverage to pry more money from a new Warner Brothers contract.

When the bank holiday went into effect, Hollywood got scared. No one could be certain what would happen. On his last day in office, economic advisors had told Herbert Hoover plainly that the U.S. banking system had stopped functioning. The major studios immediately conferred and, in an effort to survive the crisis, proposed a general waiver of one-half salary to their employees, including every star on every lot. With the unprecedented conditions then in play, the Academy of Motion Picture Arts and Sciences acceded to the plan and issued an Emergency Bulletin, agreeing to reduced pay for AMPAS members for an eight-week period from March 6 to April 30. Warren signed his agreement on March 14, and his salary was cut from $1,200 to $600 with the check dated March 11. Banks did indeed reopen the following Monday, and the system began to stabilize.

Quickly, a dispute arose within the emergency committee of the Academy. Once the banks

When Warner Brothers announced *42nd Street* in 1933, Warren William (right) was supposed to be among the cast. He never made it into the film, but later that year he headlined the studio's other iconic musical, *Gold Diggers of 1933.* He is seen here outside the Warner lot with Dick Powell (left) and an unidentified onlooker.

reopened, the outlook was far better than expected; confidence returned almost immediately and there was no general panic to withdraw money. Seeing this, the Academy felt that they might have been hasty in their agreement to the salary reduction and issued another bulletin claiming that money withheld under the waiver would now have to be paid by the studios. In comparison to many other Warner Brothers stars, Warren was severely underpaid. At the beginning of April, his contract extension kicked in, raising him to $1,300 a week, but he was still well below where a performer of his caliber should be. On *Gold Diggers of 1933* (shot mostly in February and March) Warren received top billing, but he was not the best-paid member of the cast — Ginger Rogers ($2,000) and character actor Ned Sparks ($1,250) were receiving more. With his representative from William Morris, Warren decided to use the opportunity to make an effort to break his contract with Warner Brothers and start again. After taking a voluntary reduction in his contract prior to his success with *The Mouthpiece,* he felt entirely justified in attempting to recoup some of the income that he had given away.[44]

After a conference with the William Morris people, Warren decided on a course of action. His attorney drafted a letter to Warner Brothers dated April 18, stating that since the studio had not abided by the terms of the revised Emergency Bulletin to pay back salaries, the waiver he had signed was null and void. Further, they demanded the immediate payment of back wages, which now amounted to $3,750. Foolishly, Warners sent the full sum only dating from April 10, and Warren began to worry that William Morris—and more specifically Ben Boyar, his New York agent—were not putting proper emphasis on his case. He set out to find someone new to agitate on his behalf.[45]

During the entire fiasco Warren was working double duty at the Burbank studio, simultaneously filming his limited part in *Gold Diggers* and starting work on *Goodbye Again* (then known as *Always Goodbye*) with director Michael Curtiz. Warner Brothers was planning a complete work stoppage in April but postponed the halt in production until both films could be completed. When they wrapped, Warren used his vacation time to find another attorney and a knowledgeable local agent. The new attorney, Austin Sherman, referred Warren to Michael (M.C.) Levee, a powerful figure in films during the 1920s, who had recently opened an agency to represent actors. Starting in Hollywood as a prop man, Levee worked his way up through various studios as assistant superintendent, business manager, production manager and eventually as president of his own concern, United Studios. He also helped found the Academy of Motion Picture Arts and Sciences, and had recently stepped down as the third president of the organization to start the M.C. Levee Agency. With his connections and a reputation as a fair and honest man, he quickly assembled a superb roster of clients, including Mary Pickford, Joan Crawford, Bette Davis, Paul Muni, Cecil B. DeMille and Leslie Howard, Warren's great friend from *Out of a Blue Sky* on Broadway. Mike Levee was a perfect fit for the low-key actor from Minnesota: forthright, plain-spoken and genuine. Levee was engaged as Warren's new agent and the two men became lifelong friends as well as business associates.

This is just one of many formal portraits that Warren took with his surrogate children, wirehaired terriers Jack and Jill. The caption reads: "Jack and Jill say 'hello' to Betty and Bobby Lyon with Uncle Woogie." Warren's wife Helen gave him the nickname "Woog" when they were dating. Courtesy Barbara Hall.

In the meantime, Warner Brothers consummated a deal with Columbia Pictures for Warren to be loaned out for Frank Capra's new project, *Lady for a Day* (then known as *Apple Annie*), set to begin shooting on May 10. On May 1 he was advised in writing that when he returned from vacation he would go directly to work for Columbia on *Lady for a Day*. Warren's new police dog Mike Levee saw an opening and pounced. The next day he sent Warner Brothers a correspondence demanding payment of the actor's remaining back salary in full by May 6 or they would consider his contract void and refuse to honor the loanout. Having made a complicated deal to loan Warren, Guy Kibbee and Glenda Farrell to Columbia in place of the previously promised Loretta Young, Warners executives needed to make sure this embargo didn't scuttle their production schedule. In an effort to salvage the Columbia deal, they tried to offer a compromise: If William would go to work on the Capra picture, they allowed that it would "in no matter prejudice your rights to contend that your contract ... has been terminated."[46] Again Mike Levee and Warren refused to budge. When May 6 came and went with no payment of back salary, the agent advised the studio that his client was no longer bound to them, and would refuse to work. With the Columbia production starting on the 10th, he then asked if they would like to negotiate a new contract. They had little choice; Jack Warner's own intransigence gave Warren the leverage to beat them at their own game. If the studio had simply paid the back salary in a timely fashion, they could have kept one of their biggest stars on the meager salary from his original contract, but now they would have to accede to his demands.

Mike Levee, Austin Sherman, Roy Obringer and Jack Warner set up a conference at the Columbia studio on May 9, working late into the night to have a contract that would satisfy everyone and be executed in time to keep Frank Capra's shooting schedule intact. During the session, Levee begged Jack Warner to put Warren in more prestigious films with larger budgets and longer schedules. Although 1932 had been a good year for him, most of the films had not been true "A" vehicles, but quick, economical "A-minus" or "B-plus" efforts. Jack Warner personally "promised faithfully" that he would see to it that Warren was given "a few excellent parts" during the year.[47] Quite the opposite was the case; Warren's three biggest films during the rest of his contract were all made outside Warner Brothers. After a marathon barter session, the document was signed just before midnight, allowing Warren a significant boost in salary, from $1,300 to $1,750 a week, and with much larger annual increases than before. It likely rankled Jack Warner no end.[48]

That evening, just hours before the new contract was inked, a telegram went out to Ben Boyar, Warren's agent in New York. The tersely worded cable could not have been more plain: "I have not secured representation by you while in California and as our agreement has expired I no longer want you to represent me or act on my behalf."[49] Boyar was incensed. His original 1931 agreement with Warren explicitly stated that he would continue to receive a percentage of the actor's salary as long as his studio contract was renewed or renegotiated. But Levee was an astute businessman who had made sure that the old Warner Brothers contract was not merely renegotiated, but rather voided and replaced by an entirely new document. Boyar, of course, could not take the situation lying down. He quickly asserted his rights by filing a lawsuit in California. The action took over a year to navigate the courts, and on July 28, 1934, it was decided in the actor's favor. Undaunted, Boyar filed an appeal that dragged on a further three and a half years, ending in November of 1937, with the same result. Warren was free of his useless, long distance agent, and recovered court costs from him to boot.

Change was the watchword for Warren in 1933. In addition to his contract and representation, Warner Brothers began to tinker with his screen persona, allowing for a greater dimension in his performances, but curtailing the roles he'd become known for. Following *The Mind Reader*, the sleazy, disreputable Warren William was nearly gone. Only *Bedside*, released early in 1934, remains as one of his unmistakably iconic pre–Code performances.

First Warren had a nifty little comedy part in Warners' outstanding follow up to *42nd Street, Gold Diggers of 1933* (completed before his new contract was negotiated). He played a staid New York banker — a type he knew very well from dealings with his Uncle Alvin — who tries to break up the romance of his kid brother (Dick Powell) with a dancer (Ruby Keeler), but winds up falling for a "low woman" of his own (Joan Blondell). Oddly, the story was not seriously removed from Warren's own experience with his family's reaction to Helen, and the escapade where Alvin — the wealthy banker — tried to convince him to remain single by offering him a spot in his will. In fact and fiction, the girl won out.

In spite of being the nominal star of *Gold Diggers,* Warren's contribution is rarely remembered or appreciated next to the formidable talent assembled in the film. Busby Berkeley's outrageous choreography, Al Dubin and Harry Warren's lively score, Powell and Keeler's breezy musical style, Blondell's duly famous "Forgotten Man" set piece, and the repartee of Warners' strangest duo, Guy Kibbee and the dry, sloe-eyed Aline MacMahon all pushed Warren into the background. The film was a massive hit for the studio when it opened in June, but the glow did not reflect strongly on Warren; this was a mere stopover for the star. He did endure "Warren William Day" on July 3 at Grauman's Chinese Theatre, where he appeared in person to provide a prologue for the film and address the audience. The next day he had far more fun when he attended an airship rally and got to ride in the gondola of one of the great Zeppelins. Helen stayed safely below with both feet on the ground and her heart in her mouth.[50]

Goodbye Again, based on a popular stage play starring Osgood Perkins, was an opportunity for Warren to tackle a broad, full-fledged comedy for the first time since *The Dark Horse.* Critics generally noted that while Warren was very good in it, he was not up to the standard set by Perkins on Broadway. *The Christian Science Monitor* said what everyone was thinking. "Warren William struggles with woeful unsuccess for Osgood Perkins' sprightliness."[51] It was only to be expected, with Perkins having perhaps 200 performances to hone his timing and delivery, while Warren enjoyed just one. His performance in *Goodbye Again* is amusing but as often happened when he was called on to do broad comedy, he strayed occasionally over the top. His instincts needed modulation from a director who understood comedy, an area where the immensely talented Michael Curtiz was weak. After finishing *Goodbye Again* and navigating his contract renewal, Warren would find the perfect director to elicit his greatest comic performance.

In 1933, being loaned out from one of the major studios to Columbia Pictures for a Frank Capra film was like being sent to Texarkana on a working vacation: unexpected, uncalled for, and downright depressing. The studio had not yet climbed out of the low-rent area that the majors derisively called Poverty Row, and Capra was not the American institution he later became. It was so bad that later in 1933 when MGM boss Louis B. Mayer needed to punish the young Clark Gable for demanding more money, he loaned him to Columbia for *It Happened One Night.* Gable's first comment on arrival at Columbia studios was: "I always wanted to see Siberia, but damn me — I never thought it would smell like this!"[52] Warren likely did not object so strenuously, but it couldn't have been a hopeful situation when he reported on May 10 to work with the 35-year-old director.

After a series of unmemorable, low-budget programmers, Capra was only just showing his development with films like *The Miracle Woman* and *The Bitter Tea of General Yen. Lady for a Day* was based on a short story by Damon Runyon, the New York writer whose tales of eccentric criminals, bawdy dames and Gotham nightlife were already legendary. Capra originally wanted either James Cagney or William Powell for the role of Dave the Dude, the crook with a heart of gold, but both stars were out of Columbia's financial reach. "Cohn [head of Columbia studios] had as yet nothing to trade for a star," the director recalled in his autobiography. "Therefore casting was limited to performers 'going up' (not yet contracted), and those 'going down' (contracts cancelled). From this freelance pool we selected Warren William to play Dave the Dude. He was rugged, handsome, wore clothes well — and played the part beautifully."[53] Clearly Capra did not remember everything perfectly. Warren was then at or near the height of his fame and sporting a new contract from Warner Brothers. But he was correct about one thing — Warren *did* play the part beautifully.

The story is Damon Runyon's seedy, metropolitan version of *Pygmalion.* Apple Annie (May Robson) is a washed-up old street vendor, selling apples to the New York gentry. Her best customer is a superstitious big-time gambler, Dave the Dude (Warren), who believes that Annie gives him good luck. When her daughter is set to unexpectedly arrive after many years abroad, Annie reveals that she has passed herself off to the daughter as a wealthy dowager. In order to save his good luck meal ticket from the shame of exposure, Dave the Dude embarks on a reclamation project worthy of a Brooklyn-born Henry Higgins.

Warren's fifteen years in New York coincided exactly with the era that Runyon wrote so observantly of. From the wings of Broadway's Golden Age, he had encountered the sights, sounds and characters of Runyon's New York: bootleggers, petty crooks, gamblers, scam artists and street people. He met the noted swindler Nicky Arnstein while working on *Fanny,* and was introduced to people high and low through his sister Pauline. He was likewise not above putting the brim of his hat down and knocking on a speakeasy door to take the occasional drink himself. When once asked about donating money for a Christmas tree for less fortunate people during the run of his Broadway hit *Twelve Miles Out,* he said: "Yes, we might dedicate it to all the poor rum-runners daring their lives in the cold night to provide liquids for our Christmas feasts!"[54] Dave the Dude was his splendid composite of those slangy, quick-talking guys on the make that the actor remembered so well. Here, Warren proved that his highly trained speaking voice was not just for grandiloquent pronouncements. He worked hard to forget his Academy diction, adopting instead an appropriately gravelly Brooklyn accent; Dave could dress like a Dude, but no amount of haberdashery could ever cover his low-born origins.

Capra elicited an engaging and surprisingly warm performance from his star, curtailing his natural inclination to push the comedy over the top, and allowing a cynical humanity to come through. It was an indication that with a director and writer who cared about the project and lavished thought and attention on it, Warren could be as good as any actor in Hollywood. He had to go to lowly Columbia Pictures to prove that his range was more than just the conglomeration of reprobates, users, con men and lechers that he'd been playing for the last two years. Capra himself felt that Warren may have become *too* likable in the role. "That's the trouble with actors — they've read the end of the script, so they always want to play the last scene."[55]

It is a sad circumstance that one of Warren's finest performances is again in service of a story that places clear focus on the female lead; in spite of his star billing, *Lady for a Day* is about Apple Annie, not Dave the Dude. The star turn of May Robson, then seventy, was a feel-good reclamation story and received enormous press coverage that reinvigorated her career. Following *Lady for a Day* she enjoyed status nearly on a par with the great MGM star Marie Dressler. Warren himself modestly called the film "May Robson's picture" whenever he spoke of it.[56] As usual, the man from Minnesota was snowed under by the plaudits lavished on the "lady" of *Lady for a Day.* Critics observed that he was good, as always, but nothing more. In some ways he was trapped by his own consistency. Mordaunt Hall's only comment was, "Warren William tackles the role of Dave with his usual skill."[57] Edwin Schallert limited his appraisal to three words, albeit kind ones, when he called Warren's characterization "well-nigh perfect."[58] Viewed today, Robson's portrayal of Apple Annie is still very solid, but has not aged as well as

Frank Capra's *Lady for a Day* was one of Warren William's biggest hits, and one of three pictures he starred in which were nominated for a Best Picture Oscar. The former Broadway star saw his share of Damon Runyon characters during his time in New York, and performed smartly as "Dave the Dude," the swindler and strong-arm man with a heart of gold. May Robson (right) was "Apple Annie."

Warren's Dave the Dude. It remains one of his finest all-around performances; sharply observed, wry, funny and above all, human.

Lady for a Day became an enormous hit for Columbia, grossing over $600,000 in its initial release. It also received four Academy Awards nominations: Best Screenplay, Director, Actress and Picture of 1933, but nothing for Warren. It was likely the best chance of his career for a nomination and he had been shut out. It is doubtful that it bothered him, but the ego of any performer can usually stand some stroking now and then. If he did covet the attention, it is entirely unlikely that he would have admitted it. It didn't matter; the Academy Awards of 1933 weren't appreciative of the film. None of the nominations resulted in an Oscar, and Capra himself was publicly humiliated when he mistakenly responded to Will Rogers' call for Frank Lloyd to collect his Best Director statue. The loser had to slink back to his table in front of an unprecedented array of Hollywood talent, all wondering who the upstart Columbia director thought he was.

When *Lady* wrapped on June 5, final details were taken care of with relation to Warren's new contract. Because the agreement of May 9 was quickly executed in order to save the Columbia loan-out, Warners wanted a more detailed and professional document. It was essentially under the same terms as before, but explicitly superseded all previous deals and made the validity of Ben Boyar's lawsuit so much the harder to prove.

After *Lady for a Day* opened in September 1933, Warren was off movie screens for six months. After having fifteen features parade through the nation's theaters over the previous two years, it was a positive drought for his growing fan base. The absence was not the fault of his studio, but rather the strong-willed independent producer Samuel Goldwyn. In the summer of 1933, Goldwyn was preparing the American debut of his latest protégée, the Russian actress Anna Sten. The film was *Nana*, based on a story by Émile Zola, about a gold digger and her tragic love affair with a wealthy man. Goldwyn wanted either Warren or George Brent for the part of Nana's lover Colonel Andre Muffat, and on June 29 he exercised an option with Warner Brothers to obtain Warren's services, paying the studio $5,250 for the privilege. It would be Warren's second consecutive picture on loan, but working for the lavish-spending Goldwyn was considerably more prestigious than spending time in the backwater of Columbia's Gower Street studio.

Goldwyn was hoping to mold Sten into a new Greta Garbo (something Warners also tried with Lili Damita, to no avail) and spared no expense on the production. After only three weeks of shooting on a six-week schedule, Goldwyn had already invested over $400,000 in the film. It was a far cry from the "B-plus" pictures that Warren was regularly making at his home studio, which typically cost in the neighborhood of $160,000 and took three or four weeks to complete. Goldwyn, however, did not like what he was seeing in the projection room from director George Fitzmaurice. He had only one chance to put over his new star; there would never be another opportunity for a top-notch debut that would cement her image in the public mind. Rather than risk failure, he made the expensive decision to scrap the entire production and start over again with a new director and cast. On September 9 he terminated Warren's services and restarted the film with Dorothy Arzner as director and Lionel Atwill taking the part of Colonel Muffat. For one of the rare times in his long career, Goldwyn's instincts proved dead wrong: the new version released in theaters in 1934 was a dismal failure. American audiences didn't care at all for Sten and nobody cared for *Nana*. Without seeing the unused footage, no one knows for certain, but it is unlikely that the original cast would have made a difference in the public's reception of the film. Unfortunately for film historians, every foot of film shot was destroyed at Goldwyn's direction.[59] It would have been fascinating to see what the Warner Brothers star was doing with the extra time and attention George Fitzmaurice had to bestow on the production. On the only other occasion when they worked together, *Arsene Lupin Returns* at MGM, the director evoked a smart, snappy performance that almost stole the film.

Just two weeks after *Nana* skidded to a momentary halt, Warren was back at Warner Brothers for what is possibly his sleaziest role, the despicable Bob Brown in *Bedside*. Brown is a liar, a cheat, a philanderer, a drunk and — oh, yes — a murderer. There is nothing compensatory about the character except Warren's uncanny knack of keeping your skin from crawling while he's on screen. The man is a snail leaving a slimy trail in his wake until he's forced by circumstances to admit his crimes and shortcomings — not because it's the right thing to do, but because his back is against a wall of spikes. They even have to dig in and draw blood before he confesses his transgressions.

The film begins with Brown failing to show up at his regular job as an X-ray technician in a doctor's office. When the office nurse Caroline (Jean Muir) calls to check up on him, we get a look at his squalid, bankrupt life. Hung over and passed out after an all-night bender, Brown struggles to answer the phone. Caroline implores him to get to the office or risk losing his job. He's so broke that he has to barter with the laundry woman for a clean shirt, trading the only thing he has to his name — the scanty lingerie and high heels left behind by the previous night's conquest. At the office his manner with a female patient stamps him as a cheap gigolo, to the irritation of Caroline who is blindly and foolishly in love with him. The young girl can't help trying to save the wayward wretch and loans him $1,500 to finish the medical schooling he flunked out of once before. Bob promptly loses the money in a poker game on the train out *of town*, then covers up his losses by purchasing a fake medical degree from a morphine addict. Shortly after, he opens an office where he hires Caroline as his nurse and recklessly bluffs his way through patient consultations. All the while he's two-timing the lovestruck girl, who gradually begins to understand his repulsive scheme. It isn't long before he inadvertently kills a famous opera singer by performing minor (and utterly unnecessary) surgery on her throat. After this he still isn't dissuaded from his rapacious course until finally it is Caroline's life that is in jeopardy on the operating table.

If you want to examine Warren William's personal magnetism, this is the place to do it. Bob Brown is so ugly, so base, so downright disgusting, that it is only Warren's inherent charm that keeps us from hissing him off screen like some cheap serial villain. And only Warren could get away with these sordid acts and still elicit the final line of the movie from his nearly dead girlfriend: "Oh Bob, you're marvelous!" Where else in Hollywood could we see such splendid insanity?

The absurdity of *Bedside* is neither deliberate or thought-provoking. It is rather the result of a hastily constructed, careless script that is long on cheap melodrama and devoid of any transformative character arcs. Choices define character, and the only willful choices that Bob Brown makes are hurtful and selfish ones. His one and only "redemptive" decision — to admit his transgressions because Caroline will die otherwise — is really no choice at all, but rather the result of lazy writing. Surely, even on the relentless Warner Brothers assembly line, someone could have taken an hour to figure out how to make Brown's supposed turnaround more integral to the character. Or perhaps not; *Bedside* finished in mid–October after only seventeen days of shooting. That line was moving awfully quick.

Bob Brown — and *Bedside*— got no sympathy from the New York press: "Even a Warren William couldn't make this character anything but a cad," was a common refrain.[60] The *Herald-Tribune* was deadly harsh in their assessment: "The film is lacking in any trace of dramatic value." Others still noted Warren's yeoman's effort to craft something worthwhile out of such useless material. "Mr. William is characteristically interesting as the charlatan," offered the *Times*, while the *Mirror* observed "Mr. William, always effective, does what he can to make the character sympathetic."[61]

Far more memorable than *Bedside* was the historic event that transpired during the making of the film. It would do no less than affect the lives and careers of every actor that subsequently came into the Hollywood film industry, and Warren was among a tiny handful of men sitting within the heart of it.

That season the federal government was working with various industries in an effort to curtail the continuing economic depression. New regulations were put in place across the country in transportation, construction, banking, retail and many other concerns. The National Recovery Act was now drafting new codes to also regulate the film industry, which included a proposition for limiting actors' salaries. Many members of the actors' division of the Academy of Motion Picture Arts and Sciences were unhappy with their representation at the meetings with N.R.A. representatives and decided to discuss what to do about the situation. Late at night on the first Sunday in October of 1933, a high-powered cast of Hollywood notables gathered at the home of actor Frank Morgan. Among the talent assembled at the meeting were Eddie Cantor, Boris Karloff, George Raft, James Cagney and Warren William. It was the birth of the Screen Actors Guild.

Following that first informal meeting, Warren was among a small group of fourteen men who took a bold step and resigned their membership in AMPAS. With him were Adolphe Menjou, Fredric March, Kenneth Thompson, Paul Muni, Chester Morris, George Bancroft, James Cagney, Boris Karloff, Robert Montgomery, Frank Morgan, Gary Cooper, Ralph Bellamy and George Raft. On October 3 the fourteen sent a telegram to the deputy recovery administrator in charge of their case: "We the undersigned express unqualified opposition to ... the producers code and any form of salary control board as being in direct violation of the principles of the N.R.A. All the undersigned, who are members of the Academy of Motion Picture Arts and Sciences, have this night resigned and are forming an actors' organization which will be open to all motion picture actors."[62] No one could then predict the comprehensive success of SAG in the film and television industry and the vital importance it would command for many thousands of actors great and obscure over the years. Warren often served as an officer in the early days of the Guild and was justly proud of his opportunity to be among its first members. It was the greatest expression of the dedication to community service, charity and social intercourse that he learned from his father, and persists as a testament to his professional conscience to this day.

Aside from a few minor elements in upcoming releases, *Bedside* is the swan song of Warren's primary pre–Code persona. By the time it is released in the spring of 1934, a new morality movement is taking hold in cinema and the kinds of rogues that the actor was so adept at portraying were being left behind. At the studio that summer there was some confusion as to where to take him next. First he accepted a role refused by Edward G. Robinson in a quick potboiler based on a story by Ben Hecht called *Upperworld*. He plays a wealthy industrialist who has an affair, inadvertently murders a man and gets off scot-free — then returns to his incomprehensibly forgiving wife. But while *Upperworld* was inconsequential, his next film, *Smarty*, is as disagreeable as can be — misogynistic, provoking, cheap and emasculating.

The ignoble heart of *Smarty* is contained in its original title, *Hit Me Again*, so called after the final line of the film, when Joan Blondell has been physically beaten by Warren and gets such a sexual charge out of it that she begs him for more. It is a profoundly distasteful story, with two men being upbraided and cuckolded by a woman until one of them finally learns how to be "manly." Blondell and Warren play Vikkie and Tony, a wealthy couple who have a minor problem: Vikkie is a shrewish harridan who makes her loving husband's life a living hell by goading, humiliating and gelding him. It is a role that no male star concerned about his career image would have taken, especially at the height of his powers. Alas, as Tony, Warren powders his wife's back at her command, passively watches her shamelessly flirt in his presence, admits that he will never marry again because "it hurts too much," and endures an amount of marital browbeating designed specifically to enrage the men in the audience.

Oh, and did I mention this is a comedy?

The moral of F. Hugh Herbert's script (from his original story) seems to be that women are only to be dominated and that any other arrangement is perverse. Tony, meanwhile, is portrayed as an ineffectual sissy, out of step with the times. After he's prodded, pushed and baited into divorce, he returns to the scene of the crime, still under the spell of his ex-wife, but finally beginning to learn his place in the modern world: "I had the wrong technique," he tells her. "I've been going to the movies and there the girls are different. They get kicked around and pushed in the face with grapefruit and they love it." It isn't until Vikkie's behavior has offended the senses of every man — and woman — in the audience that Tony explodes, acting out their desire to see her put in her place. He tears her dress off, slaps her face and drags her to the bedroom, then tells her, "I swear, I'll hit you so hard!" Blondell rapturously replies: "Show

Officers of The Screen Actors' Guild 1935-36

Above Right to Left:

James Cagney
1st Vice-President

Ann Harding
2nd Vice-President

Chester Morris
3rd Vice-President

Above

Kenneth Thomson
Secretary

Boris Karloff
Assistant Secretary

At Right

Warren William
Treasurer

Noel Madison
Assistant Treasurer

The Screen Actors Guild was formed in 1933 and Warren William was among the original 14 men who quit the Academy of Motion Picture Arts and Sciences to start the new union. He was the 63rd paid member and spent many years as an officer of the Guild. Courtesy SAG.

me," and after a short offscreen pause, she then commands: "Tony, dear — hit me again!" It is just barely possible that screenwriter Herbert found this all sexy or arousing. If so, one can only hope that he was not married. One person who did not find any of this amusing or appropriate was the eminently married star of *Smarty*. The man who respected women as he did found it all terribly disturbing. "Never in reality or playacting have I been called on to lay violent hands upon a woman," Warren said of a scene where he strikes Blondell, making no effort to conceal his distaste. His dignified manner would never allow him the luxury of violent anger, much less a physical outburst directed at a woman. "I was so self-conscious that I made the most complete mess of the scene for half a dozen takes, and I never could convince myself that it wasn't just acting." He called the shooting of the sequence "the most embarrassing moment of my life," and added, with much chagrin, "I never want to go through such an experience again."[63] After it was finally over, the thoroughly shaken star invited Blondell and her husband George Barnes—chief cameraman shooting the film —for lunch in order to make amends.

The script of *Smarty* endured incessant censorship from the Production Code office, proving here that they had some teeth even before the upcoming crackdown on morals in Hollywood. *If* in this case they were simply enforcing the rules of good taste, one would almost applaud them, but prudishly removing veiled references to marital sex while blithely ignoring domestic violence is hardly a public service. Such myopia proves (if it ever needed proving) that those cheap moralists were simply a pack of puritan scoundrels masquerading as arbiters of the public good.

Worse even than *Smarty* itself is the film's pressbook, where exhibitors were encouraged to sponsor a newspaper contest soliciting stories about spousal abuse — "But Make 'Em Funny" was the impossible demand. There were also articles to be planted in local newspapers with titles like "Smacking of Wives Will Check Divorce, Thinks Claire Dodd" and "Most Women Need a Good Sock Once in a While." The truly devoted theater manager could order a mechanical display in which Warren's motorized arm slaps Joan Blondell again and again. Even for 1935 this is despicable insanity.

Smarty really was taking Warren's willingness to play any part — and his submission to strong women — entirely too far. There is no question that movie-going audiences would have blanched at the idea of James Cagney or even William Powell being taught how to treat women by a woman. Men who go to movies most often want to project themselves onto the screen, fantasizing about doing and saying things like Gable or Bogart. Warren might have been secure in his masculinity, but he failed to take into account the audience's vicarious stake in the star's persona. His blithe lack of interest in participating in his own career arc was now undermining his opportunity to create a lasting and coherent self-portrait. To men he was not manly enough and women grew to respect him less and less for his weakness. Warren's single-minded insistence on being himself — even if it meant looking like a weakling and a cuckold — was driving him to leading man oblivion.

Warner Brothers was not blind to Warren's indifference and compliance. Instead of attempting to bolster the image of their important star, they took advantage of the actor's distaste for conflict and quickly assigned him to yet another useless and subservient part in a Kay Francis soap opera known as *Dr. Monica*. It was a double dip from which he never recovered.

The stage version of *Dr. Monica* had been a modest Broadway hit the previous year. It had only three players— all women — and centered on an affair one was having with the husband of her friend, pediatrician Dr. Monica Bradin. There was an illicit baby, some hoary melodrama and tears a-plenty, but no men: John Bradin, the nearly contemptible, cheating husband, was only talked about. When the studio purchased *Dr. Monica* from the author Marja Szczepkowska, they naturally decided to expand it and include the husband — a thankless, artless role that was manufactured and originally mooted for Joel McCrea, but subsequently dumped into the lap of the studio's preternaturally sympathetic cad and mountebank. Warren and Mike Levee couldn't have been too happy about it. After the enormous success of *Gold Diggers* and *Lady for a Day*, they expected better from the studio, but many stars found themselves poorly served by Warner Brothers' often incomprehensible choices.

When Warren accepted *Dr. Monica*, he signaled to the studio and the public that he was not a star of the first rank — at least not the kind of star that audiences were warming up to in 1934. Gable, Cagney or even Eddie Robinson — in the unlikely event that it was even offered to them — would have rejected it outright, and for good reason. Warren not only received second billing to Kay Francis, but also was unquestionably there simply to personify a character that the author had deemed irrelevant. Jean Muir and Verree Teasdale meant more to the story than he did. As John Bradin, Warren has almost nothing to do, disappearing from view for long stretches, enduring derision and scorn from the women of the cast and being asked to perform a perfectly ridiculous love scene in white sailing togs and scarf. It was inferior, boring, and borderline degrading. In his *New York Times* review, Mordaunt Hall observed, with crystal clarity, that while Warren does all that is possible to make the role interesting, "there is really little need for his presence." Another New York columnist said of John Bradin: "The man is— well, one might almost say, vile."[64] But the actor played good soldier and turned in a solid, professional performance. The only noteworthy element in the production is that it was Warren's first modern appearance since *Plunder* without his moustache. Perhaps he hoped no one would recognize him.

The film itself is a fairly daring story of infidelity, the final production of Warren's career before the lid was snapped down on the pre–Code era. Only months later, the idea of a married man fathering a baby out of wedlock — much less without being morally flogged for it — would be inconceivable. In spite of the soon-to-be-unique story, the film is long on melodrama and short on genuine emotions or logic. Dr. Monica, in fact, routinely delivers babies while wearing her best high heels.

Reviews were generally sympathetic to Warren, who was praised for good work in a "thankless" role, although all agreed that it was— as Phil Scheuer of the *Los Angeles Times* said —"of, by and for women." A Kay Francis soaper was no way for Warren to parlay his recent successes into greater acclaim. In fact, it tacitly informed the public and critics that he was not to be taken seriously as a star in his own right. "What's the story behind Warren William?" was the question asked by one critic that season. "He handled strong roles as in *The Match King* and *The Mouthpiece* with a skill that put him close to the top of the Hollywood pile, and then accepted without struggle a series of weak parts which made him a mere foil for women stars— the sort of thing that nearly ruined Clark Gable," the writer astutely observed.[65] At the same time, Warners was featuring Cagney in tailor-made vehicles like *Jimmy the Gent* and *The St. Louis Kid,* while Robinson was the focus of his recent offerings from the studio. All three men were essentially indentured servants, but Cagney and Robinson were treated as valuable, salable commodities, while the man from Minnesota was being carelessly handled and having opportunities squandered. Warren was not helping himself, and changes were in the wind that would limit his opportunities for the kinds of films that had made him successful and unique.

12

The Town That Forgot God

What was that sound just heard in Hollywood? It was sex getting the knock-out blow![1]

During late 1933, another public discussion was brewing about Hollywood morals. The Legion of Decency, an organ of the Catholic Church, again trotted out the well-worn accusations of immorality, and *The Payne Fund* issued the results of a study titled "Motion Picture and Youth," which alleged negative influence from films on America's children. As usually happens when a minority threatens the enormous profits generated from the vast majority, Hollywood's power brokers sat up straight in their chairs, folded their hands in front of them and listened to the lecture. Rather than risk boycotts and an angry press, they again decided to voluntarily manage their content as they had in the past. "In all sincerity Hollywood for once seems to be very intent of 'reforming,' as it is called. Secretly the producers are seeking an 'out,' and a chance to make good in a new way," the *Los Angeles Times* reported in June. "Nothing is admitted officially, and conceding anything to the adversary is frowned upon. But it is understood that during the past week in the Hays office in the east, the matter of improvement has been pretty thoroughly threshed out, and that a moratorium on the drive against movies is to be arranged, in order for them to clean house." To avoid undue controversy, industry insiders agreed to return to a stricter adherence to the Production Code of 1930, hewing closer to the spirit of the guidelines and returning the envelope to previous boundaries. "The spice box has been completely shut up," the *Times* said. "The lid has been clamped on tight. Will Hays has been given once again almost autocratic power, it is said, to rule what comes out of the movies. It's going to be the safest and sanest era ever in the movies."[2]

In spite of that ominous pronouncement, a stricter imposition of the Production Code was little more than a nuisance to the studio heads, and a relatively modest change in method of operations for writers and directors. Producers big and small simply chose a new style of picture to mount, turning more often to mystery, drama and comedy to fill those gaps. "Warner's new program [for 1934] is marked by the absence of sophisticated and sex dramas, showing that censorship has had its effect," reporters observed.[3] The studio simply avoided the subject of sex as if it were the Maginot Line. Had studios been given time to push the envelope even further, the imposition of the strict measures about content might have been maddening. But considering the *de facto* sociological restraint already prevalent — most "adult" subjects were routinely implicit rather than explicit — and the fact that the Code as enforced since 1930 had always maintained quite a few teeth, the shift was more an adjustment than wholesale change. What we consider true "pre–Code" product today was only a fraction of Hollywood's output in the early 1930s.

As for Warren, the assumption that those conscienceless, sociopathic hawks he excelled at playing were killed off by the imposition of the Code is only partially true. After *Bedside*, released just before the July 1934 crackdown, Warren never had such a role again. However, prior to *Bedside* he hadn't been seen in his quintessential cad persona since *The Mind Reader* in the spring of 1933. Between, he careened among musical, drama, mystery and comedy and made some of the most popular films of his career, including *Gold Diggers of 1933*, *Lady for a Day* and *The Case of the Howling Dog* (released in the fall of 1934). And without prompting from Code authorities his persona was already turning towards the mystery, comedy and character roles that would sustain him in the future. Few people at the time were wondering what happened to the Warren William of 1932.

The problem with the reinvigorated Code as it related to Warren was not that it eliminated characters he excelled at, but that the new paradigm undermined his uncanny capacity to wring sympathy from the audience no matter how hard they tried to dislike him. In the pre–Code era, shady characters were allowed the opportunity to be complex and ambiguous. Then, a simple metaphorical balancing of the scales was usually enough to quell objections at the Hays office — we mustn't forget that Warren was killed or imprisoned in many of his famously "immoral" roles, including *Skyscraper Souls*, *The Mouthpiece*, *The Mind Reader* and *The Match King*. The Code, however, obliged writers to be certain that there was no ambiguity in evil, and actors like Warren had little choice but to play these reductivist concoctions as they lie. After 1934 he occasionally played villains, most certainly, but not ones who had any pretense of depth or dimension; they were most often plot devices personified and reduced to caricature. The unfortunate result was that his singular quality, the ability to create nuance not just within the characters, but between he and the audience, is eliminated from his quiver and rarely used again. He commented on the problem in 1943: "The average so-called villain has got his nice points and certainly is a lot more human than those boys with the noble brows. That's the way I'd like to play a villain, but Hollywood wants you to set fire to your mother, poison a few children and give an imitation of the Prince of Darkness before they are convinced you're playing the role with conviction."[4] As base as his pre–Code constructions were, they had the advantage of revealing facets that hinted at something deeper.

As 1934 was beginning, Warren and Helen were thinking hard about putting down deeper roots in the California soil. He was now well established on America's theater screens and his new contract with Warner Brothers was paying him $1,750 a week at a time when the average individual was taking home less than $1,500 *a year*. His weekly salary would jump to $2,250 in May and be near $3,000 by the middle of 1935. That season Warren was still looking for his first ship. He'd tried a boat called *Common Sense* during the shooting of *Lady for a Day*, but did not buy it. He was finding it difficult to balance what he wanted with the cost of a new vessel. "They don't have sales any more as they did during Prohibition, when they auctioned off all those rum runners," he lamented. "Those were the days!"[5] After searching high and low at marinas and dealerships he finally purchased a 43-foot schooner called *Pegasus* from the great silent film star Richard Barthelmess. Anxious to get out on the water, he quickly outfitted the boat, hired a Chinese cook and seaman that he facetiously called his majordomo, and shook down his new vessel. He might have wanted to check the new acquisition in more detail; only a few weeks later, Warren was lost at sea when the boat's auxiliary motor failed during a trip to Catalina Island. After reaching the island and calling Helen from the town of Avalon, he and his friend, Warner Brothers still photographer Scotty Welbourne, made an effort to sail back to Los Angeles. En route the wind died completely and the two (along with Warren's cook) were becalmed for hours in the Pacific.[6] Helen called out the Coast Guard, but the wind finally kicked up and Warren limped back to Avalon under sail before any harm was done. Warner Brothers publicity had a field day with the story, but conveniently left out the fact that Warren was mercilessly teased about his seamanship in the local press and among his friends.

Pegasus was Warren's home away from home. He purchased the ship from the great silent film star Richard Barthelmess and sailed it from Los Angeles to Mexico, Hawaii and many points between.

There was also the matter of a new house to consider. For two years the Krechs had been living in a rented house on a hillside in Los Feliz, overlooking the Los Angeles skyline and the ocean beyond. But the couple was becoming more and more interested in the patter of little feet and decided that they needed a change. "We moved from our apartment to a house when we annexed three dogs," Warren explained. "And now we feel we must have still more commodious quarters."[7] Only two months later the pair took possession of four more energetic wire-haired terriers, bringing the total padding around the Los Feliz house to seven. The childless couple who lavished love and attention on their pets concocted an idea for introducing their new "children" to the community. They sent out invitations for a christening ceremony to be held at the home of Mike Levee and invited a veritable who's who of Hollywood to bring their dogs along for an impromptu show. Among the guests were the Leslie Howards, the Edward G. Robinsons, Hal Wallis, William Powell, Joan Blondell and many others. The Williams became very involved in the dog scene in LA, attending and participating in shows, charity events and regularly touting animal rights causes. After a day in Levee's garden, Warren and Helen relished the chance to find a home with grounds to let their growing kennel run and play. That spring while Helen was spending part of each week searching for a new house, Warren was shooting long days at Paramount playing Julius Caesar in Cecil B. DeMille's *Cleopatra*.

Cleopatra was far and away the biggest production of Warren's career, a massive historical epic in the DeMille mode: if it could be done simpler, complicate it; if it could be done faster, slow down; and if it could be done cheaper, spend the extra money. It was Hollywood filmmaking at its most muscular and extravagant, a concoction of high entertainment and low art. Warren was chosen as Julius Caesar after the director considered "every available actor in Hollywood" for the part, including Adolphe Menjou, Charles Laughton and John Gilbert.[8] It was a vitally important part in one of he biggest films of the year; Warren would receive second billing only slightly smaller (of course) than the titular star, Claudette Colbert, who was just then coming off her Oscar-winning performance in *It Happened One Night*. The man from Minnesota with the perfect diction and Roman profile made an outstanding Caesar, although DeMille's insistence that the script contain modern vernacular speech made for a few cringeworthy moments.

The public loved *Cleopatra*, making it one of the top box office hits of 1934, and Academy voters nominated the film for a Best Picture Oscar, Warren's second in less than a year. Critics were generally positive, although many commented that those modern dialogue touches destroyed the visual verisimilitude that DeMille had worked so hard to craft. And of course the focus was squarely on Colbert with her extravagant gowns, exotic hairstyle and erotic performance. Warren, they barely mentioned; the *Hartford Courant* said he gave "magnificent support," and Mordaunt Hall simply allowed that he "shined in his role." The film most certainly raised his profile, but very few took sincere notice. Even DeMille himself was puzzled by Warren's lack of acclaim: "Perhaps he was overshadowed in the public mind by the other talent in *Cleopatra* or by the fact that Caesar is killed halfway through the story, but I have always felt that neither the critics nor the public did justice to Warren William's performance. I have seen other fine actors portray Julius Caesar; I have never seen any that surpassed Warren William."[9] DeMille might not have been so confused if he knew how easily Warren tended to disappear when placed adjacent to charismatic, beautiful women.

Nineteen thirty-four was the year that began a clear change in the public perception of the actor. For movie audiences of the late 1930s and '40s, the image of him as a cad and reprobate was gradually winnowed away as he found a new metier in mystery and detective films. By the end of the 1930s Warren's name would be synonymous with those roles, and to this day fans from that era recall him first as the gumshoe, the shamus or the shyster. It began with *The Mouthpiece*, still his most popular starring role, but became the dominant portrait in his gallery after he again stepped into William Powell's shoes to take over the role Powell abdicated after 1933's immensely popular *The Kennel Murder Case*: S.S. Van Dine's popular detective Philo Vance.

Warren was a natural choice following Powell's departure after four appearances as the dapper detective. He was playing many parts stylistically similar to Powell, and had already followed him once, into *The Dark Horse*, when Warner Brothers substituted Warren to avoid a lawsuit from the writer of the original film, *High Pressure*. *The Dragon Murder Case* was the sixth film made featuring Vance (Basil Rathbone took a turn in 1930), and gave movie fans a new look for Warren William: urbane, sophisticated, intellectual and finally on the right side of the law.

Only Jack Warner seemed to have expectations of success for the project, with directors Michael Curtiz, Archie Mayo, Mervyn LeRoy and Alfred Green each turning it down before journeyman Bruce Humberstone was finally assigned to the film.[10] *The Dragon Murder Case* is a tangled welter of murder mystery clues, customs and clichés, with Humberstone walking through the proceedings quickly, but with little sense of urgency. The camera mostly sits still while the actors move in and out, talking a lot but not showing us much. *Dragon* could have used Del Ruth or LeRoy's knack for spicing up the narrative with pieces of character business or cinematic flourishes. In the end it comes off as solid entertainment, but without any dash to keep it alive. Following the Curtiz-directed classic *The Kennel Murder Case*, this entry was clearly a step down, but the Warners publicity department put a big push behind Warren's maiden entry, playing up his name and likeness in advertising. They also managed to get him an honorary membership in the Protective Order of Police for Los Angeles County and a gold star as a detective on the regular city police force of Los Angeles.

Warren again performed as a very solid analogue to William Powell, being possessed of many of the same qualities of voice and style. Although he doesn't have the presence that Powell exhibited in the other entries, his Vance is equally urbane and sophisticated, while maintaining just enough of a sense of humor to keep him human. Box office was good and critics were laudatory, but only up to the direct comparison to Powell's Vance. "Not as easy and smooth in the role as Bill Powell," was a common refrain, but Warren was also described as "attractive and entertaining," "creditable," and "debonair and plausible."[11] *The Dragon Murder Case* convinced Warners executives that there was a new path on which to take Warren following the change in the Production Code, and it turned out to be where he would spend a good portion of the rest of his career.

One afternoon during a break in the filming of *The Dragon Murder Case*, Helen Krech took her husband on a trip "over the hill," as they say in Hollywood, to a sleepy, out-of-the-way district of Los Angeles known as Encino. Nestled in the San Fernando Valley, Encino was then a tiny enclave of a few thousand residents, boasting wide-open spaces unheard of elsewhere in Los Angeles. It was named for a small parcel of land donated to Mission Indians by the Spanish government: Rancho Encino, "The Ranch of the Evergreens." There, standing among eight wooded acres, was a house that Helen had seen and loved, and she expected that Warren would feel the same. The couple piled in their new Packard roadster and trouped almost ten miles straight out Ventura Boulevard, over the rim and down into the valley. At Encino Avenue they turned left and trundled down a beautiful tree-lined road until they hit a dead end. There, Warren fell in love for just the second time in his life.

Warner Brothers photographer Walter Lippman took this casually posed portrait just months after War-ren and Helen acquired their permanent home in Encino, California. The couple paid $32,000 for the eight-acre ranch, then spent $10,000 remodeling the house and environs. Courtesy Barbara Hall.

In spite of the relative distance from the bustle of Los Angeles, Encino seemed to the actor far nearer to his boyhood home in Minnesota than to the pressures of Hollywood. Everywhere he looked on the land, Warren saw beckoning nature: beautiful eucalyptus trees, walnut groves, great conifers, nearby orchards and massive oaks, some as old as 500 years. A brook eased its lazy way through the property and the smell of orange blossom flavored the air with an intoxicating tang. Warren was immediately swept away by the possibilities of the place: room for gardens, entertaining and parties; open space for the dogs to roam and play, outbuildings to serve as a personal workshop and the opportunity for blissful solitude. That day Warren wore out the pet saying he used whenever he encountered something new and exciting: a single word, spoken like a doorbell chime, was repeated again and again: "*Hel*-lo!"[12] Before May was out, negotiations were finished, papers were signed, and the ranch became the new home of Warren and Helen Krech. Being mostly frugal with their money—and with Warren having just received a renewal of his contract at $2,250 a week—the couple was comfortable enough to pay the agreed-upon price of $32,000 in cash for the property, making closing very easy.[13]

As Warren was getting ready for his next film project, he took the time for what he expected would be a most pleasant task: the remodeling and outfitting of his newly purchased home and environs. He burned the candle at both ends that summer, personally drawing up plans

Warren and Helen's wirehaired terriers Jack, Jill and Babs occasionally got into a neighbor's chicken coop until this kennel was erected to keep them honest. The Krechs raised and showed wirehairs for many years; dogs were a constant presence on the grounds of their eight-acre ranch.

Checking the lay of the land at their new home are Warren, his wife Helen, and Jill, one of their feisty wirehaired terriers. Warren is just 40 years old and Helen is already 57.

for the contractors to work from, then shooting long days (and nights) at Warner Brothers and spending any free time, vacations or days off at home supervising and helping out in any way he could. At the onset, he and Helen decided that it would be sensible to move in right away, so that she could oversee the renovations while he was working. Naively, the Krechs expected the remodeling work to proceed smoothly and methodically; in fact, it went as it always does:

slowly, painfully and with great difficulty. Each new change begot another change, seemingly without end. After just a few weeks Warren and Helen were left with only the living room and one bedroom intact, those rooms fulfilling all domestic necessities with the rest of the house having been torn apart around them. While the kitchen was renovated, the refrigerator sat in a corner of the parlor. Meals were prepared in the pass pantry on a propane hot plate salvaged from one of Warren's old boats. As if the remodeling tribulations of the new homeowners weren't enough, Warren and Helen then endured a series of unexpected and irritating occurrences seemingly designed just to make life difficult for them. That summer, the normally mild Southern California weather produced an unusual amount of rain, slowing progress on exterior work. Jack and Jill got into their new neighbor's chicken coop and killed nineteen hens. Warren lost the hand-drawn plans for his private second floor suite. Their cook quit without notice. The living room fireplace backed up and belched smoke throughout the house. Warren could not find the pair of black shoes he needed to complete an ensemble he was wearing in his new film. It was a nettlesome, maddening, irksome season in Encino.

It took until January, but when all was said and done, the ranch was exactly what he and Helen wanted it to be. At a cost of $10,000 they rehabbed the main house (there were two on

Warren and Helen hired artist Walter Bruce (center) to decorate the cabanas next to their swimming pool with this mural. On the back of the photo Warren wrote: "28 monkeys on walls — a pirate ship — two pirates. You can see many other things. Still feeling punk — worth the backache." Courtesy Barbara Hall.

Nattily attired, Warren checks the sextant in his "chart room," a secret alcove above the master bedroom in his home. The room, which he designed with maps and other nautical appointments, was his favorite retreat, and very rarely photographed.

the property), erected servants' quarters, installed a swimming pool and cabanas, planted groves of citrus fruit, outfitted a patio and deck, and created a nine-hole putting and chipping golf course, tennis courts and a recreation room. One of the garages was equipped as his machine shop, where Warren could indulge his diminutive Edison, while Helen got a grand garden and massive walk-in closet with multiple full-length mirrors. The dogs—now down to just four, Jack, Jill, Cheekie and Babs—had a large, fenced kennel to keep them out of mischief and away from the local fowl. And after redrawing his plans, Warren got his secret attic retreat. Above the couple's bedroom, accessed by a unique set of curved stairways that doubled as dressers, was a simulated ship's hold, complete with portholes, marine appointments and a compass painted on the floor. He spent many a day there, looking at charts, drawing travel plans, and generally playing the role of merchant seaman that he loved in his youth.

In April of 1934, just before the purchase of the Krechs' new property, Warner Brothers purchased the rights to a novel that had been serialized in *Liberty* magazine during January, *The Case of the Howling Dog.* The writer was Erle Stanley Gardner, and the character that Warner Brothers brought onto theater screens for the first time the following spring was the immortal Perry Mason. Although they again momentarily considered Edward G. Robinson for the role, Warren's performance in *The Dragon Murder Case* convinced them that they had the perfect man to play Gardner's iconic lawyer. So convinced was the studio that the ingenious attorney would make a splash that they contracted the author for six Mason adventures, starting at $10,000 for the rights to *Howling Dog* and rising to $25,000 for the final (then unwritten) entry in the series.

Warner Brothers decided to put somewhat more attention than usual into *The Case of the Howling Dog*, wanting to start the series with a quality offering. Bette Davis was originally assigned to the film, but bowed out with less than a week remaining before shooting began on June 19, presumably not wanting to be paired with her supposed tormenter again.[14] The studio recast Mary Astor in the role and assigned the director of *The Jazz Singer*, Alan Crosland, to the project. Crosland wasn't Michael Curtiz, the heavyweight director of the classic Warner Brothers era, but he was a fine craftsman who had been making movies since 1914 and knew how to tell a story with economy and simplicity. That didn't stop Jack Warner from putting his own

At the height of his fame, Warren's image was plastered across theater marquees, printed on cigarette cards, used to sell lip balm and tooth powder, and featured on premiums like this 1934 cardboard standee.

two cents in about how the film should be handled. He ordered Crosland to look at a print of *The Mouthpiece*, telling him, "We want to play Warren William with the same mood and feeling—and a great deal of the tempo" as in his great success of 1932. His notes about *The Case of the Howling Dog*, in fact, show how involved in the small details of film making Warner was, despite his reputation as an ivory tower executive. "We want plenty of animation out of William," he insisted. "Don't let him cross his eyes through the picture. Let him do one or two twists of the mustache and three pinches of the nose and about four pulls of the ear. Also, have at least half a dozen shruggings of the shoulder and fourteen quick look-backs with the camera behind him." In a backhanded effort to placate Crosland for such indelicate advice, he then apologized, saying that he really wasn't trying to direct the movie but rather, "I'm telling you just what to do."[15] Aside from Warner's input, the production benefited from Crosland's sure hand. The film he turned out was devoid of many of the cinema clichés that had become so prevalent in recent whodunnits and detective stories. It was in fact a different animal altogether: a slick, stylish hybrid of courtroom drama, murder mystery and legal procedural all in one. It was hailed as mature, honest and dramatic, and Warren was given better marks as Mason than he was as Philo Vance. As Warner Brothers predicted, *The Case of the Howling Dog* performed very well at the box office, inviting sequels and launching the classic icon on decades of popularity.

Mason became a staple in Warren's repertoire with four pictures over a two-year period. Warner Brothers continued to follow the template of each Mason novel but the scenario writers

Warren soaks up the sun while reading the script for *The Case of the Curious Bride*, his second film as Perry Mason. He was the first man to play the iconic lawyer (in 1934's *The Case of the Howling Dog*).

could never decide exactly how to portray him; in *Howling Dog* he's the professional, immensely successful head of a massive office of operatives. *The Case of the Lucky Legs* (1935) verges on slapstick comedy and Mason is played as a devil-may-care alcoholic who isn't above chiseling his clients out of large fees when they're over a barrel. (When he's told that a case he's handling will be more complicated than expected, he's relieved. "Good. I was afraid that it was going to be so simple that I wouldn't be able to swing much more of a fee out of it.") Far from the sober, meticulous character known from his television appearances, Warren's Perry Mason is often larcenous, frivolous, comedic, caddish, profligate, and regularly operates on the shady side of the law. In *The Case of the Velvet Claws* he drugs an unsuspecting witness into insensibility to keep the police from questioning her. At the finale of *The Case of the Howling Dog* he engineers the acquittal of Mary Astor on a murder charge that he knows her to be guilty of simply because he believes her to have acted in self-defense. And in almost every film he regularly takes the law into his own hands by stealing evidence, obstructing justice and generally ordering people around with no authority whatsoever. Mason's respect for law enforcement, however, is boundless; when there's a knock on the door of his office while he's being questioned by the police during *Lucky Legs,* he tells the detective: "You go, Johnson. Maybe you'll get shot."

Most notable of the Masons is 1935's *The Case of the Curious Bride.* Second in the series, it is distinguished as the final "A" production, with Michael Curtiz directing, and the adorable Claire Dodd as Della Street (a role she reprised in 1936's *The Case of the Velvet Claws,* where she and Mason finally get married). While the film itself is a snappy little mystery with some neat in-camera blur transitions and Perry's amusing penchant for cooking and gastronomy, there is the matter of it offering a new face on the cinema landscape: Errol Flynn makes his American film debut in a small part. It is doubtful that anyone suspected at the time that this insignificant bit player would begin one of Hollywood's greatest star rises the following year. And no one—certainly not Warren himself—could see that the young man who plodded awkwardly through his three minutes of screen time would inadvertently drive a wedge between him and the studio that would result in the cancellation of his contract and the gradual decline of his career.

13

Smarty

"Necessity is the mother of invention," the saying goes. For Warren William, this couldn't have been more true: It was a necessity that he invent.

From his earliest days, the mind of the Minnesotan was curious, inquisitive, restless, questioning and ingenious. His interest in technical solutions to practical problems was an expression of his personal character: self-contained, only marginally socially minded, with equal parts doer and thinker. For him there was nothing better than the process of engineering something new: the birth of a creative idea, the single-minded pleasure of solitary thought and planning followed by hours alone, putting it all together in his machine shop retreat. "I'm afraid I am antisocial," he explained. "An actor's place is on the stage. On screen I am a heroic fellow. Off the screen I am not heroic, nor do I want to have to pose and pretend. I go where don't have to pretend — home.[1] I spend all my spare time in the work shop, doing things around the place."[2] For Warren, the Hollywood life was a chore. Over a bench press in his garage was where he enjoyed the fruits of his fame.

In New York and in the early years in Hollywood, when he and Helen first rented an apartment, then a house with a modest workshop, there was very little opportunity for Warren to indulge in building his ideas. While living in New York his never-ending stream of engineering concepts did not diminish. During that time he drew up plans and built a model of a showboat that he called a "marine theater," with a circular performance stage and a new system of footlights.[3] "You see," he reasoned, "all of the old-time riverboats are narrow and long. If you staged a show at one end, the people in the seats at the back would be so far away they wouldn't see anything at all. And I thought it would be a great idea to build a circular stage right in the middle of the boat so that everyone would get a good view."[4] He likewise made sketches for a novel lighting scheme to be used in common areas of apartment buildings. But with no practical place for hands-on building, few of these things ever went beyond the planning stages. The last time he was able to make mock-ups of his ideas was when he had his personal tinkering shop back in Aitkin, where he made family furniture, pulled apart disused machinery and cobbled together his bicycle-driven boat "The Pirate."

When Warren purchased his Encino ranch in 1934, one of his first projects was to create the machine shop that he had always wanted. He still owned and maintained the hand tools that he had acquired as a boy and now he had a place of his own to use them. He chose one of the ranch's storage sheds for the shop and augmented those quaint old relics with a brace of modern power tools: drill press, lathe, circular saw, arc welder, belt sander, grinder, water stone and anything else he would need to complete his mechanical inspirations. During the months of remodeling his new house and environs, Warren involved himself directly in many of the projects, working tirelessly to make the house exactly what he and Helen wanted. Once the dust settled in the winter of 1935, he was finally able to repair to his sanctum — and make no mistake, that is exactly what it was — and begin the inventive output that continued until

An inveterate amateur inventor, Warren cooked up this stunningly dangerous motor rig during the spring of 1933. A list of what could go wrong with the device would be enormous.

he could no longer drive a nail or turn a screw. In short order, things began rolling out of the William workshop with such startling frequency that the Hollywood press took notice.

When Warren first arrived in California, articles about him were invariably divided into two camps. In one he was known as the quiet man who loved home life, never complained about anything and steadfastly refused to toot his own horn or proclaim his greatness. According to the other, the sea was the key to his character. It exemplified his image as a loner and was usually accompanied by the belief that Warren could give up the fame and the fortune for a life on the water. Both were terribly dull copy, not the least because Warren was so stoic and reserved when it came to talking about himself. "The only thing you'll get by coming to my house is a good lunch," he once told a columnist in search of a story.[5] The situation vexed Helen. "I know Warren is not easy to write about," she said. "Not so long ago a woman magazine writer complained to me that it was difficult to do stories on him because there is no purple past, present, or future connected with him. As far as we both can see, that is lamentable, but we do not propose to do anything about it merely to provide sensational copy!" After 1934, however, the press finally had something to hang a story on. From then on, the Minnesota man became invariably known as "The Gadgeteer" in every magazine and newspaper article about him. Warren likely enjoyed that notoriety and was more comfortable with it than any acting plaudits he received.

On a visit to his home for an interview, feature writers would almost instantly find their "angle" when they encountered the welter of clever labor-saving devices that their subject whipped up in his garage workshop. First was the telephone he had installed at the entrance to the ranch on Encino Avenue. Built at the end of a boom with a counterweight, it dropped down to the window of any car that drove up to the front gate. From there the visitors could announce themselves and gain admittance when a lever was thrown to open the gate by remote control. On the far side of the ranch, there was an automated drawbridge built of huge timbers designed with the precise opposite function — to keep out the unwanted celebrity seekers who regularly drove unannounced onto the property. Seeing these unique contraptions built by their subject, writers knew immediately that they had a hook.

Inside the grounds there were examples of the actor's ingenuity around every corner. When he noticed that his pups were tearing up the lawn outside the entrance to their doghouse, he built a new rotating split-level version made from discarded studio arc lights. "The whole affair is mounted on a central shaft," he explained. "It revolves at will. The value is that the dogs can run every day or so, on new grass. The grass keeps fresh and green all of the time." When the same dogs again got in Dutch with one of his neighbors over some dead chickens, he outfitted the offending pooch with a wide tin collar designed to stop his wanderlust. "He can't do more than get his nose through anything with that on," Warren chuckled.[6] But the local feud was not so easily quelled, and later turned ugly. In March of 1935 someone — presumably the offended neighbor — threw acid in the eyes of Jack and Jill, resulting in some serious damage that eventually blinded one of them.[7] After the incident was reported in the press, mail and packages containing toys and treats for the unfortunate pooches deluged Encino for a month.

"They keep coming at me all the time, ideas for new gadgets," Warren complained. "I really never get a full night's sleep." Almost every day there was a new contrivance from the shop: he designed sunglasses with a thin horizontal slit in the lenses for reading in strong sunlight. In his bedroom were a series of rotating valets housed in what he called his "tower closet." Here he could scroll through his immense wardrobe of shoes, hats, ties and socks at the twist of his wrist. For his clothes he also designed a system of number-coding his ensembles, ensuring

When Warren got to Hollywood, he took up many hobbies. In addition to his penchant for inventing, he indulged in fencing, boating, tennis, golf, flying, swimming and archery. This was taken in 1935, while he was working on *Don't Bet on Blondes.*

that each item worn for a film (where he regularly provided the wardrobe) would never be lost or missing when it came time to be on the set. Far ahead of his time, he also had a specially built storage tank that used solar power to heat water for use on the property. He hated time being wasted, unless it was wasted on leisure. To that end he installed an intercom system throughout the property for his landscapers to use instead of having to return to the house for instructions. "Whenever there was a call for anybody, all we could do was blow a whistle. Everybody stopped working and headed for a telephone. It didn't make sense."[8]

Among his most useful devices was the construction of an enormous rolling picnic table built on the chassis of an old car. The inspiration for his "movable feast" came when Warren saw the beat-up chassis of a vintage Chevy in Los Angeles. The car still had a working engine and steering column, and Helen was positively mortified when Warren purchased it and drove the skeletal remains home through the streets of LA wearing his dirtiest dungarees and sweatshirt.[9] She did not like the real world getting too close a look at the real Warren William. Back in his shop, Warren changed the steering column, added a base platform, table, benches and a bright yellow canopy. He also installed an electrical system to power percolators, grilles, hot plates and warming trays. When guests arrived he could literally drive it out to any area of the ranch and be ready to serve, seat or cook for dozens of people.

There were custom barbecue grills, dressers that doubled as stairways, storage units for the produce grown at the ranch, flexible lights, special closets, electric toothbrushes, concealed lock boxes and a photoelectric sundial. The tractor that carried him around the grounds was equipped with a motor that could be used to power pumps, saws and other devices by connecting drive belts to a main capstan. In 1943 he invented a massive, vacuum-operated "lawn sweeper" that gobbled up leaves and twigs with suction power. It was an idea well ahead of its time, although the machine was bulky and *very* loud until Warren replaced the gas motor with one powered by electricity. He made the switch after hearing the sweeper power-up when he was almost a mile from the house. "I was far away when I heard a noise like a cement mixer," he laughed. "I finally decided they were building a road in the hills. When I reached home I found it was the sweeper." Mortified, he quickly went to work. "I think the neighbors have been punished enough," he declared upon installation of the new, quieter motor."[10] The sweeper was one of only a handful of devices that he tried to patent. Although many articles claimed he had received one, no paperwork appears under his name in the U.S. patent office.

Engineering and amateur inventing were among Warren's great passions. One of the creations that came from his workshop were these sunglasses, designed with slits to allow clear reading in strong light. He's seen here on the set of 1935's *Satan Met a Lady.*

There was always a practical solution to any problem in the Warren William house. He mounted this picnic table on the chassis of an old Ford so that it could simply be driven out to any location on the ranch for an impromptu party.

Warren's most ambitious project was the self-contained recreational vehicle he built in the winter of 1935, and it never failed to impress anyone who saw it. The story of its construction gives amusing insight into his character: The hundreds of hours he spent outfitting his moving apartment were all in the service of getting an extra hour's sleep in the morning.

Although it has been repeated many times, it is not true that Warren invented the first practical mobile home. That distinction goes to a midwestern bacteriologist and amateur inventor named Arthur G. Sherman. In the summer of 1929, just before the stock market crash, Sherman constructed a little house that he could tow behind his car on family vacations. There was so much interest in his gimmick that he was persuaded by friends and clients to build others. The following year he exhibited his handiwork at the Detroit Auto Show and quickly found himself in a lucrative business fabricating trailer homes. The idea was so successful that big manufacturers began to produce lines for the expanding market. By 1935 the industry estimated that there were over 150,000 trailers on the road, with more being built every day. In addition to mass-market product, thousands of people were building their own trailers from specifications in automotive journals and trade publications.

Early studio calls were the bane of Warren's existence. Six, sometimes seven days a week, forty weeks a year, the actor was obliged to drag himself out of bed in the early morning and make the hour commute from Encino to the Warner Brothers lot in Burbank. The notorious late riser told Gladys Hall in 1937: "My one aim in life, my one philosophy, is to save myself the slightest unnecessary exertion. I believe in reducing the high pressure of life to a minimum, and I believe that to save time for leisure is one way to reduce pressure." When the amateur inventor saw print coverage of the new trailer homes, he immediately recognized a golden opportunity to "reduce pressure." If he had such an apartment on wheels, he could prepare for work while he was en route, rather than having to arrive early enough for makeup and wardrobe. And if he could shower and shave, too—well, so much the better. So, the inveterate tinkerer set out to create an ambitious and complex mobile apartment that would allow him to do just that.

Warren began by changing the rules. While tow-behind trailers were well established by this time, self-contained RVs were quite scarce. It would be a great amount of work, but Warren wanted an all-in-one drive and park caravan. He first purchased a medium-sized panel delivery truck with the structure and space for everything he needed. Inside, he set about the process of fabricating and adapting the various parts needed to make the vehicle a functional house on wheels, calling on many of the ideas in pleasure craft design with which he was familiar. There was an ivory leather couch on one side, with space underneath to hold extra bedding and clothes, and a deep bookshelf nearby. Opposite was a copper wash basin and toilet with running water provided from a large storage tank. Towels and washcloths were provided, just as they would be in any other powder room, allowing the owner to wash and ready himself for arrival at the studio. Next to this, a dressing table folded down from a panel in the wall, revealing a lighted mirror and an outlet for running his electric razor, portable radio and fan. The dressing table was hinged and collapsed in sections, doubling as a valet that would fold clothes and keep them in perfect press. Another panel revealed a small bar, with liquor, mixers, glasses and openers, just above a small gas range powered by propane and flanked by a tiny pantry for utensils. There was also a deep, open closet for costumes and clothing changes he would need that day, made necessary by the fact that the actor provided his own wardrobe for his films. In later years there was a telephone, operated via radio frequency. The space was finished in a light tan, with carpeting of dark chocolate brown, and a beige curtain dividing the space between the driver and the apartment. The attention to detail that Warren lavished on the project was amazing, and it was certainly the most ambitious project of his amateur-inventing career.

"All this serves the purpose of saving time and effort," he revealed to *Modern Screen* magazine a few years after the contraption was built. "I can sleep an extra hour in the morning.

My house man drives me, and I dress and shave and make up as I'm on my way to the studio." He could now drive right on to the set, with everything at hand; no running to the dressing room, commissary or wardrobe department. "And it's lots more convenient than a trailer," he enthused. "You don't have to keep looking around to see if it's still with you." Warren refused to let *Modern Screen* or any other publication take pictures of the truck, however. He was usually reluctant to even discuss the project, claiming that the anonymity of the vehicle was a defense against aggressive autograph hounds who often accosted him at red lights when he drove around town in his touring car. "But the delivery truck fools them completely," he said. "I can park it anywhere downtown without anyone giving me a second glance. I guess they figure I'm just a deliveryman for a florist or a meat market."[11] His continuing incredulity at fame and desire for a reasonable level of privacy still trumped the pride of his accomplishment. Typically for him, the entire endeavor was a practical exercise and the ultimate satisfaction of it was enjoyed neither on the road nor in the press, but in bed for that extra hour.

In the end, the irony of spending so many hours slaving laboriously on something that was supposed to save time, effort and unnecessary exertion was not lost on him. "It's all very paradoxical," he mused. "My goal is to do everything in moderation and nothing excessive. But I am excessive about my gadgets. They ride me breathlessly. They defeat the very purpose for which they are conceived."[12]

In 1938 Warren impulsively shuttered his workshop. "I've made 138 inventions and that's all I'm going to invent for posterity," he announced. "Not that I don't enjoy inventing, but it has gotten that I don't do anything else." There is almost no doubt that Helen was more than a little stir-crazy sitting at the ranch while her husband tinkered in the garage, and told him so. "In the past two years my wife and I haven't been out more than five evenings and we never go on weekend trips. When I'm not working on a picture, I'm in my shop experimenting, but from now on it's going to be different."[13] The arrangement lasted a few months, long enough to see some shows, attend a premiere or two and do a little dancing at the Copa before the ineluctable call of invention returned Warren to the shop and consigned Helen to the wilds of Encino once again. It was no contest. Invention was too perfect a fit for Warren William's character.

14

*The Man in
the Iron Mask*

In August of 1934, Universal was preparing the classic Claudette Colbert melodrama *Imitation of Life*, based on the novel by Fanny Hurst. Paul Lukas was signed to play Colbert's beau Steven Archer, another limited male role often assigned to the second leads of Hollywood, but clearly not meant for real stars. Men like Lukas, George Brent, Ricardo Cortez and—shudder—Lyle Talbot almost appear to have been born to look and sound good, but not take focus from a female lead. John Stahl, the director of *Imitation of Life*, had a difficult time casting the Archer role, looking for someone who could play the troublesome character: a reserved and proper scientist who could also be romantic and worldly. By the time cameras rolled on the second day of filming, the director knew they had made a serious mistake in casting Lukas. Immediately Stahl and his producer brainstormed about who could be called in on short notice to fill the part. It may have been Colbert (who was most certainly consulted), fresh off a pleasant experience with Warren on *Cleopatra*, who suggested he might be their solution. Universal's Henry Henigson contacted Warners and a deal was quickly reached with the studio for Warren to immediately start shooting. Universal expected to use him for three weeks, but Mike Levee wanted a premium for emergency services and wrangled an extra week's pay from the studio. On August 9, just two days into filming, the substitute Steven Archer reported for duty. To save face for Lukas, Universal planted a story saying that Warner Brothers wanted him for a film called *King of the Ritz*, and that the two studios had then engineered a swap (even though Lukas had already begun shooting on Stahl's set). Warner Brothers did not make *King of the Ritz*.

Imitation of Life is one of the grand soap operas of classic Hollywood. Colbert plays Beatrice Pullman, a destitute widow with a young daughter who takes on a similarly single African American maid with a daughter of the same age. Bea and Delilah become friends and wildly successful business partners while their children grow up in different worlds. Jessie Pullman attends college and finishing school, enjoying the fruits of a wealthy mother. Meanwhile, Delilah's daughter, the very light-skinned Peola, disavows her black heritage by "passing" as white. When Peola's self-loathing charade is discovered, she cruelly disowns her mother and disappears. The resultant melodrama—in spite of political reservations from some quarters—has broken the hearts of generations of filmgoers.

Warren has the unenviable part of Colbert's near-perfect (read: boring) paramour Steven Archer, who has the misfortune to also attract Bea's daughter Jessie with his charms. Here Warren must not only reject one woman, but is in turn rejected by the other. Naturally, the staid, sober scientist takes it all in stride, being the perfectly understanding and unruffled victim of circumstance. God forbid a Warren William character (or the actor himself) should advocate on his own behalf.

Warren's performance beside Colbert and Louise Beavers (as Delilah) in *Imitation of Life* is, as always, solid, sincere and professional. He excels in a thankless part, but again, the picture is not for him — everyone recognized that it would be "the joy of women audiences."[1] In a way, Warren's Academy training was too deeply instilled; he believed in the idea that an actor must give everything to the play and took deeply to heart the idea of ego being secondary to the material. Harkening back to his days as a fledgling actor in the Theatre Guild production of *John Hawthorne,* he remembered their motto: "The play's the thing."

Although *Imitation of Life* became a box office smash and an Academy Award nominee, it continued to devalue Warren's image as a star in his own right. The man who had just completed his third Oscar-nominated film in fifteen months neither received tremendous attention nor sought the important roles others might have leveraged from such a string of excellent work. He professed an ever so slight interest in playing the title role in the upcoming Warner Brothers filming of the runaway best seller *Anthony Adverse,* but could not bring himself to beg for it.[2] Now, when casting directors (or Warner Brothers producers) were looking for a strong, capable man to carry a picture, they increasingly relegated Warren to an afterthought. He was the man who supported women, not the other way around.[3]

Warner Brothers next pushed Warren into a forgettable programmer in support of Barbara Stanwyck called *The Secret Bride,* wherein the daughter of a governor (Stanwyck) has a clandestine marriage to the state's attorney general (William). Naturally, there is a murder and some other shenanigans that implicate the governor and complicate the marriage. The waste of those two stars in a scenario like this reminds us that even in the Golden Age of Hollywood — with stars sometimes in as many as six or seven films a year — not all of them could be gems. *The Secret Bride* was mere product, and another installment in Jack Warner's series of broken promises to Mike Levee. The biggest of those unfulfilled pledges involved the young Tasmanian actor who was about to begin his film career in Warren's second Perry Mason outing, *The Case of the Curious Bride.*

History tells the lore of Errol Flynn's incredible rise to Hollywood stardom when he was plucked from the ranks of minor Warner Brothers contract players and given his break as the star of 1935's *Captain Blood.* But, like other Hollywood lore — for example, the possibility that Ronald Reagan might have been the star of *Casablanca*— there is more going on behind it.

In June of 1934, Jack Warner was still wrestling with what to do with Warren William. His new likeness as a detective-mystery star was coming into focus on *The Dragon Murder Case* and the incipient Perry Mason series. But Warren and Levee were still unhappy about the films he'd been presented with since signing his new contract thirteen months earlier, when the studio head had promised better films but instead delivered a cheap mélange of second leads, B pictures and the disastrous *Dr. Monica.* But hope was on the horizon when the studio elected to mount a remake of 1923's version of the swashbuckling pirate novel *Captain Blood.* In an effort to mollify their dissatisfied (but still largely cooperative) player, Warner Brothers publicly announced that Warren would be the star of the upcoming production.[4]

Warren and Levee were excited by the idea of a heroic role in a big-budget picture, but it is doubtful that Warner Brothers ever truly intended to feature Warren in *Captain Blood.* It was a common practice of studio publicity departments to excite interest in projects by placing blurbs about them in the press well before production began. This regularly resulted in ballyhoo for films that never got made, or were completed with players other than those who were announced. As a star at a major studio, Warren himself was subject to dozens of such erroneous press clippings. Among the films he was mooted for but never made it into were: *Larceny Lane* (a proposed sequel to *The Public Enemy*), *King of the Ritz, Beauty Incorporated, A Midsummer*

Night's Dream (he was supposed to play Theseus), *42nd Street*, *Doctor X*, *The Great Profile*, *Delilah*, *Three Loves Has Nancy* and *The Blue Moon Murder Mystery*. Like Reagan with *Casablanca*, Warren likely had the unfortunate luck to simply be a momentary stand-in for an embryonic studio production.

There is another reason to question the sincerity of the *Captain Blood* rumor. By 1934 Warren was just reaching forty years old, hardly the age to take on the persona of a swash-buckling freebooter swinging across the bounding main. Of the subsequent men who were announced as Peter Blood, Robert Donat — who dropped out due to a scheduling conflict — and Errol Flynn, both were in their twenties and had no stylistic baggage to overcome with audiences. The idea of Warren William, already deeply etched in the public consciousness as a modern businessman, lawyer or detective, leading a group of cutthroat pirates would have been too much for Warner Brothers to risk on such a project. They quietly removed his name from the production schedule and continued to assign him to their cut-rate William Powell–style vehicles.

In the end, whether or not Warner Brothers actually intended for Warren to portray the swashbuckling sea captain is irrelevant; he believed it, and the loss of *Captain Blood* as a starring vehicle was the insult that finally shook his imperturbable resolve. From late 1934 until the end of his contract in June of 1936, the actor was more vocal in his complaints and less accom-modating in his actions with the studio. He and Levee began talking about looking for a new contract elsewhere. If Warner Brothers wasn't going to live up the bargain Jack Warner himself had promised, they would test the market in the world outside.

Warren's next assignment was an unwelcome signpost in his relationship with Warner Brothers. Levee and his star read it as exactly what it turned out to be: a warning of a steep downturn ahead. It solidified Warren's pique at what he considered cavalier treatment of his career by the powers that be — a complaint echoed over and over again by various Warners stars through the years — and widened the rift between them. Far from placating him over the loss of *Captain Blood*, putting him in *Living on Velvet* was a clear demotion of his star status on the lot. Only months removed from the twin successes of *Cleopatra* and *Imitation of Life*, he was placed in a subordinate role to George Brent and billed third in a limp, undistinguished film that is far beneath the talents of everyone involved.

Living on Velvet concerns a young pilot, Terry Parker (Brent), who crashes his private plane, killing his sister and parents. Grief-stricken, Terry allows his pent-up guilt and rage to turn him into a self-absorbed creep, and his resulting death wish eventually endangers innocent men when he recklessly disrupts a local air show. His old pal Gibraltar (Warren) is there to greet him when he lands, taking Terry home in an attempt to reconstruct some semblance of the friend he once knew. As Gibraltar, Warren is the precise flip side of all those pre–Code cads he played: an overgrown Boy Scout without any hint of guile or self-interest in him. When he introduces Terry to his girl, Amy (Kay Francis), Gibraltar knows almost immediately that there is a romantic spark — as infinitesimal as it is between Brent and Francis — and nobly steps aside to allow it to turn the incredibly tiny engine of this story. Alas, once Terry and Amy are married, the newlyweds can't seem to agree on how to live; will it be her model of bland normalcy, or his freewheeling insouciance? Eventually Terry's guilty conscience once again rears its head. Indulging his mewling death wish, he again cavalierly puts innocent people at risk, this time when he plows his car into the entrance of an amusement park, narrowly missing the wholesale slaughter of families with young children. No one in the script takes him to task for this obscene behavior, and warming up to such a lout is well nigh impossible.

The *Living on Velvet* script originally called for Terry to die in the wreck, leaving Gibraltar to pick up the pieces with Amy. It would have salvaged some semblance of propriety for the project, but Warners chickened out at the last minute. Hal B. Wallis sent off a memo on November 13 insisting on re-shooting a happy ending where Terry survives and returns, changed, to his wife.[5] Just a week before it wrapped, Jack Warner endorsed the change — perhaps out of simple spite — and Warren did not even get the satisfaction of being the consolation prize for Kay Francis.[6] The ultimate theme of the reedited picture, exemplified by Terry's capitulation to Amy's desire for stability (that conformity is good and necessary), seems so unnatural, contrived and arbitrary, that it resembles the censorious punishment meted out to crooks and cads in Warners' crime pictures. He's emasculated, but — probably only momentarily — happy.

Living on Velvet is clearly designed as a Kay Francis vehicle, but the picture is given over to Brent as Terry. Among the least convincing bad boys in the history of film, Brent is nonetheless the focus of the narrative, and undeniably the one audiences are (inexplicably) supposed to root for. Warren is reduced to a handful of scenes in which he dutifully obeys the rule of the movie best friend: be noble, be sympathetic, and be milquetoast. It is so obviously an inferior, place-holding role — wasted on a quality star when it could have been played by almost anybody — that Warren could hardly mistake the message that Warners was trying to send. Why they were doing it was another matter entirely. While he certainly could have refused the assignment, it was still not in his nature; he preferred to be professional but not without making his displeasure obvious. Typically, he did his level best to shine in his limited scenes, putting in solid and subtle work in spite of the clear downgrade he'd received from his employers. The film's treatment of Gibraltar is, in fact, a metaphorical capsulation of Warren's career at Warner Brothers to that point. The decent, hardworking man does the selfless thing time and again: excuses his friend's fickle behavior, plays the good soldier in love by stepping aside without complaint, then quietly accepts his place as the low man in the triangle. At Amy and Terry's wedding, he is the perfectly unruffled best man. But when the ceremony is over, the camera pulls back in a long truck following the couple down the aisle and out of the chapel, while Gibraltar — and Warren — recede in the distance, left at the altar.

During the production of *Living on Velvet*, disaster struck the Warner Brothers Burbank studios. On the night of December 4, 1934, a fire broke out in the machine shop near the stage where Michael Curtiz was shooting the Paul Muni vehicle *Black Fury*. In spite of efforts of a large group of extras to stop it, the flames quickly spread to an adjacent property warehouse where it gained terrible energy. Out of control, the blaze ravaged fifteen acres and destroyed almost $500,000 worth of studio property before it was extinguished. Among the many famous firefighters pressed into service that night, Warren passed buckets and toted valuable commodities out of harm's way, along with Bing Crosby, Dick Powell and Helen Morgan. Production was temporarily moved to the old Sunset Boulevard studios while Burbank was rebuilt.[7]

Final re-shoots of *Living on Velvet* wrapped late in 1934, and just before New Year's Day the Warners advertising department began placing coverage in trade publications for the early March release. With Warren clearly in a supporting role — his screen time is roughly one-third of Brent's — the actor was billed third behind the two principals, an obvious decision considering the circumstances. However, Warren's reconstructed contract of 1933 — the one that resulted from Warner Brothers' refusal to pay back salary following the Emergency Bulletin reductions — provided that the actor would receive no less than first feature billing in any production he made at the studio. Warren and Mike Levee, eager now to get out from under Warner Brothers' careless attitude towards the actor's livelihood, immediately seized on the legal infraction. On January 4, Levee called Roy Obringer to complain about the situation, since repeated in other print ads, and to reiterate his client's displeasure at this shabby treatment. Levee likely did not get the response he was hoping for—conciliation and assurances of better roles ahead—and he and his client decided to use the breach of contract as an escape clause. It was an inopportune time for Warren's attention to be diverted, with he and Helen at last moving into their new home following months of remodeling. Nonetheless, on January 8—just a week before their first official day as residents in Encino—Warren mailed a letter to Obringer at the studio. The stationery reflected his momentarily limbo between residences, with no address below the simple and elegant script spelling out "WARREN WILLIAM" centered at the top of the page:

> Gentlemen,
>
> [On] December 29th, 1935[8] ... you advertised a picture entitled *Living on Velvet* and gave me second feature billing, which is an outright violation of my contractual rights with you....
>
> I consider that irreparable damage has been done to my standing in the motion picture industry by this type of advertising and by your reassigning other pictures that have heretofore been publicly announced as vehicles intended for me. I make particular reference to Rafael Sabatini's *Captain Blood*.
>
> I am sure that litigation in a matter of this type is unwarranted and as long as you so very apparently consider me unimportant to your forthcoming production schedules, I can most certainly see no valid reason why you should object to giving me my release. My manager, Mr. M.C. Levee, is hereby authorized to execute same for me and I ask that you handle the details of the cancellation of my contract with him.[9]

The letter did not get the desired result, which would have been an outright release from the contract, but it did open communication channels. In a letter dated January 11—Warren and Helen's twelfth anniversary—Obringer attempted to smooth over the situation, calling the billing on *Living on Velvet* "a mix-up." Meetings were held, arguments boiled over and dirty laundry was aired. After everything was settled, Warner Brothers had promised better treatment, but Warren and his agent were still dubious of any change in the road ahead. Meantime, even critics were on Warren's side. One astute scribe simply said of *Living on Velvet:* "Warren William deserves better than this."[10]

On January 16, in the middle of a five-week vacation that started just before Christmas, the Krechs spent their first official day as permanent residents of Encino. During the summer they had sometimes divided their days between a rented house on Carnavan Road and the new ranch, supervising work as it went on around and under them. At last, Warren was able to tell the studio office that they could now send his mail to 4717 Encino Avenue, his new home. He had two weeks to enjoy the settled, still feel of calm that must have enveloped him and Helen after six months of noise and clatter. After that, nothing remained static at the Krech house for long. For the next twelve years, there was always some new project, clever remodel or unfinished upgrade bubbling from the mind of the master of the house.

With Warren's troubles from *Living on Velvet* smoothed over, Warner Brothers continued offering lackluster assignments in B programmers. As always they took the most obvious path—the same one that led Cagney and Robinson into endless gangster pictures, Kay Francis into increasingly cheap soap operas and Errol Flynn into tights and doublets again and again. Warren was now a detective, and the studio could think no further than that.

By his third installment, Perry Mason was flipped permanently off the A-side on the Warners budget list. *The Case of the Lucky Legs* and *The Case of the Velvet Claws* were both snappy and amusing but were knocked off quickly and for little money. Warren's final episode as Mason was delivered into the hands of William Clemens, a journeyman director who was only on his third assignment after an apprenticeship cutting low-budget westerns for *Looney Tunes* producer Leon Schlesinger. There was a fun and entertaining little comedy called *Don't Bet on*

From his boyhood, Warren loved the sea. He combined his passion for boats and engineering by experimenting with models in the swimming pool on his Encino ranch.

Blondes (also known as *Wife Insurance*), with Warren as Odds Owen, the owner of a Lloyd's of London-style insurance agency that indemnifies policy holders against highly unusual occurrences. Contracted by southern Colonel Guy Kibbee to make sure that his daughter (the lovely Claire Dodd) doesn't marry within the year, Warren proceeds to upend his business and his bachelor ways by making her *his* wife. "After doing several of those detective parts I was delighted when *Don't Bet on Blondes* came along. No actor should play serious roles continuously," Warren offered in an interview with the *New York Evening Herald*. "The real benefit of a change to comedy is in the relaxation of tension. It keeps an actor's talent flexible and gives his work naturalness." Producer Hal Wallis rode herd over Robert Florey, the director of *Don't Bet on Blondes,* constantly asking for more speed in the dialogue and pacing. Florey was regularly berated for turning out dailies that were "flat and slow"; line producer Nathan Levinson remarked to Wallis in their ongoing correspondence that the director "does not know all he should know about talking motion picture production."[11] In spite of all the troubles, *Don't Bet on Blondes* remained a favorite of Warren's own films throughout his career.

The critics do not single out Warren for praise in the late Warner Brothers films as they had in the past. He is most often mentioned as solid and professional, but the aura of "a new star in Hollywood" is over. He is still well positioned in gossip columns, magazines and feature articles, but his star has perceptibly faded. He is gradually being convinced that he must take a more active hand in his career or risk being forgotten by producers and the public.

In August of 1935 the carefully controlled and generally unemotional Warren reached his professional breaking point. When he finished *The Case of the Lucky Legs*, the studio gave him his latest assignment, the lead role in another Kay Francis soap opera, *I Found Stella Parish*. A script was furnished and Warren took it home, studying his role as an enterprising newspaper reporter who solves the riddle of a famous actress's mysterious disappearance. After the fiasco of *Living on Velvet, I Found Stella Parish* was at least an A production with Warren in a starring role, better than the increasingly cheap Perry Mason entries and other B pictures being assigned. Unfortunately, Warner Brothers' often inscrutable ways were about to be again demonstrated; when Warren reported for work on Thursday, August 15, he had a shock in store. During his short hiatus, the studio had inexplicably reassigned the lead role to the newly signed British actor Ian Hunter, and demoted Warren to a supporting role that would keep him out of the film for almost an hour.[12] The normally reserved actor was livid. He could not believe that studio executives would be so callous and uncaring as to continue to undermine his career this way, especially after he had been the dutiful soldier in taking on other parts that were clearly less than prestigious. Only a few months earlier Warren's annual contract had been renewed at $2,750 a week and now his employers seemed to be doing everything they could to sabotage one of their most expensive assets. Warner Brothers was clearly more interested in building up a new contract player than maintaining the popularity of a star in whom they had already invested a tremendous amount of time and money. Here, well and truly, Jack Warner's word was proven to be worth nothing. "He'll shake your hand on Friday and tell you you're set for two years," producer Bryan Foy once lamented, "then go to New York, call on Monday and fire you."[13]

Warren refused to participate in the film. Even the most modest of men can be prodded once too often. He must have felt like the continually emasculated husband in *Smarty*, pushed finally to the point of pushing back. He called Mike Levee, told him the situation and removed himself from the lot. *I Found Stella Parish* could go on, but not with him in a nakedly subservient and degrading part. No matter the consequences, he was right to take matters into his own hands. The part of Steven was exactly the kind of meaningless, ineffectual third-wheel character that was destroying his image. He would have been the screen no more than a few minutes near the beginning and the end of the film, in which time the leading lady throws him over for the ponderous and stuffy Ian Hunter. Hardly a recipe for public acclaim.

In response to Warren's very legitimate complaints, Jack Warner had him suspended and thrown off the payroll. Two days later, Warren returned to the studio in an effort to hammer out a compromise. He met with producer William Koenig and the film's director Mervyn LeRoy, but no one was budging until Warren suggested that he be given an unpaid layoff rather than play the part. Koenig took the proposal to Roy Obringer and Jack Warner. While the studio head allowed that he was willing to meet Warren halfway, he didn't feel that the studio should have to be deprived of his services beyond the term of his normal vacation time, paid or not. Obringer and Warner then devised an equitable solution that actually worked out in Warren's favor. They proposed that their dissatisfied player be suspended for the amount of time that his replacement, Paul Lukas, spent shooting *Stella Parish*, with the term of his contract correspondingly extended. Although Warner sometimes used this ploy to artificially extend the contracts of certain stars, in this case it was an excellent deal for the actor. He was not obliged to appear in the offending film, and had the added caveat of the studio legally absolving him of any liability resulting from his refusal to work.[14] That afternoon, Obringer tried to telephone Levee but the agent was out. Coincidentally, however, Warren was in Levee's office at that very moment, and spoke to Obringer about the deal. After listening to the proposal, he told the studio lawyer to send a contract with the terms they discussed and that he and Levee would consider it. Knowing they had come out very equitably, Warren and his agent agreed to the settlement and by Monday, August 19, the row was over. Levee announced to the press that things had been settled amicably, saying that Warners had "kindly" agreed to a one-time loanout in replacement for Warren's appearance in *Stella Parish*.[15] The loanout was not actually part of the deal and it never happened. It's too bad, since the final five films on Warren's contract—all at Warner Brothers—are among the worst of his career.

When he returned to work in September, the studio teamed him with Dolores Del Rio in *The Widow from Monte Carlo*, an odd trifle that at least had the saving grace of finding the actor for once billed above his romantic co-star. Part comedy, part intrigue, part melodrama, *The Widow from Monte Carlo* succeeded in nothing except blurring audience focus and dragging Warren more securely into cheaper pictures. Director Arthur Greenville Collins' unimaginative staging and lack of invention was typical of what Warren could expect during the last part of his service with Warner Brothers. Earlier in his career he was often under the supervision of the A-list Warner storytellers: three times with Curtiz, four times with Roy Del Ruth, twice each with Archie Mayo and Mervyn LeRoy, as well as in loanouts with Cecil B. DeMille, Frank Capra and John Stahl. In his final eighteen months he was largely relegated to the second string talent: William McGann, William Clements, Robert Florey and William Dieterle.

In 1934, MGM's enormous success with Dashiell Hammett's *The Thin Man* had other studios scrambling to duplicate their breezy comedy-mystery hit. Warner Brothers was in the sweepstakes with the Philo Vance series and their schizophrenic attempts to refashion Perry Mason in a similar vein. Then in the winter of 1935, producers Henry Blanke and Hal Wallis decided to dust off the studio's own Hammett property, *The Maltese Falcon*, which had been languishing at the script department since it was initially filmed in 1931 with Ricardo Cortez. Although the novel was clearly of a different stripe from the charming fluff of the MGM film, the producers stubbornly forged ahead to reinvent *The Maltese Falcon* as a screwball farce in order to chase the box office of *The Thin Man*. The idea was not altogether illogical but it was immensely stupid. There is very little room for screwball comedy in Hammett's novel, and without the time, money, script, and appropriate casting or director, the project was doomed from the start.

If Blanke had gotten his way, film history would have had the fascinating proposition of seeing William Powell or Spencer Tracy as Sam Spade in *The Maltese Falcon*. Luckily for both men, Blanke's June memo directing Wallis to try to secure the services of either star went unfulfilled. "In case you can't get William Powell, Spencer Tracy would also be excellent for the part. He and Davis would make a marvelous team," he futilely directed.[16] The actors were spared the ignominy of appearing in this puerile production, eventually extruded onto the screen as *Satan Met a Lady*. Warren was not so lucky. When Powell and Tracy had the good sense to balk, or the good fortune to have MGM refuse, the unlucky actor was assigned to this incoherent, unruly, directionless mess that began shooting on December 2.

On the set with Warren was his old nemesis Bette Davis, now in the early stages of becoming a Hollywood icon following her successes in *Of Human Bondage, The Petrified Forest* and an Oscar-winning performance in *Dangerous*. In spite of their previous problems, there was no trouble between the two actors; on set, Davis complained incessantly of everything except Warren. The actor was in a position to stand by and agree with her anger, even if he was put off by her haughty manner. Everyone in fact was unhappy with the entire sordid mess, including producer Wallis, who almost immediately complained of the script in a memo: "We're going to throw the plot right out the window, what there is of it." Wallis also endured months of debate and uncertainty about the movie's title, which was finally chosen after the exasperated producer started an informal contest to name the picture. An office boy named Howard Clausen got a $25 bonus when he submitted the utterly incomprehensible winning entry over a list of sixty others, including the producer's own suggestions *Beware of Imitations, Every Girl for Herself*, and *Men on Her Mind*. (Almost all the alternate titles refer to the Brigid O'Shaughnessy character, rather than Spade himself.) Since the film was inexplicably originally known as *The Man with the Black Hat*, Warren was forced to wear an absurd black Stetson — which he promptly "lost" six times — until the title was changed during filming due to legal complications. Wallis quickly told director William Dieterle to drop the hat, saying it looked "screwy" — a little late, since Warren wears it in almost every scene.

The picture vaguely follows the story of the classic book (with Spade now known as Ted Shayne), but the script by Brown Holmes — in which Shayne comes off less as a hardbitten pragmatist and more as simply a self-absorbed lout — broadens the characters to cartoonish proportions. Dieterle was a terrible choice to direct; he was technically adept, but his comedic instincts were virtually non-existent. He simply allows the cast to grotesquely overplay the humor — a particular problem since Warren usually went ballistic when allowed to modulate his own comedic choices. Here he careens from semi-serious to downright outrageous — hanging from a doorjamb claiming to be King Kong at one point — and back again. Everyone, in fact, is so aimless that one gets the impression that Dieterle was simply checking the lighting and letting the camera run. After a break for Christmas, the project wrapped on December 28. That evening, Warren attended a gathering to designate his neighbor Al Jolson the unofficial "Mayor of Encino." He was happy to have the whole thing over.

Only the *Washington Post* offered anything positive, unfathomably stating that in *Satan Met a Lady* "all the true Hammett facility and wit have been translated to the screen," while simultaneously insisting that *The Thin Man* had failed to do justice to the author.[17] The critics who saw the film while sober were merciless. Bosley Crowther termed it a "cynical farce of elaborate and sustained cheapness," *Time* magazine dubbed the film "a frayed tassel from Hollywood's lunatic fringe,"[18] and words like "asinine" and "atrocity" were tossed around like so many nickels. It fared so poorly at the box office that a Warners executive later insisted that they had to give out dishes wherever *Satan Met a Lady* was playing. By the time John Huston's 1941 version was released, *Satan Met a Lady* was blissfully forgotten. Humphrey Bogart's portrayal became immortal, and Warren's merely a bizarre footnote.

After *Satan Met a Lady* wrapped, Warner Brothers teamed Warren with his old friend

Gene Lockhart, the man who had helped end his newlywed drought on Broadway with a part in *The Wonderful Visit*. The film was *Times Square Playboy*, and Warren had the added pleasure of Gene's wife Kathleen also appearing in the film. The Krechs and the Lockharts were fast friends, often visiting each other for parties, or dinner and billiards. Their young daughter June — later to be a fine actress herself — remembered well the very tall man with impeccable manners and a winning smile. His rapport with children, in fact, was quite good; any comments from family and friends who knew him as youngsters uniformly indicate that he enjoyed playing and kidding with them, usually treating them as equals. Warren's nieces Barbara and Patricia recall their uncle and the occasional famous friend playing with them under the dining room table in the family home at Port Washington, New York. Warren's decision not to have children seems entirely to be a consequence of marriage rather than personal desire. "I'm sure he would have liked to [have had his own children]," Barbara insisted. "Because he was that kind of person. He was such a giving man that he would have made any child just a *wonderful* parent."[19] Warren never seemed to indicate any displeasure with the situation, however, perfectly content to instead divide his time between his work, his hobbies and Helen.

Times Square Playboy was based on a play by the theatrical giant George M. Cohan, and concerns two old friends from a small town: Victor (Warren), a successful stockbroker and bon vivant in Manhattan, and Ben (Gene Lockhart), married and happy back in the tiny town of Big Bend. When Vic is about to finally marry after many years of bachelorhood, he invites his parochial friend to the big city to be his best man. As the fish out of water, Ben misunderstands the intentions of city slickers (including Vic's future wife and in-laws), causing many problems along the way. Hilarity does not ensue, but mild amusement puts in an appearance, chiefly through the easy rapport and genuine warmth evident between Warren and Gene Lockhart. While they are wonderful together, once again a director allows Warren to overplay the humor. The script likewise needed work, with the construction being too scattershot to sustain interest, and the characters surrounding the two men mostly one-dimensional plot contrivances. Director William McGann, in his only work with Warren, fails to spice up scenes with the proper blocking or visual character cues that might have helped hold the audience's attention. It was a competent but lazy studio effort, typical of the lack of polish put into the actor's vehicles at this time.

While working with his friends Gene and Kathleen on *Times Square Playboy* was a pleasure, Warren was still steaming about his recent treatment from Warner Brothers. On the set he was unlike himself: testy, sensitive, and ready for a fight. Before shooting started on *The Gentleman from Big Bend* (so-called in its script stage), the actor made a request for some changes in dialogue. In the script the two friends are portrayed as older men, with Ben in particular feeling as though life has lately passed him by. Vic, on the other hand, is marrying a girl of twenty. The old friends banter with each other about age, taking turns playfully upbraiding each other. Warren was now 42 years old, and becoming increasingly aware of the trend towards youth on the screen. He did not want to be thought of as "old," and asked that the script be clarified so that it didn't appear that he and Gene — a mere three years older — were supposed to be men between fifty and sixty. When it came time to shoot the main scene in question, Warren found that the script had not been changed. With his dander up from previous indignities, the actor stopped the entire production on Stage One of the Vitagraph lot and refused to continue unless the offending dialogue was removed. McGann was clearly irritated, thinking that everything had been taken care of earlier. He eventually had to call in producer Bryan Foy to mediate, but Warren was spoiling for a fight. "I can't change lines on the set without an okay," the director insisted, to which Warren immediately shot back: "Better start talking it over with someone else, then." As the argument escalated, Foy arrived and brought up the actor John Boles as an example of a young star having played an elderly man in his recent picture, but Warren was having none of it. "Listen, I don't care about what John Boles does—I'm only looking out for myself." "What about Warner Brothers?" Foy asked, irritated. "That's a question we could go into at length—that's something I could write a *book* about!" was the star's indignant reply. The producer then argued that Warren's objections concerning the age question were absurd, but he discovered that there was no getting around the normally accommodating actor this time. "I could object if you wanted to cut my head off, couldn't I?" Warren asked, astonished. It was at this point that Foy turned up the heat. "Warner Brothers would be in a position to probably get damages if the whole thing has to be done over again." "That's your look-out," Warren blustered. "You'll see you can't frighten me with that argument."[20] As the two men went back and forth, it was clear that Warren was looking for an excuse to express his displeasure with the studio, and Foy was the man available. By the time things were cleared up, the lines were changed and Warren had blown off some steam while reasserting a bit of the hard-won clout that Warners was stripping from him. Clearly he was no longer interested in accommodating the will of an organization that did not have his best interests at heart.

Upon release, *Times Square Playboy* came and went, alternately described as "amusing" and "dull" by critics, which is about as accurate and succinct as can likely be managed.

In late January, Warren finished his final appearance as Perry Mason in *The Case of the Velvet Claws*, and on the 31st Warner Brothers advised him that he would have seven weeks off before he needed to return to the studio. The Williams quickly packed up their rolling apartment and trekked 350 miles to a rustic retreat in Rim Rock, Arizona, known as Beaver Creek Ranch. Nestled snugly in the exotic desolation of Coconino National Forest, the area reminded Warren of the magnificent topography he had encountered for the first time as a young soldier in New Mexico. There, he and Helen relaxed, visiting the local cliff dwellings and the red rocks of Sedona. He also had time to consider the near future. His contract with Warner Brothers was only a few months away from renewal, and Mike Levee was looking outside Warner Brothers for options. After all that they had done to him recently, Warren's instinct was to leave the studio if possible, and take his chances elsewhere. It would be a sticky problem, however, since the option of renewal was with the studio, not the artist. If Warner Brothers wanted him to stay, there was nothing he could do about it.

In late February, Warner Brothers decided to recall Warren for a part in a new big-budget Busby Berkeley musical called *Stage Struck*. The studio was hoping to recapture some of the magic of *Gold Diggers of 1933*, bringing in Joan Blondell and Dick Powell to fill out the cast after they had first considered Pat O'Brien and Ruby Keeler, and then the bizarre pairing of Al Jolson and Olivia de Havilland. Levee sent the script out to Arizona on March 3, with Warren directed to report back to the sound stage by March 9. *Stage Struck* needed selling to Warren from the very beginning. Except for the "mix-up" of *Living on Velvet*, *Stage Struck* would be the first time since *Beauty and the Boss* that Warren would be billed below his male co-star. Levee pushed hard to justify taking the assignment in his letter accompanying the script. "[Your] character, in my opinion, in many respects is more interesting than that of Dick Powell. I think the part will get a great many laughs and I think that this type of character will be a welcome change for you. I would very much rather see you go into something like this than another class 'B' picture."[21] In some ways the agent was right. As the theatrical producer Fred Harris, Warren has some of the best lines in the movie, and essays a solid light comedy performance. But the role continued the now precipitous erosion of his star status; Warren does not appear in the film until almost 25 minutes have elapsed, and he is clearly in a supporting position to Blondell and Powell. In the script, Harris could be looking forward to Warren's own future when he is discussing a famous actor of yesteryear: "Where is Reginald Hempstead?" he asks an aide. "I don't know, sir." "That's right. You don't know. Nobody knows. Oblivion."

Stage Struck is a uniquely odd mélange of comedy, musical and character elements and includes Warren's only direct participation in a musical number on film. The song is "The Body Beautiful," featuring manic, surreal choreography by Berkeley wherein a low-rent novelty act known as the Yacht Club Boys dress as *faux* acrobats and perform incredible athletic feats for Fred Harris with the aid of some camera tricks. While Warren drops the occasional rejoinder to the song's questions, he is bopped on the head, tripped, wrestled with and pushed around until the grand finale, when the heads of the four singers detach from their bodies and snake directly into the camera. Let me repeat that: their heads pop off and wriggle toward the audience. Eccentric does not begin to describe it.

Stage Struck fared almost as poorly as *Satan Met a Lady* with audiences and critics. Warren was mercifully absent from most reviews, and even the Yacht Club Boys were thought better than future husband-and-wife Dick Powell and Joan Blondell. The duo was married shortly after shooting wrapped, and upon release Frank Nugent summed up the film against that backdrop. "[*Stage Struck*] will be, we suspect, about as welcome a gift to the Powells as a clock for their mantelpiece, a carving set or a waffle iron, and is just about as novel as a contribution to musical comedy."[22]

Stage Struck was the absolute limit to Warren's celebrated reserve. He believed now that Warner Brothers was doing nothing less than destroying his career. Over the last year they had pushed him into terrible choices that compromised his image and status. But Warren himself made many of those choices possible by not being an active participant in his professional life. With his distaste for conflict and pathological avoidance of what he considered the immodest exercise of his personal ego, the actor contributed mightily to his own gradual decline. Additionally, on screen things were changing; the image of men was becoming less ambiguous and more heroic. The modern, complicated man that Warren played was being replaced by the stalwart, iconic image of Errol Flynn, Clark Gable and (eventually) John Wayne. Rogues were out. Square-jawed, unflappable men of action were in. At the age of 42, Warren, with his Old World manners, cultured voice and aristocratic looks, could not jump the gap into the new paradigm. He was starting to be left behind.

In April, while *Stage Struck* was still shooting, Warren and Levee resolved to leave Warner Brothers at any cost. The agent quietly sniffed around various studios to see what might be available if they were able to avoid renewing with Warners. On April 24, he sent a letter directly to Jack Warner, laying his cards on the table.

> My dear Jack:
>
> You had in WARREN WILLIAM a personality who could very easily have been as popular as Bill Powell is today. He started off like "a house a-fire" because you put him in a few fine outstanding motion pictures.
>
> ... In view of the fact that Warren is so unhappy in his present association — only because of the type parts he is compelled to play — won't you please let him go upon the completion of his present term instead of exercising the option? Unless it is your intention to give him far more important parts and consideration ... it most certainly is a bad investment for you to exercise the option....

At $3,250 a week for his next annual extension due in June, Jack Warner could not dismiss the logic of Levee's argument. Warren's parts could be played by any number of lower paid con-

Preparing for a scene in his final Warner Brothers film, *Stage Struck*, Warren (far left) stands alongside co-star Dick Powell. Looking on closely (left of stage) is director Busby Berkley. Other members of the crew are unidentified.

tractees like Paul Lukas, Ian Hunter or George Brent. The parties began discussing the business of severing their relationship once *Stage Struck* was finished. Warner Brothers had brought him to Hollywood and made him a star. He appeared in 33 films during the 63 months he was under contract. Now, they no longer had a use for him. The screen was changing, and to Roy Obringer and Warner, Warren already seemed old-fashioned. The present tense of the studio was in James Cagney, Edward G. Robinson and Bette Davis; the future belonged to Errol Flynn, Humphrey Bogart and John Garfield. The evolving Warner Brothers style didn't countenance Warren's *laissez-faire* post–Code construction.

But Warner Brothers did not let Warren go without first sticking the knife in just a little deeper. The studio had the sole power to renew or dismiss the contract under which Warren served the corporation. As such they had the power to control his fate and any possible deals that Levee had investigated. With a handful of secret offers on the horizon, the studio decided to leverage their power and get something in return for their "consideration." They demanded that Warren buy his way out of the contract. The actor and his agent reluctantly agreed; they would pay $10,000 for the privilege of leaving Warner Brothers and the shabby treatment he had endured in 1935.[23] Additionally, the petty powers-that-be in Warner Brothers saw to it that

A notorious homebody, Warren appears bored and tired at this Hollywood party, circa 1936. Even the company of two beautiful women (unidentified) doesn't prevent him from looking as though he wished he were elsewhere.

Warren was not featured nor touted in *Stage Struck* publicity once it hit theaters. He was absent from the cover of the pressbook and received scant attention inside. Some cast lists provided by the Warners press department had Warren placed fifth or sixth behind Frank McHugh and newcomer Jeanne Madden. Once he was no longer a studio property, his former employers acted as if he never existed.

All that spring Levee had been looking for a deal that would allow his client to star in the kind of prestige productions to which Warner Brothers had been increasingly reluctant to assign him. He had meetings with RKO for Warren to play the lead in *Beauty, Inc.*, a vehicle originally announced for William Powell about a businessman who builds an empire in the cosmetic industry. Word of the RKO assignment found its way to the press, and industry wags expected him to sign a long-term contract with the studio. But Levee had a few other irons in the fire.

During the previous months Levee had also been in negotiations with Emanuel Cohen's newly formed production company Major Pictures for the actor's services. Cohen had been the head of production for Paramount from 1929 to 1935, during which time he pulled the studio from the brink of bankruptcy and put it solidly into the black. For his efforts, the Paramount board had him fired. It wasn't long before Cohen bit back. The fledgling independent

Warren contemplates what to do next — take the plunge or not. He was so fond of the water that family members refer to him as "a fish."

producer made deals for contracts with three of Paramount's biggest stars, Gary Cooper, Bing Crosby and Mae West. Paramount found themselves over a barrel: if they wanted to retain the rights to the trio, they needed to accommodate Major Pictures. The arrangement Cohen struck with Paramount reflected his position of strength: The studio financed and distributed each production, taking a percentage of profits from the gross receipts. It was almost a no-lose situation for the producer, and by the summer of 1936 he was preparing his first film under the Paramount deal, *Go West, Young Man.*

The blue chip investment of Major Pictures was Mae West. Cohen had signed the star late in 1935 after the studio had failed to renew her option, promising her $300,000 per picture. The vivacious but aging actress had helped keep Paramount alive during the early '30s, and was handsomely rewarded for it. In 1935 she was the second highest paid resident of the United States (after publishing magnate William Randolph Hearst), with an income of $480,000, and seemingly at the height of her popularity. She would pull double duty as the writer and star of *Go West, Young Man,* making most actors hardly anxious to sign onto the project. West was well known for narrowing the spotlight to include her and little else.

On June 22, 1936, the filming of retakes on *Stage Struck* ended and later that week Warren received his final check from Warner Brothers in the amount of $458.33. With his client at last a free agent, Levee consummated the deal with Cohen. Warren was signed for three pictures, including a co-starring role in *Go West.* Although the year-long contract was non-exclusive, it left no room in the actor's schedule for *Beauty, Inc.* Levee tried to make space for the picture, but by January RKO could wait no longer and the talks melted into nothing.

On the surface, Warren's deal with Major Pictures and Cohen looked like a good one. He and Levee had every reason to believe that the move from Warner Brothers—albeit without the security of a long-term contract—would be a good one. He would command better roles in higher budget productions, and more money for less work—three films that year instead of his usual six or seven. And although he still eschewed big publicity and personal ballyhoo, deep down Warren was interested in claiming those roles and the financial stability—and personal autonomy—that went with them.

Production of *Go West* was supposed to begin in July of 1936, but the script that West had "written" and that Cohen had submitted to the MPPDA for approval was rejected. (Director Henry Hathaway described West's contribution to the film thus: "She got credit because she wrote a couple lines."[24]) The pompous head of the MPPDA, Joseph Breen, was quoted in the press as saying of West's character in the film, "The whole flavor is that of a nymphomaniac." It was true, of course, as was the way with every Mae West character, so during the summer Cohen and Breen hammered out changes to the story that would be acceptable to the MPPDA. Meantime, the erstwhile Warners star had some fun at the 55th annual Actor's Fund Benefit show at the Pan Pacific Auditorium. On the evening of June 28 he reunited with his old pal Frank Shannon to recreate a scene from their Broadway hit *Twelve Miles Out,* to the delight of the star-studded audience.[25] Warren and Helen then spent a leisurely July sailing to Mexico on the newly refurbished *Pegasus,* returning when Breen relented on the acceptability of West's script and the production finally began in August.

Go West, Young Man was based on Lawrence Riley's play *Personal Appearance* about the antics of the sex-crazed movie star Marvis Arden (West) as she crosses rural America on a publicity tour in support of her new film *Drifting Lady.* She's accompanied by her PR agent, Morgan (Warren), who has been directed by the studio to make sure that she does not break a clause in her contract that forbids her from marriage for five years. Naturally she can't help trying to obliterate the document with an endless series of carnal opportunities, obliging Morgan to deftly perform *romanticus interruptus* at each turn.

The company first trudged to location shooting at the Lake Norconian Resort, in Riverside County near San Diego. Astride the town of Norco, it was built in the late 1920s as "The Resort Supreme," and for a short while it was. From its opening in 1929 until the Depression closed it in 1933, it hosted vacationing Hollywood stars, national golf tournaments, speedboat races, and Olympic-qualifying swimming events and was featured in half a dozen major films. Following reorganization and a new influx of money, the resort reopened in 1935 and was still a versatile place to shoot, with great mountain vistas, beautiful lake views, a spectacular golf course and the quaint town of Norco nearby. The cast and crew, including Warren, director Henry Hathaway and West, celebrated the launch of Major Pictures' first film — and Emanuel Cohen's birthday — on August 5 with a huge party at the resort. Filming continued through most of the month and then the company returned to Los Angeles for studio work.

Warren reported to the Major Pictures lot, a rented space in the General Service Studio, amid a clamor of construction; new stages, executive offices and dressing bungalows were being erected during, between and around productions that summer. Located in Hollywood at Santa Monica Boulevard and Las Palmas, the facility had been built in 1919 by a former employee of Charlie Chaplin, and was a popular destination for independent producers, including Harold Lloyd and Howard Hughes. Studio space was often at a premium, and General, then owned by AT&T, was an alternative to other large studios like United Artists, just down the street. All the Major Pictures films were shot there, which was okay with Warren; it was a few miles closer to Encino than the Warner studio in Burbank, resulting in extra sleep for the late rising actor over the following year.

In September, Warren's maiden production outside Warner Brothers was finished, but not without some bruises and scrapes along the way. As always, West proved to be difficult. Director Hathaway politely termed her "taxing to work with," and there were a few painful moments on the set between the actors. In one scene, West was required to punch Warren and send him reeling. Hathaway wasn't satisfied with the shot West gave Warren and begged her to punch harder. "It doesn't look right," the director screamed. Having already endured a few painful takes, Warren mournfully asked, "What do you want her to do, shove her fist clear through my head?"[26]

Although *Go West, Young Man* has some serious defects as a comedy, it benefits from one of Warren's most engaging post–Code performances. As Morgan, the publicity agent-wrangler-romantic foil of West's Marvis Arden, he practically steals the film, and in the process makes you wish it were more worthy of his larceny. It is one of the only times in his career where he played second chair to a strong female presence — and not many were stronger than Mae West — and came out sparking brighter than the star.

West's adaptation maintains surprising focus on her male lead, a rare occurrence in her career. She should be given great credit for the generosity with which the final film treats Warren. "She had final cut on everything," Hathaway explained. "And anything she wanted out, it was out."[27] The finished movie has Warren on screen almost as much as West, and allows him some wonderful comedic business to spice up his scenes. These clever bits and personal observations add dimension to Morgan, rounding off rough character edges that might be evident without them. The director also curtailed Warren's tendency to play his comedy in broad strokes, eliciting a subtle and charmingly nonchalant performance that he rarely achieved with lesser directors in the Warners machine. Just watching Warren's face through the picture is a genuine pleasure. His simple communication of exasperation, insouciance, bemusement, irritation or satisfaction is truly entertaining. His Academy training in pantomime is glowingly evident here and it is a shame that Hollywood directors rarely used these comedic tools to greater effect.

The character of Morgan is an immaculate evolution of the pre–Code persona that Warren honed during his years at Warner Brothers. Like James Cagney going from gangster to G-man, he's now the good guy who knows all the bad guy's tricks. Here Warren does not use his devious

Warren brings a launch alongside his yacht, *Pegasus.* He was among Hollywood's preeminent sailors, along with Humphrey Bogart, Errol Flynn and James Cagney. Courtesy Barbara Hall.

talents to seduce the star, but rather to make sure no one else seduces her. There seems no doubt that Hathaway and West understood the connection between the kind of amoral, unregenerate hucksters Warren had excelled at playing during the early '30s, and the somewhat more ethical but equally underhanded character they needed to spar with Marvis Arden in *Go West.* For the first time, a director properly modulates Warren's character between humor and deviousness, and allows him to be likable not merely because of his mysterious rapport with the audience, but because of a dormant sense of decency and humanity buried deep in the cynical press agent.

Although the script could have used a professional rewrite, the real problem with *Go West, Young Man*, is the star herself. By 1936, West's style — and her popularity — were in eclipse. The sexually predatory image that had captivated audiences during the past few years had grown old and hackneyed and, not to be unkind, so had Mae West. Without the novelty of naughtiness she had long cultivated, she comes off as frankly pathetic — a wooden, sexually repellant, preposterous figure out of step with the rapidly changing tastes of the American public. Rewritten to feature the male lead, and mounted with a more intriguing starlet (let's imagine Carole Lombard, for instance), *Go West, Young Man* could have become a minor gem of screwball comedy. As it stands, it is merely a professional and competent misfire.

As West's popularity was decreasing, so was her box office. *Go West, Young Man* received generally positive reviews, but the public stayed away. It was a shame, since they would have had the opportunity for once to see Warren stand toe to toe with one of the most powerful

This portrait was taken in the library of Warren's Encino home just after he left Warner Brothers for Major Pictures in 1936. The three films he made there were forgettable, but the deal led to a contract with Metro-Goldwyn-Mayer.

women in Hollywood and come out on top. Many critics noticed, at least. The *Los Angeles Times* hailed him for one of the best performances in recent films,[28] while the *New York Times* review was indicative of the plaudits that bubbled up through West's pervasive presence: "Warren William, as the press agent, is, of course, deserving of the most special mention of all. He is the only player who has ever come close to stealing a picture from Mae West."[29]

In November, Warren started shooting his first headlining movie with Major Pictures, *Outcast*, adapted from the novel *Happiness Preferred*. Essentially a "B" programmer with an "A" cast, the film follows the travails of Dr. Phillip Jones (Warren), unjustly accused of murder in the accidental death of one of his patients. After acquittal, he retreats to a small town where he is unknown and tentatively resumes his practice. It isn't long before trouble comes in the guise of the dead woman's sister-in-law Margaret (Karen Morley), who still believes Jones to be culpable. Following the advice of kindly Anthony Abbott (Lewis Stone), Margaret discovers the innocent truth about Jones. Unfortunately, the town uncovers his true identity and the supposed "murderer" is nearly lynched by the locals. The film was widely praised and remains a sincere but flawed indictment of mob violence, as much as it can be when the victim is a good-looking white-collar wasp. Robert Florey directed (his fourth effort with Warren) with adequate pictorial flourish but little sense of drama; the script was co-written by future MGM boss and noted Hollywood liberal Dore Schary. *Outcast* did marginal business (it didn't have the sensationalism of Fritz Lang's *Fury*, released the year before) and critics again undervalued Warren's professionalism and competence. He was now trapped by his consistent excellence in unremarkable roles — good enough to notice, but not challenging enough to excite you.

By now the country was beginning to feel more confident of economic recovery. Little by little, America was crawling out from under the black cloud of doubt and uncertainty. The Depression — or as it might have been called then, "The Crisis" — was chronic, but it was no longer a looming emergency that might erupt at any moment. In early 1937, just as Warren and Helen were driving down to Mexico for a vacation, the Ohio River Valley sustained the worst flooding in American history to that point, with almost 1,000 dead and half a million homeless. Until hurricane Katrina welded a political component to the tragedy, floods like those in the 1937 season came and went — each time there was a new, bigger one, the previous horror was forgotten. The national consciousness has only so much room for heartache.

While Warren was shooting *Midnight Madonna*, the final film in his three-picture deal with Cohen, Levee was working his contacts to secure his erstwhile star a deal with Hollywood's number one studio, Metro-Goldwyn-Mayer. It was the solemn wish of every actor of the era to secure a contract with MGM — it meant money, prestige and the backing of a supreme array of talent behind the cameras and in the press. Levee believed that if Warren were with MGM, he would be able to climb back to the front rank of film actors. The studio had the will, the power and the money to revive his career by putting him in quality productions that were beyond the desire of Warner Brothers and out of the reach of Emanuel Cohen. He had assurances that Warren would be featured in some fine films, and he believed that things were looking up. In April, Levee's diligence paid off: Shortly after Warren finished *Midnight Madonna* he became the property of MGM studios.[30] His new contract was worth only $1,750 a week to the actor at 40 weeks' work, approximately $65,000 a year, far below what he would have been earning at Warner Brothers, which makes one wonder if Levee was not bargaining on the Bizarro world. But the prestige of MGM and the opportunity to work in a less pressurized environment were very important. Also, everyone was now aware of the gradual decline of Warren's career. Jimmy Fidler embarrassingly included him in his column under the section titled: "In need of good

There were four overriding passions in Warren's life: his wife Helen, sailing on the open sea, inventing, and his beloved dogs Jack, Jill and Babs. This photo was snapped at home during the time he was under contract to MGM.

pictures to bolster fading prestige."[31] And when *Midnight Madonna* opened, *The Washington Post* remarked: "Warren William should step back up by several notches because of *Midnight Madonna*. He has been the victim of a couple bits of unfortunate casting and direction."[32] But the story of a big-time gambler with a heart of gold ultimately meant nothing to the movie-going public and MGM would soon prove that Warren meant little to them.

15

Imitation of Life

When Warren reported to his new studio, his first assignment was to an adaptation of the Rudolf Friml operetta *The Firefly*, which Jeanette MacDonald was mounting as her first solo vehicle at MGM after many enormously successful teamings with Nelson Eddy. The production, a lavish historical drama of spies and intrigue during the Napoleonic era, was among the biggest of Warren's career. There were 30 major sets, a spectacular wardrobe collection, 500 extras and the usual lavish MGM detail. However, the nexus of attention was MacDonald and her co-star, the wooden baritone Allan Jones. Warren, as the villainous De Rougemont, is a mere afterthought. The shoot was very smooth, with reasonable hours and the pleasure of a polite and professional co-star in MacDonald, but once again the film and the part were not what he was expecting. In spite of a full court press from the Metro publicity department and some nice reviews, *The Firefly* failed to make a solid profit for MGM, and delivered no profit for Warren. His contribution to the film, when mentioned, was lukewarmly noted as "chiefly supporting the star," and allowing that he "heads a good supporting cast." Being back in a period piece for the first time since his sophomore Warner Brothers effort *Honor of the Family* drew some curious reactions. "I contemplated Warren William rather uneasily in costume as a Napoleonic Colonel," one critic wrote. "It was hard not to chuckle at the first sight of this modern figure under a period cocked hat, but that perhaps was not Mr. William's fault."[1] *The Firefly* did establish his viability for period roles, something few producers had contemplated with his success in the modern idiom. As his career turned more and more to character parts in the succeeding years, it gave casting directors the confidence to put him in historical films like *The Man in the Iron Mask*, *Arizona* and *Lillian Russell*.

In the few years since its inception, when Warren and thirteen other actors resigned AMPAS, the Screen Actors Guild had grown into a union 6,000 members strong. Warren had worked diligently to help its success, serving on the board of directors, helping to organize charity events and attending to various functions of the organization. By May of 1937 the ultimate strength of the union had not yet been tested, but that spring the Guild was prepared for a strike. Ostensibly SAG was looking for greater security for its junior members, demanding more money for the stock, extra and bit players, but more than that it was looking to establish itself as the sole bargaining agency for actors throughout Hollywood.[2] As a staunch supporter of the union cause, Warren was in favor of the strike, and ready to go out on the picket lines to get what he felt was right. The strike never came. With just the threat of a walkout, the studios fell in line, each signing a formal contract that meant the legitimization of the Screen Actors Guild. The ploy had worked: Not only did SAG achieve its goal of security for tens of thousands of actors in the succeeding years, but in that moment it also created a permanent, indisputable authority to negotiate for all screen actors. The success of the Screen Actors Guild, and the benefits bequeathed to each new generation as a direct consequence of the courage of those original fourteen men, should not be underestimated.

Meanwhile, Warren and Levee were discovering that MGM was going to be no better, and in some ways far worse, than Warner Brothers. Returning from a fishing trip off Catalina, Warren found his next assignment was another of those thankless milquetoast roles that had already damaged his star image. *Madame X* was the third screen reiteration of the tearjerking 1910 play by Alexandre Bisson, about a wayward mother who commits murder and is defended by a lawyer who is—unbeknownst to him—her own son. Gladys George was the infamous *Madame X* this time, and Warren played the old-fashioned husband who disowns her because of marital indiscretions. As Bernard Flouriet he is billed third behind John Beal, and literally and figuratively disappears from the screen for long stretches during the course of the narrative. Although *Madame X* is reasonably entertaining as a lightweight weeper, the public probably forgot Warren was even in the film halfway through. If the quiet, self-possessed actor ever had nightmares about his career dwindling down to almost nothing, *Madame X* is presumably the exact kind of production his subconscious would have invented to torment him.

Things looked up slightly when MGM decided to create a sequel to the classic 1932 film *Arsene Lupin*, where John Barrymore played the jewel thief Lupin and his brother Lionel was the detective who matches wits with him. Melvyn Douglas played the now-retired Lupin this time around, while Warren was a recently retired police detective who is privately on the trail

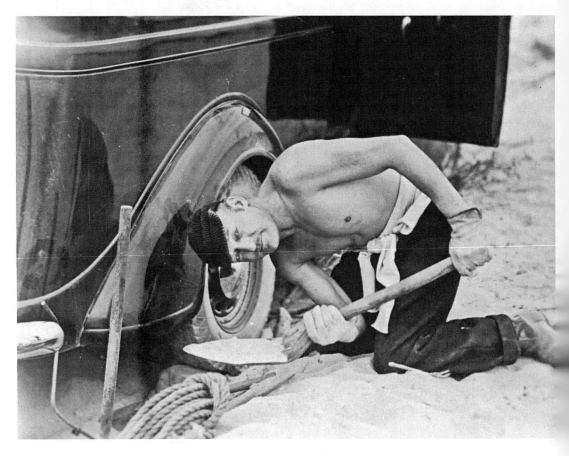

In spite of his refined and gentlemanly image, Warren William was an avid outdoorsman who loved to get his hands dirty with honest labor. He kept himself in tip-top physical shape this way throughout his Hollywood career. Courtesy Barbara Hall.

of the notorious French cracksman. There was no reason that Warren could not have played the lead in this picture; he had the sophistication, presence and intellect to pull it off. His eventual casting as the Lone Wolf at Columbia was essentially a domestic version of Lupin, but Metro executives were not thinking of him as a leading man, in spite of any assurances to the contrary. It was clear that Warren was going to get no breaks from the studio during his tenure there.

Arsene Lupin does afford Warren his best part at MGM. He crosses swords with Douglas and comes out almost equal to the dapper, urbane thief. In spite of being billed third behind Douglas and Virginia Bruce he has a juicy part and some wonderful scenes; he and Douglas, in fact, have some very solid chemistry. Warren reconnected here with director George Fitzmaurice, who had so much trouble on Sam Goldwyn's *Nana* four years earlier that it got both men replaced. Virginia Bruce became a close friend of the Williamses after this picture and their next, *The First 100 Years.*

The story of the friction between a career woman and her old-fashioned husband makes up the scenario of *The First Hundred Years.* The film is littered with arbitrary plot elements, cheap contrivances and a generally monotone delivery. In support, Warren and Binnie Barnes have some real life in them, but Robert Montgomery and Virginia Bruce manage nary a spark

The situation might be more serious than he thought: no windshield, no tires, no seats, no doors, no engine. This is exactly when the amateur inventor's mind would percolate with ideas of how to use the discarded hulk. Courtesy Barbara Hall.

as man and wife. Frank Nugent was not unduly unkind when he lead his review with this bon mot: "Nobody has ever discovered a way of yawning politely. If somebody had we should certainly infringe his copyright today on behalf of *The First Hundred Years*."[3]

In April, with a contract renewal looming and no hope of better choices at MGM, Warren advised Levee to have him released from the contract. "Warren William has decided that MGM has given him roles just as mediocre as those at Warmer Brothers," the *Hartford Courant* reported, "and will freelance at the end of his current contract."[4] The pair fully expected to have been treated far better than at Warner Brothers, but it was quite the opposite case. "I left Warner Brothers for MGM because they gave me such awful parts," was Warren's lament in the spring of 1938. "But MGM was much worse." He added, naively, "Now I'm only going to make good A pictures."[5] Levee got the studio to loan his unhappy client out to Universal to fulfill the final picture on his contract,[6] but it was too late; by that time, Warren was no longer a leading man. Rather than bolster him, MGM accelerated the downward arc of his career by deliberately placing him in weak, secondary roles, and featuring him behind tepid, lackluster stars like Robert Montgomery and Allan Jones. Less than a year earlier he was still mentioned as an important star on a par with Tyrone Power, Robert Taylor and James Stewart,[7] but now he was being painted as the odd man out. "I feel like the forgotten man of pictures," he complained immediately after breaking his MGM deal. His agreement with Universal paid him

This is Warren as he saw himself—just plain old Bill Krech from Minnesota. No fancy cars, jet-set lifestyle or tabloid affairs ever beguiled this sincerely modest man. Courtesy Barbara Hall.

$1,500 a week, less even than what he was drawing at Metro.[8] Columnist Sheilah Graham was brutally honest about what was happening to Warren and others who had begun the slow ebb of their career status. It had been going on since the advent of the star system in 1910, when Florence Lawrence broke away from her nameless career as "The Biograph Girl" and became the first well-known movie star. "Every time a new star is created an old star begins walking the plank toward oblivion. A few short years ago Ruby Keeler, Constance Bennet, Kay Francis and Warren William were names guaranteed to pile up a box office score. Where are they now?" Graham asked. "The majority have been forced into 'B' pictures. Others willingly play second fiddle to the stars who have ousted them."[9] In this observation the savvy columnist was an oracle. Warren was now consigned to do both.

At Universal, *Wives Under Suspicion* (from a play by Ladislas Fodor, author of *Beauty and the Boss*) offered Warren his first starring role in over a year. As crusading District Attorney Jim Stowell, he revels in obtaining capital convictions, counting them off on an abacus made of tiny skulls. When he begins to suspect his wife of adultery, Stowell gets the urge for homicide himself. It was a quick B picture, assigned by Universal to James Whale after a series of box office failures over recent years. The director of *Frankenstein* described *Wives Under Suspicion* as one of his "punishment pictures," but in spite of his restrictions in cast, crew, schedule and budget, he did his best to turn out something professional. Whale moved quickly on the set,

Warren sets up housekeeping on this 1937 camping trip into Nevada. He developed a love for the American southwest while he was stationed in New Mexico during the First World War. Courtesy Barbara Hall.

Three of the world's ten best-dressed men: Warren appears with Douglas Fairbanks, Jr. (center), and Adolphe Menjou (right) on the Universal lot while he was filming *Wives Under Suspicion* (1938). Warren regularly appeared on "Hollywood's best-dressed" lists during the 1930s.

hoping to re-establish his credibility in the industry. *Suspicion* began on April 8 with a budget of approximately $250,000 (still almost double some of Warren's Warner Brother vehicles) and twenty days to shoot. The director finished in sixteen days and $30,000 under budget. In spite of his unhappiness on the project, Whale got along well with Warren. The actor likely knew of his director's quiet reputation as a homosexual, but Warren was quite liberal about such issues. He had met many gay friends of his sister Pauline,[10] and couldn't help but encounter all kinds of personalities during the fabulous Roaring Twenties in New York. Additionally, the two men were not dissimilar in character. "Whale never followed a policy of rigorous self-promotion," his biographer James Curtis wrote. "Socially, he had a small sphere of friends, maintained a regular routine of little variation ... and entertained scantly."[11] When Whale scored a prestige assignment the following year on *The Man in the Iron Mask*, Warren was in the cast with the director's blessing.

In the middle of 1938, Warren was tired. By the time he finished *Wives Under Suspicion* he had been working almost continuously for seven years. It was his first starring role in over a year and it disappeared with barely a notice. The best the press could manage was to say he had given a "thoughtful and highly intelligent performance."[12] His disillusionment with the studio system was at its height and he began thinking seriously about a return to the stage as a way to bring the enjoyment back to acting. He fielded an offer from producer John Wildberg to star in Dorothy Bennet and Link Hannah's new play *Writers Cramp*, which Wildberg wanted to tour the country before it opened in New York.[13] During the summer, he and Katherine Alexander, along with Rod La Rocque (star of the film version of Warren's stage hit *Let Us Be Gay*), rehearsed the comedy, waiting for a schedule from the producer. Nothing came of the opportunity. The next year rumors also spread that Warren would return to the stage when he was mooted for a production at Milwaukee's beautiful Pabst Theatre under the direction of right wing kook Myron Fagin. This one also failed to materialize. It wasn't until October that Warren's name again appeared in the trades, when he signed a deal to go to Columbia Pictures for the series that would become his bread and butter for the next five years.

The summer of 1938 saw Warren weighing his options and taking time

The Lone Wolf was the essence of suave. In nine films from 1939 to 1943, Warren portrayed Michael Lanyard, the reformed thief who now used his illicit skills for good causes instead of helping himself. Among those who appeared in the series with him were Ida Lupino, Rita Hayworth, Lloyd Bridges, Victor Jory, Henry Wilcoxon, Sheldon Leonard, Ann Savage and his old friend Thurston Hall.

off from the grind of picturemaking. He had no pressing interest in going back to contract work, and Mike Levee was sure that he could get Warren quality roles on a picture-by-picture freelance basis. While Levee sniffed out deals and manned the phones, Warren took the opportunity to enjoy California sunshine, while sailing, fishing and playing golf. Unfortunately, it was scarcely time to remove himself from the screen. After the fiasco at MGM, he needed to steady the ship of his career. But never let it be said that Warren did not do things his way. This was the summer that he announced (temporarily, it turned out) that he was quitting the invention business to devote more time to Helen and the well-being of their marriage. "Now, I'm going to have some fun," he enthused.[14] The pair were indeed a different couple that season, appearing regularly at events and openings all over Los Angeles. In July they hosted a massive party for civilians to "meet the stars" sponsored by a major fan magazine. Hundreds came to the ranch to enjoy the couple's hospitality, meeting other famous faces such as Anita Louise, Glenda Farrell, Marian Marsh, Wayne Morris, Henry Wilcoxon and Jack La Rue. At about the same time he was continuing his charity work with the Tailwaggers Foundation, helping stage a series of events designed to raise money for a hospital and shelter for dogs. He spoke at a reunion of World War I nurses, rode in the American Legion Pageant, played in Mount Sinai's annual Comedians vs. Leading Men charity baseball game, and attended a benefit for the Salvation Army. He and Helen were seen at a cocktail party for the Viscount and Viscountess Berard-Alais, high tea at Aileen Beaver's home, the Motion Picture Polo Game and Horse Show, and a gam for the Antarctic explorer David Abbey Page. Helen hosted her own high tea for wives of visiting Phi Kappa Alphas, and the couple attended Helen Hayes' debut in *Victoria Regina* at the Biltmore Theatre. On August 18, the great drama of the Williams' summer unfolded while Warren was fishing on the boat of his friend, William Kreider. Looking for marlin south of Catalina Island, Kreider snagged something and reeled in the catch. When it came into view, the sportsmen saw not a marlin, but a 200-pound shark at the end of the line. After several tense and bloody minutes in which the two men bludgeoned the animal with spikes, they landed it and Warren stepped up to remove the hook from the dead fish. Except that it was not quite dead and quickly took a bite out of Warren's left index finger and hand. "Those teeth sounded like a buzz saw," he sheepishly recalled when interviewed about the incident.[15] The wound was not serious — although it might have been — and his doctor stopped by the house to examine it and thread seven stitches, telling Warren to stay home for a few days. Helen, entirely used to his exploits, had the last word. "Not even a hero to the fish, and only a husband to me," she said.

16

The Lone Wolf Strikes

After a summer devoted to leisure with Helen, it was finally time to go back to work. While Warren had been enjoying himself on the town, Mike Levee was working with Columbia on a deal to bring him back to the screen in a role that was tailor-made for him. The character was the gentleman thief Michael Lanyard, a.k.a. the Lone Wolf, created by Louis Joseph Vance in 1914. Since 1917 Lanyard had been featured in a series of successful film adaptations of Vance's stories, the latest being 1935's *The Lone Wolf Returns*, starring Melvyn Douglas. The late 1930s and early 1940s was a Golden Age of screen sleuths, with each studio investing in series featuring characters such as the Thin Man, Philo Vance, Perry Mason, Mr. Moto, Charlie Chan, Bulldog Drummond, the Saint, the Falcon and many more. Lanyard himself was an inspiration for the "suave crook turned honest" subgenre that counted the Saint and the Falcon as members. In the fall of 1938, Columbia resolved to bring the Lone Wolf back in a big way, with solid resources behind their maiden revival, and they wanted Warren.

On October 7, news releases announced that Columbia had signed Warren William to play the Lone Wolf in a series of films. Levee had engineered a very solid deal: Warren was contracted on a non-exclusive basis for two Lone Wolf films per year, allowing him to pick and choose freelance productions on the side while still enjoying the security of a long-term contract. It was a very happy arrangement for Warren, who was now able to avoid the pettiness of studio politics. He could work when he wanted, on the films he wanted, and be the arbiter of his own fate. Also, it is likely that he was now beginning to accept the fact that he was no longer a sought-after star, but rather took heart in the fact that he was still a sought-after character actor and featured player. Watching stars come and go in the theater and in films, he was acutely aware of the fact that nothing lasts forever. Without an overly developed ego, he would finally accept his changing fate without too much anger or resentment, but rather relief that he was still wanted and liked.

Just before he signed with Columbia, Warren decided to sell his boat and invest in a new schooner. *Pegasus* was now almost ten years old (Richard Barthelmess had sailed it for many years before Warren purchased it) and the actor was interested in an upgrade to something more modern. He consummated a sale with a buyer to make monthly installments starting in January. After February the payments stopped and *Pegasus* was quickly back in his hands. Just two years later he made a similar arrangement with a young couple who had just gotten married. Within a few weeks the newlyweds split when the husband sailed off on the boat with another woman and no payments forthcoming. *Pegasus* again returned to him. Finally by the summer of 1941 it was sold for good.

In June of that year he was rumored to be awaiting completion of a new yacht being built in Gloucester, Massachusetts. The story was that when it was finished he would fly east, then bring the ship home by sailing through the Panama Canal.[1] Although Warren was a fine fair weather sailor, he was hardly the man to attempt such a feat and Helen knew it. She often worried of "maritime dangers," especially when Warren had been involved in more than his fair share.[2] Besides the incident where he was becalmed off Catalina Island and running the *Cutlass* aground in New York, there were occasional examples of him having trouble with navigation. He once supposedly set sail for Ensenada, in Baja California, just south of San Diego, and after twelve hours at sea instead wound up in Santa Barbara, ninety miles north of LA.[3] The story is probably apocryphal — how could an experienced sailor not know which direction he was going with the continent of North America at his right at all times? — but still, the idea of him on the Atlantic at the whim of Mother Nature scared Helen. The boat was instead delivered to the Williams in July of 1941. There was talk of breaking the new vessel in with a trip to Honolulu, but it is unlikely that Helen assented to that adventure either.

Back at Columbia in November, Warren began work on the first of nine films he would mount as the Lone Wolf, creating the character that indelibly etched him in the minds of an entire generation of filmgoers. Michael Lanyard was a perfect fit for the actor: a welcome combination of humor, sophistication, insouciance, intellect and masculine charisma, while not forgetting a hint of larceny that is never far from the surface. It was a neat mash-up of all of the roles Warren had played over the years stuffed into one satisfying package. The very first scene of the Warren William *Lone Wolf* era sets the tone for the series: At night on a rain-soaked street, two gunmen quietly accost the reformed crook. "Stick-up?" he sleepily asks. When they indicate that it isn't, he lowers his voice, resignedly. "Murder?" It is neither robbery nor homicide, but it is the beginning of a nifty little crime film suffused with comedy called *The Lone Wolf Spy Hunt*. Warren's initial effort, based on 1929's *The Lone Wolf's Daughter*, concerns Lanyard's efforts to break up a local spy ring, while his daughter (Virginia Weidler) does her best to get herself into trouble again and again. Everything was right about the studio's relaunch of the series. Ida Lupino is gorgeous and funny as Val Carson, the man-eating daughter of a Senator who does her best to trap Lanyard into marriage. She mugs, argues, fumes, coos and woos with great agility; her scenes with Warren crackle with comic timing and chemistry, as one then the other gets the romantic upper hand. The script, by the well-known whodunit writer Jonathan Latimer, deftly balances mystery, intrigue, screwball comedy and action, while his dialogue keeps things attractive even when there isn't much action going on. It was the first film for stage director Peter Godfrey (later with Warner Brothers) and he worked very nicely, increasing the pace to a breakneck finale while keeping the audience fully invested in the story. Then there was the casting of sultry Rita Hayworth as Karen, the femme fatale who vamps Lanyard and bedevils his would-be fiancée, Val Carson. It was here, in *The Lone Wolf Spy Hunt*, that Howard Hawks reportedly first saw Hayworth and offered her a part in *Only Angels Have Wings*, the film that began her rise to fame in the 1940s.

Critics greatly enjoyed this reiteration of the Lone Wolf, although it was inevitably compared to *The Thin Man* in spite of Lanyard's far older pedigree. "Should be in there with this sort's current spy scare," said B.R. Crisler, noting the tendrils of war hysteria seizing Hollywood.[4] And of *Spy Hunt* one reviewer noted "Warren William's subdued manner greatly benefits him." However, in spite of the positive response to the film and good box office, Columbia decided that a change was in order if the series was to have the room to branch off into other plots and locales. For the second installment, *The Lone Wolf Strikes,* Lanyard's daughter is jettisoned, leaving the former thief and adventurer to go wherever intrigue will take him: Washington, New York, London, Miami, Egypt. Another major change is the cast, with Eric Blore taking over the role of Lanyard's valet Jameson from the very dry Leonard Carey, there to stay for Warren's full run of films through 1943 and beyond. Blore was ubiquitous in the early '30s as the fussy waiter or impudent butler of many comedies, and offered comic relief in many Astaire–Rogers classics, including *Flying Down to Rio*, *Top Hat* and *Swing Time*. Their team-up was a sharp bit of casting, with the two becoming friendly off screen and clearly enjoying each other's company. The second film also cemented the two men who would become Lanyard's nemeses for the series, Sergeant Dickens (Fred Kelsey), and Inspector Crane (Thurston Hall, Warren's old friend from *Sign of the Leopard* on Broadway). With these basic characters and a wide variety of Columbia guest stars, the Lone Wolf reappeared on movie screens regularly for the next five years.

After *The Lone Wolf Spy Hunt*, Columbia gradually diminished the series in budget and resources. With *The Lone Wolf Strikes* it was already solidly in B territory and fading, but unlike some other studio series, the Lone Wolf movies never took on a cheap, tawdry look. In fact, the series was often singled out as a cut above the blizzard of mystery-detective films that populated Hollywood during those years. "Warren William is rapidly becoming the cinema's most delightful detective," Frank Nugent enthused. "Seldom do all the pieces of a puzzle fit together as they do in *The Lone Wolf Strikes* — the niftiest jools-and-robber picture since goodness knows when."[5] The producers found energetic young directors who learned their craft in Columbia's sweat shops before moving on to better things. Edward Dmytryk, the stylish director of the noir classics *Murder My Sweet* and *Crossfire* (and later one of the Hollywood Ten), helmed 1941's *Secrets of the Lone Wolf* and the following year's *Counter Espionage*. Both were distinguished by some visual flair, although the scripts were paint-by-number affairs, with Lanyard usually required to steal something in order to (a) clear his name, or (b) stop spies and saboteurs. Still, critics generally described the films and Warren's performances in generous terms. One offered: "In *Counter Espionage*, Warren William is subtle, speedy and likable, as always."[6] Andre De Toth, who later built a fascinating career making noir thrillers and cerebral westerns, was dubious about the prospects for his first American film, 1943's *Passport to Suez*. "They gave me a script; I told them it stank," the notoriously outspoken director ruefully remembered. "They said 'Good, that's what we think too. You have seven days to shoot it. Go.'"[7] De Toth went over schedule seven days on the seven-day shoot. When Columbia chief Harry Cohn berated him, he suggested that if Cohn removed a clause in his contract explicitly requiring him to produce films "to the best of his ability" that he could move faster. Cohn held his ground and De Toth turned out the most atmospheric entry of the series, although the influence of *Casablanca*, released only nine months earlier, is painfully obvious. This time Lanyard is loitering at the Yankee Hotel in Alexandria, Egypt, clearly modeled on Rick's Café Americaine, and the sleazy supporting cast dimly mirrors the various cutthroats, black marketers and opportunists played so memorably by Peter Lorre, Sydney Greenstreet and Curt Bois in the classic Warners picture. *Passport to Suez* also features the most outrageous sequence of the entire series, as the Lone Wolf pilots a rogue biplane to follow a speeding car containing Nazi spies. In his final scene as the Lone Wolf, Warren strafes the car, blasting it off the road where it explodes on an embankment, killing everyone inside. This is war, after all.

Writers came and went, with no great contributions to laud, except for Jonathan Latimer's expert dialogue on *Spy Hunt*. Dalton Trumbo took a turn with the story for *The Lone Wolf Strikes* (he made Lanyard an ichthyologist, same as Steven Archer in *Imitation of Life*), and Sidney Salkow contributed scripts for his tightly directed entries. But casting was where Warren had the greatest fun, with an old friend, stablemate or acquaintance in almost every picture. Henry Wilcoxon, Marc Antony to Warren's Caesar in *Cleopatra*, appeared in *The Lone Wolf Takes a Chance*. His friend Addison Richards turned up in *The Lone Wolf Strikes*. Regis Toomey (*Under Eighteen*) and Jean Muir (*Bedside, Dr. Monica*) reappeared for *The Lone Wolf Takes a Chance*. Thurston Hall was always on hand, and Lloyd Bridges, Don Beddoe, Fred Kelsey and other recurring Columbia contractees made the Lone Wolf stable like family.

Warren clearly enjoyed the light, breezy confection of his Lone Wolf appearances; they were simple stories that required no serious study or preparation. Playing Michael Lanyard was like slipping into a comfortable overcoat for him — the character so snugly within his metier that Warren barely ended where Lanyard began. It was another instance, however, of Warren's sense of complacency getting in the way of enduring success: With a long-term contract and regular work coming in, he was content to coast on the assignment. He never failed to work hard — the impetus to excel and to prove himself of greater talent was still there, but he would not agitate for more. As Ben Maddox described it in 1935: "He can't exploit his emotions; in fact, he would be miserable if he were a puppet on continual promenade. He says thanks, but he'll take Hollywood his way."[8] So it was that once he signed with Columbia, his career was permanently divided into two parts; B-movie star and character actor for hire. His days of glory as a leading man in important productions were behind him.

Over the next few years Warren bounced between studios, taking quality freelance assignments in support of stars like Louis Hayward, Henry Fonda, Jean Arthur, Alice Faye, Tyrone Power and Linda Darnell. Even he was aware of his fading prestige. In early 1939 he made a modest effort to locate an appropriate New York stage production, hoping, as he said, "to be discovered all over again via a Broadway show."[9] It never happened. Before he returned to Columbia for the second *Lone Wolf* film he appeared in three very different roles: once again as the dapper detective Philo Vance, as D'Artagnan in a lavish adaptation of a Dumas classic, and as a philandering boss in 20th Century-Fox's *Day-time Wife*.

After his release from MGM, Levee burned up considerable energy putting Warren's house in order. In addition to the Columbia contract he quickly secured two solid offers for his client's services. In January of 1939, Warren was signed for *The Gracie Allen Murder Case*, a comedy in which (who else) Gracie Allen vexes Philo Vance, and The *Man in the Iron Mask*, to be directed by James Whale for independent producer Edward Small.

The Gracie Allen Murder Case is an understandably schizophrenic picture. At once a murder mystery and a comedy vehicle for the great radio star, it suffers from divided loyalties. Writer Nat Perrin's radio background is nakedly obvious as Gracie spouts off facile one-liners (she calls the detective "Fido" throughout the film), while the plot sometimes seems independent of the comedy. Warren does his best to support the star (what else is new?), although the sight of Vance reduced to a double-talking straight man is quite disconcerting. He does manage to register sublime exasperation at Gracie's antics, occasionally looking like a man trying to read small print off his chest while wearing bifocals. All in all it was good fun, but it satisfied neither Gracie Allen fans (who missed her husband George) nor mystery addicts who preferred their entertainment undiluted by humor. Least satisfied was the studio (the film was a box office disappointment), and Gracie herself, who never appeared on film, television or radio again without Mr. Burns in tow. The *New York Times* summed it up as well as possible when they offered: "Far as we are from any intention to disparage *The Gracie Allen Murder Case*, or its splendid cast ... we can nevertheless confidently state that it is probably just what you think."

In late February Warren returned to the General Service Studio to take part in his second James Whale production, *The Man in the Iron Mask*. After some time on a lower rung of the Hollywood ladder, Whale had a new opportunity to helm an A picture, but this experience was not quite as pleasant as Warren's last one. Whale was at odds with producer Small, who made his presence known on the set where he would sometimes interrupt takes and yell: "That's not right!" Whale was also cool to the star, Louis Hayward. "I think he disliked me," Hayward later mused. "I thought he disliked everyone." Things eventually got so bad between Small and his director that the producer fired him and installed writer George Bruce to shoot nine

Looking dapper in his summer suit, Warren is right at home on shipboard taking a few publicity shots with Frances Robinson for *The Lone Wolf Keeps a Date.*

days of retakes at the end of the production.[10] The sad truth of *The Man in the Iron Mask* is that it looks beautiful and is also a dreadful bore. It is the exact type of film that gives historical drama a bad name: leaden, motionless and dour. Even the beautiful Joan Bennett is wasted, appearing virtually as a series of framed portraits rather than a flesh-and-blood woman. The only real spark in the entire enterprise is provided by the two old troupers, Alan Hale and Warren William as Musketeers Porthos and D'Artagnan. Their chemistry is infectious and it is a shame that they didn't work together more often. (Both appeared in *Imitation of Life*, but were not on-screen together.) In spite of the mannered and deliberate gait of the film (it had the unfortunate luck to be released in the banner year of 1939, against such classics as *Stagecoach* and *Gone with the Wind*), it did excellent business. Warren was often singled out for his effervescent portrayal of the ultimate swashbuckler, D'Artagnan. The *Washington Post* called him "particularly able,"[11] and the *Times* said "Warren William's D'Artagnan is an effective, believable figure; the performance has surprising dash and vitality for an actor chiefly associated with knowing sophistication."[12] *The Man in the Iron Mask* reinforced Warren's viability in period roles, something that expanded his casting possibilities over the next few years.

Before returning to Columbia for his second appearance as the Lone Wolf, Warren appeared in the cheap farce *Day-time Wife* for 20th Century-Fox. It is a shiftless, distasteful jumble, following a pentagon of tawdry affairs between the principals: Businessman Tyrone Power is cheating on wife Linda Darnell with his secretary. Darnell discovers the liaison and goes to work as a secretary for Warren William to understand why. Warren, naturally, makes every effort to cheat on his wife with his new secretary, Darnell. Worlds collide. Boredom ensues.

The pathetic attempt to affect a continental attitude in *Day-time Wife* is soundly defeated by a puerile script, and by two leads who lack chemistry and are clearly unable to muster the appropriate charm to pull it off. There's little help from director Gregory Ratoff, who treats the proceedings as if he's a traffic cop guiding slow-moving cars through a small-town intersection. The picture is maddeningly mundane in content and look, never reaching an appropriate level of outrageousness or speed to sell the situations. Only Warren musters up the energy necessary to push the comedy along, and he's deliberately undermined by the star focus constantly pointed at the leads. *Day-time Wife* is so slow and mechanical that it makes the cheapest Lone Wolf entry look like the Daytona 500.

As sociology, *Day-time Wife* paints a far uglier picture of marriage and relationships in the late thirties than anything mounted in the pre–Code. Even *Smarty* never manages the nakedly cynical edge this picture strives for. The entire sordid mess excuses infidelity, belittles marriage, and demeans women, all with an immature, cavalier wink. When Darnell discovers Power's affair on their second wedding anniversary, she does not react with anger or grief, but simply accepts the idea that even in an ostensibly happy marriage, the man will find a reason to stray. All the women in *Day-time Wife*, in fact accept this axiom — and the men fulfill the stereotype, merely because the writers deem they're supposed to. So, the cheaters help the other cheaters cheat, Power blackmails Warren into a bad business deal, one wife and two secretaries are reduced to disposable objects that the men toy with, and no one pays a price for any of these transgressions. The Breen Office was right on top of things though — Power and Darnell have twin beds at home. Apparently it's okay for the movie to imply they have sex, just so long as it's not with each other.

Warren here is only able to mount a pale shadow of his pre–Code rogues gallery. His performance as Bernard Dexter is never allowed to be anything but the standard wolfish boss, and all the underlying subtext the actor could have brought to the role is lost amid the idle traffic. He's still able to gather a measure of likability in spite of his disgusting behavior, but in the end he's merely an unrepentant dog who will do it all again once his wife is out of earshot. Warren reunited here with his old friend Gregory Ratoff, who had acted with him in *Skyscraper Souls* seven years earlier, and on stage in *Out of a Blue Sky* on Broadway. It was old home week, certainly, but considering the flaccid direction of this mess, Warren would have been better off if they had remained apart.

As the 1930s were drawing to a close, the American economy was ever so slightly returning to health, while overseas Europe was spinning into war. Just a month before the release of *Day-time Wife*, Adolf Hitler's blitzkrieg attack shattered Poland's meager armed forces, and the Second World War was underway. It would be two long years before America entered the conflict, with the memories of the horrific casualties of the Great War spurring isolationist fervor. Across the nation 85 million people flocked to the movies every week and General Motors was producing one-third of all the new automobiles and trucks on Earth. The New York World's Fair showed off the incredible new fruits of science and the arts; there were robots, the introduction of Lucite, and a demonstration of the new invention of television. In early 1940, Superman and Batman — neither yet two years old — appeared together for the first time on the cover of a comic book prepared especially for the fair.

As Warren was bouncing between freelance assignments and his Lone Wolf performances he was continuing the sporadic appearances on radio that he had begun with his first broadcast on the *California Melodies* program in May of 1933. With his fantastic voice for radio, he became a regular guest on many popular programs. He appeared with Rudy Vallee on *The Fleischmann's Yeast Hour*, Bing Crosby on *The Kraft Music Hall*, Smith Ballew on *The Shell Chateau Program*, and on *Lux Radio Theater*. He was heard doing an adaptation of *The Lone Wolf Strikes* on NBC's *Good News of 1940*; just two days before Pearl Harbor he cavorted with singer Kate Smith on her weekly program. With May Robson he performed an audio adaptation of *Lady for a Day*. In 1935 Billie Burke joined him for excerpts from their Los Angeles production of *The Vinegar Tree*. Also during that decade he appeared on dozens of programs alongside Melvyn Douglas, Virginia Bruce, Bette Davis, Ginger Rogers, Fanny Brice, Kay Francis, Edward Arnold and many others.

In early 1940, there was momentary talk about Warren playing John Barrymore in a biopic about his life, *The Great Profile*. Nothing would have been more ironic than Warren playing his nettlesome counterpart after all those years of complaining about the comparisons, but after Adolphe Menjou and Fredric March were also suggested, the part was eventually played by Barrymore himself. That spring Warren instead took an assignment at 20th Century-Fox, on another biopic, this one about the popular turn-of-the-century music hall entertainer Lillian Russell. Fox put customary care into mounting this extravagant musical, which, as was common in the Golden Age of Hollywood, bears only nominal resemblance to the life of the celebrated title character. Accuracy was clearly secondary to the beautiful costumes and nostalgic songs that are the heart of the picture. The film follows young Helen Leonard from infancy through the various trials and tribulations, real and manufactured, that give birth to her great alter ego, Lillian Russell. The standard linear signposts are struck with metronomic precision: Lillian's meeting with impresario Tony Pastor, her first audition and stage successes, dalliance with the legendary Diamond Jim Brady, romances, marriage, and personal failures. As a document of late 19th century America, *Lillian Russell* is visually striking, but ultimately lifeless and static.

The general diminution of Warren's star continued. He was billed fifth behind Henry Fonda, Edward Arnold and Don Ameche, playing ardent Russell suitor Jesse Lewisohn, who the singer throws over for two separate husbands. The change in prestige did little to diminish his enthusiasm, however, and his limited scenes, especially those with Edward Arnold, shine as among the best in the film. Arnold had come from a similar background of study and experience as Warren, having grown up in New York and spent time on Broadway and in silent films before settling in Hollywood in 1932. (The two had appeared in *Three on a Match*, but not on-screen together.) Watching these two old hands, sharply exercising the style of acting that became dominant between the two wars, is a genuine pleasure. The screenwriter was William Anthony McGuire, the writer-director of Warren's great stage success *Twelve Miles Out*.

In 1939, the American western was in the meaty heart of its popular appeal. That August, Columbia chief Harry Cohn gave Wesley Ruggles the go-ahead to direct a film version of Clarence Budington Kelland's novel *Arizona,* and the money—two million dollars—to make it a prestige picture. Ruggles was anxious to recreate the success of his 1931 epic *Cimarron*, and immediately began to assemble the project. He wanted Gary Cooper, then at the height of his popularity, but the taciturn star turned down the assignment and Ruggles reluctantly settled for Joel McCrea. Then, shortly after pre-production began, German tanks entered Poland and Cohn scuttled the film, fearful that the loss of European markets would doom the project to heavy financial losses.[13] It took many months, but with $300,000 already spent and parts of the sets already erected, Ruggles convinced Cohn to continue. Cohn acquiesced—but with the caveat that the budget be brought under control. To that end, McCrea was out, and the young William Holden was in. Additionally, Warren's rare chance to perform in a Technicolor production was lost. The picture was beautifully shot, but it was shot in black and white.

A large part of the money lavished on *Arizona* went to the construction of a painstaking recreation of the town of Old Tucson, just north of the present-day city it spawned. During the spring of 1940, engineers, architects, researchers, carpenters, and laborers returned to Arizona to finish building the town in the middle of the desert. They enlisted local Indians with expertise in the making of adobe structures, and little by little everything took shape. The cast and crew arrived in April to find the location rustic, to say the least. Everything (food, water, equipment, sanitation, electricity, manpower) had to be trucked in 40 miles from Tucson. Warren couldn't help but be reminded of his year of army training in the furnace of New Mexico. The veteran of "The Sandstorm Division"—who got hives while on the shoot—saw temperatures reach as high as 140 degrees, with eighteen days of the four months on location eaten up by dust storms. Even with a team of nurses dedicated to keeping the cast and crew hydrated, Ruggles realized that he couldn't afford to lose important players to heat stroke. After a month, the director had air conditioning installed, and made sure that the principal actors and crew stayed cool and healthy.

The film opens with a magnificently photographed montage of a wagon train heading west and into the town of Tucson. Pete Muncie (Holden) is the column boss bringing in newcomers after months on the trail. Superb period detail and atmosphere create a beautifully textured portrait of the Old West, right down to the scruffy costumes and weather-beaten faces of the townspeople. Unfortunately when Muncie encounters Phoebe Titus (Jean Arthur) it isn't long before the picture veers sharply away from surprising naturalism and into standard Hollywood drama and never recovers. Naturally the two have a love-hate relationship, with the strong-willed Phoebe making every effort to tame, or at least corral Muncie. Into this typically Hollywood romance slithers Jefferson Carteret (Warren), a Confederate dandy with a smooth line and something more than cards up his sleeve. Ruggles wanted Warren for the part so badly that he tracked him down in Redwood National Forest where the Krechs were then vacationing. "You know, that guy has something," Ruggles said of Warren, "and I think he's going to be wonderful as the suave, polished Carteret." The director had to corral his wily villain again after principal shooting had finished. Happy to be at liberty, Warren quickly packed up his gear and headed due south, figuring to get in a few days of fishing off the Mexican coast. At the border he was taken aside by guards who gave him a note from Ruggles, telling him that he was to return to Old Tucson in case of retakes. It wasn't the first time filmmaking had scuttled a vacation in progress—Warner Brothers once had the Coast Guard track him down on the open sea so he could be called back to the studio. The actor dutifully turned around and promptly ran into a rare desert cloudburst that swept his car off the road and into a ditch. With the help of some locals and a team of mules, his predicament was limited to five hours on the roadside.[14]

In *Arizona*, Warren for the first time moves from mere villainy to something even worse and eminently more dangerous. Jefferson Carteret is the actor's sarcastic composite of Snidely Whiplash and William Bonney—a charismatic sociopath who crosses lines that even David Dwight and Kurt Anderson would have found obscene. He first ingratiates himself in town business by bullying the local freight handler Lazarus Ward (Porter Hall) into sharing his business with him, then brazenly takes over the entire operation with nothing more than harsh language and sheer force of will. Later, when Carteret and the skittish Ward share a dusty trail back to town, the stylish villain puts his partner's mind at ease. "I wouldn't double-cross you, partner. I'm your pal," he insists, smoothly assuaging Ward's fears. Moments later he politely asks Ward to ride up a ways to check the trail, then promptly shoots him in the back. In fact, he makes a career of shooting people in the back, blasting a hole in a stool pigeon who has betrayed him and similarly trying to ventilate Pete Muncie *during his wedding* to Phoebe. When this fails, he is beside himself with anger and spoiling for a fight—a final showdown. In one of the best scenes of this period of his career, Warren's controlled fury is positively chilling. He is sullen, taciturn and determined—and all the more dangerous because he doesn't care what happens next. The final confrontation between Carteret and Muncie is neatly played off-camera, and Warren is spared the ignominy of an on-screen death. The dastardly villain most certainly was not entitled to a bravura finale.

Jefferson Carteret has no ambiguity, no mitigating factors to soften his edges. He is a single-minded, one-dimensional construction—about as subtle as a pickaxe to the back of the neck, but still outrageously fun. Warren did not invest in the character anything more than guile and unrestrained violence because nothing else was called for. Critics appreciated his performance as perhaps the purest character in the film. The *Hartford Courant* politely called him "the nastiest villain of the year,"[15] while the *Wall Street Journal* gave him one of his best notices in ages: "Warren William ... must have had a lovely time, for the part is eminently suited to [his] talents for suave scurrility. He is smooth, masterful, skillful and vicious all at once."[16] After some kind words for Arthur and Holden, critic Nelson Bell offered this: "These two are the mainsprings of the film, but even so, do not tower too high above Warren William in the role of major villainy."[17] Meanwhile, Louella Parsons observed the descending trend in Warren's career, and his capitulation to his new status in Hollywood: "He is very smart not to sit idly by waiting for leading man roles. After all, it's these character parts that are winning the admiration of the fans all over the country."

The premiere of Arizona took place in Tucson on November 15, with the cast and crew in attendance. Warren and Helen flew to the festivities (along with thirty other celebrities and friends like Guy Kibbee, Melvyn Douglas and Rita Hayworth) and took part in the "return to pioneer days" engineered by the studio. It was a fully paid chance to get back to his beloved southwest and the desolate, quiet landscape that he loved. The film was a modest success, but ultimately did not make a profit for Columbia. It is somewhat overlong, with too few genuine thrills for a Saturday afternoon teen audience and not enough drama for anyone else. The most interesting moment in *Arizona* happens when Phoebe appears in a dress for the first time in front of her fiancé Pete. The cattle boss is playing with his pistols, and catches a glimpse of her on the sidewalk in front of him. As she comes into view he raises the barrel of the gun next to his crotch until he has a full-fledged erection. Presumably it passed by the Breen Office unnoticed.

Warren kept busy through 1940 and early 1941 with various radio appearances, three more entries in the *Lone Wolf* series and two freelance jobs on *Trail of the Vigilantes* and *Wild Geese Calling*. The first began as a dramatic western at Universal, but director Allan Dwan hastily reshaped it into a fast-paced little comedy following the terrific success of *Destry Rides Again*. In *Vigilantes*, Warren is a clandestine villain smoked out by undercover tinhorn Franchot Tone. Andy Devine, Porter Hall and Mischa Auer co-starred. It was all good fun, but nothing to get excited about.

Wild Geese Calling stars Henry Fonda as — well, Henry Fonda — a quiet, decent, hard-working boy who wants to follow the lure of the wild geese to lands of adventure. He hooks up with his old friend Blackie (Warren), a vaguely shifty sort who nonetheless has deep affection for his old pal John Murdock (Fonda). Together they endure a difficult love triangle, the rough-neck anger of a former business partner (Barton MacLane), a trip at sea through a hurricane, gunplay, frontier privation, and the ire of the local "lady of leisure." It was a sturdy part — sometimes villainous, sometimes heroic, juicily waxing and waning between decency and scur-rility. The scene where Blackie returns Murdock to his wife (Joan Bennett) by sailing his schooner through a massive storm is both exciting and instructional. It is the only time on film that Warren is seen piloting a ship. Location shoots in Lake Arrowhead, Big Bear and at the San Bernardino National forest added authenticity and delighted the avid outdoorsman.

The film received solid reviews, and any real criticism came not from the columnists, but Warren himself. Given his modest nature and Merton-ish temperament, he rarely had the courage to watch himself on screen, but for the first time in years he took the chance. "After seeing myself in *Wild Geese Calling*, I don't really see why I should ever be in pictures any more at all," the self-effacing actor complained. "I thought all the while I was giving a bang-up, knock 'em dead performance. I practically never see myself on the screen. And I shouldn't have this time!"[18] He was unduly harsh. His performance in *Wild Geese Calling* is among the more interesting of the later portion of his career. Perhaps he was mortified at the broadness of his work, but compared with the utterly spare style of Henry Fonda, anyone will appear to be doing too much.

Between assignments in the summer of 1941, Warren took a two-week vacation in the High Sierra for fishing and hunting. At that time he also professed to be writing a memoir of his experiences in France during the Great War to be called *War, as I Saw It*. It might have been a tad dry, since Warren served, but never saw any *actual* warfare. This project probably ended up like the occasional play he began but could not finish, with a tiny raft of pages stuck inside a plain brown envelope, lost to the ages. Later that season he made an arrangement with the famous automobile driver Abe Jenkins to ride with him on his attempt to break the record of 4,000 miles driven in 24 hours. Jenkins was a daredevil and speed demon who held many records for endurance and distance driving. At the Bonneville Salt Flats in Utah, Jenkins was determined to break the new record, and he was going to take Warren with him in the car.[19] There is no account of Warren as a passenger on Jenkins' run. It is once again assumed that Helen — or perhaps this time Warren himself — thought better of it.

Towards the end of the summer, Levee made a deal for Warren to return to Warner Brothers after over five years away from the studio. The film was *Wild Bill Hickok Returns*, a program western with Bruce Cabot as Wild Bill, Constance Bennett as the dance hall girl, and Warren as— well, what else?— the deadly villain of the piece. He hardly expected the feeling, but returning to Warner Brothers was surprisingly satisfying for the erstwhile contractee. His experiences since leaving the studio had made it clear to him that while Warner Brothers was no bed of roses, it was infinitely superior to many of the other places he had been. "It was just like old home week," he told Irene Thirer. "Lots of folks of my day were still around — Cagney, Bette Davis, George Brent for instance. Kay Francis was back for one picture, and I renewed an acquaintanceship with Monty Woolley who'd been playing walk-ons and bits at Metro during the years I served time there."[20] His choice of words was no error: Warren's feeling towards Warners may have been as to that of a dysfunctional family, but for him MGM was indeed more like prison.

Warren had a great time on *Wild Bill*, even though he was earning barely half of what he was taking in when he left the studio in 1936. He got to show off his significant horse-riding skills, and relished the location work near his home in Encino. "It was an easy job for me, since most of the action was on location fifteen minutes from my home and all I had to do was get in my dressing-room truck each morning, drive to the appointed place, do my stint and return in good time to superintend my two and a half acres of citrus fruit."[21] Although by this time the villains he played were most often cheap plot contrivances rather than genuine characters, his turn as Harry Farrell is more fun than anything else in the picture. When Farrell asks the crooked sheriff about bribing a local banker, the lawman tells him, "You can't get nowhere with him, he's honest." Downcast, Farrell shakes his head and sadly replies: "Yeah — that's a drawback." Critics had little to say about the film, being merely high-class Saturday afternoon stuff, but Bosley Crowther was just about right when he opined: "This picture will only be remembered as the one in which a Bennett sister slummed."[22]

After his undemanding job at Warners, Warren was quickly contracted by Universal to participate in what is almost certainly the most frequently viewed performance of his career. It was announced in the press as *Destiny*, but became better known by its eventual release title, *The Wolf Man*. The classic film tells the story of Larry Talbot (Lon Chaney Jr.), bitten by a werewolf and thus condemned to change into a werewolf himself when the autumn moon is bright. Warren was Dr. Lloyd, the local man of science among superstitious locals who fear the beast. Lloyd is the expository oracle of the film, expounding on mental illness, lycanthropy, animal wounds and psychiatry until he comes to see the stark reality of the supernatural. As a television staple and a perennial revival house favorite, *The Wolf Man* is a confirmation of the fickle nature of memory. Even though he is prominently billed, Warren is utterly erased from the memory of the millions of people who have seen the film over the intervening years. Very few are able to recall his name or role until they are prompted by the quote he delivers at the side of a mutilated victim of the beast: "His jugular vein was severed by the bite of powerful teeth!" Amidst career performances from Chaney and Maria Ouspenskaya, Warren is simply lost in the shuffle. Ouspenskaya's role as an old gypsy, in fact, may have given her more lasting fame from a single film than Warren William managed in his entire career.

The day Warren arrived at Universal City to begin work, he had a flashback to times he hoped were forgotten. Sitting on the set was a portable makeup trailer, with the name "John Barrymore" neatly emblazoned on the side. Warren had long since softened in his distaste for the joke, and he was more unhappy than angry, although he hadn't always been so charitable. Hedda Hopper reported that Warren once "exploded" when columnist Liza Wilson playfully sent a friend over to ask "Mr. Barrymore" for his autograph.[23] He developed a standard response to signature seekers who got his name wrong. "If they guess who I am, I sign. If they guess someone else, I don't," he explained. "Who do they think I am? Not just Barrymore. Everyone else — a dozen others. It's a little discouraging. Sometimes I think I probably have no personality of my own at all. Maybe that's it." Although the *Wolf Man* incident was probably a deliberate gag by some stagehands, the producers insisted that it was simply an unfortunate accident, the trailer being left over from Barrymore's recent work at the studio on *The Invisible Woman*, and Warren accepted the explanation graciously.[24] Way back to the beginning of his career he had attempted to dispense with the talk of such similarity. "I think, and hope, that people have mostly forgotten about it by now," was his wishful aspiration. The intervening 75 years indicate that the comparisons will never end until one or the other is wiped entirely from the consciousness of man.

Filming of *The Wolf Man* ended on November 25, after just 21 days shooting. "It was swell sport," Warren enthused. "The director, [George] Waggner, seemed to know all the spooky angles. It should be fun for audiences."[25] The man from Minnesota could not have been more right. It has been watched again and again by fans who relish everything about the film: the

The Wolf Man is probably Warren's most famous film but few people remember his appearance in this Universal horror classic. Left to right: Ralph Bellamy, Warren, Lon Chaney Jr., and Claude Rains.

atmospheric photography, Hans J. Salter's melancholy music score, beautiful Evelyn Ankers and Jack Pierce's groundbreaking makeup. Few, however, register more than a passing notice of Warren William, poised inquisitively over a partially devoured body, checking for teeth marks.

Just two weeks after wrapping *The Wolf Man*, Warren was appearing on NBC's radio program *Listen America* when the broadcast was interrupted for a special bulletin. It was December 7, 1941, and an American naval base had just been attacked by Japanese air forces at Pearl Harbor, Hawaii. The next day, Franklin Roosevelt declared war in his famous speech forever inscribing December 7 as a "date which will live in infamy." Once again the world was spiraling towards destruction, just 23 years after Warren and millions of other doughboys had won the war that was supposed to end all wars.

Now 47 years old, Warren was clearly not a candidate for active service, but he had no intention of sitting idly by. Between assignments for the next two years, he did what millions of other Americans did: volunteered and served on the home front. He began by attending bond drives and rallies in and around Los Angeles with friends and other stars such as Mary Astor, Gale Sondergaard and Anita Louise. The Encino ranch was always open to servicemen through the auspices of the USO, and in May of 1942 he and Helen hosted the second annual garden party and bazaar for ANZAC (Australian and New Zealand Army Corps) war relief, raising thousands of dollars that went to "General MacArthur's boys down under."[26] The most unusual aspect of his services to the war effort was his participation in the rounding up of Japanese-Americans for internment in relocation camps. John Ford, the legendary director of such Hollywood classics as *Stagecoach* and *The Grapes of Wrath*, formed an ad hoc cavalry unit as a civilian arm of the U.S. military, which included members such as the Academy Award–winning actor Victor McLaglen. The men would ride out on horseback, overseeing and supervising the movement and dispensation of those American "aliens" who were deemed potentially dangerous. For a while at least, Warren rode with them. "He was a very fair person, and it surprised the hell out of me that he would go out on horseback and round anybody up," his niece Barbara remembered, disappointed.[27] At the outset of the war, Warren's actions with this celebrity posse were most likely seen as very patriotic and necessary.

Late in December of 1941, Warren and Helen packed up and headed to New York for their first proper eastern vacation in almost eight years. They occasionally visited on short jaunts, and Warren sometimes appeared in New York for publicity tours and openings, but there had been no real chance to settle in and visit seriously with the family. "A couple years ago we had a three-day visit on a movie jaunt for *Union Pacific*," he explained. "We were in such a dither that we didn't get to see or do a single important thing. This is my first *official* holiday." Warren and Helen checked into the Gotham Hotel, with plans to stay through the New Year. They were delighted to spend time with Pauline, still in the city, raising Cain and living the childless, bohemian lifestyle that suited her so well. Her first husband had been accidentally killed in a hunting accident, and she was now getting ready for a second marriage that would eventually end in divorce.[28] Out in Port Washington, Elizabeth was raising three daughters, Liz, Bobby and Pat, each of whom loved their famous uncle and doted on him when he came to visit. The girls knew him simply as "Uncle Woog," appropriating the long-standing nickname given to him by Helen many years earlier. His fifteen-year-old niece Barbara — known to Warren as Bobby — made sure to jealously guard her time with him. "I used to get mad when we'd go places and they'd stop him for his autograph. 'Why don't they just leave him alone? He's mine!' You didn't get that much time with him, you see."[29] In upstate New York, Warren also visited with his brother-in-law Charles, likewise a great lover of the sea and a founding member of the Port Washington Yacht Club. The sailing enthusiasts engaged in good-natured arguments about everything nautical, and found common ground on another subject, their service in the Great War. "My father joined the Air Force in World War I," Barbara explained. "He was in the infantry, but he never liked to walk, so he said, 'To hell with this,' and he joined the Air Force." Warren had continued his interest in flying over the years, taking gliding lessons and contemplating the purchase of his own airplane (which Helen put the kibosh on after five years of arguing),[30] so stories of those halcyon days over France were like so much candy to the aging vet.

During the early years of the war, Warren contented himself with two *Lone Wolf* appearances a year and the occasional radio play. His career was slowing down; there was much to do on the home front, and after twelve years at the Hollywood grind he was tired and wanted a break. Late in 1942 there was movement at Fox to mount the greatest detective-murder mystery ever produced, gathering together four of the biggest shamuses in films for the first time. The project *The Four Star Murder Case* would have brought together the talents of Philo Vance (Warren), Charlie Chan (Sidney Toler), Mr. Moto (Peter Lorre), and Michael Shayne (Lloyd Nolan). Ironically, the story saw Mr. Moto helping out the other detectives— seriously —from a Japanese internment camp.[31] The idea passed away in development hell, and the screen lost a golden opportunity for future generations to look back and shake their heads in utter astonishment.

17

Outcast

In the spring of 1943, Warren was finishing up his contract with Columbia Pictures. After nine appearances as the Lone Wolf, the series was getting tired. The studio made a modest effort to revivify the franchise with more exotic locales and a change in sales strategy by eliminating the "Lone Wolf" moniker from the titles. *Counter Espionage, One Dangerous Night* and *Passport to Suez* did not convince anyone that the series was worth continuing, and Columbia put Lanyard to bed for a little while. "I think you've seen the last of me as the Lone Wolf," Warren commented in the summer.[1] For the first time in twelve years, Warren was without a studio contract and no film offers on the horizon.

In April, Warren had begun discussions with producer Henry Duffy to return to the stage, not on Broadway, but in Detroit, Michigan. Duffy was assembling a play called *The Bat*, with ZaSu Pitts and Jane Darwell, the unforgettable Ma Joad of *The Grapes of Wrath*. *The Bat* did not pan out for Warren — his schedule for the *Passport to Suez* would not allow it — but Duffy's follow-up in Detroit seemed a natural. It was *There's Always Juliet*, a neat little four-person comedy written by John Van Druten, and Warren would have the great pleasure of playing opposite Violet Heming. (It was her test, that Warren helped on early in 1931, that secured him his initial contract with Warner Brothers.) In May rehearsals began for a June opening, and after so many years away the film actor was apprehensive. "Actually it's ten years since I've been on a stage, and I must admit I'm still a victim of stage fright," he confessed. "If it weren't for the help that such a fine actress as Miss Violet Heming has given me, I'm afraid I'd be shaking in the wings." The play opened on June 6 to very nice reviews and some solid box office, but nothing to draw Warren irrevocably back to the stage. "I was so happy to get the chance to play in *There's Always Juliet*, because I had the opportunity to return to light banter and easy humor," was his relieved response after playing so many villains in recent years. In spite of only modest success, when the play closed Warren resolved to try again. "When I return to my home I'm going to take it easy and read a few plays, because this opportunity has whetted my appetite for the footlights again. I do want to do a play on Broadway this fall and I hope I can find one soon."[2]

After *There's Always Juliet* closed, Warren did not work for over a year. In January of 1944, producer Charles Washburn sent him a script for a play called *April in Shubert Alley*, but in spite of Warren's interest the production did not come off.[3] At around the same time he began to have a series of minor but chronic physical symptoms that included fatigue and lower back pain that sometimes kept him up at night. His doctor, Stanley Gordon, had no specific answers, but most likely advised a rest after years of grinding work at the film studios and at the ranch where Warren regularly plowed his own fields, sprayed his own crops and worked in his garage workshop. Helen convinced him that Dr. Gordon was right, and Warren took an extended break from work for a good portion of the next twelve months, except for the occasional war bond drive or hosting charity events at the ranch. In August of 1944, he again considered a return to the stage when the bandleader Richard Himber signed him to appear in a proposed Broadway musical called *Abracadabra*, to star El Brendel.[4] Shortly after, Himber made a deal to host a new radio program on the West Coast and *Abracadabra* was quietly shelved. Throughout the year Warren continued to have various medical troubles, occasionally being laid up by infections and chronic fatigue.

Mike Levee was still looking out for his former star, but there was little to choose from since rumors were now going around that Warren's health was poor. The possibility that a star — or even an important feature player — might be unable to complete a project because of illness after hundreds of thousands of dollars were spent on it meant that most studios regularly insured their players against just such an eventuality. It was a hedge against the possibility of winding up with half a film and having to start all over again. Any producer who heard the scuttlebutt about Warren's woes was unlikely to offer him a freelance contract without a clean bill of health from a qualified doctor who could attest to his fitness to finish the film, and thus allow them to obtain a completion bond for his services. What offers were available under these circumstances came from Poverty Row producers — those low-budget studios that operated in the margins of Hollywood, and were happy to have an important and well-known actor for a fraction of the cost he was commanding just a few years before. With shooting schedules that often lasted less than a week and little money invested, they were willing to take the risk of employing a potentially sick man without a bond to back him up. An offer came from Producers Releasing Corporation (PRC) for an interesting part in a modern adaptation of *Hamlet* called *Strange Illusion*. Healthier than he'd been in a while, Warren craved a return to work. Many stars might have balked at the short money and meager resources of PRC, but Warren's lack of ego would not allow him to look down on honest work; he took the job. Inveterate Warren William booster Hedda Hopper gave the ailing actor a little friendly publicity in her column when the signing was announced. "Warren William finally gets a good part in *First Illusion* [*sic*] with PRC, I wonder why our town forgets he's such a fine actor. All he needs is one good part. Maybe this is it."[5] A few days later the columnist received a letter from the underemployed actor, saying that the kind words in the article were "very sweet" of her.[6] In spite of everything, his gentlemanly impulses were still intact.

The budget for *Strange Illusion* was an infinitesimal $25,000 and there were just fifteen days to shoot, but Warren was excited just to be working when he stepped on to a sound stage in January of 1945 for the first time in a year and a half. His director was Edgar G. Ulmer, a fascinating figure in classic Hollywood cinema. A protégé of the great German director F.W. Murnau, Ulmer helmed dozens of atmospheric, low-budget films, using his background as an art director to maximize his limited resources. Within the choking restrictions of time and money, he turned out such minor classics as *The Black Cat*, *Bluebeard* and *Detour*. *Strange Illusion*, in fact, was shot directly between the latter two productions.

This updating of *Hamlet* has James Lydon — Henry Aldrich himself — standing in for the Danish prince. Ulmer begins *Strange Illusion* with ghostly figures lurking Paul Cartwright (Lydon) through a fever dream while his voice-over tells the tale: a murdered father, a new man taking a place in his mother's affections, and danger to the family that only he can see and prevent. The danger turns out to be Warren as Brett Curtis, a suave con man with a sour whiff of modernity — pedophilia — and an axe to grind against the Cartwrights. With the help of a local psychiatrist, Curtis plans to marry Paul's mother and steal the family fortune, completing the job he began when he engineered the murder of the elder boy's father.

As entertainment, the picture is a reasonable mélange of detective story, shallow psychiatry and suspense, but Ulmer's visual style is really the heart of the film. In spite of a dearth of time and money, Ulmer finds ways to spice up the proceedings, featuring simple but clever set-ups to indicate subtext or merely keeping things moving through the exposition-laden script. The real novelty in *Strange Illusion*, however, is the surprisingly modern pathology of the character of Brett Curtis. Warren's performance allows a sense of morbidity in Curtis that prefigures much of the post-war noir psychology that later seeped into many studio productions. The touches are sometimes subtle — as when Ulmer allows his camera to capture the perverse thoughts behind Warren's eyes as he watches Paul's sixteen-year-old girlfriend Lydia swimming in the family pool. Here, in the disconcerting creepiness of Brett Curtis, the pre–Code is well and truly gone, replaced by something neoteric and distasteful. Curtis' interest in Lydia is not just the result of an over-developed sexual drive, but rather springs from a repellant, aberrant psychology that cannot be controlled. Warren's willingness to go to even darker and uglier places in character puts in mind that if he had lived longer he might have had the opportunity for a career revival, playing an entirely different kind of villain, steeped in post-war disillusion and nuclear angst.

In spite of lingering health troubles, the 51-year-old Warren of *Strange Illusion* looks quite good. Compared to his Warner Brothers contemporaries Bogart, Flynn and Robinson at his age, he appears downright virile. We even get to see the only known footage of him playing tennis, showing a loose, effortless style acquired from years of practice — and still able to jump the net after taking the set. (Serious, debilitating deterioration of his health was almost two years away.) Film audiences may have wondered why he was stuck at this tawdry little studio, working for almost no money. "Warren William manages a sinister atmosphere as the villain,"[7] the *Los Angeles Times* said, while *Time* magazine made a dead-on observation when they called the film "small change, but honest coin."[8]

During most of 1945, Warren was continuing to battle fatigue, respiratory infections and a general pain in his limbs. Dr. Gordon was still at a loss to understand what he was going through, but ordered tests. The actor was a compliant patient. When he was still able, however, Warren continued to tend his gardens and work in the orchards. Helen kept her husband's condition as quiet as possible, knowing full well that if word got out to the press, Warren's career would be utterly finished, at least while he was still sick. Even within the family, she was careful not to reveal too much. She told Warren's sister Elizabeth simply that Warren was ill, but never discussed the increasing seriousness of his condition. His niece Barbara still recalls the family's disappointment at not being informed of Warren's slow deterioration. "My mother was very concerned," she remembered. "She was talking to Auntie Helen, and Uncle Woog was losing weight, but Auntie Helen didn't say anything about being diagnosed with any kind of disease or anything. Which would be like Auntie Helen. She didn't tell you anything that she didn't want to." In this case, the highly protective guardian of her husband's career and privacy made the choice to keep most everybody out of the loop while she dealt with a very difficult situation.

Fortunately, at this time the Krechs were financially stable. Never particularly extravagant, they had banked a solid nest egg from Warren's many years of lucrative employment, and did not absolutely need him to continue working. There was also the annuity that Warren invested in almost twenty years earlier; it began to pay on his 50th birthday in December of 1944.[9] Their careful planning for just such circumstances would hopefully carry them through this rough patch.

In July, Warren accepted a part in *Fear*, another low-budget quickie on Poverty Row. Essentially a retelling of Fyodor Dostoyevsky's massive novel *Crime and Punishment* compressed into 64 minutes, this dreary production has none of the compensatory flourishes that distinguished Ulmer's *Strange Illusion*. The wooden Peter Cookson stands in for the famous literary murderer Raskolnikov, while Warren injects the proceedings with a dash of class as the police detective who suspects him. His low-key performance as he plays cat and mouse with Cookson is surprisingly fun to watch, considering the amazingly low production values and low-rent talent around him. Here, despite having been relegated to a lower rung of the Hollywood ladder, Warren focuses all his professional experience, refusing to sleepwalk through this sad, tawdry mess. Director Alfred Zeisler is not entirely to blame for the static camera and unimaginative staging. With only about $25,000 and six days to shoot, Zeisler needed to move quickly, and was unfortunately not in a creative league with the miracle worker Edgar Ulmer. The production looks and feels exactly like what it is— a cheap programmer designed to play for a few weeks, deliver a couple dollars profit and fade into obscurity.

Just after Warren finished shooting *Fear* at Monogram, the United States Air Force dropped the first tactical atomic bomb on the Japanese city of Hiroshima. Just months earlier the Allies had achieved victory in Europe when Germany surrendered, but the empire of Japan promised to continue hostilities to the bitter end. Three days later, on August 9, 1945, the bitter end came when a second nuclear warhead destroyed the city of Nagasaki. The Second World War — at long last — was over.

Just three months after the war ended, an excellent opportunity presented itself to Warren. A Turkish émigré named Ali Ipar was preparing an independent production called *Accusation* to be shot in Mexico in both Spanish and English versions. Ipar, the dilettante son of a wealthy import-export magnate, was assembling an American cast and had already signed Warren's old friend Virginia Bruce (*Arsene Lupin Returns, The First Hundred Years*). Bruce was also undergoing a change in her fortunes; working in Mexican movies was most certainly not something that any star did when they had work being regularly offered in Hollywood. It is entirely possible that Bruce introduced Ipar to her unemployed actor friend, and in November he was signed for the producer's maiden production. "Mexico bound is Warren William, as one of the first of the more important stars to consider a proposition from the industry south of the border," the *Los Angeles Times* reported. "He will play the lead in *Accusation* which is to start about mid–January."[10]

In January, Warren headed south with Bruce, Richard Arlen and Rose Hobart to begin filming the English-language version of *Accusation*. Things did not go well from the very start. Initially there were difficulties with the exchange of money from Ipar's accounts. After weeks of delay the troubles appeared to be solved, but then a dispute arose between competing motion picture unions that delayed things further when they went on strike. Ipar himself appeared unconcerned, seeming far more interested in Virginia Bruce than in film production. The two were seen regularly at nightclubs, restaurants and concert halls, appearing very close to each other while the rest of the cast waited and wondered if their green producer really had the money for the movies he wanted to make. Eventually Warren realized that the project was not to be. In all his years in Hollywood he had never had to worry about problems like this and it vexed him. He said goodbye to Bruce and returned home. Ipar made good on the money promised the cast and continued to hope that the films would eventually be made. "They have all been tremendously good sports about our difficulties," Ipar said of his stalwart cast on his return to Los Angeles in March. "My brother is still in Mexico City and will report as soon as the strike is settled. I'm hoping to reassemble my cast and return there — if I do not receive encouragement for this, I will produce the film in Hollywood."[11] There was no film. Ipar's producing career ended before it began, although something did come out of it all: He became Virginia Bruce's third husband.

Warren's health was still degenerating very slowly. His niece Barbara visited her uncle and aunt in the spring of 1946, and remembers being surprised at how slim and gaunt he appeared.[12] At this time Warren's doctors were still at a loss to understand his condition, and he had nothing more than his own body's immune systems to fight against the unknown disease that was beginning to consume him. His niece described Warren's illness as "long and hard," but the worst was still many months into the future.

In January of 1946, Levee made a clever deal for Warren to return to acting without having to circumvent studio doctors. The project was a syndicated radio program, co-created by Warren himself, to be known as *Strange Wills*.[13] The producer was Teleways, a small company with studios in Los Angeles, who also offered such syndicated fare as *Danger*, *Chuck Wagon Jamboree* and *Sons of the Pioneers*. Also involved in the package was producer Charles Michelson, a broadcasting bigwig with a hand in the radio programs *The Shadow* and *Nick Carter*. A pilot was made on January 15, and while Warren was cooling his heels in Mexico City, a Teleways sales force was hawking the series to independent stations across the country. By the summer of 1946, the program had been sold in enough regions to produce a full series. Warren made his way to Teleways' Los Angeles studio to begin his first serious foray into radio.

Strange Wills is an anthology of short radio dramas, with each story revolving around a peculiar bequest or codicil in the last will and testament of a client of attorney John Francis O'Connell (Warren). O'Connell is typically reminiscing about his career from the distance of time, recalling interesting and exciting instances that stand out in his memory. There was the very first case of O'Connell's career, where he falls in love with an heiress who will only inherit ten million dollars if she promises never to marry. In another he tells the story of a will etched on the back of a woman who turns out to be his great-great grandmother. O'Connell must be a highly successful lawyer, since in various episodes he impulsively travels to the moors of Scotland, pilots a plane from America to the West Indies and visits England, France and South America. In *The Prince of Broadway*, he enlists and has a tour of duty during World War II. During the episode *Emeralds Come High*, he treks through the jungles of Colombia — there to encounter headhunters who are thwarted by Patsy "Bubbles" Moran, the burlesque queen he's travelling with. There is time travel, hypnosis, eugenics, pirate treasure, murder on the moor, and a dramatic last-minute call to the governor's office — in other words, the sheer undiluted fun of a medium in which anything could happen at any moment.

At this point, radio was a perfect fit for Warren. Although not in the best of health, he could enter the studio in Los Angeles and record many of his parts in one day. Unfortunately, *Strange Wills* never overcomes its weak scripts. Each is a trifling diversion, and Warren sounds like he's knocking them off not with enthusiasm, but sheer professionalism.

While *Strange Wills* was being recorded in the summer of 1946, Helen Krech passed her 68th birthday. Around that time she discovered an awful complication to the blissfully happy life that she and her husband had been living for over twenty years. It began a steep decline in the fortunes of the Krechs, one from which they would not recover.

18

Bedside

In the summer of 1946, Helen found a lump in her right breast. Then, as now, the indication was clear: The possibility of cancer was very high. With her stalwart husband supporting her, she entered the hospital where Stanley Gordon coordinated the surgery and biopsy to determine what they would do next.

Advanced schirrous carcinoma was the diagnosis. Although it may not have been readily apparent with the techniques in use at the time, it was already too late for Helen to long survive the cancer that was attacking her body. The atrophic tumor had begun forming months earlier and was likely already spreading to the other parts of her body.

A radical mastectomy was called for. After decades of happiness, good fortune and prosperity, Warren and Helen now needed to call on their reserves of strength and love for each other. The surgery was quickly scheduled, and Helen went to the hospital on August 17 — just two days before the premiere of *Strange Wills*—for surgery she might not survive. (The type of cancer with which Helen was afflicted runs high among older women who have never had children.)

Ostensibly, Helen's operation was a success. The mass was removed. It is unknown if doctors understood — or if Helen and Warren were aware — that the cancer was continuing to grow into carcinomatosis and moving through her body. If it were apparent, they would have known that the slow-moving disease would leave her only a few years to live. The couple returned home where their beloved ranch now seemed more like an isolating retreat than the private escape they had always loved. Jack and Jill were still there, but both were now elderly, one blind and feeble and the other simply tired.[1]

For months Helen convalesced, regaining her strength. While he was watching over her, Warren decided to purchase the rights to *Strange Wills* from the Teleways corporation and make a deal for the program to leave syndication and instead appear in a more lucrative run on one of the major networks. Warren William Radio Productions was created, and episodes of the series were re-recorded and repackaged under the name *I Devise and Bequeath*. A contract was signed with NBC, but only a handful of episodes were produced and there is no record of their having run on the network. The circumstances behind the failure of *I Devise and Bequeath* are still puzzling, but after just one syndicated series, *Strange Wills* was gone.

During Helen's illness, Warren was also waiting for a new project to come to maturity. Out of the fiasco of *Accusation*, producers David Loew (son of theater magnate Marcus Loew) and director Albert Lewin offered him a part in their upcoming *The Private Affairs of Bel Ami*. In April, columnist Edwin Schallert announced: "Warren William, who went to Mexico City for the Ali Ipar picture *Accusation*, is apparently due to gain some benefit from his jaunt, even though the film didn't come off. Loew-Lewin have engaged this actor for one of the most important roles he has had in Hollywood in latter days. This is the heavy in *Bel Ami*."[2] Like Hedda Hopper, Schallert also sympathized with Warren's recent inability to get work in Hollywood. "William, a most competent actor, has been in one of those doldrums, or air-pocket periods, the last year or so, that can happen to the player without rhyme or reason in moviedom, and this assignment promises new impetus." *Bel Ami* promised to be a prestige production, and although Warren would be playing a small part, it was a return to activity, and an opportunity to attempt to quiet those long-standing rumors about his health. It wasn't until early 1947 that Loew and Lewin were ready to begin production with a superb cast that included George Sanders and Angela Lansbury. There were also two old friends from Warren's Warner Brothers days, Marie Wilson, who played Effie in the execrable *Satan Met a Lady*, and Ann Dvorak, Warren's co-star from 1932's *Three on a Match*. Dvorak, looking beautiful and performing well, had recently been in England, driving an ambulance truck during the war (echoes of *Stepdaughters of War*), and was just beginning to re-establish her Hollywood career.

The film, based on a Guy De Maupassant novel, has Sanders playing Georges Duroy (nicknamed "Bel Ami"), a Parisian version of the kind of nonchalant, acid-tongued scoundrel he excelled at in films like *The Picture of Dorian Gray* (also directed by Lewin) and *All About Eve*. Warren is Laroche-Mathieu, a newspaper editor and public servant who despises everything Duroy stands for—from his coarse personality to his cavalier treatment of women. Although Laroche-Mathieu has just a handful of scenes, his presence pervades the film as the greatest adversary of the title character.

The Private Affairs of Bel Ami is a tiresome bore, with the script never evidencing the deeper emotions that Georges Duroy supposedly acquiesces to in the moments before his death, making him merely a disagreeable, obnoxious lout. It is also terribly dry, unconscionably formal and needlessly stagy, with Lewin's camera either standing maddeningly still, placed too far away from the action or failing to capture any particle of drama that accidentally drifts into the production. Apparently Lewin decided that any film with such literary pedigree must maintain the utmost seriousness and gravity, thus consigning the entirety of French society in the age of Degas, Toulouse-Lautrec and the Folies Bergère to a humorless, tedious existence.

Most critics were lukewarm, but Bosley Crowther was positively cold. "Really, it is incredible that a picture could be made from a Guy De Maupassant novel and be as tiresome as this. But there's no denying the evidence. And there's no denying the fact that it takes more to make a man intriguing than persistent protestation that he is. This is the history of a scoundrel— but what a monotonous prig! And what a lifeless history it is that the picture unfolds! Everybody, from Mr. Sanders right on down—the whole lot of them are as utterly artificial as the obvious paint-and-pasteboard sets."[3]

As fine an actor as Sanders is, he lacks the capacity to wrestle sympathy from an audience when playing a cad. He simply does not hint at anything more complex, and does not possess a sense of personal warmth necessary to explain why anyone would like him. Warren's innate ability to convey emotional possibilities under the villain's actions—and his simple likability—would have made him a natural for the role of Bel Ami in younger days. It's a shame that Sanders did not ask the aging actor for some insight, since it is unlikely that Warren would offer any advice unless he was politely asked.

The Private Affairs of Bel Ami became Warren's swan song to Hollywood. When it wrapped in January of 1947, the actor had nothing on the horizon and his health was continuing to deteriorate. His final scene on the silver screen comes in the closing moments of the film, after Duroy has been fatally shot in a duel in the French countryside. Warren looks at the mortally wounded scoundrel—the cheap, one-dimensional imitation of all those magnificent bastards he essayed—and lets an ever-so-slight smile of satisfaction cross his face. Then he turns his back to the camera and walks slowly into the mist, out of Hollywood forever.

During most of 1947, Warren could not work. He tired easily, and was having severe bone pain, unable to walk or stand for extended periods. There were bouts of nausea, continuing infections, headaches and numbness in his limbs. Tests and medical treatment — still unable to properly diagnose his condition — were now winnowing away the Krechs' savings. The couple had to consider breaking up their beloved ranch and selling off parcels to stay ahead of their debts. It was a difficult decision, but these were people who were raised to take responsibility and look after themselves and others. Arrangements were made to move from the main house at 4717 Encino, into their servants' quarters in the 4657 building. The plat of land around 4717 was split from the body of the ranch and sold off. Staff was let go. The house continued to drift towards a dour, sad tone.

On May 19, Warren managed an appearance on the CBS radio program *Screen Guild Players*, in their adaptation of the superb post-war film *The Best Years of Our Lives*. Standing in for Fredric March (alongside Dana Andrews, Virginia Mayo and Cathy O'Donnell), Warren performed smartly, and customarily donated his earnings to Motion Picture Relief Fund for the Motion Picture Country Home. His charity work during the postwar years was a major endeavor, including many events for Cedar's Sinai Hospital, the Anti-Vivisection League and numerous Episcopal organizations.

In the summer, Geraldine Hasskamp — daughter of one of Warren's five aunts — trekked from sleepy little Aitkin to Los Angeles to visit her famous cousin. When she arrived with her children Marsha, Thomas and Steven after days on the road, she found the house shuttered, the servants gone and the ranch dark and gloomy. Fortunes were changed. Only ten years earlier, when Warren's aunt Marcia Ross was in financial trouble with an Aitkin bank, she asked her nephew to help take care of the debt. The flush movie star immediately bailed her out to the tune of many thousands of dollars. But now things were different.[4] Warren was unexpectedly in the hospital and Helen was running the ranch on an austerity plan. While Geraldine visited her cousin in the hospital, the three children rattled around the ranch, swam in the pool and played with the dogs that were still resting in the comfortable nooks they knew so well.

For the rest of 1947, illness and fatigue continued to plague Warren, with doctors still unable to diagnose his condition properly. Cancer was certainly suspected, but if it was cancer, where was it attacking the system, and how far along was it? In October, Warren marshaled his strength and went into a Los Angeles studio to record an audition tape for a new radio series to be called *United States Postal Inspector*.[5] The show was the brainchild of producer-director Robert Webster and was written by Ken Cripine, an alumnus of *Strange Wills*. Warren was postal inspector Jefferson Black, who cracks "one of the vilest schemes ever perpetrated," wherein a grave monument company plans to swindle the parents of dead soldiers. The series was modeled on the same design as *Strange Wills*, with each episode to be a different case from Black's archives. Warren sounds a little tired in the pilot, like a sleepy man using muscle memory to drive a car home through familiar surroundings. *United States Postal Inspector* may have had potential, but the precipitous decline of the health of its star scuttled it before it was even started.

Southern California was enjoying an abnormally warm fall and winter late in 1947, with temperatures climbing regularly into the low 80s. That holiday season, two curious ailments made their way up the West Coast from Los Angeles to Sacramento, San Jose and San Francisco, then into Oregon and Washington. First was Q fever (so called because it came from Queensland, Australia), a relatively harmless form of typhus. Following Q fever was a fast-moving disease that presented flu-like symptoms — gastrointestinal upset, inflammation of the nose and throat, and general aches and pains—that would put the infected person in bed for days. The Los Angeles Health Department dubbed the condition Virus X, and by late December there were over 200,000 cases reported in the greater Los Angeles area alone. Errol Flynn contracted it, as did Bing Crosby and numerous other stars, whose productions had to be shut down for fear of sending out an entire company. It was not fatal, except perhaps to the very young or the very old—or to someone who was already weakened by another condition. In November, Virus X infiltrated the ranch in Encino and infected its owner. With his constitution already compromised, Warren's ability to fight off the disease was problematic.

On December 2, Warren passed his 53rd birthday. He was thin and weak and continually tired. Virus X was draining his meager resources. Later that month he was admitted to Cedars Sinai Hospital for observation and another battery of tests. It was on December 15, 1947, that Dr. Gordon finally received the information he'd been searching for.[6] The diagnosis was grave: multiple myeloma, an incurable cancer of the bone marrow. In myeloma, cancer cells adhere to structural cells in the marrow, then gradually invade the hard outer part of the bone, eventually infecting all the large bones of the body. Along the way they create many small lesions, giving the disease the name *multiple* myeloma.[7] The condition was then often underdiagnosed or was discovered very late in the term, and Warren fulfilled the profile. With the cancer already well in force, he was told that three years was the average survival rate from onset. There was no way to tell exactly how long he had to live. One can only imagine the scene between patient and doctor—not to mention Warren and Helen—when the prognosis was given.

After years of modern investigation, the causes of multiple myeloma are still vague and imperfectly understood. However, there are studies that indicate the very real possibility that Warren's personal passions contributed to his own undoing: His love of nature and inventing may have killed him.

According to current research, there are a group of environmental factors that appear to raise the odds of contracting myeloma. Each points directly to an area that Warren was intimately involved with during his years in Encino. One study concluded, "Agricultural occupations ... exposure to herbicides, insecticides ... and various dusts ... appear to be risk factors for the disease."[8] Throughout the late 1930s and 1940s, Warren regularly worked the citrus orchards and walnut groves on his ranch, riding out on his tractor, cultivating, tilling, and spraying his crops with chemicals to control insects. DDT, the infamous pesticide that was eventually banned by the United States government as unsafe, is also linked to myeloma. Introduced in 1945 (after Warren was already sick, apparently), the insecticide became an immensely popular product both for agricultural applications and in the home. Although there is no direct evidence that Warren used DDT at the ranch, his interest in having the latest tools and substances for his work would have undoubtedly drawn him to the new and extremely effective product. *Time* magazine reported on potential side effects of DDT as early as 1949, mentioning that no less an authority than the U.S. Army had warned that there were no data on the long-range effects of the chemical. "But the public, delighted with DDT, kept right on spraying closets, beds, kitchens and household pets. Whole communities were engulfed in artificially created DDT fogs."[9] It is entirely possible that as Warren was working to get better, DDT was slowly continuing to poison him. Another study almost drew a picture of the long-time inventor and tinkerer: "Agricultural occupations and jobs in which workers are exposed to wood dust increase the risk of developing multiple myeloma."[10] Sequestered in his small workshop, regularly sawing, drilling, sanding and planing wood for his hundreds of inventions, exposed him to a large amount of dust and particulate matter over the years. He rigged a power saw in his workshop during 1934 and once commented: "It's fun playing with that for an hour or so a day."[11] It's no coincidence that he also attended a conference on the uses of waste sawdust in 1939. The damn stuff was in his blood.

Helen still did not tell the family how serious Warren's condition was. Although she mentioned to Elizabeth and Pauline that he was losing weight and had "a problem with his blood," she never gave them the diagnosis that would have told them that their brother had only a short time to live.[12] Neither of them was able to see him before he died. Remaining family members still resent the fact that Warren's sisters never got to say a final goodbye to the brother they admired so much.[13]

Palliative care was now all that Helen and the doctors could offer Warren. He was seriously weakening and almost entirely confined to the house. At least four doctors (Stanley Gordon, N.H. Robin, L.A. Newman and Martin Stein) were attending him, and there was also a nurse to look after his daily needs. As time went on, the athletic, 6'3" outdoorsman became so thin that she sometimes carried him from room to room rather than transfer him to a wheelchair and out again.

As 1948 proceeded, the Virus X infection proved a serious complication to Warren's prognosis and his health grew steadily worse. Pneumonia set in. Most of his time was spent in bed, often under an oxygen tent, and with regular care from Helen and his nurse. At 70, Helen was herself being taxed by the physical and mental stress of taking care of her husband and the ranch on her own. By September 2 it was clear that time was limited, and Warren called two of his closest friends, business manager Mitchell Frug and attorney Glen Still, to the house for the signing of his will. Via a very simple document, he left everything to the woman he loved so dearly for over thirty years. In the event that Helen were to predecease him, his sisters and nieces would inherit the bulk of the estate, with a small gift going to Frug and another to the Anti-Vivisection Society of America. He could hardly leave without helping the animals that had stood in for his own children over all those years. One can picture his loyal wire-hairs sitting vigil at the bedside, wondering when their master would get up and take them to roam over the lush estate they called home.

The next day Helen drafted her own will, and all the legal pieces were in place.

On Friday, September 24, 1948, Warren William could no longer fight off the diseases that were ravaging his body. At 2:35 in the morning, with Helen sitting at his side, his heart simply stopped.

Intermission: Out of a Blue Sky

On March 20 of 1948, as the 1947 Academy Awards were underway, a tired and weakening Warren William rested at home. He had only six months to live.

At the Shrine Civic Auditorium in Los Angeles, an 82-year-old engineer named Thomas Armat was pulled momentarily from obscurity and given the recognition he had eschewed for most of his life: He was awarded a special Oscar for his contribution to the development of the motion picture industry. Like most people, Warren William the actor likely never heard of Thomas Armat. It's a shame, since Warren William the amateur inventor surely would have been fascinated by him, and for good reason; Armat was largely responsible for Warren's fame and fortune.

Near the end of the 19th century very few people in the world, much less the inhabitants of the tiny midwestern town of Aitkin, Minnesota, could have envisioned the cinema industry that would soon revolutionize communication and the arts, and through those, drive the social

P2189-17

Warren loved trees so much that he once said that visiting a lumber mill would be "like going to a slaugh-terhouse." He personally tended the groves and orchards on his eight-acre ranch, using the skills he learned growing up in a small Minnesota lumber town. The DDT and other pesticides he sprayed on his crops almost certainly contributed to the cancer that killed him.

development of America during the following century. Thomas Armat was one of those select few.

At precisely the time Warren Krech was born in December of 1894, Armat was engaged in a race with inventors in Europe and America to be the first person to perfect the projection of motion pictures on a screen. During the first six years that movies were in existence, their audience had been limited to a single viewer peeping into Thomas Edison's revolutionary motion picture machine, the Kinetograph. While Edison stubbornly preferred to wring maximum profits from the per-person coin drop of the Kinetograph, exhibitors clamored for a projection system that would allow the exploitation of a mass audience. At the Bliss School of Electricity in Washington, DC, Armat met a classmate named Charles Jenkins. The two became friends, and the pair decided to set about creating a practical machine for throwing sequential photographic images on a screen. Jenkins had previously failed in his own attempt at a projection system, but Armat felt that together they could solve the problems that Jenkins had encountered. Simultaneously, other engineers, inventors and tinkerers around the world were working on the very same idea, each hoping to capture the all-important patent and the presumed riches to follow.

Armat and Jenkins got there first. They received U.S. patent number 673992 for their projection mechanism, and there started an acrimonious series of disputes, arguments and lawsuits with other inventors which lasted for over twenty years. In time, Armat bought out Jenkins' interest, becoming the sole holder of the patent they had submitted, and for many years he defended it against all illegal encroachment. While the wealthy Armat enjoyed the fortune associated with being the man who kicked off motion picture exhibition in America, he never courted the fame. By the time Warren made it to Hollywood, the patent war had long ended, and Armat was just another footnote in the history of Victorian cinema.

That night the glittering stars of the silver screen watched, probably indifferently, as Armat accepted the thanks of the Academy of Motion Picture Arts and Sciences for his service. Perhaps few understood what his contribution meant to their fame and fortune. There is little doubt that Warren would have appreciated the significance of Armat's work, and would rather have received Armat's special award for invention than any acting award the Academy might have proffered. Had he been on hand, the amateur engineer would have most certainly applauded longer and louder than anyone in the house.

Later that year, on September 30, only six days after Warren died, Armat also passed into memory. As the digital revolution enfolds the world, it won't be long before any semblance of the motion picture system he devised enters entirely into the realm of the obsolete. Mechanical projection of film as pioneered a century ago will be as quaint to future generations as dirigible travel is to us. Like all inventors— whose goal is progress— Thomas Armat and Warren William Krech wouldn't have it any other way.

The molding and shaping of Warren William's memory began the next day with dozens of obituaries in newspapers throughout the country. Each observed Warren in a different way, reflecting how his image and focus changed among audiences during his time in Hollywood. The *New York Times* chose to accent his mature film persona when they wrote: "Warren William, the suave sleuth of dozens of mystery films, died today at his home in suburban Encino after a long illness. Mr. William ... starred and featured in sixty films, notably the Erle Stanley Gardner mysteries and 'Lone Wolf' series."[14] The *New York Herald Tribune* writer was troubled to remember a little further back, to Warren's bygone characters: "Warren William was well known to the moviegoers of the 1930s as a handsome, suave, dark-haired matinee idol with much of the appearance of a young John Barrymore. In his earlier days Mr. William leaned to the more amiable types of villainy — swindler, shyster, murderer, seducer, double-crosser, heartbreaker, and generally unmitigated scoundrel."[15] The *Los Angeles Examiner* went in a different direction, featuring a straightforward shorthand bio: Minnesota upbringing, service in the war, Broadway, Hollywood and personal interests, all neatly wrapped up in a 200-word package. According to the Associated Press, "he played the ideal man about town, although he was one of the town's most home-loving figures."[16] Tiny Aitkin, privy to the secret, unadorned life of their old friend, was left to present the most personal tribute. "It was with regret and shock that the people of Aitkin received the news of the death of Warren William, one of Aitkin's favorite sons, who had achieved fame on stage and screen."[17] In all, about ten pieces of information were distilled and served to readers with their morning coffee. After a moment's consideration they laid the paper aside and thus began the long process of decay and interference that gradually scratched Warren William from our episodic memory.

19

Veils

Helen Barbara Krech was now alone for the first time in almost 30 years. The dogs, the surrogate children that she and her husband doted on, should have been a great comfort to her. But they were aging and failing at the same time as Warren had been. They only seemed a reminder of what she had just been through.

Helen broke the news to Pauline and Elizabeth, still back in New York unaware of how serious things were. Warren's younger sister immediately boarded a westbound train in order to be in Los Angeles by Monday afternoon, when services were to be held at the St. Nicholas Episcopal Church of Encino. Helen's brother Charles, his wife Florence and his son Homer also motored in from their home in Albany, New York, to look after the ranch while Helen was gone. Once the services were over, she would be travelling east. Pauline, ever the non-conformist, stayed put in New York.[1] Perhaps she believed that she'd be able to speak with Warren through the mists of the afterlife, as her spiritualist grandfather Ernst had.

On Monday, the Reverend Harley Wright Smith presided at a simple memorial service for the modest, charitable man who never let fame go to his head. A host of Hollywood celebrities, neighbors, friends and acquaintances came through to pay respects: His *Lone Wolf* compatriots Eric Blore and Thurston Hall were there, along with Genevieve Tobin, Grant Mitchell, Alan Mowbray and many others. Honorary pallbearers included longtime stalwarts Mike Levee and Gene Lockhart, as well as Porter Hall, John Litel and animation pioneer Walter Lantz.

After the services, as per his wishes, Warren William Krech was cremated. His final request was to have his ashes spread in Manhasset Bay on Long Island Sound, at a spot near the Execution Rocks Lighthouse where he often sailed from the Port Washington Yacht Club. In early October, Helen gathered her strength for her cross-country trip, back to tiny Port Washington where the couple had enjoyed so many days with his family. While attorney Glenn Still was attending to the legal affairs, including Warren's life insurance—valued at half a million dollars—Elizabeth and Helen packed up what she would need for the journey east. They left Frank, Florence and Homer to care for the house, bundled up the ashes of the man both women loved and took the three-day pilgrimage by rail to Long Island, New York.

Back home, Helen and Elizabeth brought the earthly remains of Warren back to the sea, the only fitting place for it to end. With their three children sitting on the pier, Elizabeth and her husband Charles put Helen on the boat and set out on the bay. It was cold and windy that afternoon, with choppy seas and submerged rocks making navigation around the lighthouse difficult and dangerous.[2] The crew wisely decided to simply moor the boat at a nearby spot where the lighthouse provided a picturesque backdrop. There, where he was most at home, the final words for a beloved brother, cherished friend and faithful lover were offered. Then Warren William Krech drifted literally into history.

There was some tension at the Lyon household while Helen was staying there in the weeks following Warren's death. Elizabeth never quite warmed up to her sister-in-law, a consequence of Freeman and Frances' personal antipathy towards Helen during the time they lived with the Lyons, beginning in 1920. Elizabeth did not appreciate losing close ties with her brother for those years, and continued to blame Helen. She was also terribly unhappy about not being advised of the severity of Warren's condition in time to visit him before he passed away. Nonetheless, after almost thirty years, Helen was family and she was treated as such.

Shortly after the disposal of Warren's remains, Helen began complaining of shortness of breath and heart palpitations. On November 25, it was severe enough for her to see a local doctor about it. After just a few questions, it is likely that the doctor was able to diagnose Helen's condition. She was suffering from acute myocarditis, a potentially fatal enlargement of the heart, possibly the result of radiation treatments for breast cancer. It was not the biggest of her worries: The cancer that had attacked her in 1946 was also now entwined throughout her body as a carcinomatosis. She had perhaps a month to live.

While she was made as comfortable as possible, Helen saw her final holiday season pass before her. Just after Christmas she was admitted to Manhasset Medical Center, weak and barely able to breathe. On New Year's Eve at 2:00 A.M.— the same hour as her husband's death — Helen Nelson, a.k.a. Helen Ferris, a.k.a. Helen Krech, a.k.a. Helen William, died from congestive heart failure. Her personal fantasy lived on even after she was gone: Her obituary in the *Los Angeles Examiner* claimed the 71-year-old Helen to be just 54.[3]

Helen was also cremated. She had asked that her ashes be spread with her beloved husband's. The boat did not go out, and Helen did not mingle eternally with Warren. Elizabeth instead scattered her sister-in-law's remains off the Manhasset municipal pier, with little fanfare.[4]

Half of Helen's assets, now reduced to almost $400,000 from the estate taxes following Warren's death, were given not to her brother, but to her nephew Homer. This unusual bequest led to long-time speculation among the family that Homer was not her nephew, but rather her son, having been raised by her brother and sister-in-law. It seems entirely unlikely, since Homer was born in 1930, meaning he would have almost certainly been Warren William's son as well. If that were true — and leaving aside the seemingly heartless idea that the couple would have agreed to give him up — Warren's own last will and testament would have reflected it. But Homer was the beneficiary of a mere 5.5 percent of his estate, just equal to what business manager Mitchell Frug and the Anti-Vivisection Society of Los Angeles received combined, making the idea highly suspect. Helen left her remaining assets to Warren's sisters, and divided her jewelry collection — almost $8,000 worth of watches, necklaces, brooches and cigarette cases — among Pauline, Elizabeth and the three girls. The estate lingered on until December of 1950 when it was finally closed for good.

Warren's sister Pauline endured many health problems, the death of one husband and divorce of another, but continued to live her life on her own terms until she passed away during the 1960s. Elizabeth raised three lovely children and passed away far too soon, in 1960, at the age of 58. Warren's nieces, still devoted to their famous uncle, love to reminisce about him, but many others of the family are sadly unaware or uninterested in the details of his life and career. The Krech family name survives through the children and progeny of Alvin Krech, the turn-of-the-century power broker and financier who has likewise been forgotten by history.

In 1958, a small group of merchants from the Hollywood Chamber of Commerce sat together talking about a unique publicity idea designed to drum up business and beautify their neighborhood. The scheme had been pitched by a local contractor as a way to drum up some work for his company, and involved creating plaques honoring celebrities which would be embedded in sidewalks throughout the area. After the Chamber approved the idea and raised seed money from local shops, the Hollywood Walk of Fame was born. The council appointed to assign the first stars on the Walk consisted of eight people, and they would choose among important contributors from the fields of film, television, music, radio and theater.

During the following months, 1,558 people were chosen to be immortalized in the first installation of plaques. Among those initial inductees laid down in early 1960 was Warren William, the Minnesotan who had carved out a sliver of personal fame in the world's greatest medium of mass entertainment. His star sits at 1559

Among the 1500 original stars chosen for installation on the Hollywood Walk of Fame in 1960 is this plaque dedicated to Warren William at 1559 Vine Street. The mercurial nature of fame means that thousands who read the name have no idea of his career or life.

Vine Street, a quarter of a mile south of the famed corner of Hollywood and Vine, in sight of the Capitol Records building. He shares the street with the famous and the famous forgotten: Colleen Moore, Alec Guinness, Fred Stack, George Carlin, Brian Donlevy, John Wayne, Richard Rowland, Andrea King, Michael Jackson and perhaps twenty others. The tread of feet across his brass and terrazzo plaque is incessant, and most often oblivious.

20

Nocturne

Shortly after Warren died, television began its inexorable march as the dominant communication and media device on earth. It quickly supplanted stage, screen and radio as the preferred entertainment of the mid-twentieth century, and programming was needed to feed the voracious appetite of the public. Movies—the overwhelming majority of which remained unseen following their original releases ten and twenty years earlier—became a TV staple. For the first time, new fans could discover the forgotten actors of yesteryear, or encounter long unseen gems of those stars who were still active. But in the early 1950s the Hollywood Production Code was still in force, meaning that those racy, bawdy, risqué, pre–Code classics of Warren William's star era could not be released to television. The very films in which he excelled—whether as the magnificently amoral cad, or the king of licentious innuendo—went unseen during the years when new generations were rediscovering James Cagney, Clark Gable and Joan Crawford. Even the Falcon, the Saint, Charlie Chan, the Thin Man and their brethren appeared with a plurality of geometric proportions compared to the Lone Wolf. Warren did not have the single picture that might have kept him alive, as *Watch on the Rhine* did for Paul Lukas, or *Disraeli* for George Arliss. Without that periodic reminder—a recognition cue for our episodic memory—Warren simply faded out of the regular recall of the people who once knew him. And new generations simply never saw him at all.

That Warren's career is now even being unearthed and revived is remarkable; his rediscovery is happening without the benefit of a significant fan base, regular television appearances or a mainstream star vehicle. This archaeology testifies to his unquestionable relevance as an essential model for the modern construction of greed and heedless ambition, human qualities intrinsic to any era. His dominant film persona is as resonant now as it was 75 years ago. You can trace a crooked line from David Dwight or Kurt Anderson to Sydney Greenstreet's soap tycoon in *The Hucksters*, through Everett Sloane harassing poor Ed Begley in *Patterns*, and on to Michael Douglas in Oliver Stone's *Wall Street*. The only difference from then to now is found in the innate humanity of Warren's characters, something we no longer seem to want in our villains—at least the ones whom we perceive as taking advantage of *us*. We might like a scoundrel, but we do not want to feel pity for *the enemy*.

It is a sad fact that if Warren's ruthless businessmen have granted him the renewed post-mortem interest of fans, his subservience to strong female characters was largely responsible for the gradual downfall of his living fame. His personal attitude of equality toward women, his own unshakable security in his manhood and his lack of interest in forging a clear public image led him to accept the disastrous assignments *Smarty*, *Dr. Monica* and *Living on Velvet*. Even today's women—not so fundamentally changed from their 1930s counterparts—would be unlikely to respect him in those roles. As a flesh-and-blood man they might appreciate Warren's respect and support—but watching him on the big screen would be another matter. From the distance of history, however, modern audiences can allow themselves to ignore those pictures and focus solely on the work that fits their interest and enjoyment. In this way we constantly create our own augmented filmographies of the great stars; Humphrey Bogart is *Casablanca* and *The Maltese Falcon*, but not *The Two Mrs. Carrolls* or *Conflict*; Errol Flynn invariably conjures *The Adventures of Robin Hood* and *Captain Blood*, but never *Cry Wolf* or *Green Light*. Contemporary audiences have no such luxury; they are obliged to see *everything* pass before them and make judgments based on a more complete picture of a career. When Depression era audiences saw Warren as subservient, or ineffectual, or passive, they could not un-see it. And when the man of action was becoming more and more entrenched in popular culture, Warren was not even portraying his opposite number — the intellectual, thinking man — but rather one who let women run his life by making no choice at all. The Historic Eye — the one that decides where future generations look — can not only point at or away from people, but also at only selected moments of their lives, allowing a newly manufactured image that is sometimes equally truthful, eminently false, or just plain salable. The Warren William of *Employees' Entrance* or *Skyscraper Souls* has relevance to new audiences, and we watch. The one who starred in *The Secret Bride* is unmemorable and we pay no attention. Both personae are products of Hollywood, and history, and commerce. Neither image — nor, I dare say this book — bears a *true* resemblance to the real, flesh-and-blood man.

The conspiracy of fame is a ruthless enterprise. It is made up of thousands of details integral and circumstantial; any one of those details can create an icon or relegate them to a mere footnote in history. Only a supreme few are powerful enough to forge a legacy and infiltrate the overburdened minds of succeeding generations. In the complete portrait of Warren William there is no legacy, only a career. What we are doing when we see him on screen is simply watching a man work. If he has a legacy at all, it is not in his craft, but in the incredible success he had in remaining true to himself. While many resolve to make their lives subservient to their work, Warren had the exact opposite goal: He would control his career, not the other way around. His loyalty was to his personal identity. At the nexus of greed and idolatry he maintained a sense of humility and proportion; he chose reality over fantasy and was satisfied to create a well-rounded person, rather than the mere image of one. In a way, this quality may explain the reason why there is an inherent humanity in those base, corrupt, praetorian scoundrels Warren excelled at. Consciously or subconsciously he would never fully erase himself from the characters he played, no matter how unlike him they were.

For all his years on stage and screen, Warren William Krech refused to become what audiences, or his studio bosses, or even his wife wanted him to be: Warren William, movie star. As a result he almost certainly sacrificed greater fame and glory, but maintaining his personal integrity made him far happier; he rarely wavered from a determination to remain, simply and plainly, his own man. In Hollywood — the nirvana of fakery — *that* is a most singular accomplishment.

Chapter Notes

Chapter 1

1. Bob Chatelle, "Aitkin, Minnesota: An Introduction," Aitkin Area Chamber of Commerce, 1996, April 4, 2008, http://users.rcn.com/kyp/aitkin.html.
2. "Aitkin, Minnesota — Our Heritage," 2006, April 13, 2007, www.aitkin.com/fest/history.htm.
3. Ibid.
4. Barbara Hall, interview with the author, August 12, 2009.
5. Otto E. Naegele, "Biographical and Narrative History of Ernst Wilhelm Krech and Matilda Krech," unpublished monograph, April 1944. Mr. Nagle, a former student of Ernst and friend of the Krech family during their years in Minnesota, sent this short biographical sketch to Warren William late in 1944.
6. Patricia Lyon, interview with the author, July 12, 2009.
7. Shepherd Krech, *A History of the Krech Family to 1960*, self-published, 1960.
8. Ibid.
9. Ibid.
10. Ibid.
11. Ibid.
12. Kenneth Carley, *The Sioux Uprising of 1862*, 2d ed., St. Paul: Minnesota Historical Society, 1976.
13. "Seasons in Time," Aitkin County Historical Society, 1995.
14. Naegele, "Biographical and Narrative History of Ernst Wilhelm Krech and Matilda Krech."
15. Krech, *A History of the Krech Family to 1960*.
16. *Time*, May 14, 1928.
17. A.C. Klee, "Newspaper History," *Aitkin Age*, 1971.
18. "Aitkin, Minnesota — Our Heritage," 2006.
19. "Aitkin History Page," Minnesota GenWeb Project, no date, March 22, 2007, www.geocities.com/Heartland/Valley/8119/aitkhis.htm?200722.
20. Deed Record, Aitkin County.
21. Bob Chatelle, "A Year in the Life of Aitkin Minnesota," Aitkin Area Chamber of Commerce, 1996.
22. "Seasons in Time."
23. Carlisle Jones, "Krech's Bad Boy," Warner Brothers Studio bio, 1932.
24. *Aitkin Republican*, December 21, 1899.
25. Grace Kingsley, "Early Loves of Stars Revealed," *Los Angeles Times*, February 19, 1939.
26. Klee, "Newspaper History."
27. Ibid.
28. Connie Pettersen, interview with author, August 2008.
29. "Seasons in Time."
30. Jones, "Krech's Bad Boy."
31. Ibid.
32. *Aitkin Age*, February 7, 1918.

Chapter 2

1. Jones, "Krech's Bad Boy."
2. J. Maurice Ruddy, "Warren William: The Squire of Encino," *Screen and Radio Weekly*, May 19, 1935.
3. *Aitkin Age*, May 1908.
4. "Seasons in Time."
5. "Warren Krech in N.Y. Play with Mrs. Barrymore," *Aitkin Age*, July 7, 1928.
6. *Los Angeles Times*, March 1936.
7. *Los Angeles Times*, August 6, 1936.
8. Jones, "Krech's Bad Boy."
9. "Warren William Talks," *New York Times*, July 24, 1932.
10. *Aitkin Age*, circa 1936.
11. *Duluth News Tribune*, August 28, 1915.
12. "June Weather and June Graduates," *Aitkin Independent*, June 5, 1915.
13. Mark Dowling, "Just to Oblige," unidentified magazine article, circa 1935, Wisconsin State Historical Society clipping file.
14. Harry Lang, "Warren William," *Movie Mirror*, April 1933.
15. Ibid.
16. Gladys Hall, "Life Story of a Dangerous Man," author's manuscript, 1932.
17. Allen Churchill, *The Theatrical Twenties*, McGraw-Hill, 1975.
18. *Movie Classic*, September 1931.
19. Audition notes for Warren Krech, American Academy of Dramatic Arts, October 26, 1915.

Chapter 3

1. Audition notes, 1915.
2. Christine Arnold Schroeder, American Academy of Dramatic Arts, correspondence with the author, May 12, 2008.
3. Catalogue for the American Academy of the Dramatic Arts, New York City, 1915.

4. "An Actor from Minnesota," January 24, 1931, clipping from unidentified New York newspaper.

5. Memo from Hal Wallis to Alan Crosland during the filming of *The Case of the Howling Dog*, June 1934.

6. Schroeder correspondence, May 12, 2008.

7. Schroeder correspondence, May 19, 2008.

8. Sid, "Happenings in Hollywood," *Hartford Courant*, March 8, 1936.

9. Schroeder correspondence, May 9, 2008.

Chapter 4

1. Jones, "Krech's Bad Boy."

2. *Movie Mirror*, November 1932.

3. Jones, "Krech's Bad Boy."

4. *Movie Mirror*, November 1932.

5. World War I draft registration card of Warren Krech, March 3, 2008, http://content.ancestry.com.

6. *Movie Mirror*, November 1932.

7. Jones, "Krech's Bad Boy."

8. "These May Serve Country" *Aitkin Age*, June 1917.

9. "Cannot Comply Here," *Aitkin Age*, September 1, 1917.

10. "Aitkin County Selective Soldiers Soon to Leave," *Aitkin Age*, September 15, 1917.

11. "Reception to Be Given Departing Soldier Boys," *Aitkin Age*, September 15, 1917.

12. "Aitkin County Selective Soldiers Soon to Leave."

13. "Young Soldiers Are Honored by Citizens," *Aitkin Age*, September 22, 1917.

14. "Soldier Boys Given Rousing Send Off Before Going to 'Can' Kaiser," *Aitkin Republican*, September 20, 1917.

15. "Aitkin County Selective Soldiers Soon to Leave."

16. "Aitkin County's First Drafted Men Have Gone," *Aitkin Age*, September 22, 1917.

17. Ibid.

18. "Soldier Boys Feel They Have Backing of Folks at Home," *Aitkin Republican*, September 27, 1917.

19. Ibid.

20. "Aitkin Contingent to Go to New Mexico," *Aitkin Age*, September 29, 1917, letter from Warren Krech.

21. "Aitkin County's First Draft Boys Are Now Hardly in Touch with Each Other," *Aitkin Age*, October 1917.

22. "Camp Cody — Deming, New Mexico," no date, May 17, 2007, http://www.zianet.com/kromeke/camp-cody/CW01.htm.

23. "First Contingent Men Are Separated," *Aitkin Age*, February 20, 1918.

24. "Aitkin County's First Draft Boys Are Now Hardly in Touch with Each Other."

25. "Aitkin County Boys at Camp Cody," *Aitkin Age*, November 3, 1917.

26. "World War I History — 34th Division," March 16, 2004, May 17, 2007, http://www.34infdiv.org/history/wwihist.html.

27. "World War I History," 2004.

Chapter 5

1. Ben Maddox, "Don't Try to Explain Warren William," *Photoplay*, October 1935.

2. Patricia M. Lyon, interview with the author, July 20, 2009.

3. Minnesota census record, 1895.

4. Death record, Nassau County, New York.

5. Marriage certificate, state of Minnesota, January 30, 1902.

6. Ruth Biery, "The Man Who Can't Talk," *Photoplay*, February 1933.

7. Ibid. The story of Warren and Helen's first meeting has been told many times in fan magazines and feature articles. Details of the afternoon and evening agree with remarkable consistency.

8. "Don't Try to Explain Warren William."

9. Synnott and Clark, "Influenza Epidemic at Camp Dix, N.J.," *Journal of the American Medical Association*, November 30, 1918.

Chapter 6

1. Jones, "Krech's Bad Boy."

2. Ibid.

3. Hall, "Life Story of a Dangerous Man."

4. Maddox, "Don't Try to Explain Warren William."

5. Jones, "Krech's Bad Boy."

6. "Warren William Talks," *New York Times*, 1932.

7. Ruddy, "Warren William: The Squire of Encino."

8. "Two Players, in Person, a Mystery Hit," *Washington Post*, July 24, 1932.

Chapter 7

1. "The A.E.F. Coming and Going," *Stars and Stripes*, June 1919.

2. *Movie Mirror*, November 1932.

3. In his Warner Brothers studio bio, Carlisle Jones places Warren's return on July 4. The record of the 34th Infantry Division lists the 109th Engineers as sailing from St. Nazaire on June 17 and returning to Newport News on June 29.

4. "Look at This Who's Who of Hollywood," *Lima Sunday News*, July 16, 1933.

5. *Hartford Courant*, August 5, 1934.

6. "Local News," *Aitkin Independent Age*, July 19, 1919.

7. *Duluth News Tribune*, September 14, 1919. The family stayed in New York for four weeks, leaving on August 13 and returning to Aitkin on September 14.

8. "Last Night's Play," *Columbus Enquirer-Sun*, November 1, 1919.

9. "*I Love You* at Springer Opera House Tonight," *Columbus Journal*, October 31, 1919.

10. "At the Nesbitt," *Wilkes-Barre Times*, September 13, 1919.

11. Freeman Krech, letter to E. C. Knieff, September 30, 1925.

12. "Warren William Practices Lines Before a Mirror," *Satan Met a Lady* pressbook, Warner Brothers, 1936.

13. Jones, "Krech's Bad Boy."

14. "*Independent-Age* Changes Hands Today," *Aitkin Republican*, January 1, 1920.

15. "Virtues and Activities Extolled," *Aitkin Age*, May 13, 1920.

Chapter 8

1. Lang, "Warren William."

2. *Aitkin Independent Age*, April 3, 1920.

3. Nathan Ward, "The Fire Last Time," *Free Republic*, December 2001, March 6, 2008 http://www.freere-public.com/focus/f-news/577915/posts.

4. *Marion Daily Star*, September 17, 1920.

5. Jones, "Krech's Bad Boy."

6. "Theater Guild Is New York Triumph," *Dallas Morning News*, June 6, 1921.

7. Alexander Woolcott, "The Play," *New York Times*, January 24, 1921.

8. *Movie Mirror*, 1932.

9. "A Sermon in a Storm," *New York Times*, November 1, 1922.

10. *Movie Mirror*, 1932.

11. George Jean Nathan, "The New York Stage," *New York Times*, December 4, 1921.

12. "Movieland Notes," *Davenport Democrat and Leader*, September 10, 1922.

13. Jones, "Krech's Bad Boy."

Chapter 9

1. Maddox, "Don't Try to Explain Warren William."

2. Ibid.

3. Barbara Hall, interview with the author, July 30, 2009.

4. Jones, "Krech's Bad Boy."

5. Marriage certificate, New York State records.

6. Barbara Hall, July 30, 2009.

7. J. Maurice Ruddy, "Warren William: The Squire of Encino."

8. *Aitkin Independent Age*, March 31, 1923.

9. Barbara Hall, August 12, 2009.

10. "Warren William Talks," 1932.

11. Lang, "Warren William."

12. Jack Warner to Sam Bischoff, interoffice memo, June 14, 1935.

13. *New York Times*, March 16, 1924.

14. Katharan McCommon, letter to the dramatic editor, *New York Times*, February 24, 1924.

15. Gertrude Linnell, letter to the dramatic editor, *New York Times*, February 20, 1924.

16. John Corbin, "Among the New Plays," *New York Times*, May 4, 1924.

17. John Corbin, "Among the New Plays," *New York Times*, April 27, 1924.

18. Jones, "Krech's Bad Boy."

19. Corbin, "Among the New Plays," May 4, 1924.

20. Hilda Couch, letter to the dramatic editor, *New York Times*, May 25, 1924.

21. M. L. Malevinsky, letter to the dramatic editor, *New York Times*, June 1, 1924.

22. "With the Plays and Players," *Westfield Leader*, July 23, 1924.

23. "With the Plays and Players," *Westfield Leader*, July 9, 1924.

24. "Bright Comedy at the Wilbur," *Boston Daily Globe*, January 6, 1925.

25. Stark Young, "*Nocturne* Is Interesting," *New York Times*, February 17, 1925.

26. "Re-Enter Goodman," *New York Times*, March 29, 1925.

27. Alice Rohe, "A New Theater Movement Starts in New York," United Press, syndicated in the *Winona Republican-Herald*, April 13, 1925.

28. Stark Young, "The Stagers First Venture," *New York Times*, March 25, 1925.

29. Gladys Hall, "Life Story of a Dangerous Man."

30. Otheman Stevens, "Vinegar Tree Player Shows Superb Poise," publication unknown, June 1931.

31. "Actor Thinks About Hiking for a Part…" clipping from New York City newspaper, 1933, New York Public Library.

32. Gladys Hall, "The Gadgeteer," manuscript for article in *Modern Screen*, June 14, 1937, Gladys Hall collection, Margaret Herrick Library. The manuscript contains margin notes written by Warren.

33. John Chatterton, "Warren William," clipping from unidentified magazine, 1935, New York Public Library.

34. Jones, "Krech's Bad Boy."

35. John J. Daly, "Footlights and Shadows," *Washington Post*, May 10, 1925.

36. "New Plays," *Time*.

37. Herbert G. Goldman, "Fanny Brice: The Original Funny Girl," Oxford Books, 1993, pp. 124–25.

38. *New York Post*, September 22, 1926.

39. Gilbert Gabriel, *New York Sun*, September 22, 1926.

40. *New York Times*, October 3, 1926.

41. Letters and correspondence between the company and Actor's Equity, April 1927.

42. Percy Hammond, *New York Herald Tribune*, April 25, 1928.

43. Edward Cushing, *Brooklyn Eagle*, June 25, 1928.

44. On November 2, 1936, *The Washington Post* reported that Warren beat out Clark Gable for his role in *Let Us Be Gay*. At that time Gable was a complete unknown just returned from an unfruitful trip to Hollywood.

45. Barbara Hall, interview with the author, August 12, 2009.

46. Barbara Hall, August 12, 2009.

47. *New York Times*, August 3, 1930.

48. Burns Mantle, "Heroines Have Tough Breaks on Broadway," *Chicago Tribune*, October 19, 1930.

49. Brooks Atkinson, "Ghosts of the War," *New York Times*, October 7, 1930.

Chapter 10

1. "Lines from a Scrapbook," *New York Times*, January 25, 1931.

2. Unknown New York newspaper, January 24, 1931, New York Public Library clipping file.

3. "Warren (Slim) William," unidentified newspaper clipping, 1937, New York Public Library.

4. *Washington Post*, February 14, 1937.

5. Brian Herbert, "Speaking of New Men," unidentified magazine article from late 1931, Wisconsin Historical Society clipping file.

6. Barbara Hall, July 30, 2009.

7. Patricia Lyon, June 20, 2009.

8. Years later an overzealous publicity hound claimed that this flight was the same one that killed Notre Dame football coach Knute Rockne. According to the story, Warren had a premonition of disaster and deplaned. Rockne was indeed killed on the last leg of the same New York–Los Angeles flight — but during the following week, on March 31, 1931.

9. Hubbard Keavy, "Keavy Gives Some First Impressions," *Hartford Courant*, June 7, 1936.

10. "When It's Zero Hour in Hollywood," *Hartford Courant*, August 14, 1932.

11. "Seventh Jones Subject Finished," O.B. Keeler, *New York Times*, April 26, 1931.

12. Robbin Coons, "Hollywood Sights and Sounds," *Winona Republican-Herald*, September 2, 1931.

13. *Los Angeles Times*, May 2, 1931.

14. Grace Kingsley, "Paul Muni to Act Scarface," *Los Angeles Times*, May 21, 1931.

15. Edwin Schallert, "Airy Billie Burke Charms," *Los Angeles Times*, July 1, 1931.

16. Stevens, 1931.

17. Nelson B. Bell, "New Cinema Offerings," *Washington Post*, January 17, 1932.

18. Bell, January 17, 1932.

19. Eileen Creelman, "Warren William on Vacation Here Before Starting Ben Hecht's *Upperworld*," unidentified New York newspaper article, New York Public Library clipping file.

20. Roy Obringer, memo to Darryl Zanuck, September 10, 1931.

21. *Washington Post*, December 29, 1933.

22. Norbert Lusk, "Dove, Costello in Dull Stories," *Los Angeles Times*, November 22, 1931.

Chapter 11

1. Grace Kingsley, "Warren William Starred in Story of Courts," *Los Angeles Times*, May 21, 1931.

2. Eileen Creelman, "Warren William on Vacation Here," unidentified New York newspaper, New York Public Library clipping file.

3. "A Strong Film," *Washington Post*, May 15, 1932.

4. Mordaunt Hall, "Shrewd Strategy of Crooked Lawyer," *New York Times*, April 21, 1932.

5. Mordaunt Hall, "The Blackleg Lawyer," *New York Times*, May 1, 1932.

6. *The Westfield Leader*, May 11, 1932.

7. Unidentified newspaper article, Wisconsin State Historical Society clipping file.

8. Mae Tinee, "2d of Lawyer Cycle of Films Has Barrymore," Chicago Tribune, May 13, 1932.

9. Memo from William Koenig, February 25, 1932.

10. John C. Moffitt, "The Life Story of William Powell," *Hartford Courant*, April 2, 1933.

11. Frederick Lewis Allen, "Since Yesterday," 1939, Perennial Library, 1972, p. 44.

12. *Los Angeles Times*, June 4, 1932.

13. "Who's Who This Week in Pictures," *New York Times*, October 2, 1932.

14. Barbara Leming, *Bette Davis: A Biography* (New York: Simon & Schuster, 1992), 103.

15. Lawrence J. Quirk, *Fasten Your Seat Belts: The Passionate Life of Bette Davis* (New York: William Morrow, 1990), 56–58.

16. *Boyar v. Krech*, 10 Cal.2nd 207, court decision issued November 26, 1937. The opinion of Judge J. Langdon spells out Warren's early contract troubles in some detail.

17. "Warren William's Dilemma," *Hartford Courant*, October 2, 1932.

18. "Herding's Design Stirs Interest," *Los Angeles Times*, July 10, 1932.

19. "Warren William's Dilemma."

20. "Warren William," *Movie Mirror*, November 1932.

21. Hall, "Life Story of a Dangerous Man."

22. Philip K. Scheuer, "Loews Tells Tall Story," *Los Angeles Times*, August 8, 1932.

23. Louella Parsons, syndicated in *The Washington Post*, September 30, 1941.

24. *New York Post*, April 1, 1933.

25. "Player's Rise to Note Rapid," *Los Angeles Times*, July 9, 1932.

26. *Washington Post*, November 12, 1932.

27. "Seek Garbo for Film Role," *New York Times*, August 16, 1932.

28. Frank Partnoy, *The Match King: Ivar Kruegar, The Financial Genius Behind a Century of Wall Street Scandals* (New York: PublicAffairs, 2009), 217.

29. *The Match King* was completed at a cost of $154,713.

30. Not everyone thought Warren was particularly subtle. When a columnist wrote that Warren and Warner Baxter were "the two biggest hams in Hollywood," Baxter confronted the writer, telling him, "I don't mind you calling me a ham, but don't tie me up with Warren William ever again!"

31. Mae Tinee, "*Match King* Is a Thrilling Film That 'Gets' You," *Chicago Tribune*, December 17, 1932.

32. Norbert Lusk, "*Match King* Unconvincing," *Los Angeles Times*, December 18, 1932.

33. "Warner Stars to Feel Blow of Salary Ax," UPI, August 6, 1932.

34. Warren's salary log from Warner Brothers shows no pay reduction during the summer of 1932.

35. Matthew Kennedy, *Joan Blondell: A Life Between Takes* (Jackson: University Press of Mississippi, 2007), 51.

36. "Army Training Found Valuable," *Los Angeles Times*, February 14, 1933.

37. "*Employees' Entrance* on Strand Bill," *Hartford Courant*, January 30, 1933.

38. Muriel Babcock, "Warren William Dominates *Employees' Entrance*," *Los Angeles Times*, February 3, 1933.

39. *Hartford Courant*, January 30, 1933.

40. "Fortune Telling Racket Exposed in New Picture," *Los Angeles Times*, May 8, 1933.

41. "*The Mind Reader*," www.tcm.com, accessed December 21, 2007.

42. Mae Tinee, "*Mind Reader* Scores High in Every Detail," *Chicago Tribune*, April 8, 1933.

43. Frederick Lewis Allen, *Since Yesterday* (1939, Perennial Library Edition, New York: Harper & Row, 1972), 78.

44. Warren was so irked by the entire situation that in March he demanded a repayment of three dollars that the studio deducted from his check for the Motion Picture Relief Fund, since he had already personally paid the fee.

45. J. Langdon, opinion in the case of *Boyar v. Krech*, 10 Cal.2nd 207, November 26, 1937.

46. Letter to Warren William from Warner Brothers, dated May 5, 1933.

47. M.C. Levee, letter to Jack Warner, April 24, 1936. Levee references the meeting in his letter requesting Warren's release from the studio.

48. On January 12, 1934, Roy Obringer sent a memo to Jack Warner outlining the contract dispute with Warren, and enumerating the money lost. It appeared to have no other function than to irritate the studio head.

49. Langdon, *Boyar v. Krech*.

50. *Los Angeles Times*, July 4, 1933.

51. *Christian Science Monitor*, September 8, 1933.

52. Frank Capra, *The Name Above the Title* (New York: Macmillan, 1971), 165.

53. Capra, p. 149.

54. *New York Sun*, December 19, 1925.

55. Joseph McBride, *Frank Capra* (New York: Simon & Schuster, 1992), 300.

56. Eileen Creelman, "Warren William on Vacation Here," unidentified newspaper article, clipping file of New York Public Library, circa November 1933.

57. Mordaunt Hall, "May Robson as a White-Haired Cinderella," *New York Times*, September 8, 1933.

58. Edwin Schallert, "*Lady for a Day* Excellent," *Los Angeles Times*, October 2, 1933.

59. Michael Freedland, *The Goldwyn Touch* (London: Harrap, 1986), 130.

60. *New York Sun*, date unknown, *Bedside* clipping file, Warner Brothers Archives.

61. *Bedside* clipping file, Warner Brothers Archives, dates unknown.

62. "Film Actors Quit Academy Over Code," *New York Times*, October 3, 1933.

63. "Warren William in First Rough House Role, Hits 'Em Hard," *Smarty* pressbook, p. 12, Warner Brothers archives, 681B_F000261_001.PDF 12.

64. Unidentified newspaper clipping, Warner Brothers Archives, USC.

65. Mark Dowling, "Just to Oblige," unidentified magazine article, clippings collection of the Wisconsin Historical Society, circa November 1934.

Chapter 12

1. Edwin Schallert, "Producers Ban Lurid Sex Scenes from Future Films," *Los Angeles Times*, June 17, 1934.

2. Schallert, June 17, 1934.

3. Mollie Merrick, "Censorship Threat Tones Down Films," *Hartford Courant*, June 19, 1934.

4. Charles Gentry, "Warren William Finds Time for Comedy," *Detroit Evening Times*, June 1943.

5. *Washington Post*, May 17, 1936.

6. Some sources say he was with the marine artist Tom Manners, who was a consultant at Warner Brothers and a member of the Cape Horners sailing group with Warren.

7. Grace Kingsley, "Hobnobbing in Hollywood," *Los Angeles Times*, December 13, 1933.

8. Robert S. Birchard, *Cecil B. DeMille's Hollywood* (Lexington: University Press of Kentucky, 2004), 276.

9. Cecil B. DeMille and Donald Hayne, ed., *The Autobiography of Cecil B. DeMille* (Englewood Cliffs, NJ: Prentice Hall, 1956), 337–338.

10. Clive Hirschhorn, *The Warner Brothers Story* (New York: Crown, 1979), 147.

11. Reviews from *The New York Daily News*, August 22, 1934, *The New York Evening Journal*, August 23, 1934, and other unidentified newspaper clippings, Warner Brothers Archives.

12. Telephone interview with Barbara Hall, August 29, 2009.

13. *Hartford Courant*, April 14, 1935.

14. A June 14, 1934, memo from Jack Warner indicates that there were other problems with Davis relating to *Howling Dog*: "Be sure that Davis has her bulbs [breasts] wrapped up. If she doesn't do it we are either going to retake or put her out of the picture." There is a possibility that her dismissal had more to do with unwrapped "bulbs" than with her co-star.

15. Jack L. Warner, memo to Sam Bischoff, June 14, 1934.

Chapter 13

1. "Warren William Rarely Seen in Person by Public," *Los Angeles Times*, July 22, 1934.

2. Gladys Hall, "The Gadgeteer."

3. "An Actor from Minnesota," 1931.

4. Hobart, "Warren William — Actor and Arborphile," unidentified San Francisco newspaper article, circa 1939, New York Public Library clipping file.

5. Chatterton, 1935.

6. "The Gadgeteer."

7. *Washington Post*, March 3, 1935.

8. "Warren William, Actor, Gadgeteer," unidentified newspaper article, circa 1943, New York Public Library clipping file.

9. Barbara Hall, August 12, 2009.

10. "Warren William, Actor, Gadgeteer."

11. Unidentified newspaper clipping, February 10, 1935, collection of New York Public Library.

12. "The Gadgeteer."

13. "William Quitting Gadget Inventing," *Washington Post*, March 2, 1938.

Chapter 14

1. Edwin Schallert, "Film Hailed in Premiere at Pantages," *Los Angeles Times*, November 28, 1934.

2. "Actor Thinks Aloud About Hiking for a Part Selected All by Himself," unidentified newspaper article, New York Public Library clipping file.

3. When *Photoplay* polled their readers to "cast" *Anthony Adverse*, they chose Warren for the supporting role of Brother Francis.

4. Mollie Merrick, "Censorship Threat Tones Down Films," *Hartford Courant*, June 19, 1934. The article mentions the Warners production schedule for 1934–35, noting: "*Captain Blood*, Rafael Sabatini's pirate novel, will star Warren William."

5. Herve Dumont, *Frank Borzage: The Life and Films of a Hollywood Romantic* (Jefferson, NC: McFarland, 2006), 233.

6. Clive Hirschhorn suggests that Warren's Warners contract "was in its last stages, and Jack Warner saw no reason why, in the circumstances, he should emerge a winner." *The Warner Brothers Story*, p. 148.

7. "Fire Sweeps Film Studio," *Los Angeles Times*, December 5, 1934.

8. Warren's letter of January 8, 1935 incorrectly dates the *Living on Velvet* ads as appearing on December 29, 1935; the actual date is December 29, 1934.

9. Warren William, letter to Roy Obringer, January 8, 1935.

10. Unidentified newspaper review in *Living on Velvet* file, Warner Brothers Archives.

11. Memo from Nathan Levinson to Hal Wallis.

12. "New Breach Jolts Films," *Los Angeles Times*, August 20, 1935.

13. James R. Silke, *Here's Looking at You, Kid* (Boston: Little, Brown, 1976), 119.

14. Memo from Roy Obringer to M.C. Levee, August 17, 1935.

15. A letter from Jack Warner to Levee dated August 17, 1935, says that they "kindly agree" to Warren's refusal to appear in *Stella Parish*.

16. Memo from Henry Blanke, June 5, 1935.

17. *Washington Post*, August 10, 1936.

18. *Time*, August 3, 1936.

19. Interview with Barbara Hall, August 12, 2009.

20. Transcript of conversation on the set of *Times Square Playboy*, January 17, 1936.

21. Letter from Mike Levee to Warren William, March 3, 1936.

22. Frank S. Nugent, "The Strand Presents Another Back Stage Musical," *New York Times*, September 28, 1936.

23. George Shaffer, "Actor Warren William Is an Inventor, Too," *Chicago Tribune*, June 10, 1936.

24. Rudy Behlmer, *Henry Hathaway* (Lanham, MD: Scarecrow Press, 2001), 147.

25. Marshall Kester, "Curtain Ready to Rise on World's Largest Stage," *Los Angeles Times*, June 28, 1936.

26. George Shaffer, "Experts Differ on K.O. Punch of Mae West," *Chicago Tribune*, September 5, 1936.

27. Behlmer, p. 148.

28. "Best Performances in Current Pictures," *Los Angeles Times*, December 6, 1936.

29. J.T.M., "Mae West at the Paramount in *Go West, Young Man*," *New York Times*, November 19, 1936.

30. On April 17, 1936, *The Chicago Tribune* announced Warren's casting in his first MGM production, *The Firefly*.

31. Jimmy Fidler, *Washington Post*, January 30, 1937.

32. "East Film Play," *Washington Post*, July 24, 1937.

Chapter 15

1. Unidentified newspaper clipping, Hunt Stromberg collection, Herrick Library, Los Angeles.

2. AP wire story, "Actors in Polling Favor Film Strike," *New York Times*, May 9, 1937.

3. Frank S. Nugent, "*The Adventures of Robin Hood*—Other Films," *New York Times*, May 13, 1938.

4. *Hartford Courant*, March 25, 1938.

5. *Hartford Courant*, April 21, 1938.

6. James Curtis, *James Whale* (Metuchen, NJ: Scarecrow Press, 1982), 167.

7. John Scott, "Films Moan Need of More Leading Men," *Los Angeles Times*, October 17, 1937.

8. Sheilah Graham, "List of Stars Suspended by Studio Grows," *Hartford Courant*, April 8, 1938.

9. Sheilah Graham, "Rising Stars Mean Doom for Favorites of Today," *Hartford Courant*, July 24, 1938.

10. Interview with Barbara Hall, August 12, 2009.

11. Curtis, *James Whale*, 1982, pp. 169–70.

12. Mae Tinee, "Film Favorites at New Heights in This Movie," *Chicago Tribune*, June 27, 1938.

13. *New York Journal American*, May 1, 1938.

14. "Warren William Quitting Gadget Inventing," *Washington Post*, March 2, 1938.

15. Hedda Hopper, "In Hollywood," *Washington Post*, September 7, 1938.

Chapter 16

1. *Los Angeles Times*, June 18, 1941.

2. *Los Angeles Times*, May 28, 1933.

3. *Los Angeles Times*, May 19, 1938.

4. William R. Meyer, *Warner Brothers Directors*, Arlington House, 1978, p. 136, quoting *New York Times* critic B.R. Crisler.

5. Frank S. Nugent, "The Screen," *New York Times*, February 5, 1940.

6. Unidentified newspaper review, New York Public Library clipping file.

7. Andre De Toth, *De Toth on De Toth*, edited by Anthony Slide (Boston: Faber & Faber, 1996), 46.

8. Maddox, "Don't Try to Explain Warren William."

9. *Hartford Courant*, January 7, 1939.

10. Curtis, *James Whale*, pp. 171–74.

11. *Washington Post*, September 7, 1939.

12. "*Man in the Iron Mask* seen as Comparative Success," *Los Angeles Times*, July 25, 1939.

13. "*Arizona*," Turner Classic Movies website, www.tcm.com/thismonth/article/?cid+150885, accessed December 21, 2007.

14. Hedda Hopper, "Hedda Hopper's Hollywood," July 3, 1940.

15. *Hartford Courant*, December 29, 1940.

16. *Wall Street Journal*, February 7, 1941.

17. Nelson B. Bell, *Washington Post*, February 15, 1941.

18. Irene Thirer, "By His Mustachios You Shall Know Warren William's Status," unidentified newspaper article, December 1941, New York Public Library clipping file.

19. Hedda Hopper, "Hedda Hopper's Hollywood," August 21, 1941.

20. "By His Mustachios You Shall Know Warren William's Status."

21. Ibid.

22. Bosley Crowther, "The Screen: Ordinary Western," *New York Times*, February 7, 1942.

23. Hedda Hopper, "Hedda Hopper's Hollywood," November 20, 1940.

24. Gregory Mank, *The Wolf Man* (Universal Filmscripts Series), MagicImage, 1993, from repro of *The Wolf Man* pressbook, p. 5.

25. "By His Mustachios You Shall Know Warren William's Status."

26. "Bazaar Proceeds Go to MacArthur's Men," May 11, 1942.

27. Hall, 2009.

28. Ibid.

29. Ibid.

30. Ibid.

31. Thomas M. Pryor, "Notes on the Film Scene," *New York Times*, August 16, 1942.

Chapter 17

1. Charles Gentry, "Warren William Finds Time for Comedy," *Detroit Evening Times*, June 1943.

2. Gentry, "Warren William Finds Time for Comedy."

3. *New York Times*, January 22, 1944.

4. *New York Times*, August 12, 1944.

5. Hedda Hopper, "Looking at Hollywood," *Chicago Daily Tribune*, May 26, 1944.

6. Letter to Hedda Hopper from Warren William, Margaret Herrick library, Hedda Hopper Collection.

7. "Father's Death Avenged by *Hamlet* of Present," *Los Angeles Times*, February 13, 1945.

8. *Time*, August 20, 1945.

9. *Los Angeles Times*, March 30, 1939.

10. Edwin Schallert, "John Garfield Sought for Sam Wood Feature," *Los Angeles Times*, November 27, 1945.

11. "Mystery Concerning Virginia Bruce Cleared," *Los Angeles Times*, March 22, 1946.

12. Hall, August 20, 2009.

13. "The *Strange Wills* Radio Programs," http://www.digitaldeliftp.com/DigitalDeliToo/dd2jb-Strange-Wills.html, accessed September 6, 2009. This is the only source that lists the Teleways corporation and Warren as co-creators of *Strange Wills*.

Chapter 18

1. Interview with Tom Hasskamp, September 2008.

2. Edwin Schallert, "William in *Bel Ami*," *Los Angeles Times*, April 24, 1946.

3. Bosley Crowther, *New York Times*, June 16, 1947.

4. Interview with Steve Hasskamp, August 17, 2008.

5. Sources differ on the recording date for *U.S. Postal Inspector*. Some indicate that it may have been recorded in February 1947.

6. Warren's death certificate, dated September 25, 1948 (District #1901, Registrar's #15503) indicates the disease was "discovered" on December 15, 1947.

7. "Intro to Myeloma," 2002–2006, Multiple Myeloma Research Foundation, www.multiplemyeloma.org/about_myeloma/, accessed August 30, 2007.

8. "Intro to Myeloma."

9. *Time*, April 11, 1949.

10. Enitza D. George, M.D., "Multiple Myeloma, Recognition and Management," American Academy of Family Physicians, http://www.aafp.org/afp/990401ap/1885.html, April 1, 1999, accessed March 21, 2008.

11. Ruddy, "Warren William: The Squire of Encino."

12. Hall, August 12, 2009.

13. Ibid. "Pissed off" is the way Elizabeth's daughter Barbara put it. "I don't think it was nice."

14. *New York Times*, September 25, 1948.

15. *New York Herald Examiner*, September 25, 1948.

16. Associated Press obituary, printed in the *Minneapolis Morning Tribune*, September 25, 1948.

17. "Warren William Dies of Rare Blood Disease," *Aitkin Independent Age*, September 24, 1948.

Chapter 19

1. Pauline's niece Barbara Hall says Pauline did not attend her brother's memorial service. "I don't think she gave a rat's ass about memorial services or things like that!"

2. Hall, August 12, 2009.

3. "Mrs. William Dies 98 Days After Actor," *Los Angeles Examiner*, January 1, 1949.

4. Hall, August 12, 2009. Other sources indicate that Helen's remains were returned to California and rest in Forest Lawn Memorial Park. Unless the memory of those who were there is faulty, Helen's ashes are not in the Columbarium of Memory, but rather in Long Island Sound, regardless of what any marker on the Memorial Terrace might say.

Bibliography

Books

Allen, Frederick Lewis. *Only Yesterday*. New York: Harper and Row Edition, 1957.

_____. *Since Yesterday*. New York: Perennial Library Edition, 1972.

Behlmer, Rudy. *Henry Hathaway*. Lanham, MD: Scarecrow Press, 2001.

Birchard, Robert S. *Cecil B. DeMille's Hollywood*. Lexington: University Press of Kentucky, 2004.

Capra, Frank. *The Name Above the Title*. New York: Macmillan, 1971.

Carley, Kenneth. *The Sioux Uprising of 1862*, 2nd ed. St. Paul: Minnesota Historical Society, 1976.

Chatelle, Bob. *A Year in the Life of Aitkin Minnesota*. Aitkin Area Chamber of Commerce, 1996.

Churchill, Allen. *The Theatrical Twenties*. New York: McGraw-Hill, 1975.

Curtis, James. *James Whale*. Lanham, MD: Scarecrow Press, 1982.

DeMille, Cecil B., and Donald Hayne, *The Autobiography of Cecil B. DeMille*. Englewood Cliffs, NJ: Prentice Hall, 1959.

De Toth, Andre. *De Toth on De Toth*. Boston: Faber & Faber, 1996.

Dumont, Herve. *Frank Borzage: The Life and Films of a Hollywood Romantic*. Jefferson, NC: McFarland, 2006.

Freedland, Michael. *The Goldwyn Touch*. London: Harrap, 1986.

Goldman, Herbert G. *Fanny Brice: The Original Funny Girl*. New York: Oxford University Press, 1993.

Hirschhorn, Clive. *The Warner Brothers Story*. New York: Crown, 1979.

Kennedy, Matthew. *Joan Blondell: A Life Between Takes*. Jackson: University Press of Mississippi, 2007.

Krech, Shepherd. *A History of the Krech Family to 1960*. Self published, 1960.

LaSalle, Mick. *Dangerous Men*. New York: Thomas Dunne Books, 2002.

Leaming, Barbara. *Bette Davis: A Biography*. New York: Simon & Schuster, 1992.

Mank, Gregory. *The Wolf Man* (Universal Filmscripts Series). Absecon, NJ: MagicImage, 1993.

McBride, Joseph. *Frank Capra*. New York: Simon & Schuster, 1992.

Meyer, William R. *Warner Brothers Directors*. New Rochelle, NY: Arlington House, 1978.

Partnoy, Frank. *The Match King: Ivar Krueger, The Financial Genius Behind a Century of Wall Street Scandals*. New York: PublicAffairs, 2009.

Quirk, Lawrence J. *Fasten Your Seat Belts: The Passionate Life of Bette Davis*. New York: William Morrow, 1990.

Seasons in Time. Aitkin County Historical Society, 1995.

Sennett, Ted. *Warner Brothers Presents*. Secaucus, NJ: Castle Books, 1971.

Silke, James R. *Here's Looking at You, Kid*. Boston: Little, Brown, 1976.

Magazine and Newspaper Sources

"An Actor from Minnesota." January 24, 1931, unidentified New York newspaper, New York Public Library clipping file.

"Actor Thinks About Hiking for a Part...." 1933, unidentified New York newspaper, New York Public Library clipping file.

"Actor Thinks Aloud About Hiking for a Part Selected All by Himself." unidentified newspaper article, New York Public Library clipping file.

"Actors in Polling Favor Film Strike." AP wire story, *New York Times*, May 9, 1937.

"The A.E.F. Coming and Going." *Stars and Stripes*, June 1919.

"Aitkin Contingent to Go to New Mexico." *Aitkin Age*, September 29, 1917, letter from Warren Krech.

"Aitkin County Boys at Camp Cody." *Aitkin Age*, November 3, 1917.

"Aitkin County Selective Soldiers Soon to Leave." *Aitkin Age*, September 15, 1917.

"Aitkin County's First Draft Boys Are Now Hardly in Touch with Each Other." *Aitkin Age*, October 1917.

"Aitkin County's First Drafted Men Have Gone." *Aitkin Age*, September 22, 1917.

"Army Training Found Valuable." *Los Angeles Times*, February 14, 1933.

Associated Press obituary, printed in the *Minneapolis Morning Tribune*, September 25, 1948.

"At the Nesbitt." *Wilkes-Barre Times*, September 13, 1919.

Atkinson, Brooks. "Ghosts of the War." *New York Times*, October 7, 1930.

Babcock, Muriel. "Warren William Dominates *Employees' Entrance*." *Los Angeles Times*, February 3, 1933.

"Bazaar Proceeds Go to MacArthur's Men." May 11, 1942.

Bedside clipping file, Warner Brothers Archives, dates unknown.

Bell, Nelson B. "New Cinema Offerings." *Washington Post*, January 17, 1932.

_____. *Washington Post*, February 15, 1941.

"Best Performances in Current Pictures." *Los Angeles Times*, December 6, 1936.

Biery, Ruth. "The Man Who Can't Talk." *Photoplay*, February 1933.

"Bright Comedy at the Wilbur." *Boston Daily Globe*, January 6, 1925.

"Cannot Comply Here." *Aitkin Age*, September 1, 1917.

Chatterton, John. "Warren William." 1935, unidentified magazine, New York Public Library clipping file.

Christian Science Monitor, September 8, 1933.

Coons, Robbin. "Hollywood Sights and Sounds." *Winona Republican-Herald,* September 2, 1931.

Corbin, John. "Among the New Plays." *New York Times*, April 27, 1924.

_____. "Among the New Plays." *New York Times*, May 4, 1924.

Couch, Hilda. Letter to the dramatic editor, *New York Times*, May 25, 1924.

Creelman, Eileen. "Warren William on Vacation Here." Circa November 1933, unidentified newspaper article, New York Public Library clipping file.

_____. "Warren William on Vacation Here Before Starting Ben Hecht's *Upperworld*," unidentified New York newspaper article.

Crowther, Bosley. *New York Times*, June 16, 1947.

_____. "The Screen: Ordinary Western." *New York Times*, February 7, 1942.

Cushing, Edward. *Brooklyn Eagle*, June 25, 192.

Daly, John J. "Footlights and Shadows." *Washington Post*, May 10, 1925.

Dowling, Mark. "Just to Oblige." Circa November 1934, unidentified magazine article, Wisconsin Historical Society clippings collection.

"Drafted Men Have Gone." *Aitkin Age*, 1917.

"East Film Play." *Washington Post*, July 24, 1937.

"*Employees' Entrance* on Strand Bill." *Hartford Courant*, January 30, 1933.

"Father's Death Avenged by *Hamlet* of Present." *Los Angeles Times*, February 13, 1945.

Fidler, Jimmy. *Washington Post*, January 30, 1937.

"Film Actors Quit Academy Over Code." *New York Times*, October 3, 1933.

"Fire Sweeps Film Studio." *Los Angeles Times*, December 5, 1934.

"First Contingent Men Are Separated." *Aitkin Age*, February 20, 1918.

"Fortune Telling Racket Exposed in New Picture." *Los Angeles Times*, May 8, 1933.

Gabriel, Gilbert. *New York Sun*, September 22, 1926.

Gentry, Charles. "Warren William Finds Time for Comedy." *Detroit Evening Times*, June 1943.

Graham, Sheilah. "List of Stars Suspended by Studio Grows." *Hartford Courant*, April 8, 1938.

_____. "Rising Stars Mean Doom for Favorites of Today." *Hartford Courant*, July 24, 1938.

Hall, Gladys. "The Gadgeteer." Manuscript for article in *Modern Screen*, June 14, 1937, Gladys Hall collection, Margaret Herrick Library.

_____. "Life Story of a Dangerous Man." author's manuscript, 1932.

Hall, Mordaunt. "The Blackleg Lawyer." *New York Times*, May 1, 1932.

_____. "May Robson as a White-Haired Cinderella." *New York Times*, September 8, 1933.

_____. "Shrewd Strategy of Crooked Lawyer." *New York Times*, April 21, 1932.

Hammond, Percy. *New York Herald Tribune*, April 25, 1928.

Herbert, Brian. "Speaking of New Men." Late 1931, unidentified magazine article, Wisconsin Historical Society clipping file.

"Herding's Design Stirs Interest." *Los Angeles Times*, July 10, 1932.

Hobart, "Warren William — Actor and Arborphile." Circa 1939, unidentified San Francisco newspaper article.

Hopper, Hedda. "Hedda Hopper's Hollywood." July 3, 1940.

_____. "Hedda Hopper's Hollywood." November 20, 1940.

_____. "Hedda Hopper's Hollywood." August 21, 1941.

_____. "In Hollywood." *Washington Post*, September 7, 1938.

_____. "Looking at Hollywood." *Chicago Daily Tribune*, May 26, 1944.

"*I Love You* at Springer Opera House Tonight." *Columbus Journal*, October 31, 1919.

"*Independent-Age* Changes Hands Today." *Aitkin Republican*, January 1, 1920.

J.T.M., "Mae West at the Paramount in *Go West, Young Man*." *New York Times*, November 19, 1936.

"June Weather and June Graduates." *Aitkin Independent*, June 5, 1915.

Katharan McCommon. Letter to the dramatic editor, *New York Times*, February 24, 1924.

Keavy, Hubbard. "Keavy Gives Some First Impressions." *Hartford Courant*, June 7, 1936.

Keeler, O.B. "Seventh Jones Subject Finished." *New York Times*, April 26, 1931.

Kester, Marshall. "Curtain Ready to Rise on World's Largest Stage." *Los Angeles Times*, June 28, 1936.

Kingsley, Grace. "Early Loves of Stars Revealed." *Los Angeles Times*, February 19, 1939.

_____. "Hobnobbing in Hollywood." *Los Angeles Times*, December 13, 1933.

_____. "Paul Muni to Act Scarface." *Los Angeles Times*, May 21, 1931.

_____. "Warren William Starred in Story of Courts." *Los Angeles Times*, May 21, 1931.

Klee, A.C. "Newspaper History." *Aitkin Age*, 1971.

Krech, Alvin, obituary, *Time*, May 14, 1928.

Lang, Harry. "Warren William." *Movie Mirror*, April 1933.

"Last Night's Play." *Columbus Enquirer-Sun*, November 1, 1919.

"Lines from a Scrapbook." *New York Times*, January 25, 1931.

Linnell, Gertrude. Letter to the dramatic editor, *New York Times*, February 20, 1924.

"Local News." *Aitkin Independent Age*, July 19, 1919.

"Look at This Who's Who of Hollywood." *Lima Sunday News*, July 16, 1933.

Lusk, Norbert. "Dove, Costello in Dull Stories." *Los Angeles Times*, November 22, 1931.

Maddox, Ben. "Don't Try to Explain Warren William." *Photoplay*, October 1935.

Malevinsky, M.L. Letter to the dramatic editor, *New York Times*, June 1, 1924.

"*Man in the Iron Mask* Seen as Comparative Success." *Los Angeles Times*, July 25, 1939.

Mantle, Burns. "Heroines Have Tough Breaks on Broadway." *Chicago Tribune*, October 19, 1930.

Merrick, Mollie. "Censorship Threat Tones Down Films." *Hartford Courant*, June 19, 1934.

Moffitt, John C. "The Life Story of William Powell." *Hartford Courant*, April 2, 1933.

Movie Classic, September 1931.

Movie Mirror, November 1932.

"Movieland Notes." *Davenport Democrat and Leader*, September 10, 1922.

"Mrs. William Dies 98 Days After Actor." *Los Angeles Examiner*, January 1, 1949.

"Mystery Concerning Virginia Bruce Cleared." *Los Angeles Times*, March 22, 1946.

Nathan, George Jean. "The New York Stage." *New York Times*, December 4, 1921.

"New Breach Jolts Films." *Los Angeles Times*, August 20, 1934.

New York Herald Examiner obituary, September 25, 1948.

New York Times, September 25, 1948.

Nugent, Frank S. "*The Adventures of Robin Hood*— Other Films." *New York Times*, May 13, 1938.

_____. "The Screen." *New York Times*, February 5, 1940.

_____. "The Strand Presents Another Back Stage Musical." *New York Times*, September 28, 1936.

Parsons, Louella. Syndicated in *The Washington Post*, September 30, 1941.

"Player's Rise to Note Rapid." *Los Angeles Times*, July 9, 1932.

Pryor, Thomas M. "Notes on the Film Scene." *New York Times*, August 16, 1942.

"Reception to Be Given Departing Soldier Boys." *Aitkin Age*, September 15, 1917.

"Re-Enter Goodman." *New York Times*, March 29, 1925.

Rohe, Alice. "A New Theater Movement Starts in New York." United Press, syndicated in the Winona.

Ruddy, J. Maurice. "Warren William: The Squire of Encino." *Screen and Radio Weekly*, May 19, 1935.

Schallert, Edwin. "Airy Billie Burke Charms." *Los Angeles Times*, July 1, 1931.

_____. "Film Hailed in Premiere at Pantages." *Los Angeles Times*, November 28, 1934.

_____. "John Garfield Sought for Sam Wood Feature." *Los Angeles Times*, November 27, 1945.

_____. "*Lady for a Day* Excellent." *Los Angeles Times*, October 2, 1933.

_____. "Producers Ban Lurid Sex Scenes from Future Films." *Los Angeles Times*, June 17, 1934.

_____. "William in *Bel Ami*," *Los Angeles Times*, April 24, 1946.

Scheuer, Philip K. "Loews Tells Tall Story." *Los Angeles Times*, August 8, 1932.

Scott, John. "Films Moan Need of More Leading Men." *Los Angeles Times*, October 17, 1937.

"Seek Garbo for Film Role." *New York Times*, August 16, 1932.

"A Sermon in a Storm." *New York Times*, November 1, 1922.

Shaffer, George. "Actor Warren William Is an Inventor, Too." *Chicago Tribune*, June 10, 1936.

_____. "Experts Differ on K.O. Punch of Mae West." *Chicago Tribune*, September 5, 1936.

Sid, "Happenings in Hollywood." *Hartford Courant*, March 8, 1936.

"Soldier Boys Feel They Have Backing of Folks at Home." *Aitkin Republican*, September 27, 1917.

"Soldier Boys Given Rousing Send Off Before Going to 'Can' Kaiser." *Aitkin Republican*, September 20, 1917.

Stevens, Otheman. "Vinegar Tree Player Shows Superb Poise." June 1931.

"A Strong Film...." *Washington Post*, May 15, 1932.

Synnott and Clark. "Influenza Epidemic at Camp Dix, N.J." *Journal of the American Medical Association*, November 30, 1918.

"Theater Guild Is New York Triumph." *Dallas Morning News*, June 6, 1921.

"These May Serve Country." *Aitkin Age*, June 1917.

Thirer, Irene. "By His Mustachios You Shall Know Warren William's Status." December 1941, unidentified newspaper article, New York Public Library clipping file.

Tinee, Mae. "*Mind Reader* Scores High in Every Detail." *Chicago Tribune*, April 8, 1933.
_____. "2d of Lawyer Cycle of Films Has Barrymore." *Chicago Tribune*, May 13, 1932.
_____. "Film Favorites at New Heights in This Movie." *Chicago Tribune*, June 27, 1938.
"Two Players, in Person, a Mystery Hit." *Washington Post*, July 24, 1932.
"Virtues and Activities Extolled." *Aitkin Age*, May 13, 1920.
"Warner Stars to Feel Blow of Salary Ax." UPI, August 6, 1932.
"Warren Krech in N.Y. Play with Mrs. Barrymore." *Aitkin Age*, July 7, 1928.
"Warren (Slim) William." 1937, unidentified newspaper clipping, New York Public Library.
"Warren William." *Movie Mirror*, November 1932.
"Warren William, Actor, Gadgeteer." Circa 1943, unidentified newspaper article.
"Warren William Dies of Rare Blood Disease." *Aitkin Independent Age*, September 24, 1948.
"Warren William Quitting Gadget Inventing." *Washington Post*, March 2, 1938.
"Warren William Rarely Seen in Person by Public." *Los Angeles Times*, July 22, 1934.
"Warren William Talks." *New York Times*, July 24, 1932.
"Warren William's Dilemma." *Hartford Courant*, October 2, 1932.
"When It's Zero Hour in Hollywood." *Hartford Courant*, August 14, 1932.
"Who's Who This Week in Pictures." *New York Times*, October 2, 1932.
"William Quitting Gadget Inventing." *Washington Post*, March 2, 1938.
William, Warren. Undated letter to Hedda Hopper.
"With the Plays and Players." *The Westfield Leader*, July 9, 1924.
"With the Plays and Players." *The Westfield Leader*, July 23, 1924.
Woollcott, Alexander. "The Play." *New York Times*, January 24, 1921.
"Young Soldiers Are Honored by Citizens." *Aitkin Age*, September 22, 1917.
Young, Stark. "Nocturne Is Interesting." *New York Times*, February 17, 1925.
_____. "The Stagers First Venture." *New York Times*, March 25, 1925.

Internet Citations

"Aitkin History Page." Minnesota GenWeb Project, no date, March 22, 2007, www.geocities.com/Heartland/Valley/8119/aitkhis.htm?200722.
"Aitkin, Minnesota — Our Heritage." 2006, April 13, 2007, www.aitkin.com/fest/history.htm.
"*Arizona*." Turner Classic Movies website, www.tcm.com/thismonth/article/?cid+150885 accessed December 21, 2007.

"Camp Cody — Deming, New Mexico." no date, May 17, 2007, http://www.zianet.com/kromeke/camp-cody/CW01.htm.
Chatelle, Bob. "Aitkin, Minnesota: An Introduction." Aitkin Area Chamber of Commerce, 1996, April 4, 2008, http://users.rcn.com/kyp/aitkin.html.
George, Enitza D., M.D., "Multiple Myeloma, Recognition and Management." American Academy of Family Physicians, http://www.aafp.org/afp/990401ap/1885.html, April 1, 1999, accessed March 21, 2008.
"Intro to Myeloma." 2002–2006, Multiple Myeloma Research Foundation <www.multiplemyeloma.org/about_myeloma/, accessed August 30, 2007.
"*The Mind Reader*." www.tcm.com, accessed December 21, 2007.
"The *Strange Wills* Radio Programs." http://www.digitaldeliftp.com/DigitalDeliToo/dd2jb-Strange-Wills.html, accessed September 6, 2009.
Ward, Nathan. "The Fire Last Time." *Free Republic*, December 2001, March 6, 2008, http://www.freerepublic.com/focus/f-news/577915/posts.
World War I draft registration card of Warren Krech, March 3, 2008, http://content.ancestry.com.
"World War I History — 34th Division." March 16, 2004, May 17, 2007, http://www.34infdiv.org/history/wwihist.html.

Personal Interviews

Hall, Barbara. July 30, August 12 and 29, 2009.
Lyon, Patricia. July 12 and 20 and August 11, 2009.
Pettersen, Connie. August 2008.
Schroeder, Christine Arnold. American Academy of Dramatic Arts, correspondence, May 2008.
Other Sources
Audition notes for Warren Krech, American Academy of Dramatic Arts, October 26, 1915.
Blanke, Henry. Memo, June 5, 1935.
Catalogue for the American Academy of the Dramatic Arts, New York City, 1915.
Death certificate of Warren William, dated September 25, 1948 (District #1901, Registrar's #15503).
Death record of Helen Barbara Krech, Nassau County, New York, January 31, 1948.
Deed records, Aitkin County.
Jones, Carlisle. "Krech's Bad Boy." Warner Brothers Studio biography of Warren William, 1932.
Koenig, William. Memo, February 25, 1932.
Krech, Freeman. Letter to E.C. Knieff, September 30, 1925.
Letters and correspondence between *Twelve Miles Out* company and Actor's Equity, April 1927.
Levee, M.C. Letter to Jack Warner, April 24, 1936.
_____. Letter to Warren William, March 3, 1936.
Levinson, Nathan. Memo to Hal B. Wallis, 1935.
Marriage certificate of Helen Nelson and Alan Ferris, State of Minnesota, January 30, 1902.

Marriage certificate of Warren Krech and Helen Ferris, New York State records, January 11, 1923.

Minnesota Census Record, 1895.

Naegele, Otto E. "Biographical and Narrative History of Ernst Wilhelm Krech and Matilda Krech." Unpublished monograph, April 1944.

Obringer, Roy. Memo to Darryl Zanuck, September 10, 1931.

_____. Memo to Jack Warner, January 12, 1934.

_____. Memo to M.C. Levee, August 17, 1935.

Wallis, Hal. Memo to Alan Crosland, June 1934.

Warner Brothers. Letter to Warren William, May 5, 1933

Warner, Jack L. Memo to Sam Bischoff, June 14, 1934.

_____. Inter-office memo to Sam Bischoff, June 14, 1935.

_____. Letter to M.C. Levee, August 17, 1935.

_____. Memo, June 14, 1934.

"Warren William in First Rough House Role, Hits 'Em Hard." *Smarty* pressbook, p. 12, Warner Brothers Archives, 681B_F000261_001.PDF 12.

"Warren William Practices Lines Before a Mirror." *Satan Met a Lady* pressbook, Warner Brothers, 1936.

William, Warren. Letter to Roy Obringer, January 8, 1935.

Index